CW01370247

SCARLET PASSION

SCARLET PASSION

Ferrari's famed sports prototype and competition sports cars 1963-73

ANTHONY PRITCHARD

© Anthony Pritchard

All rights reserved. No part of this publication may be reproduced, stored in a retrieval system or transmitted, in any form or by any means, electronic, mechanical, photocopying, recording or otherwise, without prior permission in writing from the publisher.

First published in June 2004

A catalogue record for this book is available from the British Library.

ISBN 1 85960 872 8

Library of Congress Catalog Card no 2004105183

Haynes North America Inc.,
861 Lawrence Drive, Newbury Park,
California 91320, USA

Published by Haynes Publishing, Sparkford,
Yeovil, Somerset BA22 7JJ, UK
Tel: 01963 442030 Fax: 01963 440001
Int. tel: +44 1963 442030 Int. fax: +44 1963 440001
E-mail: sales@haynes.co.uk
Website: www.haynes.co.uk

Styling: Simon Larkin. Page layout: Glad Stockdale

Printed and bound in Great Britain
by J. H. Haynes & Co. Ltd, Sparkford

CONTENTS

	Author's Note	7
	Colour sections	65 & 193
1	Introduction and Background	8
2	The Evolution of the Ferrari Grand Touring Car	20
3	Prototype Racing, 1962	42
4	Prototype Racing, 1963	52
5	Prototype Racing, 1964	62
6	Prototype Racing, 1965	86
7	Prototype Racing, 1966	96
8	Prototype Racing, 1967	114
9	The 250LM, 1963–68	132
10	The Can-Am Cars, 1967–72	146
11	The 312P Prototypes, 1969–71	154
12	The 512S and 512M Competition sports cars, 1970–71	166
13	The 312PB 1971–73	186
14	An Interview with Mauro Forghieri, formerly Technical Director of Ferrari Sport	226
15	An Interview with John Surtees, works Ferrari driver, 1963–66	234
16	An Interview with Brian Redman, works Ferrari sports car driver, 1972–73	242
17	Colonel Ronnie Hoare, founder of *Maranello Concessionaires*	246
	Appendix 1 Dramatis Personae: A guide to the more important personalities	251
	Appendix 2 Specifications of Ferrari prototypes, competition sports cars and GT cars, 1962–73	259
	Appendix 3 Championship Results, 1962–73	262
	Appendix 4 Ferrari Chassis Information	263
	Bibliography	269
	Index	270

The four works 512S cars line up for scrutineering at the 1970 Le Mans race. The lead car is that of Ickx/Schetty. The front two cars have short tails without fins, but longer tails with fins were fitted before the race. (FotoVantage)

AUTHOR'S NOTE

Later in this book John Surtees writes, 'The Prototype period was one that Ferrari could be justifiably proud of and I was proud to be part of it.' As an enthusiast and a writer, who was present at many of the races described and at close quarters with the cars, I share John's sentiments and it has been a delightful experience to relive this period through photographs, references and conversations with those who were directly involved with Ferrari at the time.

During the years covered by this book the racing categories changed three times. In 1962–67 Ferrari was competing with Prototypes and after 1962 there was no limit on engine capacity. For 1968–71 there were two categories of contender: Prototypes up to 3 litres and Competition Sports Cars of up to 5 litres. Maranello missed out on Prototype racing in 1968, but returned for a single, volatile season in 1969, then came the rather one-sided battle between the competition sports cars of Porsche and Ferrari. Once more, after a year, Ferrari changed direction, left the racing of the 5-litre cars to private owners and introduced a new flat-12 prototype. The categories changed again for 1972 and there was now a 3-litre capacity limited for what were now referred to as sports cars.

The years 1962 to 1973 witnessed major progress in the development of sports car racing. During these years the competing Ferraris evolved from the 'old school' of technology under the direction of Carlo Chiti, who left the company at the end of 1961, through to the very advanced, lightweight and highly sophisticated flat-12 cars of 1971–73. It was also a period that witnessed two major battles for supremacy: that between Ferrari and Ford in 1964–67 which ended with the level of success of the two teams fairly evenly balanced, and that between Ferrari and Porsche in 1970, which the German team won convincingly.

There were of course significant developments from other constructors and manufacturers. Perhaps the most important and influential car of the period was Eric Broadley's Lola GT, which ran at Le Mans and several other races in 1963. Broadley's Lola GT led directly to the Ford GT40 and its influence was also felt at Maranello. But for the involvement of Ford, prototype racing during the years 1964–67 would have been very dull indeed, simply a series of Ferrari processions. Nor should the influence of Jim Hall and the Chaparral be forgotten. These cars, raced in prototype events in 1966–67, were very advanced in construction and in aerodynamic design and Hall's pioneer work in using a high-mounted aerofoil on his Can-Am cars and on the 1967 Chaparral 2F led to a rash of similar, but rather more dubious devices on Grand Prix cars until movable aerodynamic devices were banned in 1969.

It is easy to overlook that in the years up until 1969 Ferrari struggled financially and the team underwrote the cost of racing by the sale of road cars. This inhibited both technical development and the number of prototype races in which Ferrari competed. It also placed restrictions on the amount of testing that Ferrari could undertake outside Italy. Just as Ferrari rejected Ford when the American giant negotiated a take-over, the question of control protracted negotiations with Fiat for a very long period. When the deal was finally concluded in 1969, Ferrari's financial situation was much improved, although there were still years, notably 1973, when funds were tight.

I have also covered, fairly briefly, the development and racing of Ferrari GT cars. They are germane to the story because of the commonality of engine design between these, the *Testa Rossa* sports-racing cars and early prototypes. There has been more than one book about the so-called 'Cobra-Ford War', but in reality it never happened directly and Shelby American Cobra never beat Ferrari. The only occasions on which a GT Cobra beat a GT Ferrari on the road were at Le Mans in 1964 and one hill climb. When Cobra won the GT Championship in 1965, Ferrari was no longer a contender.

Ferrari typed models by number, usually followed by a name such as 330 *Le Mans Berlinetta* and 250 *Prototipo*, which in abbreviated form reads, strictly speaking, as 330 *LMB* and 250 *P*, the number denoting the cubic capacity of each cylinder. For convenience type numbers such as these are reproduced in this book as 330LMB and 250P without the space between figures and letters. Power output figures are those claimed by Ferrari, corrected where other conflicting, satisfactory evidence is available. Clear plastic used for windscreens and windows is known as 'Plexiglas' in the United States and 'Perspex' in Britain. They are both the same chemical compound, Methyl Methacrylate, and for consistency I have used the term 'Plexiglas'. Also for convenience I have throughout referred to *North American Racing Team* as NART.

I have tried hard to make this book about the people concerned as well as the cars and I am very grateful for all who have helped me, whether they had direct Ferrari involvement or not. Especial thanks are due to Chris Amon, Richard Attwood, Peter Everingham (Secretary of the Ferrari Owners' Club), Mauro Forghieri, Mrs Anne Hoare, Antonio Ghini (Director of Communications, Ferrari SpA), the late Guy Griffiths, Pete Lyons, David Piper, Brian Redman, Jack Sears, Tommy Sopwith, John Surtees and Geoff Willoughby (Registrar of the Ferrari Owners' Club).

Introduction
and Background

Dorino Serafini drove this works-entered Tipo 166 Mille Miglia car with Carrozzeria Touring Barchetta body in the one-hour 2-litre Production Car race at Silverstone in August 1950. He finished second to team-mate Alberto Ascari at the wheel of a similar car. (T. C. March/FotoVantage)

Enzo Ferrari was the most feared, hated and respected man in Italian motor racing. He dominated his scene for 50 years. His greatness is indisputable despite his egoism, his paranoia, his ruthlessness and his callousness. Through vast experience, determination and perseverance, he built the company which became the most successful in both motor racing and high-performance car production.

Surrounding the inception of the original V12 Ferraris there is a mystery that has never been resolved. Despite the success of Ferrari's machine-tool business (and one cannot but wonder how much help in setting this up he received from Adolfo Orsi of Maserati), it was unlikely to have produced sufficient finance for the development and construction of a sophisticated and complex range of cars. That there was a financial backer whose identity remains unknown, seems probable.

At the heart of Ferrari's success was that V12 engine – and it remained so through most of the years covered by this book. According to Ferrari in his insipid and synthetic memoirs (UK edition, *My Terrible Joys*, Hamish Hamilton, 1963), he was influenced primarily by Packard's pre-war V12 touring car engine. This statement was patently untrue. Ferrari used the V12 layout for reasons of technical efficiency, the origins of which lay in the work of the great Vittorio Jano at Alfa Romeo and the subsequent development of this layout at Alfa Romeo by Giaocchino Colombo and the Spanish engineer Wifredo Ricart whom Ferrari professed to dislike intensely.

Giaocchino Colombo, acting as consultant to Ferrari and still working for Alfa Romeo, carried out the design work before joining Maranello on a full-time basis in August 1947. Colombo's original V12 design had a capacity of 1,497cc (55 x 52.5mm) with the cylinders set at an angle of 60° and with a 20mm offset between banks, which allowed side-by-side connecting rods to be used. The cylinder heads, block and crankcase were all cast in aluminium-alloy, with shrunk-in cast iron wet cylinder liners that were held in compression against the block by the cylinder heads. Two-thirds of the way down the liner, a shoulder formed a metal-to-metal joint against the cylinder wall.

The single overhead camshaft for each block of cylinders was driven by a train of gears from the nose of the crankshaft and actuated finger-follower rocker arms. To reduce the reciprocating mass of the valve gear, two hairpin springs per valve were used with the valves inclined at an angle of 60°. There were three intake ports per cylinder head. Ignition was by two Marelli magnetos driven from the rear of the camshafts (and protruding through the firewall into the cockpit) and there was a single 14mm plug per cylinder. The compression ratio was 8:1. Three Weber 30DCF carburettors were fitted, although larger-choke 32DCFs were soon substituted.

Colombo used aluminium-alloy pistons with two compression rings and two oil rings and there were short, very strong connecting rods of H-section. The big ends were split at an angle of 40°, allowing them to be withdrawn from above through the original 55mm bores. This design feature provides some evidence that originally Ferrari was not intending to increase capacity above 1,500cc. The nitride-hardened steel crankshaft was machined from a single billet and ran in seven main bearings; as on an in-line six, with its throws at 120°. The sump was T-shaped, cast in aluminium-alloy and well baffled to prevent oil surge. It was this engine that was to provide the continuous link between the first Ferraris and the Prototype GT cars that were raced as late as 1965.

The earliest engines had cam covers without ribbing or the Ferrari name. There were a large number of design shortcomings in the original engines but these were eliminated over the years, at first by Luigi Bazzi, who had been with Ferrari since early *Scuderia Ferrari* days, and later by Aurelio Lampredi and his successors. A number of changes were made to reduce loss of compression seal at the copper O-rings when the engines were hot and to reduce the frequency of blown head gaskets and water leaks. In addition larger Vandervell Thin Wall bearings were adopted.

There is uncertainty about the power output of the V12 engine in its original form. When an advance description of the new cars was published in the November–December 1946 issue of Italian magazine *Inter Auto*, a power output of 72bhp at 5,600rpm was quoted, which seems to have been erring on the pessimistic side. Other sources give the output in 1947 as 118bhp at 7,000rpm, but this appears more than a little optimistic.

The first sports Ferrari, the Tipo 125 with streamlined Touring body, seen on its debut at Piacenza on 11 May 1947. Franco Cortese led this 62-mile race, but retired because of fuel pump failure.

Transmission was by a single dry-plate clutch and a five-speed and reverse gearbox without synchromesh and mounted in unit with the engine. It is believed that only the first three cars had an exposed-gate gear-change. From the gearbox a two-piece prop-shaft ran to the final drive, which had a light-alloy casing. The chassis was constructed from oval-section tubing and substantially cross-braced. At the front the suspension was independent by a transverse leaf spring, double wishbones and hydraulic shock absorbers in unit with the upper arms of the suspension. Ferrari used a rigid axle and semi-elliptic leaf springs together with hydraulic shock absorbers at the rear. Worm-and-peg steering was used on the earliest cars.

During 1947 Ferrari built only three cars, all 125C *Competizione* sports models. Carrozzeria Touring built smooth full-width bodies on two chassis and a neat cycle-wing body on the third. The first race appearance of a Ferrari was in a 62-mile (100km) race at Piacenza on 11 May 1947 and although the cars failed on this occasion, a number of successes were gained subsequently that year in minor Italian events. Ferrari's original plan to restrict the cars to 1,500cc was abandoned because of the opposition from the 2-litre Maseratis and because of the strong likelihood of a Formula B (or Formula 2, as it later became known) being introduced for 1948.

Franco Cortese appeared with the first 2-litre car at Pescara on 15 August 1947 and took second place behind a very fast Fiat. This Ferrari, known as the Tipo 159, had the engine re-linered to 60mm and was fitted with a new crankshaft to give a 58mm stroke. Capacity was 1,902cc and the power output was 125bhp at 7,000rpm. Over the winter of 1947–48 the two Tipo 159s and the Tipo 125 had the bore increased to 60mm, giving a capacity of 1,992cc. Shortly afterwards the stroke was lengthened to 58.8mm, giving a capacity of 1,995cc, and this was to become the classic stroke dimension for all Colombo 'short-block' engines. In this form the model was known as the Tipo 166 and the power output was 140bhp at 6,600rpm.

These cars were widely raced and sold to private owners. For 1949 the famous version with the Carrozzeria Touring *Barchetta* ('little boat') body appeared and this supremely stylish body was built on Tipo 166 and other Ferrari chassis through to 1953. These cars gained numerous competition successes; including wins at Le Mans and in the Paris 12 Hours race in 1949 and in the Mille Miglia road race in 1948–49. The first touring Ferrari, the Tipo 166 *Inter*, appeared in 1948. It was powered by a single-carburettor engine developing 110bhp at 6,000rpm and available with bodies by Carrozzeria Touring or Stabilimenti Farina (Farina works). Very few of these cars were sold and they were not a serious proposition for everyday use.

The 1,500cc supercharged Ferrari Tipo 125 grand prix cars made their debut in the 1948 Italian Grand Prix held in Valentino Park, Turin on 5 September 1948. They were raced in developed form through to 1950, but their lack of success was to result in Colombo's fall from grace at Maranello and his departure from Ferrari that year. The company's V12 Formula B cars with the Tipo 166 engine were raced until the end of 1951 and dominated the formula. Development of the Colombo V12 for use in sports cars continued. During 1950 the Tipo 166 was supplemented by a new version, the Tipo 195 with 2,341cc (65 x 58.8mm) engine. It was built in very limited numbers as the *Sport* developing 150bhp at 7,000rpm and the *Inter* with a power output of 130bhp at 6,000rpm.

The Tipo 195 was an interim model and later in 1950 was replaced by the Tipo 212, with the engine bored out to 68mm, giving a capacity of 2,563cc. At this point the Ferrari 'range' becomes confusing. Ferrari's catalogue, issued in October 1950, listed two versions of the Tipo 212. The *Inter* with a single Weber 36DCF carburettor developed 130bhp at 6,000rpm, while the *Export* with the same carburettor and a higher compression ratio was claimed to have a power output of 150bhp at 6,500rpm. There was also a competition version introduced in 1951 and known variously as the *Export* or *Sport*. This version had triple Weber 32DCF carburettors and a power output of 170bhp.

There were two further stages in development of the Colombo engine in the early 1950s. In 1952 Ferrari introduced the Tipo 225 *Sport* with the bore further increased to 70mm, giving a capacity of 2,715cc. This was another interim model, but there were a number of design changes, including the adoption of 12 intake ports and Lampredi-type roller-follower rocker arms. With three Weber 36DCF carburettors the power output was 210bhp at 7,200rpm. The majority of the small production run of these cars had Vignale bodywork in *berlinetta* or *spyder* form. They were raced extensively, especially in the United States.

Early in 1952 Ferrari built the 250 *Sport* with a 2,953cc (73 x 58.8mm) version of the Colombo engine and with three Weber twin-choke 36DCF/3 carburettors, power output was about 220bhp at 7,000rpm. Vignale coupé bodywork was fitted. This car was loaned to Giovanni Bracco who ran it as a private entry in the 1952 Mille Miglia. Fortified by chain-smoking and brandy, Bracco drove an incredible race to defeat the works Mercedes-Benz 300SLs by a margin of four and a half minutes. The race had been run in the wet, which reduced speeds but Bracco averaged 79.90mph (128.56kph), fastest post-war average apart from 1949 when Biondetti, in ideal conditions, averaged 81.53mph (131.18kph) with a 2-litre Ferrari to achieve his third successive win in the race. After the race Bracco was unable to stand without support and the more generous-minded attributed this to sheer exhaustion.

From the Mille Miglia-winning car Ferrari developed the 250 *Mille Miglia* with a claimed power output of 240bhp at 7,200rpm. Some 40 of these cars with either Pinin Farina coupé or Vignale *spyder* body were built. The model represented a milestone in Ferrari history. The 250MM was exceptionally successful in its class of racing, but, also, it was powered by the Colombo engine in the definitive capacity used in the incomparable *Testa Rossa* sports-racing cars of 1958–61, the 250P Prototype of 1963 and with Pinin Farina coupé body it represented the starting point for the development of a long-lived range of GT cars.

Despite the continuous development of the Colombo engine, the emphasis had shifted at Maranello. Aurelio Lampredi, who had joined the company as assistant to Colombo, evolved a large-capacity unsupercharged V12 engine which in 4,494cc form was to challenge and finally defeat the Tipo 159 Alfa Romeos in 1951 Grand Prix racing. Although the general design principles of the Colombo engine were retained, there were many new features. The centres of the cylinder bores were spaced at 108mm, because of the greater diameter of the bores, and as a result the engine was longer and known as the 'long-block'.

Instead of separate cylinder heads, the water jackets were cast integrally with the heads. The steel liners had threaded upper ends passing through the bottom of the water jackets and these were screwed into threaded bosses surrounding the valve and combustion areas. In this way a weakness of the Colombo design, the cylinder head/block gasket was eliminated. The lower ends of the liners projected below the water jacket casting to seat in matching bores in the crankcase. There was a pair of O-rings in grooves close to the bottom of each cylinder and these formed a water seal. The blocks had bolts passing through them to attach them to the crankcase. The main function of the crankcase was to support the crankshaft, formed by a machined billet and running in seven main bearings of greater diameter than those of the Colombo engine.

The first Lampredi engines had a capacity of 3,322cc (72 x 68mm) and were used in the 1950 Mille Miglia and also to power the single-seaters entered in that year's Belgian and French Grands Prix. Lampredi next increased engine size to 4,102cc (80 x 68mm). A Grand Prix car with this size of engine was driven by Ascari in the 1950 Grand Prix des Nations at Geneva on 30 July 1950, but by the Italian Grand Prix on 3 September a 4,494cc (80 x 74.4mm) engine was ready to race. There has never been a remotely satisfactory explanation as to why engine capacity was progressively increased in this way. The first cars had single-plug engines, but twin-plug ignition was adopted on 1951 Grand Prix cars.

The 4.1-litre engine was soon adopted for both sports-racing cars and production models. The 342 *America*, intended as a fast touring car, was exhibited in chassis form at the 1950 Paris Salon and sports-racing versions followed early in 1951. Successes included wins in the Mille Miglia in both 1951 and 1953. Although it is believed that the 4.5-litre engine was installed occasionally without the press being made specifically aware of it, one of the three very handsome Pinin Farina coupés entered at Le Mans in 1953 had a 4,494cc engine and was known as the Tipo 375LM. With this car Ascari set a new lap record of 112.866mph (181.601kph). Later, in 1953, Tipo 375LM cars with the 4.5-litre engine won the Belgian 24 Hours, Nürburgring 1,000Km and Pescara 12 Hours races.

For 1954 the larger engine was offered in both production sports-racing cars and fitted to a small number of touring cars. In these engines capacity was

A man who was still making himself a legend – Enzo Ferrari seen in the 1930s when he had made his reputation as an entrant, but still had to forge it as a manufacturer.

4,523cc (84 x 68mm). The 1954 works V12 was the *375 Plus*, a brutal, ugly *spyder* bodied by Pinin Farina and powered by a 4,954cc (84 x 74.5mm) engine developing a claimed 344bhp at 6,500rpm. Driven masterfully in the wet by Froilan Gonzalez and Maurice Trintignant, a *375Plus* scored a narrow victory at Le Mans from the Jaguar D-type of Rolt/Hamilton. The last large-capacity Lampredi V12 was the 4,962cc Tipo 410 *Sport* used in the Buenos Aires 1,000Km race on 29 January 1956. In its original form this engine had been developed to power the Tipo 410 *Superamerica* road car built in very small numbers.

Lampredi had been pursuing another line of development that was originally very successful, but ultimately led to his downfall and departure from Maranello. Work had been put in hand on a four-cylinder design, which appeared in late 1951 in both Formula 2 form and, in prototype form, for the un-supercharged 2,500cc Grand Prix formula projected for 1954 onwards. The Tipo 500 1,985cc car completely dominated World Championship Grand Prix racing when it was held to Formula 2 rules in 1952–53 and Alberto Ascari won the Drivers' Championship for Ferrari in both years.

Ferrari developed competition sports cars powered by four-cylinder engines and sold these to private owners in substantial numbers. The first examples had the 2,498cc engine which were tested during 1952. Then, in the Coppa Inter-Europa race at Monza on 28 June 1953 Ferrari entered one of these and also the first of the 3-litre cars. This was the Tipo 735 *Sport* with 2,942cc (102 x 90mm) engine, developing 225bhp at 6,800rpm. The production 750 *Monza* followed in 1954 and this had a 3,000cc (103 x 90mm) engine developing 260bhp at 6,000rpm. Hawthorn/Trintignant drove a *Monza* to first place on scratch and second on handicap in the 1954 Tourist Trophy on the Dundrod circuit in Northern Ireland. They were sold in large numbers, although they were notoriously difficult-handling cars.

There was also a 2-litre four-cylinder Ferrari sports car, which became known as the *Mondial*. This had the 1,985cc (90 x 78mm) engine used in the 1952–53 Formula 2 cars and in sports form it developed 170bhp at 7,000rpm. Ascari/Villoresi drove the prototype into second place in the Casablanca 12 Hours race held on 20 December 1953 and Vittorio Marzotto finished second with it to Ascari (Lancia D24) in the 1954 Mille Miglia. In 1956 Ferrari introduced the improved 2-litre *Testa Rossa* (not to be confused with the V12 cars bearing the same name) and the final version was the *Testa Rossa* TRC introduced for 1957. For this the factory claimed a top speed of 153mph (246kph).

During 1954 Ferrari continued to race Lampredi-designed four-cylinder Grand Prix cars in two forms. The 2,498cc (94 x 90mm) Tipo 625 in its original form differed little from the prototype first raced in 1951, although a number of engine developments were seen during the year. Lampredi also developed the Tipo 553, known as the *Squalo* because of its shark-like appearance and it first appeared in the 1953 Italian Grand Prix with a 1,997cc (93 x 73.5mm) engine. The 1954 version had a 2,498cc (100 x 79.5mm) engine developing 250bhp at 7,500rpm. The *Squalo* featured a short 7ft-wheelbase (2,135mm) and pannier fuel tanks; the handling was sensitive and most drivers disliked it.

In 1954 the Ferraris were no real match for the Maserati 250F or the Mercedes-Benz W196 and, after dominating World Championship racing for two years, the Ferrari team won only two Championship races in 1954; the British Grand Prix, in which Gonzalez and Hawthorn took the first two places, and the Spanish race at Barcelona in October which Hawthorn won with an improved version of the *Squalo*. Although Lampredi was planning a six-cylinder Grand Prix car, this was not even on the drawing board in 1955 and the only win that year was Trintignant's victory in the Monaco Grand Prix after the retirement of faster cars.

Lampredi did produce a six-cylinder sports car, but by then he had lost Ferrari's confidence and the Maranello 'Machiavelli' was looking for an opportunity to replace him. It came during 1955; the only year between 1947 and 1980 when the works did not race V12 cars. The first six-cylinder car was the Tipo 118 *Le Mans* powered by a 3,747cc (94 x 90mm) engine, basically the Tipo 625 Grand Prix unit with two cylinders added and developing 310bhp at 6,000rpm. The sole European victory of the six-cylinder cars was in the 671-mile (1080km) Tour of Sicily held on 3 April when Piero Taruffi won with a Tipo 118, averaging 65.86mph (106.00kph) in a drive that lasted over ten hours.

By the Mille Miglia on 1 May Ferrari had ready the Tipo 121 *Le Mans* with 4,412cc (102 x 90mm) engine developing 360bhp at 6,300rpm. These cars handled like the 750 *Monza*, but worse. In the Mille Miglia Umberto Maglioli drove a good race with a Tipo 121 to finish third behind Moss/Jenkinson and Juan Fangio with 3-litre Mercedes-Benz 300SLR cars. At Le Mans Eugenio Castellotti set a cracking pace with a 121LM, led at the end of the first hour and attained 175.6mph (282.5kph) on the Mulsanne Straight, but retired in the fifth hour because of engine problems. Several of these cars were sold in the United States, but the last works entry was in the short, 130-mile (209km) Swedish Grand Prix for sports cars in August when Castellotti drove one into third place.

As an interim measure Ferrari produced a larger-capacity version of the four-cylinder *Monza*, with a 3,432cc (102 x 105mm) engine developing 280bhp at 6,000rpm. Castellotti/Taruffi drove the first car in the Tourist Trophy on the Dundrod circuit on 17 September 1955, but it handled badly and they finished a poor sixth. Castellotti/Robert Manzon appeared with the same car in the Targa Florio, the last round in the World Sports Car Championship held on 16 October. They ran very well and were holding second place behind Moss/Collins (Mercedes-Benz 300SLR), when they had to stop for a wheel-change and dropped back to finish third. If they had held second place, Ferrari would have won that year's Sports Car Championship by the narrowest of margins. The final result was: Mercedes-Benz, 24 points; Ferrari, 22 points.

Following Ascari's death at Monza in June 1955 and largely because of Lancia's perilous financial position, the Turin team withdrew their exceptionally promising D50 V8 Grand Prix cars from racing. After protracted negotiations, the complete *équipe* was handed over to Ferrari on 26 July 1955 and the Lancia technical team, headed by Vittorio Jano, joined Ferrari. Ferrari also received an annual contribution of 50 million lire over five years from Fiat to assist his racing programme. Enzo Ferrari now rid himself of Aurelio Lampredi whom he had once rated so very highly. Lampredi then joined Fiat where he carried out significant development work on twin overhead camshaft production engines.

Lampredi's departure marked the end of a very important period in Ferrari history and the new era was marked by the appearance of two sports car engines, one a revival of the traditional V12 and the other a new V6 design. Although Ferrari always tried to credit his son Dino as the inspiration behind the V6 and named the design for him, Jano had overall responsibility for the concept and design of the new engine. He and his associates at Lancia had carried out many years' development work on V6 engines, which powered the Aurelia saloon and GT coupé, as well as the Lancia sports cars raced in 1953–54.

Ing. Andrea Fraschetti, formerly of Lancia, became head of the design office in late 1955 and he developed a new 60° V12 engine typed the 130S, which powered the

Nuvolari with his Tipo 166 Spyder Corsa at the start of the 1948 Mille Miglia at Brescia. An elderly woman offers his companion Scapinelli a bunch of flowers. Nuvolari drove like a demon, but a combination of mechanical problems and his excessively hard press-on tactics forced his retirement.

Tipo 290 *Mille Miglia* where the aim had been to incorporate the best features of Colombo and Lampredi designs. The cylinder dimensions were 73 x 69.5mm (3,491cc). There was a single overhead camshaft per bank of cylinders, with Lampredi-style roller-rocker cam followers, hairpin valve springs, larger valves, Lampredi-type screwed-in cylinder barrels, twin-plug ignition and four distributors. Colombo-type connecting rods with the big ends split at an angle were used. Lubrication was dry-sump. There were 12 separate inlet ports as on Lampredi engines and Lampredi-developed Colombo engines. With three Weber twin-choke 40DCF carburettors the power output was 320bhp at 7,300rpm.

Throughout the 1956 European season Ferrari raced both the Tipo 290MM cars and Tipo 860 *Monzas* and there was confusion for the spectator, as both types were fitted with almost-identical Scaglietti-built bodies. These two types largely dominated the year's sports car racing. The main exception was the Le Mans 24 Hours race which had been postponed until the end of July because of changes to the circuit following the 1955 disaster and there was a 2,500cc capacity limit, except for production cars. Because of its special rules the race was not a round in the Sports Car Championship in 1956. Ferrari fielded cars fitted with four-cylinder 2,498cc engines. These were not fast enough to challenge for the lead and the sole finisher driven by Gendebien/Trintignant took third place.

A typical privately owned sports-racing Ferrari of the 1950s. This Tipo 340 Mexico was owned by Briggs Cunningham and had Vignale bodywork. Apart from the general shape, it is possible to identify Vignale's work by the 'portholes' on the front wings. Bill Spear is at the wheel at the 1953 British Grand Prix meeting at Silverstone. He finished fourth behind a trio of works Aston Martin DB3S cars. (T.C. March/FotoVantage)

For 1957 Ferrari produced a version of the 290S with twin overhead camshafts per bank of cylinders with a claimed power output that varied from 330 to 350bhp. These cars failed at Buenos Aires, but the race was won by a single-cam 290MM shared by Masten Gregory, Perdisa, Castellotti and Musso. By the Sebring 12 Hours race in March Ferrari had developed the Tipo 315 *Sport* based on the four-cam 3.4-litre car, but with the engine capacity increased to 3,783cc (76 x 69.5mm) and a claimed power output of 360bhp at 7,200rpm. Both works entries failed and Maseratis took the first two places.

By the Mille Miglia on 12 May another development was ready, the Tipo 335 *Sport* with a 4,023cc (77 x 72mm) engine having a power output of 390bhp at 7,800rpm. Piero Taruffi's 335S won on his 14th drive in the famous race, with second place going to von Trips with a 315S. Gendebien finished third with the latest 250GT. About 25 miles from the finish de Portago, lying fourth, crashed his 335 *Sport* into a crowd of spectators. De Portago, co-driver Ed Nelson (his ski instructor) and ten onlookers were killed. That the cause was a tyre failure, probably caused by an earlier kerb-crunching incident, was undoubted.

There were three repercussions. The Mille Miglia was never held again; two Ferrari Tipo 335S cars were impounded during a government enquiry and Ferrari, already unhappy with the Belgian Englebert tyres, which he had been contracted to use since pre-war days, switched to British Dunlops for 1958. In August 1957 Andrea Fraschetti was killed during a testing accident at Modena and *Ing.* Carlo Chiti, formerly with Alfa Romeo, took his place.

It was known that the *Fédération Internationale de l'Automobile* intended to impose a capacity limit of 3,000cc or 3,500cc in Championship sports car racing from 1958 onwards, but it was not until October 1957 that the precise capacity was announced. Would-be entrants were forced to speculate and Maserati built and raced in the Mille Miglia an experimental V12 3,490cc car. Ferrari was convinced that there would be a 3,000cc limit and also built and raced experimental cars. In late 1957 Ferrari formally announced the new car as the Tipo 250 *Testa Rossa*. For this model Maranello reverted to the familiar V12 2,953cc Colombo engine already used in the company's GT cars. The *Testa Rossa* had been well tested and developed before the 1958 season.

In a sense the wheel had turned full circle: Ferrari had started by racing Colombo-designed V12 cars and now some ten years later had reverted to what was largely the original design. The works raced *Testa Rossas* for four seasons and private owners were still campaigning them successfully in 1962. As announced by Ferrari in November 1957, the *Testa Rossa* had a single overhead camshaft per bank of cylinders, six Weber twin-choke 38DCN carburettors, twin-plug ignition and a power output of 300bhp at 7,200rpm. The works cars had a de Dion rear axle, but the cars sold to private owners were usually fitted with a rigid rear axle. With the V12 cars Ferrari won the Sports Car Championship in 1958, finished second to Aston Martin in 1959 and won again in 1960.

After the withdrawal of Aston Martin from sports car racing at the end of the 1959, the only challengers to Ferrari supremacy were the works Porsche team entering 2-litre cars and the American *Camoradi* team, which raced Tipo 61 'Bird-cage' Maseratis. The Camoradi team would have beaten Ferrari, but for the combination of Maserati unreliability and, sometimes, inadequate preparation. Ferrari was now also running V6 cars and these will be discussed shortly. Ferrari won the World Sports Car Championship with 22 points, the same total as Porsche, but although both had achieved two outright wins and a second place, Ferrari had two third places and Porsche none.

The *Commission Sportive Internationale* had decided

that the World Sports Car Championship would only be held in 1961, if a minimum of five races could be staged. It would, however, be the last of the series, and from 1962 there would be a *Gran Turismo* Championship. While the Sebring 12 Hours, Targa Florio, Nürburgring and Le Mans races were definitely to be held, the total of five could only be put together by adding the Pescara race which was eventually limited to four hours (and half-points only) because of the very hot weather in southern Italy during the summer. Until the last moment there were doubts as to whether this race would be held and, so, whether there would be a Championship at all.

Although Ferrari had been reluctant to build rear-engined cars, arguing rather inanely that 'the horse always pulled the cart', by 1960 the factory had been building experimental rear-engined prototypes. In 1961 Ferrari raced both front and rear-engined cars. It was a year of transition for the team, but fortunately for Ferrari, if not for the sport, the only real opposition came from the works Porsche 2-litre entries, and Maranello won the last World Sports Car Championship easily.

Ferrari had introduced the first V6 *Dino* in Formula 2 form at Naples in 1957 and raced these cars in Grand Prix form from 1958 onwards. The first race appearance of a *Dino* sports car was at Goodwood on Easter Monday 1958 when a car with a 1,984cc (77 x 71mm) V6 four overhead camshaft, twin-ignition engine developing 195bhp at 7,800rpm was entered for Peter Collins to drive. There was also a 2,962cc version, which Hawthorn raced at Silverstone the following month.

In an interview in June 1958 Enzo Ferrari said that

he considered the V6 engine in four overhead camshaft, twin-ignition form was far too expensive to build for sale to private owners. He added that a V6 car with a single overhead camshaft per bank of cylinders and single-plug ignition might prove a saleable proposition and while concluding that he had no immediate intention of building such a car, this simpler variant of the *Dino* was running before the year was out.

The new model, typed the *Dino* 196S, had the cylinders at an angle of 60° and in general design it resembled a six-cylinder version of the *Testa Rossa* and had the same cylinder dimensions as the car raced by Collins at Goodwood in 1958. With three Weber twin-choke 42DNC carburettors power output was 200bhp at 7,200rpm. The chassis was a shorter version of that of the *Testa Rossa*. Ferrari also built a version of this engine in somewhat detuned form with 9:1 (instead of 9.8:1) compression ratio, smaller-choke Weber 38DCN carburettors and a power output of 175bhp at 7,500rpm. It is believed that this was intended to power a GT model that was not proceeded with.

The V6 cars scored no successes in 1959, mainly because Ferrari was too heavily committed to his Grand Prix programme, developing and racing the *Testa Rossa* and the increasing demands for GT car production and race preparation. For the 1960 European season, there was also a sports V6 model with a 2,417cc engine (the *Dino* 246S) and in 1960 Ferrari built a 2,710cc (90 x 71mm) V6 engine known as the 276S. The team raced the 2.4-litre cars regularly, but the only success was second place by von Trips/Phil Hill in the 1960 Targa Florio with a *Dino* having coil spring independent rear suspension.

In February 1961 Ferrari announced the exciting rear-engined 246SP, powered by the original four overhead camshaft 65° V6 engine in 2,417cc form. With three twin-choke Weber 42DCN carburettors and a 9.8:1 compression ratio, power output was 270bhp at 8,000rpm. The five-speed gearbox was mounted behind the engine and there was independent suspension front and rear by double wishbones and coil springs. Dunlop disc brakes were fitted front and rear. The 246SP

16 Scarlet Passion

featured a similar body to that of the 1961 version of the *Testa Rossa* and although the former had its engine at the rear and the latter at the front, they were difficult to distinguish except by close inspection. Technically, there was much in common between the 246SP and the Formula 1 V6 1,500cc cars of the time.

Richie Ginther, Ferrari's test driver, said that the 246SP was 'the best handling sports car that he had ever driven' and despite giving away half a litre it was as fast as the latest *Testa Rossa*. The first race appearance of the new car was at Sebring where the single entry retired. With the same car von Trips/Gendebien won the Targa Florio on 30 April from strong Porsche opposition. On 28 May Phil Hill with a 246SP set a new sports car lap record of 91.70mph (147.55kph) in the Nürburgring 1,000Km race.

When the World Sports Car Championship came to an end in 1961, Ferrari had established itself as the most successful constructor and entrant of competition sports cars in the history of the sport. It is interesting to note that at this point Ferrari had built 248 cars in 1959, 306 in 1960 and 441 in 1961; Ferrari had produced a total of only 1,680 cars in 15 years. With the start of the new era of racing in 1962, the only V12 in the range of competition Ferraris was a GT car. Soon however Maranello was again to race V12 Prototypes powered by developments of the original Colombo design. One point does need stressing; in the period 1962–68 Ferrari was almost desperately short of money and the company operated its competition programme on a 'shoe-string'.

In late 1961 the company ceased to be legally known as *Scuderia Ferrari* and its name was changed formally to *Societa per Azioni Esercizio Fabbriche Automobile e Corse (SEFAC Ferrari)*. In English this means 'Company limited by shares for car manufacture and racing'. At the end of 1961 there was the notorious 'palace revolution' at Maranello and a number of leading Ferrari personalities slipped their collars from the grip of the tyrant. Carlo Chiti and team manager Romolo Tavoni set up *Societa per Azioni Automobili Turismo e Sport* (ATS), with backing from a group headed by 24-year-old Count Giovanni Volpi di Misurata. Mainly because of inadequate finances, the results of their efforts were the hopelessly underdeveloped and ill-prepared ATS V8 Formula 1 car raced in 1963 and a few promising, but equally unsuccessful, prototype GT cars.

Another important figure to leave was brilliant young engineer Giotto Bizzarrini who had been responsible for the development of the 250GT SWB and the 250GTO. He joined the Iso concern in Milan where he developed the exciting Chevrolet-powered Iso Grifo GT car, a number of which were later built by him in his own works and under his own name. Others on the administrative side of the company also left, but some sort of reconciliation was achieved and two, Ermanno Della Casa and Frederico Gilberti, relented, returned to Ferrari and were promoted.

The dissidents had given Ferrari an ultimatum that the pressures and stresses at Maranello had to be reduced or they would quit, but the true reason has never been known with certainty. It has usually been attributed to Laura Ferrari's meddling in the operation of the company. Unlike Enzo, she attended races with former team manager Amoratto and undoubtedly gave Tavoni a hard time – but, for that matter, so did everybody else. Although Ferrari stood by his wife, Maranello issued a statement in February 1962 that 'Signora Ferrari will no longer be connected with the Ferrari racing *équipe*.'

Ferrari's racing programme in 1962 suffered badly as a result of the resignations. This was not as obvious in prototype and GT racing, in which the team faced no serious opposition, but was very marked in Formula 1. Lack of development of the Grand Prix cars, coupled with the fact that the British Coventry Climax and BRM V8 engines were now fully raceworthy, resulted in Ferrari failing to win a single World Championship race that year. In the Constructors' Cup Ferrari slipped from winning in 1961 to fifth place behind BRM, Lotus, Cooper and Lola.

At the start of 1962, Ferrari and other entrants still regarded sports car racing as unchanged apart from the absence of a World Championship. Ferrari's line-up of sports cars for 1962 represented developments of existing models. Soon the definition of a GT prototype was to be clarified and the whole face of racing was to change, largely because of the entry of Ford and the emergence of a closely-fought battle between Ford and Ferrari.

In late 1962 the American Ford company opened negotiations with a view to entering into what amounted to a financial partnership with Ferrari. It was to run from 15 July 1963 to 31 December 2000 and, according to Franco Gozzi, the sum of 12.5 billion lire was to be paid and there were also to be share options. Ford was planning to totally revamp its image and the addition to the group of the world's greatest competition car manufacturer would have given it a tremendous boost. From the outset Enzo Ferrari was insistent that he retained absolute autonomy in the construction and management of the racing cars. Ford carried out very detailed investigations of the company (what, today, lawyers would call 'due diligence') and there were very protracted negotiations.

When the draft agreement was being considered in detail, Enzo Ferrari realised it stipulated that if he wished to increase expenditure on racing, he would have to obtain approval from Dearborn. In the words of

On the left of the photograph is Luigi Chinetti, who became America East Coast agent and ran the very successful NART. With him are Piero Taruffi and the Ferrari 212 Export they drove to a win in the 1951 Carrera Panamericana Mexico road race.

18 Scarlet Passion

Top During 1955 Ferrari raced Lampredi-designed six-cylinder cars. This is Castellotti with his 4.4-litre Tipo 121LM at Le Mans in 1955. He led early in the race, but these cars were under-developed and unreliable, and he soon dropped out because of engine problems.
(T. C. March/FotoVantage)

Bottom Mike Hawthorn at the Karussel banked corner during the 1958 Nürburgring 1,000Km race. The car is a V12 3-litre Testa Rossa and Hawthorn, partnered by Peter Collins, finished second behind Stirling Moss/Jack Brabham at the wheel of an Aston Martin DBR1.

Franco Gozzi, 'Ferrari felt cheated, betrayed. He disputed the document and scribbled on it, and when the head of the American delegation tried to reply, saying that the partner always had to be informed, he flew into a rage.' That day, 20 May 1963, the negotiations were terminated, but six years later Ferrari was to tie the knot with a much more accommodating partner.

During the years covered by this book Ferrari was still very much a 'family'. It tended to be very inward-looking and developments that took place elsewhere could easily pass it by. Many a Ferrari driver was treated by Enzo as his favourite son, but if a driver became 'political' (which meant being 'critical'), he rapidly became the black sheep of the family and was soon shown the door.

By 1968 Ferrari was in serious financial difficulties, the result of the high costs of competing in three different categories, Grand Prix racing, Prototype GT racing and the 1,600cc Formula 2, which had come into force in 1967. There had been discussions with Gianni Agnelli, head of Fiat, which for some years had been providing support for Ferrari's Grand Prix programme through the Italian Automobile Club. It was not until 18 June 1969 that the agreement that settled the future of Ferrari was reached. Fiat took a 51% shareholding in Ferrari, Enzo Ferrari continued to control racing activities, but Fiat had 'influence' in the development and production of the road cars. On Enzo Ferrari's death in 1988, Fiat acquired a further 39 per cent of Ferrari shares. The remaining ten per cent of the shares were vested in Piero Lardi Ferrari, Enzo Ferrari's illegitimate son.

Ailing Fiat Auto does not now own the shares in Ferrari, but these belong to a Fiat holding company. In June 2002 the Italian Mediobanca purchased 34 per cent of the issued shares at a price of around US$772 million, but then sold on ten per cent to the German Commerzbank and two per cent to the Banca Popolare Emilia Romagna. It has long been rumoured that Fiat will float Ferrari on the Italian stock exchange. Ferrari holds the shares in Maserati, but it is possible that if flotation takes place, Maserati will be 'de-merged' and retained by Fiat.

Despite the Formula 1 domination of Ferrari and Michael Schumacher during the period 2000–2004 and the continuing high demand for Ferrari road cars, there must be serious doubts about the viability of Ferrari as an independent company in the deepening world recession. In 2002 Ferrari made a profit of US$120 million and over US$100 million was ploughed back into funding the Grand Prix team. The Formula 1 cars provide immense publicity for Fiat Auto, but if Fiat Auto is sold, which seems possible, then the pressure being exerted by present shareholders to reduce expenditure on racing would fall on less stony ground. That Ferrari will survive is undoubted, but in what form is a very different matter.

Principal Ferrari Successes, 1950–61

	No. of times held	No. of times won by Ferrari
Drivers' World Championship, 1950–61	12	5
World Sports Car Championship, 1953–61	9	7
Mille Miglia Road Race, 1948–57	10	7
Le Mans 24 Hours Race, 1949–61	13	5

The Evolution
of the Ferrari Grand Touring Car

Mike Parkes at the wheel of the 250GTO entered by Maranello Concessionaires, but not in the team's usual colours, in the GT race at the International Trophy meeting at Silverstone in May 1963. He won after a close struggle with Graham Hill ('Lightweight' E-type Jaguar). (T. C. March/ FotoVantage)

The first Ferraris for the road were built in 1948 and Ferrari road cars in various forms have always been available since then. The early road cars were detuned versions of the competition sports models, sometimes with a longer chassis, and as this was the heyday of the Italian coach-building industry, some very fine-looking bodies were built on these chassis. It was not practical, indeed feasible, to use these Ferraris on a daily basis. They often suffered from plug trouble, the revs had to be kept up, the suspension was harsh and the roadholding was rather too primitive for most ordinary drivers to handle at any sort of high speed.

Although the bodies were usually beautifully styled, quality was not a strong point. The trim was poor, the aluminium-alloy structure developed rattles, the panelling cracked and accident damage was exorbitantly expensive to repair. They were really only 'weekend' cars, although amateurs often drove them in competitions; Italian hill climbs, the high-speed Tour de France and rallies such as the Lyon-Charbonnières.

It was only in the mid-1950s that Ferrari gave serious consideration to the development of practicable touring cars and, in a separate category, GT models built specifically for competition work.

The 250 Mille Miglia *and* Europa GT

The inspiration for a new era of GT Ferraris was the 250MM competition sports car built in 1953 and powered by the Colombo V12 engine in its classic 2,953cc (73 x 58.8cc) form. A number of these cars were fitted with very stylish Pinin Farina coupé bodies and if the engines had not been so fiery, they would have made admirable fast touring cars. For 1954 Ferrari developed the 250 *Europa* GT, but instead of using the Colombo engine, the company opted for a Lampredi 'long-block' power unit of 2,963cc (68 x 68mm) and it was the only Ferrari model ever built with 'square' cylinder dimensions.

Quite why Ferrari chose this engine with specially cast cylinders is difficult to understand, for Ferrari had no foundry and most castings were done for him by the Maserati metal company, which had been independently run by Adolfo Orsi's sisters since the previous year. It would have been substantially cheaper to use the Colombo engine from the outset. On a compression ratio of 8.5:1, with single-plug ignition and three Weber 36DCZ carburettors, power output was 200bhp at 6,000rpm. A new type of four-speed gearbox was fitted and the coupé body by Pinin Farina was a rather less dramatic version of that used on the 250MM. These cars were rather on the heavy side for competition work and only about 20 were built. One, with right-hand drive, was delivered to the Swedish ambassador in Paris (at that time you drove on the left in Sweden). Whatever the reasoning at the time for using a 'long-block' engine, Ferrari soon changed his mind and reverted to the Colombo design for the next generation of GT cars.

The First Ferrari 250 GTs

After the Le Mans disaster in 1955, there was criticism of the high speeds being attained by competition sports cars and the familiar comment that they were only Grand Prix cars with full-width bodywork, full electrics and a larger engine. It was an argument that had been put forward for some time, and not one with much merit, but there was a response from the *Fédération Internationale de l'Automobile*, which introduced a GT Championship for 1956. Ferrari had already developed the 250GT model and this had been exhibited at the Geneva Salon in March 1955. It was available as a touring car and also as a competition model or *berlinetta*. The name, meaning 'little saloon', had been applied in Italy to sporting coupés for some while, but it was increasingly used to describe competition coupés, especially those from Maranello.

Ferrari's latest models used the 2,953cc Colombo engine, and both touring and competition cars had similar bodies styled by Pinin Farina. In standard form, with three twin-choke Weber 36DCZ carburettors and 8.5:1 compression ratio, the power output was 220bhp at 7,000rpm. The competition cars usually had a higher compression ratio and hotter camshafts. Transmission was by a dry twin-plate clutch and four-speed gearbox with Porsche baulk-ring synchromesh.

A typical early Ferrari touring car: this is a c1951 2.3-litre Inter *model with Ghia coachwork.*

The chassis was similar to that of the 250 *Europa*, except that there was coil spring instead of leaf spring front suspension.

The bodies of the touring cars were built in Pinin Farina's Turin works, but the competition cars were the work of Scaglietti and represented his interpretation of Pinin Farina's design. The competition cars lacked trim, they had half-bumpers instead of full bumpers, often there were Plexiglas windows instead of glass, air scoops in the bonnet, Plexiglas fairings over the headlamps and they sounded noisier and ran hotter (both inside and out). There was at this time no clear-cut detailed specification for the competition cars – Ferrari was still feeling his way – and through to 1957 some were completed by Zagato who built a few bodies on these chassis with its striking 'double-bubble' roof line.

Little was seen of the competition *berlinettas* in 1955, but they made their mark the following year. A works-supported car with very smooth Scaglietti body (chassis number 0503GT) ran in the 671-mile (1,080km) Tour of Sicily held on 8 April. Belgian driver Olivier Gendebien was at the wheel partnered by his brother-in-law Jacques Wascher. Peter Collins won with a Tipo 860 Ferrari from Taruffi (300S Maserati) and Villoresi (1,500cc OSCA). Despite a puncture and clutch problems Gendebien brought his *berlinetta* across the line in fourth place, just over half-an-hour behind the winner, and won the *Gran Turismo* class.

The same car with the same drivers ran in the Mille Miglia held on 28–29 April. It was a thoroughly miserable race held in torrential rain and after the retirement of the works Maseratis, factory-entered sports-racing Ferraris took the first four places. Gendebien/Wascher faced stiff opposition in the *Gran Turismo* class from a total of ten Mercedes-Benz 300SLs, two of which were works cars and all of them were under the care and control of Mercedes racing manager, Alfred Neubauer, former works driver Karl Kling and an army of mechanics.

Neubauer had expressed the cautious view that with an element of luck one of the works Stuttgart entries could win the race outright. Instead Gendebien thrashed the German opposition, despite the heavy rain flooding the interior of the *berlinetta* and Gendebien leaving the road four times and spinning wildly at high speed three times. Wascher must have been a very brave and trusting man! Gendebien finished fifth overall, won the *Gran Turismo* class and was almost seven minutes ahead of the first surviving 300SL driven by Prinz Metternich/Einsiedel.

The Tour de France rally was held between 17–23 September and included speed tests at Mont Ventoux hill climb, the Comminges circuit (five laps), Peyresourde hill climb, Le Mans (12 laps), Rouen-les-Essarts circuit (eight laps), Reims circuit (12 laps), an acceleration test at Aix-les-Bains circuit and culminated in ten laps of the Montlhéry circuit. It was to become a Ferrari monopoly, for, already, Ferraris had won in 1951 and finished second in 1952–53.

The Marquis Alfonso de Portago, partnered by his friend and ski instructor Ed Nelson, drove a Ferrari *berlinetta* chassis number 0557GT and faced a horde of 300SLs including a car driven by Stirling Moss accompanied by former racing motorcyclist Georges Houel. The Ferrari drivers scored a brilliant victory, although it has to be conceded that Moss's second-place 300SL had its problems, including an intermittent engine misfire. Gendebien, partnered on this occasion at the wheel of Ferrari 0357GT by one Ringoir (who subsequently bought the car), took third place. His Ferrari was a 1955 250 *Europa* GT with standard Pinin Farina body.

Pinin Farina had exhibited a *berlinetta* with very neat, balanced lines at the 1956 Geneva Salon and Scaglietti adopted this body for a run of competition coupés laid down in January 1957. The precise number of these cars built is not known, but they were seen frequently in competitions. Following the cancellation of the 1957 Monte Carlo Rally because of the fuel crisis caused by the Suez fiasco, the first important rally of the year was the Sestriere event held in Italy between 24 February and 1 March and incorporating speed tests at the Modena, Imola and Monza circuits. Lena/Palanga with a 1956-build Scaglietti-bodied *berlinetta* chassis number 0629GT won their class and finished sixth overall.

On 14 April the Tour of Sicily was held in heavy rain and initially veteran Piero Taruffi led with a Maserati 300S, but he lost time after colliding with a wall and Gendebien/Wascher were able to go ahead with their works GT Ferrari (0677GT) and won at an average of 66.48mph (106.97kph), only six minutes slower than Collins's winning time with a sports-racing Ferrari the previous year. By 1957 this arduous race was attracting only a reduced entry; it severely disrupted traffic in Sicily, but it was mainly as a result of the Mille Miglia disaster that it was not held again.

Gendebien, again partnered by Wascher, drove another brilliant race in the last Mille Miglia. It is believed that the engine of Gendebien's 250GT was modified to the same level of tune as the *Testa Rossa* then under development, but, apparently still on three carburettors. He finished third overall, winning the GT class at 94.2mph (151.6kph), and the car was so fast that on parts of the circuit the drivers of the larger-capacity sports-racing Ferraris had great difficulty in overtaking it. There were no GT Ferraris at Le Mans, but in July the Reims 12 Hours race was held for *Gran Turismo* cars. The Ferraris completely dominated the event, Gendebien, partnered by Paul Frère, won with his usual 250GT at 104.02mph (167.39kph) and they were followed across the line by another four of these cars.

There were GT races before the German Grand Prix, won by Wolfgang Seidel with Ferrari *berlinetta*, chassis number 0607GT, and the sports car Swedish Grand Prix, won by local driver Curt Lincoln with a 250GT. The one-hour Coppa Inter-Europa at Monza on 8 September had originated as a saloon car race, but from 1956 onwards it was held for GT cars. In 1956 Zampiero (Mercedes-Benz 300SL) had won from Luglio with his Zagato-bodied 250GT chassis number 0515GT, a very stylish coupé with 'double-bubble' roof, but Luglio with another Zagato-bodied car, chassis number 0665 GT, won the 1957 race from other Ferraris driven by Lualdi and Taramazzo.

In the Tour de France held between 16–22 September with the usual speed tests the Ferrari *berlinettas* completely outpaced the obsolescent Mercedes-Benz 300SLs. Gendebien/Lucien Bianchi were the winners with 0677GT (now sold to Gendebien), and Trintignant/Picard (0733GT) and Lucas/Malle (0747GT) with their Ferraris took second and third places ahead of the 300SL shared by Stirling Moss and Peter Garnier, Sports Editor of *The Autocar*. The third-place Ferrari was the latest version of the 250GT *berlinetta*, which was to be formally announced at the Paris Salon the following month. It was still bodied by Scaglietti, but changes included a lengthened nose, the headlamps under Plexiglas covers and other detail changes. It was with good reason that the model became popularly known as the *Tour de France*.

Because of the relatively small number of serious sports car contenders and the growing interest in GT cars, it was becoming increasingly common for a GT class to be included in World Championship sports cars races. There was no GT class in the 1958 Buenos Aires 1,000Km race held on 26 January, but Maurice Trintignant partnered by Picard (0733GT) drove a

The 250 Mille Miglia *with Colombo-designed V12 2,953cc engine was a sports-racing car with Pinin Farina coupé body. It was also the progenitor of a long line of competition Grand Touring cars. This car belonged to C. W. Hampton, a great enthusiast and founder of the Hamptons chain of estate agents.*

The Evolution of the Ferrari Grand Touring Car 23

250GT into eighth place, nine laps behind the winning *Testa Rossa*. In the Sebring 12 Hours race on 22 May Kessler/O'Shea with their 1958 *berlinetta* won the GT class and finished fifth overall behind the winning *Testa Rossa* of Peter Collins/Phil Hill.

Gran Turismo racing was becoming increasingly popular and dominated by Ferrari. The Pau Grand Prix meeting traditionally held over the Easter weekend featured three three-hour GT races and in the largest-capacity event Gendebien with his 'old' 1957 Ferrari won from 1958 250GTs driven by Seidel and Munaron. The urbane Belgian had competed in six events with this Ferrari and won them all. Another French GT race was held at Montlhéry on 13 April and André Guelfi, Moroccan former Gordini driver, won with his 250GT at 88.26mph (142.01kph) from Noblet and Peron with other 250GTs.

At the delightful and difficult high-speed Spa-Francorchamps circuit in the Belgian Ardennes on 18 May the Royal Belgian Automobile Club held its annual sports car Grand Prix over a distance of 132 miles (212km). In the class for GT cars up to 3,500cc Portuguese driver Hermanos da Silva Ramos with 0749GT was the winner and Wolfgang Seidel and André Guelfi took second and third places. The Nürburgring 1,000Km race was held on 1 June and as usual there were a large number of entrants and a large number of classes. Kessler/Picard with the latter's 1958 *berlinetta* led the over 1,600cc GT class until Picard went off the road and then Leon Dernier/'Beurlys' with their Belgian-

24 Scarlet Passion

entered 250GT went on to win the class from two other Ferraris.

The Mille Miglia was dead, but an attempt was made to keep it alive by running it as a rally held on 21–22 June. It was a parochial Italian event and Taramazzo, partnered by Gerini, won with his 1958 *berlinetta*. Much more important was the Reims 12 Hours race for GT cars held at the French Grand Prix meeting on 6 July. Ten Ferrari 250GTs were entered and Gendebien, again partnered by Paul Frère, and still with 0677GT, were the winners. During the race a stone broke the windscreen and so both this and the rear window were removed. They averaged 106.05mph (170.63kph); other Ferraris occupied second to fifth and seventh positions overall.

A three-hour GT race was held on the newly-opened, hilly, tortuous Circuit des Charades in the hills behind Clermont-Ferrand on 27 July. The Ferraris were expected to dominate the race, but this ignored the Lotus factor. The Lotus-Eleven Climax in 1,100cc form with full-width windscreen and other equipment was homologated as a GT car. Many Continental entrants considered this to be unfair, as it was an out-and-out sports-racing car. They conveniently overlooked the fact that well over 200 Lotus Elevens had been built, whereas Ferrari only *claimed* that sufficient 250GTs had been built for homologation.

A Lotus Eleven had won the 1,300cc class at Reims and now in the Auvergne, the combination of the sheer skill of Innes Ireland and the Girling disc brakes of the Lotus humbled the Ferraris. Maurice Trintignant finished second with Picard's *berlinetta* chassis number 0901GT, which was rumoured to have a full *Testa Rossa* engine. Willy Mairesse was third with a white Ferrari, chassis number 0969GT, while Olivier Gendebien who had to make a refuelling stop because the tank of his 250GT was not big enough to run through a three-hour race, took fourth place ahead of da Silva Ramos with yet another Ferrari.

In the Tour de France Olivier Gendebien/Lucien Bianchi were at the wheel of a new 250GT, chassis number 1033GT, which differed in minor detail from earlier models. As before Gendebien competed in the speed tests, while Bianchi drove most of the road section, to win the GT category for the second year in succession. Trintignant/Picard finished second with 0901 and other Ferrari drivers occupied the next three places. At the Coupe du Salon meeting held at Montlhéry on 5 October Lucien Bianchi, with what was probably Gendebien's new car, won the short GT race from two French-entered *berlinettas* and with an Austin-Healey in fourth place.

A new GT Ferrari was the 250GT *Spyder California*, only too obviously by its name intended for the

Left *With this much-modified 250GT bodied by Scaglietti, Olivier Gendebien, partnered by brother-in-law Wascher, finished third in the 1957 Mille Miglia and won the GT class.*

Below *In 1958 the Mille Miglia was held as a high-speed rally and was won by Luigi Taramazzo with this Scaglietti-bodied 250GT Berlinetta Tour de France.*

American market. Pinin Farina based the design on that of the *berlinetta* but it was built as usual by Scaglietti and exhibited in definitive form at the 1958 Paris Salon. The *California* was intended primarily for road use, but was to score two race successes of some significance. A change that occurred around this time on the 250GT was the relocation of the sparking plugs outside the vee of the engine. The *berlinetta* in 1959 form had slightly modified bodywork with raised, uncovered headlamps.

Ferrari's first GT success in 1959 was in the Sebring 12 Hours race on 21 March. Richie Ginther and Howard Hively shared a *California* and drove it into ninth place overall and a win in the 3,000cc GT class. Although the Tour of Sicily had been axed, the Targa Florio went from strength to strength and in the 1959 race held on 24 May, Porsche entries took the first four places. Le Pira/Siracusa drove a 1956 250GT into ninth place. In the Nürburgring 1,000Km race 'Beurlys'/Blaton and Bianchi/Blary with their *berlinettas* took the first two places in the 3,000cc GT class. The class-winning car was one of the latest 1959 250GTs, chassis number 1321GT and that driven by Bianchi/Blary was Gendebien's car. Gendebien co-drove a works *Testa Rossa* with Phil Hill and finished second overall behind Moss/Fairman (Aston Martin DBR1).

An interesting Italian event for GT cars held on the Sunday after Le Mans, 28 June, was the Lottery Grand Prix over a distance of 186 miles (300km) on the Monza road circuit with a first prize of over one million lire for the punter who drew the race number of the winning car. Although the race started in fine conditions, torrential rain fell during the second half and this substantially reduced lap speeds. Sixteen *berlinettas* ran in this race and they took the first 12 places. Alfonso Thiele (1389GT) won at 97.84mph (157.42kph) from Carlo Abate (1333GT) and Willy Mairesse (0969GT). Lucien Bianchi crashed heavily with Gendebien's car, which was returned to the factory for a rebuild. Another GT race at Monza was the three-hour Coppa Inter-Europa held on 13 September and Thiele and Abate again took the first two places, but on this occasion Noblet was third with his *berlinetta*.

The Tour de France was held to the usual, well-established formula between 18 and 25 September. Following Bianchi's crash at Monza with Gendebien's car, the pair drove one of the latest interim cars (chassis number 1523GT) and Gendebien scored his third successive win and Ferrari's fourth. Mairesse/Berger finished in second place with their 1958 *berlinetta* and de Lageneste/Schild were third. A Porsche took fourth place. About 100 of the long-wheelbase 250GTs were built between 1955 and 1999.

Graham Whitehead with his Ferrari 250GT SWB at the British Empire Trophy meeting at Silverstone in July 1961. Alongside the Ferrari is Graham Hill with the Équipe Endeavour Jaguar E-type and Bruce McLaren with another E-type follows. (T. C. March/FotoVantage)

The Short-Wheelbase 250GT

The definitive new 250GT exhibited at the Paris Salon was breathtakingly stylish and resembled the interim model first seen at Le Mans apart from the deletion of the rear quarter-lights. The wheelbase had been shortened to 7ft 10.5in (2,400mm) and kerb weight reduced to about a ton in its lightest form. The engine, with the 12-port outside plug *Testa Rossa* cylinder head, was still running on three Weber 40DCN twin-choke carburettors and developed 260bhp at 7,000rpm. These cars, known as the SWB (short wheelbase), were built in two forms; for competition work the cars had an all-aluminium-alloy body, and for road use the body was steel with aluminium-alloy doors, bonnet, roof and boot panels. Although the GT regulations permitted body changes, the new model required homologation because of its shorter wheelbase and it was well into 1960 before this was achieved

In 1960 the Buenos Aires 1,000Km race was revived and was held on 31 January. Gavazzoli/Todaro brought their 1957 *berlinetta* across the line in ninth place overall and won the GT category, the first of many 250GT successes that year. There was a strong entry of SWBs at Sebring on 26 March, but they were not yet homologated and victory in the 3,000cc GT category went to Scarlatti/Serena with a 250GT *Spyder California* who finished eighth overall. Works Porsche sports-racing cars took the first two places overall, but Hugus/Pabst (1785GT), Sturgis/d'Orey (1539GT) and Arents/Kimberly (1773GT) with their SWBs finished fourth, sixth and seventh.

Giotto Bizzarrini was largely responsible for the development of the SWB and at the Le Mans Practice Weekend he brought one along in *Testa Rossa* six-carburettor form. In the Targa Florio on 8 May Lenza/Maglione finished ninth overall with SWB chassis number 1791GT, but Lualdi/Scarlatti in tenth place with a 1959 *berlinetta* won the GT class. In the Nürburgring 1,000Km race Carlo Abate/Colin Davis, eighth overall, won the over 2,000cc GT class with a 1959 car and other Ferraris took second and third places. Jack Fairman with an Aston Martin DBR1 dominated the Rouen Grand Prix on 12 June and won both heats. Ferrari GT cars, however, took second, third, fourth, fifth and seventh places.

By the Le Mans race on 25–26 June the SWB had been homologated in the GT category and on the Sarthe circuit they dominated their class. Tavano/'Loustel' with their SWB finished fourth overall, averaging 105.009mph (168.960kph) compared with the 109.193mph (175.691kph) of the winning Ferrari *Testa Rossa*. Other SWBs driven by Arents/Connell,

26 Scarlet Passion

'Elde'/Noblet and Hugus/Pabst finished fifth, sixth and seventh overall.

Rob Walker and Dick Wilkins had acquired a right-hand-drive SWB, chassis number 2119GT, and they entered this in a few events for Stirling Moss. This car made its debut in the Tourist Trophy, run at Goodwood as a three-hour race for GT cars on 20 August and Moss, listening to a commentary of the race on the Ferrari's radio, won easily from Roy Salvadori and Innes Ireland with Aston Martin DB4GTs. In the three-hour Coppa Inter Europa held at Monza on the morning of the European Grand Prix there was another Ferrari landslide. Carlo Abate with his SWB won from Guichet and Toselli with similar cars.

The Tour de France was even now more formidable than previously and starting from Nice and finishing at Biarritz it covered a distance of 3,175 road miles (5,100km), 9½ hours of speed tests on circuits in France, Belgium and Germany and seven hill climbs. It devolved into a straight battle between the SWBs of Gendebien/Bianchi chassis number 2149GT and Mairesse/Berger (2129GT). Mairesse elected to use a smaller wheel and tyre size, running on Pirelli Cinturatos on the road and Dunlop racing tyres on the circuits, while Gendebien used racing Dunlops throughout.

Mairesse had two road accidents (one at night nearly wrote the car off) and one on a circuit. By the end of the event, there was hardly a body panel undamaged on this Ferrari and it was running far from *au point*. Gendebien's SWB broke a piston and time lost on repairs dropped it out of contention as it was limited to 6,500rpm due to engine vibration caused by using a lighter than standard replacement piston. Despite their problems Mairesse/Berger won on scratch from Schlesser/Loustel and Tavano/Martin with other SWBs. Gendebien and Bianchi derived some consolation by winning the Paris 1,000Km race for GT cars at Montlhéry on 23 October from Mairesse/von Trips, Schlesser/Simon and 'Loustel'/Tavano, all with SWBs.

There was no worthwhile opposition to the Ferraris in GT racing and neither the Aston Martin DB4GTs as raced in various forms between 1960 and 1963, nor the Jaguar E-type raced from 1961 onwards could match them. Ferrari was content to make only minor changes early in 1961 and these included the fitting of quarter-lights in the doors. So if a SWB has quarter-lights in the doors, it is a 1961 car and if it hasn't, it probably isn't. During the year Ferrari also built a small number of *Competizione* cars with larger valves, 46DCL Weber carburettors and paired exhausts. Buyers of these cars included Rob Walker/Dick Wilkins and *Équipe Endeavour/Maranello Concessionaires*.

The first race of the year was the Sebring 12 Hours and with their SWB Denise McCluggage/Allen Eager finished tenth and won the 3,000cc GT class. They had

The Evolution of the Ferrari Grand Touring Car 27

led the GT class overall for many hours and what made their performance all the more remarkable was that Eager had never driven in a race before. At the Le Mans Practice Weekend Mike Parkes with a works SWB lapped in 4min 9.2sec, 122.32mph (196.81kph) and was sixth fastest overall. Later Jo Schlesser crashed heavily with this car, injuring himself quite badly. There were only two SWBs entered in the Targa Florio on 30 April and the organisers would not run a class for them, so they competed with the sports-racing cars and were well down the list of finishers. In the Nürburgring 1,000Km race on 28 May Carlo Abate/Colin Davis with their private SWB finished fourth overall and won their class ahead of Willy Mairesse/Giancarlo Baghetti with a works car.

A total of eight SWBs ran at Le Mans on 10–11 June and the most interesting of these were two cars that failed to finish. Fernand Tavano and Giancarlo Baghetti drove what amounted to the first Ferrari 250GTO prototype. The body was by Pininfarina (as the company was known from 1961) and it closely resembled the production *SuperAmerica*.

The 3-litre engine was to *Testa Rossa* specification with similar camshafts, six twin-choke Weber carburettors and dry-sump lubrication. Tavano and Baghetti drove it and although it was in seventh place at the end of the second hour, it developed starter motor problems, and later retired with engine trouble.

The 250SWB *Competizione* driven by Stirling Moss and Graham Hill was faster and almost as interesting. Rob Walker and Dick Wilkins also owned this car, which was one of a very small number built and carried chassis number 2735. The entrant was *NART* (North American

28 Scarlet Passion

Racing Team). In his superb book, *Stirling Moss: My Cars, My Career* Moss said, '... we averaged over 118mph [about 190kph] for the first 1½-hours, howling along the Mulsanne Straight at 7,700rpm. It felt fabulous. After 21 laps my best time was 4min 8sec and that night we lay third overall, leading the GT category by miles.

'Suddenly, in the tenth hour, the car lost all its water and boiled dry. Unbelievably, *NART* had not removed its standard road-going fan, and since we had been holding high revs for so long, one of the fan blades had flown off and slashed clean through a radiator hose.' Noblet/Guichet drove their SWB into third place behind a brace of *Testa Rossa*s, averaged 110.241mph (177.38kph) and won the 3,000cc GT category.

Moss scored a minor win with the *Competizione* in the 25-lap race GT cars at the British Empire Trophy meeting at Silverstone. Following an engine rebuild the car had been driven back from Maranello and arrived at the circuit on rain tyres on the afternoon before the race! There were also arguments with the scrutineers about its homologation. The following day Mairesse with his 1960 SWB won the six-hour race at the Auvergne circuit. Seven SWBs ran in the four-hour Pescara Grand Prix, the final round in the World Sports Car Championship, on 15 August. The two fastest runners, Mairesse and Abate retired – the latter ran out of fuel on the last lap when in second place overall – and Arents/Hamill were fourth overall with their SWB and won the GT class.

On 19 August Stirling Moss with the *Competizione* scored his seventh win in the Tourist Trophy, again run at Goodwood as a three-hour race for GT cars. Mike Parkes with the similar car entered jointly by *Équipe Endeavour/Maranello Concessionaires* took second place. During September Stirling Moss travelled to Maranello to test the 'hack' 250GTO 1962 prototype. The Tour de France was held between 14–23 September and out of 117 starters there were only 46 finishers, the event concluding with a two-hour road race round Corsica. Ferrari SWBs took the first four places in the order Mairesse/Berger, Gendebien/Bianchi, Trintignant/Cavrois and Berney/Gretener. It was Ferrari's sixth successive win in the event and the seventh since it had first been held in 1951.

In the Paris 1,000Km race for GT cars at Montlhéry on 22 October Mexican bothers, Ricardo and Pedro Rodriguez won with a SWB from four other SWBs and with an Aston Martin in sixth place. Moss rounded off his season with the Walker/Wilkins car by winning the 112-mile (180.21km) GT Nassau Tourist Trophy in the Bahamas in December. On 11 February 1962 Moss raced a GT Ferrari again in the Daytona Continental three-hours race. This was a very special *berlinetta*, in effect another prototype of the soon-to-be-announced 250GTO with *Testa Rossa* engine, the SWB chassis and a body that resembled that of Pininfarina's *Superfast II* production model. Chinetti's *NART* entered this car and Moss drove it into fourth place behind a trio of sports-racing cars, winning the GT class by a very comfortable margin.

The 250GTO

Only 13 days after the Daytona race, Ferrari announced the arrival of the 250GTO at his annual press conference. The chassis was similar to that of the SWB, but lighter; there were some suspension modifications and the body was another dramatic design by Pininfarina and built by Scaglietti. The lines were lower and sleeker than those of the SWB, making the GTO look longer. There was a small, low, elliptical air intake set in a smoother, more aerodynamic nose and there

Left *Stirling Moss won the GT race at the July 1961 Silverstone meeting with this SWB Berlinetta jointly owned by Rob Walker and Dick Wilkins. He also won the Tourist Trophy at Goodwood in August 1961 with this car.* (T. C. March/FotoVantage)

Below *Stirling Moss at the wheel of the* NART-*entered prototype 250GTO is seen on his way to fourth place in the 1962 Daytona Three Hours race.*

were three shield-shaped inlets on the nose covered by detachable panels. The windscreen and cockpit had been moved back slightly to give better weight distribution. The tail sloped smoothly, but was cut off in accordance with the aerodynamic theories of Professor Wunibald Kamm and had a recessed rear panel. As seen at the Ferrari press conference, there was no spoiler on the tail, but this was added by the time the model was raced. Sliding Plexiglas windows were fitted (the SWBs had wind-up glass or Plexiglas windows).

The engine was in *Testa Rossa* tune with six Weber 38DCN carburettors, dry-sump lubrication and an output of 300bhp at 7,500rpm. The exhaust system consisted of three equal-length pipes on each side of the engine, which merged into single tail-pipes. The transmission incorporated a five-speed all-synchromesh gearbox. Wide nine-inch rear wheels were fitted and there was no engine fan. The competition versions of the SWB were in the minority, but the 250GTO had no such split personality and all 33 of the original type built were out-and-out competition cars.

The point has to be made that the intrinsic quality of these cars, especially the bodies, was not of the highest. As the model was intended for competition work, the panels were extremely light and these cars developed creaks and rattles very early in their life. Another constructional problem that affected all Ferrari's road cars was that the bodies were not built up on the chassis, but constructed on a production line at Scaglietti and then transported to Maranello for mounting on the chassis. Neither was mechanical quality always of the highest, especially when production-line workers were under pressure to complete cars to meet racing deadlines.

The 250GTO was homologated immediately and the *Commission Sportive Internationale* accepted it as a development of the SWB, just as the 'Lightweight' E-type and the Project 214 version of the Aston Martin DB4GT were accepted the following year. Special bodies could be fitted provided that they weighed not less than 95% of the original car. The 250GTO was to prove invincible and remained unbeaten until Le Mans in 1964, by when Ferrari regarded the model as obsolete and it *should* have been superseded by a much more radical GT car from Maranello. Race debut for the 250GTO came at Sebring on 24 March, when Phil Hill and Olivier Gendebien drove a *NART* entry. They finished second and won the GT class. An interesting entry at this race was the Daytona GTO prototype, which Ed Hugus/George Reed drove into eighth place overall.

Soon 250GTOs were in private hands and deliveries to Britain included one jointly owned by British Ferrari agents *Maranello Concessionaires* and Tommy Sopwith's *Équipe Endeavour* (usually driven by Mike Parkes). Another was for the *UDT-Laystall Racing Team* (this would have been driven by Stirling Moss but for his dreadful crash at Goodwood on Easter Monday, but was thereafter usually raced by Innes Ireland) and *Bowmaker Racing*. (*Maranello Concessionaires* also owned this car, which was not delivered until August). Col. Ronnie Hoare of *Maranello Concessionaires* and Ireland collected their cars from Italy and drove them back in time for the Easter Monday meeting at Goodwood. After Moss's crash, the *UDT-Laystall* car non-started in the 15-lap Sussex Trophy, but Parkes with the *Equipe Endeavour/Maranello* car finished second to Ireland's Lotus 19 and won the GT category.

In the Targa Florio on 6 May Giorgio Scarlatti partnered by Ferraro drove a 250GTO painted black with a white roof into fourth place overall and a GT class win. Mike Parkes won the 73-mile (117.46km) GT race from Masten Gregory with the *UDT-Laystall* car at the International Silverstone meeting on 12 May. The GTOs failed in the Nürburgring 1,000Km race on 27 May when Scarlatti crashed his GTO on lap six, before co-driver Ferraro could have a turn at the wheel, and Maglioli/Kochert led the GT class with their 250GTO until the starter motor failed after a routine pit stop. But Ferrari still dominated the GT class when Peter Nocker/Wolfgang Seidel with their SWB finished sixth overall and won the category from Noblet/Guichet and Oreiller/de Lageneste with similar cars.

Seven 250GTOs were entered at Le Mans, held on 15–16 June and those of Guichet/Noblet and 'Elde'/'Beurlys' took second and third places overall and first two places in the 3,000cc GT class. One 'GT' Ferrari at Le Mans was of especial interest. Count Volpi's *Scuderia Serenissima Repubblica di Venezia* entered what was to become known as the Ferrari 'bread van' and this ran in the Experimental category. Giorgio Neri and Luciano Bonacini carried out the mechanical work and Giotto Bizzarrini acted as adviser. It was built on SWB chassis number 2819 with the engine upgraded to full *Testa Rossa* specification and with unusual, squared-off bodywork by Venezuelan Piero Drogo's Carrozzeria Sports Cars based in the via Emilia Ouest in Modena. The cut-off rear of the body was inspired, as were so many other designs, by the aerodynamic principles of Wunibald Kamm.

The car originated after Ferrari refused to sell cars to Volpi because he had set up his own ATS racing-car company. According to Volpi the work was carried out within 14 days of delivery of the SWB to Neri & Bonacini. Under the then GT regulations, it should have been homologated immediately if the weight was not more than 5% less than that of the 250GT SWB. However, de Hartog and his colleagues in their book *Bizzarrini*, say that the weight was 100kg (220lb) less than the GTO. If that is correct, it should not have been homologated at all, because it would have been 20% lighter than an SWB! Carlo Mario Abate and Colin Davis drove the *Venezia* entry in the 24 hours' race and were in seventh place at the end of the second hour, before falling right down the field and retiring because of transmission problems.

In all there were three of these cars and each had a different body. The second car was built for Chris Kerrison on chassis number 2735, the second Walker/Wilkins 250GT SWB that Kerrison had crashed in the 1961 Tourist Trophy at Goodwood. It lacked the distinctive 'bread van' profile, as did the third car. *Écurie Francorchamps* had bought this SWB (chassis number 2019) second-hand from Ferrari and after 'Beurlys' crashed it heavily at Le Mans in 1960 it was eventually sent to Drogo and his colleagues for a rebuild. Drogo gave it a particularly stylish body with a sloping roofline. The Belgian team did not run the car after the 1963 Le Mans Test Weekend, but it continued to be raced by Gérald Langlois von Ophem until it was written off in a heavy crash at Spa-Francorchamps in 1964.

The International meeting at Brands Hatch on August Bank Holiday Monday, 6 August attracted a strong entry of Ferraris. In the 27-mile (43km) Peco Trophy race for GT cars, GTOs took the first three places in the order Parkes (*Équipe Endeavour/Maranello Concessionaires* dark blue car with white nose), Roy Salvadori (white car entered by John Coombs) and Innes Ireland (with the pale green *UDT-Laystall* car). The 133-mile (214km) Guards Trophy was for what the organisers still called sports cars and Abate with the *Venezia* 'bread van' drove a good race to finish fourth overall. On 18 August the Tourist Trophy was held at Goodwood as a 240-mile (386km) race for GT cars.

Mike Parkes at the wheel of the Ferrari 250GTO owned jointly by Maranello Concessionaires and Équipe Endeavour at Silverstone in May 1962. Parkes won the race from Masten Gregory (UDT-Laystall 250GTO) and Graham Hill (Jaguar E-type). (T. C. March/FotoVantage)

Above *The so-called 'bread van' Ferrari was a reworking of the 250GT SWB by Giotto Bizzarrini. It had an engine to full Testa Rossa tune and a body by Piero Drogo. Here at Le Mans in 1962, Colin Davis/Carlo Abate lead the V8 Ferrari 268SP through the Esses early in the race. Both cars retired.* (LAT)

Right *Another view of the 'bread van' which Carlo Abate drove into fourth place in the Guards Trophy at Brands Hatch on August Bank Holiday Monday, 1962. Much of the race was run in the wet and Abate performed very well.* (LAT)

Innes Ireland, Graham Hill and Mike Parkes took the first three places with GTOs. David Piper finished in fifth place with his 250GTO.

During 1961–62 David Piper had been importing second-hand Lancias, Lancia spares and the occasional Ferrari into the UK. He had asked his contacts in Italy to try to find him a good *Competitizione* SWB but, once the 250GTO had appeared, Piper realised that this was the car to buy and that an SWB would no longer be competitive. When first announced 250GTOs were in very short supply, but he approached Ronnie Hoare and asked if it would be possible for *Maranello Concessionaires* to obtain one for him and during the summer of 1962 'the Colonel' duly obliged.

32 Scarlet Passion

It was expected that the GTOs would dominate the Tour de France held between 15–23 September. As the event progressed, Lucien Bianchi and Claude Dubois with their GTO settled into what seemed an impregnable lead, but shortly after the speed test at Spa-Francorchamps they collided with a milk lorry. Although they drove on, the front of the car was completely wrecked and when they arrived for the final speed test at Reims, the scrutineers excluded the car because of the extensive damage. Victory in the GT category went to Simon/Dupeyron with a 250GT SWB and Oreiller/Schlesser, Darville/Langlois and Piper/Margulies took the next three places with their GTOs. Henri Oreiller was killed when he crashed his 250GTO at the Montlhéry meeting at the end of September.

The Paris 1,000Km race for GT cars held at Montlhéry on the 4.8-mile (7.7km) combined road and banked track circuit on 21 October was completely dominated by Ferrari. Pedro Rodriguez and brother Ricardo with a 250GTO entered by *NART* led throughout and won by a lap from Surtees/Parkes (*Bowmaker Racing*-entered 250GTO) and Colin Davis/Ludovico Scarfiotti who were two laps in arrears with the *Serenissima* 'bread van', now accepted as a GT car. Other GTOs took fourth to sixth places. Ricardo Rodriguez, a member of the works Formula 1 Ferrari team in 1962, was killed in November when he crashed his Lotus 24 in practice for the first Mexican Grand Prix.

There were no major changes to the 250GTO for 1963, partly because Ferrari was largely content with the car as it was, pending the introduction of a radical new model, and partly because development work had been delayed by strikes in Italy. The first GT race of the season was at Daytona, still a three-hour event, held on 17 January. It was another Ferrari benefit. Pedro Rodriguez, who had announced his retirement after his brother's death but changed his mind, won the race with a GTO owned by 20-year-old Mamie Spears Reynolds, an heiress to the R.J. Reynolds tobacco-empire. In second place came Roger Penske with a GTO owned by John Mecom, Jnr. A Chevrolet Corvette finished third.

At the finish of the Sebring 12 Hours race on 23 March, Ferraris occupied the first six places and Roger Penske/Augie Pabst with the 250GTO belonging to Mecom, took fourth place overall, six laps behind the winner. They were first in the 3,000cc GT category, ahead of Juan Fangio's protégé, Juan Manuel Bordeu partnered by Carlo Abate, and Innes Ireland/Richie Ginther with other 250GTOs.

Tommy Sopwith retired from motor racing at the end of 1962 and Ronnie Hoare ordered a new 250GTO to be entered only in the name of *Maranello Concessionaires*. The new car was not delivered by the start of the 1963 season, so Hoare borrowed the ex-*Bowmaker* car back from its new owner, Prince Zourab Tchokotoua. At Goodwood on Easter Monday Mike Parkes suffered a rare defeat when Graham Hill, with the latest 'Lightweight' Jaguar E-type entered by John Coombs, led throughout the 15-lap Sussex Trophy for GT cars. *Maranello Concessionaires* did not take delivery of their new 250GTO, chassis number 4399, until June.

Bulgari/Grana finished fourth overall with their 250GTO and won their class in the Targa Florio on 5 May. In the Nürburgring 1,000Km race on 19 May Pierre Noblet/Jean Guichet with their 250GTO took second place, on the same lap as the winning 250P prototype of John Surtees and Willy Mairesse, and won the 3,000cc GT category from two other 250GTOs. Another magnificent performance in the GT category followed at Le Mans held on 15–16 June. Carlo Abate/Fernand Tavano brought their 250GTO across the line in second place, with other 250GTOs fourth and sixth. The fastest speed recorded by a GTO on the Mulsanne Straight was 174mph (280kph) compared with 180mph (290kph) for the prototype 250P.

A combined Prototype and GT race over 129 miles

Above *'Beurlys'/ Langlois van Ophem with this 250GTO entered by Écurie Francorchamps finished in a brilliant second place overall at Le Mans in 1963.*

Right *In the 1963 Tourist Trophy at Goodwood Bruce McLaren (works Aston Martin Project 214) leads Jack Sears (Jaguar 'Lightweight' E-type) through the chicane. Following is David Piper with his 250GTO. Handling problems plagued the Aston Martins and McLaren retired because of mechanical trouble. Graham Hill and Mike Parkes with 250GTOs took the first two places.*

(208km) was held at Reims on 30 June and the 250GTOs suffered a surprise defeat. Dick Protheroe with his famous Jaguar E-type, CUT 7 – despite an engine vibration that limited him to 6,000rpm and a mud-spattered windscreen – took second place overall behind Abate's *Testa Rossa* and beat Bianchi and Noblet with their 250GTOs into second and third places in the class.

Next was the Tourist Trophy at Goodwood on 24 August. British-entered 250GTOs largely dominated this 100-lap race for GT cars. The entry included two works Aston Martin DB4GT Project 214 cars driven by Innes Ireland and Bruce McLaren, but these cars were handling atrociously because the scrutineers would not permit them to run on the wider 6½-in rims, accepted at Le Mans and fitted to production versions of the DB4GT, on the grounds that they had not been homologated. Graham Hill and Mike Parkes with GTOs took the first two places ahead of Roy Salvadori and Jack Sears with 'Lightweight' Jaguar E-types. David Piper was fifth with his 250GTO and Innes Ireland with the surviving Aston Martin finished a lurid seventh.

The Coppa Inter-Europa was revived at Monza on 8 September and was a three-hour race for GT cars. There was a race-long battle between Roy Salvadori with an Aston Martin DB4GT Project 214 and Mike Parkes at

34 Scarlet Passion

the wheel of a 250GTO. It was one of those very close races that left everyone, including the spectators, breathless. Salvadori had dropped back a fraction, but retook the lead on the last lap to win by the narrowest of margins. Lucien Bianchi, with another Aston Martin finished third and was followed across the line by a quartet of 250GTOs. It was a rare defeat for the GTO and the only win achieved by the works Aston Martin team with the DB4GT P214 cars.

Inevitably, Ferraris dominated the Tour de France held between 14–22 September. Ferrari 250GTOs took the first two places, but they were not without their travails. Six GTOs started the event, but only two finished – one of them almost hopelessly crippled. Jean Guichet, partnered by José Behra, the younger brother of the greatly lamented Jean, won outright despite badly crumpling the nose of their car. In second place came the 250GTO of Lucien Bianchi/Carlo Abate – after several accidents, including one, after a brake pipe worked loose, that demolished the front end of the GTO. The final 250GTO success of 1963 was second place by American Mike Gammino in the 112-mile (180km) Nassau Tourist Trophy in the Bahamas. Augie Pabst won with a Chevrolet-powered Lola GT, a model that was GT in name only and formed the basis of the Ford GT40.

Tommy Sopwith remembers driving the *Équipe Endeavour/Maranello Concessionaires* Ferraris on the road: 'The 250GT SWB was great fun, very fast and the only road car that was anywhere near it in performance terms was the Jaguar E-type. The original E-type that we raced in 1961 was almost a straightforward production car, it was nearly as fast as the 250GT SWB and I think that it stimulated Ferrari into building the 250GTO. On the road the E-type was a nicer car to drive because of its independent rear suspension, but on a smooth racing circuit the 250GT SWB was superior. The 250GT SWB had a better power-to-weight ratio than the E-type. The 250GTO was a much harder car to drive than the SWB.

'I remember that Ronnie Hoare went to Italy to collect the 250GTO and drove it back in time for Mike Parkes to race at the Easter Goodwood meeting. We did a season's racing with that car and achieved a great deal of success. We paid about £6,000 for it and we sold it for £6,500 at the end of the season. We thought that we'd done bloody well, but the next time that I heard of the car, I was being asked if I wanted to buy it for a $1 million – I quite wrongly said no! I think that the top price for a 250GTO was £10 million paid by a buyer in Japan.'

Jack Sears raced the *Équipe Endeavour/Maranello Concessionaires* 250GT SWB once in 1961 and GTOs four times in 1963. He raced both the *Maranello Concessionaires* and John Coombs' car. In 1970 he bought the ex-Coombs GTO chassis number 3729GT from Neil Corner and owned it for 29 years. When he raced the SWB against the E-types on their racing debut at Oulton Park in April 1961, he thought that it was great fun – he had never raced a Ferrari before. Jack comments, 'The SWB and the GTO were totally different cars.

The GTO had vastly superior handling, it was a much easier car to drive, there was no roll or other vices; the handling was neutral and it was a sheer joy. As far as the engine was concerned, you could take it up to 7,500rpm, much higher than with the SWB, and there was much more power. A good example had a power output of over 300bhp and in those days 100bhp per litre was quite an achievement. Everything about the car was better than the SWB; it was a major milestone forward in technology. Of course, the appearance of the 250GTO was staggeringly good.'

Top On a wet track Graham Hill drove the Maranello Concessionaires' 250GTO64 to a convincing win at Silverstone in May 1964. (T. C. March/ FotoVantage)

Bottom At Silverstone in May 1964 David Piper finished fourth with his 1963 250GTO. The car looks rather odd because of solid headlamp covers. (T. C. March/ FotoVantage)

An aside on the 250LM and the 250GTO64

At the 1963 Paris Salon Ferrari exhibited the 250LM intended as the 1964 GT car and very real evidence that the Prototype of 1963 *could* be the following year's competition GT car. It was in essence the 250P Prototype in coupé form. The production versions were fitted with 3.3-litre engines in place of the 3-litre unit installed in the car exhibited in Paris. The model will be discussed in greater detail later, but it suffices to say here that, for various reasons, Ferrari was unable to submit the homologation papers to the *Commission Sportive Internationale* until April 1964, when they were too late for inclusion in that month's agenda. So the 250LM was not considered for homologation until July when it was ruled that insufficient examples had been built.

There is cause for believing that Ferrari knew at an early date that the 250LM would not be homologated and that is why the 3.3-litre engine was substituted. If he believed that the car would be homologated, he would have retained the 3,000cc engine, as that is the GT category in which he would have wished the cars to run. It would have been tactically wrong to race them in the GT category with the 3.3-litre engine, as this would have put them in the same class as the Cobras.

Instead of the 250LM, Ferrari was forced to rely on the latest version of his front-engined GT car, the 250GTO64, a dramatically styled car, which in appearance resembled the mid-engined 250LM, especially from the rear, and had a very similar angular, aerofoil roof design. The sleeker nose had a wide air intake and gone were the bonnet-top inlets that had characterised the 1962–63 GTOs. The windscreen was very steeply raked and the cockpit area was further to the rear of the chassis. There were no important mechanical changes. Ferrari announced the GTO64 early in the year and it was supposedly intended only as an interim car until the 250LM was homologated. A number of existing 250GTOs were rebuilt to the 1964 specification.

Throughout the 1964 season there was a battle in the GT Championship between the Ferrari 250GTO64s and the *Shelby American* Cobras. Shelby usually, but not always raced the Daytona coupés; outstandingly glamorous cars of immense potential. Only six of these were built, but there were no homologation problems because the regulations permitted different bodywork to be fitted. The chassis was very different from that of the Cobra roadster, 'much more rigid, they handled very well, but marginally inferior to the 250GTO. The Cobra Daytona had a bit more grunt,' commented Jack Sears who drove them both.

It must also be remembered that the two marques were competing in different classes of races, the Ferraris in the up to 3,000cc class, the 4.7-litre Cobras in the over 3,000cc class, but the same class (over 2,000cc) in the Championship. Carroll Shelby's Cobra challenge, heavily backed by Ford, enlivened GT racing and he succeeded in denting, if not breaking Ferrari's stranglehold. The success of the Cobras also helped to divert attention away from the unsuccessful Ford GT40 Prototypes.

The season opened on 16 February with the Daytona Continental race now extended to 2,000km (1,243miles). Phil Hill and Pedro Rodriguez were at the wheel of the first of the 250GTO64s entered by *NART* and early in the race they trailed the latest Cobra coupé driven by Dave MacDonald/Bob Holbert. They dropped further back when the nearside front Goodyear blew on the banking and seriously damaged the bodywork, inevitable on a car with such light and flimsy panelling. This Ferrari spent a long time in the pits while the panelling was cut away and the suspension checked. During the remainder of the race Phil Hill was unhappy with the handling of the car and the wear rate of the Goodyear tyres was such that three complete tyre changes were made during the race.

The leading Cobra developed problems with the rear axle; it slipped back to second place and was eliminated from the race after it caught fire during a pit stop. Hill

The Evolution of the Ferrari Grand Touring Car 37

and Rodriguez won at 98.23mph (159.66kph) and they were at the wheel for 12hr 40min 25.8sec. Other 250GTOs took second and third places and Dan Gurney/Bob Johnson brought their roadster Cobra across the line in fourth place. Ferrari scored maximum points in the GT Championship.

Ferrari Prototypes dominated the results of the Sebring 12 Hours race on 21 March and took the first three places, followed across the line by a trio of Cobras. Pedro Rodriguez, David Piper and Mike Gammino shared the *NART* GTO64 and finished in seventh place. So the two main contenders remained on even points in the Championship. A minor event with no Championship points at stake was the 15-lap Sussex Trophy for GT cars at Goodwood on Easter Monday. Graham Hill at the wheel of *Maranello Concessionaires*' GTO, which had been rebuilt to 1964 specification, won the race by four-fifths of a second from Jack Sears with the red, open Willment-entered Cobra.

Ferrari GT cars were conspicuous by their absence from the Le Mans Test Weekend on 11–12 April, but on 26 April both GTOs and the Cobras were out in force in the Targa Florio. Shelby entered three open cars, lent another to two Italian drivers and delightfully named White Russian Prince Zourab Tchokotoua shared his private car with wealthy young American Tommy Hitchcock III, best known for his heavy crashes. Seven private GTOs ran in this race, including the 1964 cars of Ferlaino/Taramazzo and Facetti/Guichet. Cobra roadholding was primitive and on the difficult Picollo Madonie circuit with its poor surface and at many corners the drivers could only point, brake, scrabble round and squirt – and repeat this ungainly progress at the next corner. Porsche 904s took the first two places ahead of a brace of Alfa Romeo Giulia TZs; Claudio Ferlaino/Luigi Taramazzo finished fifth with their 250GTO. Dan Gurney/Jerry Grant struggled hard with their Cobra and despite suspension problems took eighth place.

Another minor GT race was the 25-lap event at Silverstone on 2 May and Graham Hill with the *Maranello Concessionaires*' car scored an impressive win in the wet from Mike Salmon (ex-works Aston Martin DB4GT) and Jack Sears (Willment Cobra roadster). On 17 May a 500-km (331 mile) race for GT cars was held on the very fast Spa-Francorchamps circuit. Mike Parkes drove a superb race with the *Maranello Concessionaires*' GTO64 to win at 124.40mph (200.16kph) from Jean Guichet and Lorenzo Bandini with similar cars. Bob Bondurant drove the highest placed Cobra, an open car, into ninth place. Again, these ill-handling brutes were out of their competitive depth on the fast, sweeping bends of this circuit in the Ardennes forest, although ex-World Champion Phil Hill had put up a spirited fight on the first lap. He was forced to stop at the pits because of a fuel blockage and dropped out of contention. Hill did have the consolation of setting fastest lap at 129.01mph (207.58kph).

The Nürburgring 1,000Km race on 31 May provided another success for Ferrari, but another disappointing performance by the open Cobras. There was a high rate of attrition among the Ferrari prototypes and the sole survivor was the 275P, which Ludovico Scarfiotti and Nino Vaccarella drove to a win at 86.99mph (139.97kph). Just over 30 seconds behind at the finish were Mike Parkes and Jean Guichet with a works GTO64. Ferrari rarely entered GT cars, but usually relied on private owners who were in receipt of works support for which they paid. The Cobras were outclassed yet again and the highest placed drivers were Jo Schlesser/Richard Attwood who brought their car to finish 23rd.

At Le Mans the *Shelby American* team scored one of its only two victories over the Ferraris during the year. Dan Gurney/Bob Bondurant with a Daytona coupé pounded their way to fourth place overall behind a trio of Ferrari prototypes. Behind them came the 250GTO64s of 'Beurlys'/Lucien Bianchi (entered by *Écurie Francorchamps*) and Innes Ireland/South African Tony Maggs (*Maranello Concessionaires* entry). Two Porsche 904 GT cars followed them across the line and Fernand Tavano/Bob Grossman finished ninth with their 250GTO64 entered by *NART*. At the beginning of the year the GTO64s raced with smoothly unbroken bonnet configuration, but increasingly a bonnet-top air scoop had been fitted and all the GTO64s at Le Mans had this feature.

The Ferraris and the Cobras met again in battle in the Reims 12 Hours race, which was held for the first time since 1958. It was open to prototypes and GT cars and started at 12 midnight on 4 July. There was a strong entry of both GTOs and Cobras, but the overall results were dominated by privately entered 250LMs. Graham Hill/Joakim Bonnier drove the winning car entered by *Maranello Concessionaires* and covered 1,521.77 miles (2,448.53km) at 126.81mph (204.04kph). John Surtees and Lorenzo Bandini finished second with a *NART* 250LM. Mike Parkes and Ludovico Scarfiotti took third place with the *Maranello Concessionaires*' GTO64 and won the GT category. David Piper/Tony Maggs finished in fourth place overall with Piper's green-painted GTO. Carroll Shelby's two Daytona coupés had retired before half-distance, so no GT Championship points for Cobra and Ferrari was opening up a gap in the leadership.

The Freiburg hill climb on 9 August was the next round in the GT Championship. Edgar Barth with a flat-eight Porsche sports car set fastest time for the 6.96-mile

On 9 August 1964 Ludovico Scarfiotti drove this 250GTO64 to a class win in the Freiburg hill climb in the Black Forest area of Germany. Surprisingly, his time was slightly slower than that of Bob Bondurant with a Cobra roadster running in the over 3,000cc class.

(11.20km) course in 6min 40.66sec. Scarfiotti with a GTO64 won the 3,000cc GT class in 6min 56.42sec and in the over 3,000cc GT class Bob Bondurant was first in 6 min 55.89sec, heading two other Shelby entries. Another hill climb included in the GT Championship was the Swiss Sierre-Montana-Crans event on 30 August. *Shelby American* Cobras took the first three places in the over 4,000cc GT class.

The Bridgehampton 'Double 500 Km' race held on Long Island in New York State was run over two days on 20–21 September and was the penultimate round in the GT Championship. The Sunday race was for GT cars over 2,000cc and prototypes and sports cars over 1,600cc. Ten Cobras were entered, most of them factory cars, and there were no GT Ferraris after the sole GTO blew up its engine in practice. Ken Miles, in fourth place with a Cobra, meant that Shelby won the GT category and maximum points.

Included in the GT Championship series for the first time was the Tour de France. The event took place between 11 and 20 September and the *FIA* now categorised the event as a race and not a rally. The event was over a distance of 3,800 miles (6,111km) and incorporated speed events at Reims, Rouen-les-Essarts, Le Mans, Cognac, Pau, Albi, Clermont-Ferrand and Monza, together with the Brabant, Mont Ventoux, Chamrousse, La Bollene and Col de Braus hill climbs and a downhill and uphill test at La Chevalerie. Four Cobras started and there was the usual large number of GTO Ferraris, all privately entered pre-1964 models. Although Cobras led in the early stages, all retired; Bianchi/Berger and Guichet/de Bourbon-Parme took the first two places with their GTOs in the GT category and it was Ferrari's ninth successive victory in the event.

The final event in the 1964 Championship series was the Paris 1,000Km race held at Montlhéry on 11 October. Shelby missed this race, for Ferrari was now unbeatable in the Championship. At the French circuit Graham Hill/Jo Bonnier with a *Maranello Concessionaires*' 330P were the winners at 96.50mph (155.27kph), but Pedro Rodriguez/Jo Schlesser finished second, two laps behind with their GTO64 entered by *NART*. Ferrari's final score in the GT Championship was 84.6 points to the 78.3 of *Shelby American* Cobra.

1965 Postscript

Quite unreasonably Enzo Ferrari bitterly resented the failure of the *CSI* to homologate the 250LM and blamed the Italian Automobile Club for not supporting him.

At the 1964 United States Grand Prix he protested by entering the team's Formula 1 cars in the name of *NART* and in white and blue American racing colours. He announced at his press conference on 12 December 1964 that the team would not be contesting the 1965 GT Championship. There is little doubt that if the 250LM had been homologated, *Shelby American* Cobra would not have won the 1965 GT Championship. It was obvious, however, that to build 100 examples of the 250LM would have been hopelessly uneconomic, for no market existed for such a large number of specialist competition cars. So Shelby's team was able to canter to an easy and hollow victory. Almost.

At the 1964 Paris Salon Ferrari launched the production 275GTB GT car with V12 3,285.72cc engine developing 280bhp at 7,000rpm and a new five-speed all-synchromesh gearbox in unit with the final drive. The elegant steel body was styled by Pininfarina,

Above As soon as the 275GTB was announced, it became available with six carburettors and lightweight body. Dumay/Gosselin with this car entered by Écurie Francorchamps drove a fine race at Le Mans, finishing second overall, winning their class and trouncing the Cobras. (LAT)

Right At Le Mans in 1965 Jack Sears and Dick Thompson brought this Shelby American Cobra Daytona coupé into eighth place and a class win. Later in the race Sears crumpled the nose of the Daytona badly when he ran into an Alfa Romeo that crossed his line through a corner.

40 Scarlet Passion

but as usual built by Scaglietti. From the moment the model was announced, it was available with six twin-choke Weber carburettors, 9.5:1 compression ratio and a power output of 300bhp at 7,600rpm. Lighter aluminium-alloy bodywork was also offered.

Ferrari did seek to have the new car homologated in the GT category and it has been claimed that by 16 March 1965, when a sub-committee of the *CSI* considered homologation, 147 examples of the model had been built. Ferrari was informed on 29 March that the application had been rejected because 'it is observed that there is a discrepancy between the minimum weight of the car as shown on the form, and its actual weight.' The *CSI* was acting unreasonably, probably through sheer pique because of what had happened the previous year. Ferrari protested publicly, issued statements to the press and, perhaps not surprisingly, the 275GTB was homologated in time for one to be entered in the Nürburgring 1,000Km race on 29 May.

Giancarlo Baghetti and Giampiero Biscaldi drove the new car, but they were slow and finished in 13th place overall. This 275GTB reappeared at Le Mans where it was entered by *Écurie Francorchamps* and Willy Mairesse/'Beurlys' drove it with speed, skill and consistency to finish third overall, first in the 4,000cc GT class and a little over 300 miles ahead of the sole surviving Daytona Cobra driven by Jack Sears and Dick Thompson, which finished in eighth place. Ferrari could be said to have made his point and the car was put on one side until December when Charlie Kolb drove it to a win in the Nassau Tourist Trophy. *Shelby American Cobra*'s win in the 1965 GT Championship was inevitable and largely unopposed. Shelby did not defeat Ferrari.

The Evolution of the Ferrari Grand Touring Car 41

Prototype Racing, 1962

Phil Hill and Olivier Gendebien drove this sports-racing 246SP to a win in the Nürburgring 1,000Km race. The 246SP was one of the most successful of all sports-racing Ferraris. (LAT)

Before the start of the 1962 season sports car racing faced an uncertain future. The World Sports Car Championship had ended, although Ferrari and others were still building competition sports cars and the official *FIA* Championship was for Grand Touring cars. The only change to the sports car regulations was a reduction in the minimum height of windscreens to approximately six inches. There was to be a sports car cup with no outright winner, but with classes for cars of up to 1,000cc, 1,001–2,000cc and 2,001–3,000cc.

The sports car cup was soon forgotten after the organisers of the Sebring 12 Hours, Targa Florio, Nürburgring 1,000Km and Le Mans 24 Hours races joined together to offer the *Challenge Mondiale de Vitesse* for what they chose to call variously Experimental cars or Prototypes with a capacity of up to 4,000cc. The term 'Prototype' gradually became accepted, but at this stage it was none too clear what it meant and it was broadly interpreted as any sports car that was not a homologated GT car. [*However, from this point onwards, in this book such cars will be referred to spelt with a capital 'P' – Prototype. Author's Note.*]

Ferrari held his press conference on 24 February 1962, rather later than usual and, almost certainly, as a result of the loss of his senior management. Since his appointment as head of the racing department, Forghieri realised that an entirely new approach was required and while he carefully formulated his plans, he was, for the time being, reasonably content to race the cars developed by his predecessors. The team was to continue to display overwhelming superiority against weak opposition in Prototype racing, but it was to be a hopelessly unsuccessful season for the Formula 1 cars.

At the press conference Ferrari displayed three different competition sports cars, all rear-engined and with a single overhead camshaft per bank of cylinders. Although previous V6 works sports-racing cars, including the 246SP, had the cylinders at an angle of 65° and twin overhead camshafts per bank of cylinders, these arrangements had now been abandoned. All three new cars had five-speed gearboxes and Dunlop disc brakes. The styling differed from that of the 1961 rear-engined cars in that the windscreen and rear decking were lower, the nose was slightly longer and there were scoops for the inboard-mounted rear brakes at the front of the rear wings. These cars looked so similar that small white lettering on the upper edge of the windscreen showed the type numbers. There were a number of engine 'swaps' with these cars and details are set out on Page 232–233.

The new cars can be summarised as follows:

Dino 196SP: 60° V6, 1,984cc (77 x 71mm), three Weber twin-choke 42DC carburettors, 9.8:1 compression ratio, single distributor and single-plug ignition. The power output was 210bhp at 7,500rpm. Apart from increased power, the engine was little changed from the original single cam per bank 2-litre V6 that was first seen in late 1958.

Dino 286SP: 60° V6, 2,863cc (90 x 75mm), three Weber twin-choke 46DC carburettors, 9.5:1 compression ratio, twin distributors and single-plug ignition. The output was 260bhp at 6,800rpm. This model was never raced.

Dino 248SP: 90° V8, 2,459cc (77 x 66mm), four Weber twin-choke 40IF2C carburettors, 9.8:1 compression ratio, twin distributors and single-plug ignition. The power output was 250bhp at 7,400rpm. Subsequently engine capacity was increased to 2,645cc (77 x 71mm) and in this form power output rose to about 260bhp at 7,500rpm. The model then became known as the 268SP. The concept of the V8 engine was in effect the V12 *SuperAmerica* with four cylinders less and the angle between the two banks of cylinders increased.

The V8 cars were the work of Carlo Chiti before he left the company at the end of 1961 and it is understood that the inspiration came from Chinetti who saw a market for these cars in the United States. Only two V8 cars were built and their poor performance in 1962 was due to lack of development. Forghieri and his small team had too many other problems to worry about. Ferrari announced the 250GTO at the same press conference.

In the absence of works Ferrari entries Joakim Bonnier and Lucien Bianchi drove this TR61 Testa Rossa to a win in the 1962 Sebring 12 Hours race. Bonnier sits placidly on the pit counter, while Bianchi leaps in for a stint at the wheel. The entrant was Scuderia Serenissima Repubblica di Venezia.

Despite the appearance of the three new competition sports cars, both the works and private teams continued to race the 246SP, which was an exceptionally successful car, combining a very competitive performance with reasonable handling. It was also by far the best looking of these early rear-engined Ferrari sports-racing cars. One of these cars was also at the 1962 Press Conference. Private teams were also still racing front-engined *Testa Rossa* cars. There was no worthwhile opposition to Ferrari in sports car/Prototype racing at this time. The only potential opposition, the latest Maseratis designed by Giulio Alfieri, lacked reliability, the result of insufficient resources to carry out a full development programme. Once again, it was not question of whether a Ferrari would win, but which one.

Daytona Continental Three Hours Race

Held on 11 January, the Daytona race was still a rather parochial event and attracted an almost exclusively American entry, which included a 246SP entered in the name of *NART* and driven by Phil Hill/Pedro Rodriguez. The 246SP set fastest lap at 108.80mph (175kph), led for a considerable while, but then dropped out because of mechanical problems. This enabled Dan Gurney with Frank Arciero's Ford-engined Lotus 19B to pull out a good lead. Then, when the Lotus broke a con-rod, Gurney was able to stop short of the finishing line and at the end of the race cross the line on the starter motor to win.

44 Scarlet Passion

Sebring 12 Hours

NART made a very strong entry of eight cars in the Sebring 12 Hours race on 23 March. With almost incredible incompetence, they failed to keep a lap chart and this was to have serious consequences. The lead *NART* entry was a 248SP, due to make its race debut in the hands of Stirling Moss and Innes Ireland, but in practice they both found that it was uncompetitively slow, and as the *NART Testa Rossa* TR61 was nine seconds a lap quicker in their hands, this was the car that they opted to drive. Bob Fulp/Pete Ryan took over the V8 and the Rodriguez brothers were at the wheel of the *NART*-entered 246SP. Graham Hill and Joakim Bonner were to have shared the TR61 entered by the *Serenissima* team, but Hill strained his back and his place was taken by Lucien Bianchi.

Ireland led away at the start, but by lap 11 Pedro Rodriguez was in front. When Innes Ireland brought the TR61 in to refuel, it had covered less than the minimum of 20 laps stipulated in the race regulations. Without any lap chart the *NART* pit was unaware of how many laps Ireland had covered, and so were the stewards until they received a protest and took the trouble to look at the official charts. First it was announced that Ireland had been give a 15-second penalty for driving into the pits area at excessive speed. Nothing was said about disqualification at this time and at a quarter-distance the Rodriguez brothers still led from Moss/Ireland. During the early afternoon Pedro Rodriguez with the leading 246SP stopped out on the circuit, not far from the pits. He started to push the car, lifted the bonnet to look at the engine and then abandoned it.

So, at half-distance Moss/Ireland had a comfortable lead. As Gregor Grant reported in *Autosport*: 'Then came a real bombshell. The stewards ordered out the black flag for the Moss/Ireland car, upholding a protest that the Ferrari had been refuelled before the specified 20 laps. This had happened over three hours earlier, and the unfortunate Moss and Ireland had been bashing their pans (sic) in to hold a lead in a veteran car which seemed as if it would run forever. Such Keystone Cops organization in a major motor race was unbelievable, and should require an official inquiry as to why the club-appointed man in charge should have cut the filler-cap seals in the first instance. Some choice language from Innes Ireland was of no avail, and the car was withdrawn.'

There was, of course, no inquiry, and the only real culprit was the *NART* team who could not organise its own pit properly. Over the years *NART*'s low standards of preparation and inefficient pit work were to become notorious. So Jo Bonnier/Lucien Bianchi went on to win the race for the *Serenissima* team at an average of 89.142mph (143.43kph) from the 250GTO of Phil Hill/Olivier Gendebien, with a Porsche 1.5-litre sports-racing car in third place. After Fulp had run out of fuel on the circuit and pushed the 248SP back to the pits, the new Ferrari rejoined the race, but, delayed by this and mechanical problems, it eventually finished 13th, all of 30 laps behind the winner.

Testing At Le Mans

The Le Mans Practice Weekend was held on 7–8 April, although Ferraris missed the Saturday. It rained from 8am on the Sunday morning throughout the day, so Ferrari times were inconclusive. One of the cars that

Left *In the 1962 Sebring 12 Hours race Ricardo and Pedro Rodriguez shared this 246SP entered by NART. They led until after half-distance when the car expired out on the circuit because of engine problems.* (Ozzie Lyons)

Right *Seen in the pits before the start of the 1962 Sebring race is the new, but uncompetitive Tipo 248SP V8 Ferrari, which Stirling Moss and Innes Ireland declined to drive. It eventually finished 13th in the hands of Fulp/Ryan. Behind it is the 250GT SWB entered by* Scuderia Serenissima Repubblica di Venezia; *Davis/Tavano led the GT class for some while with this car, but they fell back before retiring because of gearbox trouble.* (Ozzie Lyons)

Prototype Racing, 1962 45

Ferrari sent along was a 250GTO fitted with a 3,967cc (77 x 71mm) V12 engine, the Tipo 400 *SuperAmerica* touring car unit, to full *Testa Rossa* specification save that it was fitted with three larger Weber 42DCN carburettors, instead of the usual six-carburettor TR arrangement. On a compression of 8.7:1, power was claimed to be 390bhp at 7,500 rpm. A four-speed gearbox was fitted. (The standard GTO had a five-speed gearbox.)

The car looked like a standard 250GTO, except for a larger blister in the bonnet over the carburettors. It seemed that Ferrari had fully grasped what was meant by a 'Prototype'. Both Parkes and Mairesse drove the new car, but on the wet roads times meant very little. There was also a 268SP, which featured an aerofoil 'bridge' straddling the car immediately behind the cockpit and a glass panel insert in the Plexiglas windscreen, which it was hoped would assist vision in wet weather.

Targa Florio

The Sicilian road race held on 5 May was just about the only event that a prudent man would not put good money on Ferrari's chances of winning – three times in the past (1956 and 1959–60) the works cars had been beaten by the smaller-capacity Porsche opposition. In the 1962 race held over a distance of 447 miles (719 km) Ferrari entered three cars; a 248SP for Phil Hill/Olivier Gendebien, a 246SP for Ricardo Rodriguez partnered by Mairesse and a 2-litre *Dino* 196SP for Giancarlo Baghetti/Lorenzo Bandini. At this race the 246SP had a supplemental opening with a wire-mesh grille above the main twin air intakes.

Hill was practising with the V8 car when the throttle stuck open, the car ran up and over the bank alongside the road and slammed down with such force that it was to all intents and purposes a write-off. The American was uninjured apart from bad bruising. He was becoming increasingly disenchanted with the Ferrari team and after a fierce argument with team manager Eugenio Dragoni about the team's standards of preparation, Ferrari dropped him from the race. Under Tavoni, there had been far too much indiscipline in the team and it was part of Dragoni's job to manage the team with a firm hand. Dragoni was too firm and lacked tact and diplomacy. Gendebien was switched to the 246SP as an additional driver.

Mairesse was in cracking form, he covered the first lap with the 246SP in 40min 43.2sec (very close to the existing lap record), he broke the lap record on his second and third laps with times of 40min 2.3sec and 40min 0.34sec and then stopped at the end of the third lap to hand over to Rodriguez. The Mexican left the pits with a lead of 5min 50sec and he had extended this to 19min 18sec by the time he handed over to Gendebien for the final stint. Gendebien was able to cruise round for the remaining three laps and at the finish he was 12 minutes ahead of Baghetti/Bandini with the 2-litre car. The works Porsche entries were running on new, but ineffective disc brakes and Bonnier/Vaccarella with the third-place Stuttgart entry were 2min 56sec behind the winning Ferrari.

Nürburgring 1,000Km

Ferrari ran four different cars in the German race: the 246SP that had won the Targa Florio was shared by Phil Hill/Gendebien; a 268SP was entered for Ricardo and Pedro Rodriguez; Baghetti/Bandini drove the second-placed *Dino* 196SP from the Targa Florio and Mairesse/Parkes shared the 4-litre coupé seen at the Le Mans Practice Weekend. Ferrari was to take the first two places, but Jim Clark at the wheel of a 1½-litre Lotus 23 powered by the new Ford 116E Classic engine with a twin overhead camshaft cylinder head set the pace on a very wet track. He took the lead on the exit to the South turn on the first lap and stayed in front until lap 12 when he went off the road at the *Kesselchen*, overcome by fumes from an exhaust leak.

Mairesse had been holding second place with the 4-litre Ferrari and he was leading when he came into refuel at the end of lap 12. While this car was stationary in the pits, Phil Hill went past into the lead with the 246SP. The 4-litre GTO went ahead again later in the race, but then the two cars swapped places once more. At the finish Hill/Gendebien were the winners at 82.40mph (132.58kph), over two minutes ahead of Mairesse/Parkes. Graham Hill/Hans Herrmann and Jo Bonnier/Dan Gurney took third and fourth places with their works Porsche entries. Pedro Rodriguez stuffed the V8 Ferrari into a ditch early in the race and the *Dino*, which had been holding fifth place, was retired because of an oil leak at the end of lap 13 of this 44-lap race. Ferrari had won the first Nürburgring 1,000Km race in 1953, but it was the team's first victory in the event since it was revived in 1956.

Le Mans 24 Hours

A total of 15 Ferraris were entered in the 24 Hours race on 23–24 June and four of them were works cars. The works entries can be summarised as follows:

No 6: There was no official designation for this model, which is usually referred to as the 330TRI-62. It ran in what the *Automobile Club de l'Ouest* described as the Experimental class. The chassis was basically *Testa Rossa* TR61 with similar independent rear suspension. The power unit was the 3,967cc V12 fitted with six carburettors. The open body was remarkably ugly, with a large Plexiglas air scoop on the bonnet over the carburettors; aluminium-alloy windscreen surround and

46 Scarlet Passion

Willy Mairesse and Mike Parkes shared this 250GTO with 4-litre V12 engine at the Nürburgring in 1962. They finished second, 2min 21sec behind the winners. This car was exactly what organisers meant when they talked about GT Prototypes. (LAT)

a windscreen incorporating a glass panel; an aerofoil 'bridge' immediately behind the cockpit and large air scoops on the front of the rear wings to cool the brakes. Phil Hill and Olivier Gendebien were the drivers.

No 7: This was the Nürburgring 4-litre coupé, which was now also running on six twin-choke carburettors and had a larger bulge in the bonnet. Mike Parkes/Lorenzo Bandini were the drivers.

No 27: Tipo 268SP car with 2,645cc V8 engine driven by Giancarlo Baghetti/Ludovico Scarfiotti.

No 28: Tipo 246SP driven by Ricardo and Pedro Rodriguez.

At Le Mans the 330TRI Spyder of Phil Hill/Olivier Gendebien leads the 246SP of Ricardo and Pedro Rodriguez. They battled for the lead for close to 15 hours before the smaller-capacity car retired because of engine failure. The car following is the Écurie Ecosse-entered Tojeiro-Climax of Tom Dickson/Jack Fairman.

The mechanics work on the 246SP of the brothers Rodriguez in the 1962 Le Mans race. Although both Ricardo and Pedro were exceptionally fast, they were also exceptionally hard on their cars. In later years Pedro learned to match speed with restraint. (LAT)

48 Scarlet Passion

The only opposition to the Ferraris came from a trio of new Tipo 151 3.9-litre Maserati coupés; two entered by Briggs Cunningham and the third by *Maserati-France*. Although the Cunningham-entered Maseratis were front-runners in the early hours of the race, all three were out by half-distance.

During Wednesday evening practice Phil Hill with the 4-litre open car set a new unofficial lap record at 128.08mph (206.08kph) and although he was not quite so fast in the race, he lowered the official record to 3min 57.3sec, a speed of 126.884mph (204.156kph). The Rodriguez boys put up a strong challenge and held first or second place each hour from the third to the 14th, but they had over-driven their car and retired because of transmission problems. Hill/Gendebien with the 4-litre *Spyder* were now unchallenged and won at 115.244mph, covering 2,765.876 miles; on distance they were nearly 42 miles ahead of the 250GTO driven into second place by Guichet/Noblet.

The Parkes/Bandini car was plagued by problems from the start of the race. Parkes had put it into a sandbank on the first lap near the end of the Mulsanne Straight after Kerguen (Aston Martin DB4GT Zagato) had cut in front of him. It took Parkes a long time to dig the car out and after that it started to overheat and Ferrari finally withdrew it in the seventh hour. Although the V8 cars had shown poor form generally in 1962 (and were to be abandoned at the end of the year), Baghetti/Scarfiotti ran well with the 268SP, holding second place for several hours before retiring because of clutch failure. The only other sports Ferrari to finish was the *NART*-entered *Testa Rossa*, which Grossman and Roberts drove into fifth place. Ferrari had easily won the *Challenge Mondiale de Vitesse*.

Mike Parkes drove a 246SP loaned by the works to *Maranello Concessionaires* in the 50-lap Guards Trophy at Brands Hatch on 6 August, Bank Holiday Monday, and he won this very wet race from Innes Ireland driving a *UDT-Laystall* Lotus 19. It was said that Ferrari had intended sending a V8 car, but this could not be prepared in time. It was a thin story, for the 246SP was by far the more consistently successful car and had 'run rings' round the V8s all year. The 246SP, accompanied by Mauro Forghieri, had arrived in Britain on only the Saturday before the race.

In September Ferrari withdrew from all forms of racing for the rest of the year and sent the letter set out overleaf to drivers Giancarlo Baghetti, Lorenzo Bandini, Phil Hill and Ricardo Rodriguez. It was something of a publicity stunt in relation to Italy's woes and strife, but he made his point in no uncertain terms.

Phil Hill at the wheel of the 4-litre Testa Rossa-based Prototype which he and Olivier Gendebien drove to a win at Le Mans in 1962 at 115.244mph (185.428kph). Hill also set a new circuit record with this car at 126.884mph (204.156kph).

Gentlemen:

The industrial situation has rendered it once more impossible for us to finalise our racing programme, where we had hoped to produce four new Formula 1 cars for Monza [The Italian Grand Prix].

Without the co-operation of the workers, for reasons stemming from a national, not local, dispute, which began last March, we are forced to withdraw from further competition.

Within the limits imposed by reduced working hours, we shall continue to work on the prototype Formula 1 car and hope that we shall later benefit from this.

Meanwhile, if you wish, you are at liberty to compete in other marques for this season's remaining races, with the sole proviso that you respect our contracts with Dunlop, Shell, Marchal and Ferodo.

We would like to thank you for your help during this season and we are sorry that we were unable to put at your disposal Formula 1 cars as successful as our GT, sports and experimental machines.

ENZO FERRARI
President, SEFAC
Modena, 21st September 1962

There were of course no further Prototype races of any importance in 1962, but the drivers missed the United States Grand Prix and the Mexican Grand Prix, the latter being held for the first time and as a non-Championship race. The final appearance of a V8 sports-racing car in 1962 was in the Nassau speed week in December, but it performed disappointingly in the hands of Lorenzo Bandini and he finished a poor eighth in his race.

The European Hill Climb Championship

In 1962 Ferrari prepared a *Dino* 196SP which *Scuderia Sant' Ambroeus* ran in the European Championship for Ludovico Scarfiotti. He missed the first event at Faucille in France on 3 June, but soon built up a lead by winning the Parma-Poggio de Borceto (Italy), Mont Ventoux (France) Trento-Bondone (Italy) and Freiburg-Schauinsland (Germany) hill climbs and headed the Championship table with 36 points, three points ahead of Heini Walter who drove both four- and eight-cylinder works Porsche cars. At Ollon-Villars on 26 August Jo Bonnier was fastest with a Formula 1 Porsche, but this was not eligible for Championship points. Scarfiotti finished second in the 2-litre sports car class to Josef Greger (Porsche) and this was good enough to clinch the Championship with 42 points to the 33 of Walter and 25 of Greger. Ferrari did not enter the Championship again until 1965.

Left *The Ferrari V8s were never competitive. Carlo Abate/Colin Davis drove this 2,644cc Tipo 268SP at Le Mans in 1962, but retired early in the race because of transmission problems. The glass panel set into the Perspex screen was an attempt to give a clear view in wet weather, but the idea was soon abandoned. Another innovation was the aerofoil 'bridge' behind the driver. (LAT)*

Above *The works entered this 246SP for Mike Parkes in the Guards Trophy at Brands Hatch on Easter Monday. In wet weather Parkes scored a convincing win. Because it was a sports car race the Ferrari ran with a cut-down screen. (LAT)*

Prototype Racing, 1962 51

Prototype Racing, 1963

The 250P with rear-mounted V12 3-litre engine was one of the most successful of all Ferrari competition sports cars. Here in the 1963 Sebring race, the winning 250P of Scarfiotti/Surtees heads through the Webster turns. (Ozzie Lyons)

Without doubt the most successful car in Prototype racing in 1962 had been the 246SP, in fact a 1961 model. Following the failure of the V8 cars, Forghieri decided to combine the best features of what was available – the 246SP chassis with the tried, tested and exceptionally successful Colombo-based *Testa Rossa* engine. So the team extended the wheelbase of a 246SP chassis from 7ft 7.4in (2,320mm) to 7ft 10.5in (2,400mm) to accommodate the longer engine, and installed the *Testa Rossa* dry-sump engine in the same form as used in the 1961 sports-racing cars, with six twin-choke Weber 38DCN carburettors and on a 9.5:1 compression ratio developing 310bhp at 7,500rpm.

As before there were twin distributors and twin-plug ignition. Transmission was by a multi-plate clutch and five-speed, all-indirect gearbox without synchromesh, in unit with the final drive. Ferrari designed the transmission so that the final drive ratios were altered by changing the reduction gears (which transferred the

52 Scarlet Passion

torque from the engine shaft at the base of the transmission to the primary shaft). With the four available reduction gears, maximum speeds were claimed to be 131mph (211kph), 143mph (230kph), 157mph (253kph) and 178mph (286kph).

Suspension was similar to that of the 246SP, independent front and rear by double wishbones and coil spring/damper units. There were disc brakes front and rear and those at the rear were mounted inboard on either side of the final drive. The fuel tank, water radiator, oil radiator and oil tank for the dry-sump system were all mounted at the front of the car to help equalise weight distribution. Right-hand drive was retained.

After two seasons with what had become the *Bowmaker Racing Team*, John Surtees had signed up with Ferrari for 1963 and he tested the new Prototype, known as the 250P, at Monza in November and December 1962. After these successful tests Ferrari dispatched the 250P to Pininfarina to be re-bodied and in its revised form it had very smooth lines, the twin-nostril air intake of the prototype was abandoned and a large glass windscreen and bridge-type aerofoil seen on the V8 cars were fitted. The cockpit area was fully trimmed. The claimed weight was 1,520lb (689.5kg). Ferrari showed the car in this form at his press conference held at Monza in March. Surtees turned in some very fast laps and it was clear that Ferrari would again dominate Prototype racing.

Ferrari also revealed the 330LMB (or 330SA, as is now considered the correct designation) *berlinetta*. It combined a slightly modified 250GTO chassis and the *SuperAmerica* 3,967cc engine with six Weber twin-choke 42DCN carburettors, 9.0:1 compression ratio and a power output of 400bhp at 7,500rpm. It was developed from the 1962 4-litre coupé, but it had new Pininfarina bodywork that blended the lines of the very beautiful production 250GT *Lusso* of 1962–64 with 250GTO nose treatment. Originally the body lacked supplemental air intakes above the main intake, but these were adopted for the Le Mans race in June. There were also small panels on the tops of the rear wings, which permitted more wheel movement than with a standard *Lusso* body. Three of these cars were built; two with left-hand drive and one with right-hand drive, but there was also an example with a 3-litre engine.

The Sebring 12 Hours

Ferrari's first Prototype race was the Sebring 12 Hours on 23 March. A change in the Prototype rules since 1962 had been the abolition of the 4-litre engine capacity limit, which allowed Maserati to run a bigger engine in the Tipo 151 at Le Mans, and the rules at Sebring permitted Jim Hall to enter his Chevrolet Corvette-engined Chaparral for himself and Hap Sharp. Ferrari entered two 250Ps in the Florida race and Surtees/Scarfiotti and Mairesse/Vaccarella drove these, while there was a 330LMB for Parkes/Bandini. On the very abrasive Florida circuit the drivers had to restrict the speed of the 4-litre car to avoid excessive tyre wear. *NART* had acquired the 4-litre 1962 Le Mans-winning roadster and entered this for Pedro Rodriguez/Graham Hill.

Early in the race both 250Ps lost ground because of pit stops to re-attach a loose plug lead. The 4-litre SA was vying for the lead until shortly after 2pm when Parkes spun off and hit a tree. He crawled back to the pits, the body shattered; the split fuel tank dripping a trail of petrol and there was no alternative but to withdraw the car. Co-driver Bandini was reported

Willy Mairesse (seen at the wheel here) and Ludovico Scarfiotti shared this 250P in the 1963 Targa Florio. The car retired early in the race and Scarfiotti transferred to share the driving of the Ferrari team's 2-litre Dino.

to have burst into tears as the Ferrari was pushed away. At half-distance Graham Hill/Rodriguez led from Surtees/Scarfiotti and Mairesse/Vaccarella. In fifth place came Roger Penske/Augie Pabst with a 250GTO.

As darkness enveloped the circuit, the *NART* 4-litre car lost time in the pits because of repairs to the exhaust system and began to drop back steadily because the generator was not charging; the car had virtually no lights and Hill was forced to tuck in behind other cars to use their headlamps. Scarfiotti/Surtees won the race at 90.39mph (145.44kph), Mairesse/Vaccarella finished second, a lap behind, and then came Rodriguez/Hill two laps behind the winner. The Penske/Pabst 250GTO was fourth overall to win the GT class and lead two other GTOs across the line.

The Le Mans Practice Weekend

The Practice/Test Weekend was held over 6–7 April and, inevitably, Ferrari dominated both days in the absence of serious opposition. The team brought along a 250P and a 330LMB and five team drivers attended. On the Saturday Parkes (250P) lapped in 3min 47.1sec at 132.60mph (213.35kph), an unofficial record. He was also timed at 187.90mph (302.33kph) on the Mulsanne Straight, the first time that 300kph had been exceeded. Surtees was even faster with the 250P on the Sunday and lapped in 3min 45.2sec, a speed of 133.30mph (214.48kph). The SA's best time was 3min 53.3sec – 129.07mph (207.67kph) – by Mairesse on the Saturday.

Left *The 2-litre Dino 196SP entered by Ferrari in sports trim in the 1963 Targa Florio. The photograph captures the atmosphere of road racing of the time. Bandini, Scarfiotti and Mairesse shared the driving.* (LAT)

Above *A later view of the same car during a pit stop in the 1963 Targa Florio. The battered wing was very light damage by Targa Florio standards. This Ferrari would have won the race if Mairesse had not lost time in a last-lap spin. They finished second behind Bonnier/Abate with a Porsche.* (LAT)

Targa Florio

While only too often in the late 1950s and early 1960s Ferrari drivers appeared to treat the Sicilian road race as a 'demolition derby', the circuit was the most difficult used in World Championship sports car/Prototype races until its abandonment after the 1974 event.

Writing of the circuit with particular reference to the 1963 race, that very perceptive journalist Bill Gavin said, 'The little Madonie is a specialized circuit and here the special skills of the Grand Prix driver are lost, for to memorize the circuit perfectly is an impossibility and it is scarcely feasible to drive a race car round the circuit a sufficient number of times to establish braking points, ideal lines and so on. There are very few places on this vast circuit which haven't witnessed some form of

Prototype Racing, 1963 55

incident, and how the mighty have often fallen here. The strain on the car is equally as severe as that on the driver; the unevenness of the circuit, its hump backs and potholes, take their toll on all but the strongest chassis and suspensions, while the slow corners demand a great deal of the brakes, the engine, and the gearbox.'

In the 1963 race held on 5 May Ferrari entered two 250Ps in exactly the same trim in which they had been raced at Sebring and Mairesse/Vaccarella and Surtees/Parkes were to drive these. In addition there was a *Dino* 196S that ran in the class included by the organisers for Group C sports cars up to 2 litres. This was driven by Bandini/Scarfiotti, but because Vaccarella had been disqualified from driving shortly before the race, Bandini also took a turn at the wheel of the 250P that the Sicilian was to have shared with Mairesse. Lualdi/Bini drove a similar, private Tipo 196S. The main opposition came from two Porsche 2-litre flat-eight Prototypes driven by Bonnier/Abate and Maglioli/Baghetti.

At the end of the first 44.7-mile lap Scarfiotti and Parkes with the 250Ps led from Bonnier and Bandini with the 2-litre works Ferrari. By the end of the next lap the order was Parkes–Bonnier–Bandini, while Scarfiotti came into the pits with a very ragged engine after a slow lap. Mairesse took over, but the car was retired after another two slow laps. It was only later discovered that Scarfiotti had made a very heavy landing with this 250P; this had flattened the outward bulge at the bottom of the fuel system, which housed the inlet for the fuel line, and partially cut off the fuel supply.

Parkes with his 250P had a comfortable lead of over a minute when he handed over to Surtees at the end of the third lap but two laps later Surtees ran straight on at a slow corner, going off the road and damaging both bodywork and fuel tank. Spectators pushed the Ferrari back on to the road, but there was petrol spewing out of the tank and he had no choice, but to abandon the car. Scarfiotti, at the wheel of the 2-litre sports car, clouted one of the concrete markers that lined the circuit at 10-km intervals and was in second place on time when he brought the car in to be checked and a replacement wheel fitted.

Over the next two laps Scarfiotti made up ground and resumed the lead. At the end of lap eight he handed over to Bandini with an advantage of close to a minute over the Porsche of Bonnier/Abate. Mairesse took the wheel in what was soon to become heavy rain and the 2-litre Ferrari seemed set to win the race. On the last lap Mairesse spun the 196S, crunching the bonnet, and so dropped back to finish 11.9sec behind the winning Porsche. The Lualdi/Bini *Dino* crashed on lap one, caught fire and was burnt out.

Left *The 250P was a superb all-round competition car, and could – with its 250LM successor – be regarded as a rear-engined* Testa Rossa. *Ferrari faced little opposition in Prototype racing in 1963 and Surtees/Mairesse won the Nürburgring 1,000Km race with this car by a margin of over eight minutes from a Ferrari 250GTO. Here Surtees takes a tight line at the* Karussel.

Above *Ludovico Scarfiotti and Lorenzo Bandini drove this 250P to a fine win at Le Mans in 1963, taking the lead after the similar car of John Surtees/Willy Mairesse caught fire in the 19th hour of the race.*

Nürburgring 1,000Km

Ferrari entered a trio of 250Ps in the German race on 19 May. These were to be shared by Scarfiotti/Parkes, Surtees/Mairesse and Vaccarella/Bandini. Vaccarella's driving licence had been restored with almost indecent haste. He did not benefit from whatever influence had been brought to bear, for he crashed into the forest at *Hocheichen* during practice, wrote off the car and broke his arm. So only two works Ferraris started the race. Peter Lindner with his 'Lightweight' Jaguar E-type led until near the end of the first lap, but then the two 250Ps moved ahead and in the order Surtees/Mairesse and Scarfiotti/Parkes dominated the race until lap 16. At the end of the previous lap Scarfiotti came in to refuel and hand over to Parkes. It proved to be a very quick pit stop and the Englishman left the pits leading from Mairesse.

The circuit was now very slippery, the two Ferraris were lapping in close formation and as they went through the *Aremberg* curves Parkes spun, either through driver error or because he had been nudged by Mairesse. The rear end of the 250P was demolished against a bridge and Mairesse punctured his nearside front tyre on debris from the crash. By the time that the Belgian had stopped to change the wheel and stopped again at the pits for the car to be checked over, he had dropped back to fourth place and the 2-litre Porsche of Phil Hill/Joakim Bonnier was in the lead. After 19 laps Mairesse was in second place.

Prototype Racing, 1963 57

Left John Surtees at the wheel of the 250P he shared with Willy Mairesse at Le Mans in 1963. They took the lead in the fourth hour and led for almost 15 hours before the car caught fire and was eliminated.

Below Jack Sears/Mike Salmon drove this 330LMB entered by Maranello Concessionaires at Le Mans in 1963 and finished in fifth place. The body by Pininfarina combined the lines of the production Berlinetta Lusso with a 250GTO nose. Note the panel on the rear wing to allow for extra wheel movement.

Right In the Esses at Le Mans in 1963, the experimental green-painted 250LMB of Masten Gregory/David Piper passes the 250P, which caught fire while Mairesse was at the wheel. Quite how the 250P ended up facing the traffic is one of life's many mysteries. Gregory/Piper finished sixth. The front of the car is very badly burned and the accident effectively brought the career of Willy Mairesse to an end. (LAT)

On lap 20 of this 44-lap race Phil Hill went off the road at Aremberg and severely damaged the leading Porsche. So Surtees/Mairesse went on to win at 82.71mph (133.10kph) from Pierre Noblet/Jean Guichet (250GTO) and Carlo Abate/Umberto Maglioli with a TR61 *Testa Rossa*. Making its international debut in this race – and a portent for the future – was the Lola GT; this sleek coupé with rear-mounted Shelby-modified Ford V8 4.7-litre engine and Colotti trans-axle had first appeared at the London Racing Car Show in late 1962 and it had been driven by Tony Maggs at the International Trophy meeting at Silverstone in May 1963. Tony Maggs/Bob Olthoff were the drivers at the Nürburgring, but a rear wheel worked loose, damaging the driving pins, and after this had been sorted out it ran well until the distributor drive failed.

Le Mans 24 Hours

The entry list for the 24 Hours on 15–16 June included a very large number of Ferraris. The Prototypes and their fortunes in the race can be summarised as follows:

No 9: 330SA entered by Pierre Noblet and driven by Jean Guichet/Noblet. This car had a bolted-on tail spoiler. It retired in the ninth hour because of an oil leak, having held fourth place at the end of the fifth hour.

No 10: 330TRI entered by *NART* and driven by Pedro Rodriguez and Roger Penske. The 1962 winner held third place, but caught fire early on the Sunday morning because of petrol swilling around on the undertray and it had to be abandoned out on the circuit. It was another example of *NART*'s poor management.

58 Scarlet Passion

No 11: 330SA entered by *NART* and driven by Dan Gurney/Jim Hall. It had been holding third place, but developed an engine misfire and dropped back to fourth; it retired because of a broken drive-shaft early on the Sunday morning.

No 12: 330SA entered by *Maranello Concessionaires* and Colonel Hoare drove it directly from the factory to Le Mans. This SA was the car with right-hand drive and was heavier than the other examples because of the more extensive use of steel panelling. Of his drive in this race, Sears told the writer, 'The drive at Le Mans was a surprise for me. Ronnie Hoare telephoned me to tell me that he was running a 4-litre coupé at Le Mans and he wanted me to drive with Mike Salmon. This was a fantastic invitation for me and the only car of his that I had driven previously had been the 250GT SWB at Oulton Park.

Ronnie collected the car from Maranello on Italian trade-plates a few days before the race and drove it to Le Mans. He'd said, "It'll run it in and I'll enjoy the drive". It was serviced and we did the race. It had a four-speed gearbox with quite a slow gear-change and the handling was not as good as that of the 250GTO, but at Le Mans that didn't matter too much. Ronnie did everything in an amazing style, we stayed at a very nice hotel, good wines, good food, the very best was provided – we didn't get paid, but it was a joy to drive for him. His main instruction to us was "I want this car to finish. Do be careful." With that in mind, we were very careful, but we had some problems. At one stage we were slowed by a loose plug lead and water loss caused overheating but we nursed the car on, despite a sick engine and a damaged hub spline, which slowed every tyre change, and gradually worked our way up the field to finish fifth.'

Prototype Racing, 1963 59

No 21: works 250P driven by Ludovico Scarfiotti/ Lorenzo Bandini. It ran exceptionally well throughout the race and was in second place between the sixth and 18th hours. It took the lead after the retirement of Surtees/ Mairesse and won, covering 2,834.509 miles (4,560.725 km) at an average of 118.104mph (190.029kph).

No 22: works 250P driven by Mike Parkes/Umberto Maglioli. It had led briefly in the third hour of the race, but dropped to 17th place in the seventh hour because of mechanical problems and then steadily climbed back through the field to finish third.

No 23: works 250P driven by John Surtees/Willy Mairesse. They had moved up into the lead during the fourth hour and headed the race until 10.45am on the Sunday morning. As the 250P with Mairesse at the wheel swept under the Dunlop Bridge a flash of fire could be seen from the rear end. Mairesse exited from the *Esses* with the car enveloped in flames; the fire had spread to the fuel tank which had exploded. The Belgian aimed the Ferrari for the straw bales and jumped out, suffering burns on his face, shoulders and right arm. Early in the race Surtees had set a new lap record in 3min 53.3sec, a speed of 129.067mph (207.669kph). Inspection of this car at the factory revealed that a poorly fitted rubber gasket had failed to seal one of the filler caps, although the cap itself fitted properly. At speed, fuel splashed on to the rear lamp switch and resulted in the fire.

No 26: 250SA with 3-litre engine. This car had a standard 250GTO chassis, SA body and weighed 2,520lb (1,143kg). Entered by *NART*, Masten Gregory/ David Piper drove well, holding third place in the early hours of Sunday morning. This Ferrari was delayed by electrical problems and then Gregory put it into a sandbank; it dropped to tenth place, but by the finish of the race the drivers had clawed their way to sixth.

Ferrari 250GTOs driven by 'Beurlys'/Langlois van Ophem and 'Elde'/Pierre Dumay finished second and fourth and so Maranello entries took the first six places. Peter Bolton and Ninian Sanderson with a Cobra entered by AC Cars, sponsored by *The Sunday Times* and managed by Stirling Moss, finished seventh. Other significant entries were the Maserati Tipo 151, the Aston Martin Project 215 and the Lola GT. The Maserati had a 4,941cc engine and was entered by *Maserati-France* for André Simon/Lloyd Casner. It led for the first two hours; developed transmission problems and retired in the fourth hour.

Aston Martin's Project 215 Prototype was a development of the car raced at Le Mans in 1962; it was based on the DB4GT and its 3,995cc (96 x 92mm) six-

60 Scarlet Passion

cylinder engine developed 323bhp at 6,000rpm. Its only race as a works car was at Le Mans where Phil Hill and Lucien Bianchi drove it. Although it had considerable potential as a Ferrari-beater, it ran poorly before being retired in the fourth hour because of transmission problems. David Brown withdrew his team from racing at the end of the year and Aston Martin never raced again under his ownership.

The Lola GT had the greatest potential of all the also-rans and it was very shortly to be adopted as the basis for the Ford GT40. The drivers at Le Mans were Richard Attwood and David Hobbs. The Lola was still very new and underdeveloped. It had a hopelessly unsatisfactory cable-operated gear-change and was plagued by many minor problems. Hobbs crashed at 5.30am on the Sunday morning when he was insufficiently careful in changing gear and the Lola jumped out of gear at *Tertre Rouge*.

After Le Mans

Mike Parkes appeared with an experimental version of the 250P fitted with a 4-litre engine in the 130-mile (209km) Prototype and GT race at the French Grand Prix meeting at Reims on 30 June. Prospects of a walkover for the Ferrari evaporated when he had clutch problems on the first lap. Parkes managed to get the Ferrari back to the pits. He eventually rejoined the race and as he stormed round this very fast circuit in pursuit of the rest of the field, he set a new Prototype/sports car record in 2min 22.5sec, a speed of 130.32mph (209.71kph). Parkes retired and Carlo Abate won with a *Testa Rossa*.

Ferrari then loaned this car to *Maranello Concessionaires* and Parkes drove it for the British team in the sports car and GT race at the British Grand Prix meeting at Silverstone on 20 July. Parkes was unable to get the car smoothly off the line and was rammed by Chris Williams (Lotus 23). He moved into fourth place before his mangled exhaust pipes fell off, and he later retired because of an oil leak.

At Brands Hatch on Bank Holiday Monday, 5 August, *Maranello Concessionaires* entered Lorenzo Bandini with the 330SA that had finished fifth at Le Mans in the Guards Trophy race for sports cars over 2,000cc and GT cars over 2,500cc. Jack Sears was driving the team's 250GTO and was faster than Bandini in practice. Hoare asked him to take the 4-litre car round and do a few laps. He commented recently, 'I was slower than I had been in the GTO, but a little faster than Bandini. I said to Ronnie Hoare, "I'll tell you why I'm faster with the GTO; one, it has better handling; two, its five-speed gearbox is really well suited to the Grand Prix circuit here." The tight corners and camber of the track put the 330SA to a disadvantage.' Jack won the GT category and was fourth overall, while Bandini was eighth overall and won the over 3,000cc sports class.

On 15 September Pedro Rodriguez drove a 250P entered by *NART* in the sports car division of the Bridgehampton Double 500 race. This 250P had a simple tubular roll bar behind the cockpit in place of the usual 'bridge' aerofoil. Rodriguez chased Hansgen (Cooper-Buick) and took the lead when Hansgen's routine pit stop extended to over two minutes because of engine problems. He lost the lead during his own pit stop because broken spokes in one of the rear wheels necessitated a wheel-change and *NART* had no jack in the pits (tell us something new!). Rodriguez took second place, about a minute in arrears. Dan Gurney drove a 330SA in this race, but failed to feature in the results.

Rodriguez then drove the 250P in the 245-mile (394km) sports car Canadian Grand Prix held at Mosport on 28 September. He lapped the entire field except Graham Hill (Lotus 23) and won at 91.55mph (147.30kph), although he was perilously close to running out of fuel before the finish. Surtees retired another *NART*-entered 250P (it was in fact a works car) with clutch problems at about one-third-race distance. Bandini was at the wheel of *NART*'s V8 248SP, but retired when his Ferrari shed a wheel and spun into an embankment.

John Surtees appeared with his 250P in the 200.2-mile (325.4km) Riverside Grand Prix on 13 October and finished fourth behind Dave MacDonald (King Cobra), Roger Penske (Zerex-Cooper-Climax) and Pedro Rodriguez (Super Genie-Ford). It was a race for sprint cars, so the result was not at all bad. Surtees's appearance in these races was an effort by the factory to see how well (or badly) the Proto-types appeared in competition with lighter, much more powerful Group Seven sports cars. In December Rodriguez drove a 250P into second places in both the Nassau Trophy and Governor's Cup races during the Nassau Speed Week.

Prototype racing had yet to reach the peak of its competitiveness and interest and more events were added to the Championship series over the next couple of years. In the early 1960s Ferrari's stranglehold on sports car racing was such that he was moulding its future. When Prototype racing started, its definitions were unclear, but Ferrari just carried on racing his competition sports cars and developing genuine GT Prototypes in the shape of the 4-litre version of the 250GTO and the 330SA. If Ferrari had not enjoyed such a successful record in sports car and Prototype racing, and if Ford had not failed in its bid to buy the company, the Ford GT40 would never have developed and Prototype racing would have been infinitely less fascinating over the next four seasons.

Richard Attwood and David Hobbs drove the sensational new Lola GT coupé at Le Mans. The car was too new to do well, but its great potential was obvious. Hobbs crashed on the Sunday morning when the Lola jumped out of gear at Tertre Rouge. The design was well ahead of its time and formed the basis of the Ford GT40.

Prototype
Racing, 1964

The Ferrari garage at the 1964 Sebring race. No. 24 is the Maranello Concessionaires' 330P driven by Graham Hill/Bonnier, No. 21 the NART 330P of Surtees/Bandini, No. 23 the 275P of Scarfiotti/Vaccarella. (Ozzie Lyons)

In 1964 the Ferrari press conference was held on 11 January. There were two sides to this, which could be described as the sentimental and the serious. The sentimental was the presentation of gold medals to John Surtees, Mike Parkes and Graham Hill for their contribution to Ferrari racing successes in 1963, while Colonel Ronnie Hoare received a marble statue of the Prancing Horse for his efforts. The serious side was the announcement of the latest cars. The new Prototypes were developments of the 1963 250P. The 275P had a 3,286cc (77 x 58.8mm) version of the familiar *Testa Rossa* engine developing 320bhp at 7,700rpm. The 330P had a 3,967cc (77 x 71mm) version of the same engine with an output of 390bhp at 7,500rpm.

Technically, these cars were the 1963 250P with larger-capacity engines. In fact certain 275Ps were re-engined 250Ps, but the 330Ps were mainly new cars with revised bodies. The biggest difference was that the new bodies had longer tail-sections, the rear part of which was split at the axle-line, so that the part of the tail below the axle-line did not rise up when the rest of the tail was lifted. This made the cars easier to work on in the pits. The nose was also slightly lower and longer; the 'bridge-type' roll-bar was wider with straighter supports, the air scoops in the rear wings were near-horizontal and the fuel filler caps were nearer the top of the wing and fitted more flush than on the 1963 cars. Generally the drivers reckoned that the 275P handled rather better and was more manoeuvrable than the 4-litre version.

Ferrari also announced that certain Ferrari agents would race the new cars in what was now known as the Speed and Endurance World Challenge Cup.

Coupled with John Surtees's win in the Formula 1 Drivers' Championship, albeit by a narrow margin, it was to prove one of the most successful Ferrari years ever.

Sebring 12 Hours

As expected there was a strong Ferrari entry and likewise, as expected, there was little in the way of opposition for the Florida race held on 21 March. There were three works cars, 275Ps for Parkes/Maglioli and Scarfiotti/Vaccarella, while Surtees/Bandini drove a 330P. *NART* entered their new 330P for Rodriguez/Fulp. Phil Hill should have driven this with Rodriguez, but he had absconded late in the day to Shelby's Cobra team. Graham Hill/Joakim Bonnier drove *Maranello Concessionaires*' 330P.

At the end of the first lap Surtees led from Rodriguez and Graham Hill, but then Rodriguez forged into the lead; the other Ferrari drivers were content to sit behind him, knowing that Pedro was something of a car-breaker and Fulp would never be close to matching the Mexican's lap times. On lap ten Rodriguez's Ferrari shed its spare wheel – more evidence of *NART*'s poor attention to detail – and he stopped next time round to pick it up, and then pulled into the pits for it to be properly attached and for the fuel to be topped up. By the time Rodriguez rejoined the race, he was a lap behind the leaders. Surtees/Bandini lost the lead after the first driver changes, but with Surtees back at the wheel, they went ahead again. Rodriguez retired his 330P soon afterwards when a radiator hose worked loose, the car lost its water and the engine was beginning to seize up.

Surtees/Bandini, Graham Hill/Bonnier, Scarfiotti/Vaccarella and Parkes/Maglioli held the first four places at half-distance and then came Gurney/Johnson with their Shelby Cobra. An hour later Hill/Bonnier had moved up into the lead, but during the ninth hour Hill brought the *Maranello Concessionaires*' car into the pits to retire because of gearbox trouble. During the last couple of hours the Surtees/Bandini 330P spent a long time in the pits while the brake pads were replaced and the mechanics repaired defective rear lights.

This 330P resumed in fourth place, but the Scarfiotti/Vaccarella 275P was also in trouble and stopped at the pits because of clutch problems and a defective rear light. When the flag fell at 10pm Parkes/Maglioli were the winners, having covered 1,112.8 miles (1,790.5km) at 92.634mph (149.05kph), Scarfiotti/Vaccarella were second, a lap in arrears, and then came Surtees/Bandini. It had been a magnificent Ferrari demonstration, but opposition to the red cars was desperately needed if interest in this class of racing was to be sustained.

In the Ferrari garage at Sebring in 1964 Luigi Chinetti (centre in spectacles and braces) in conversation with Mauro Forghieri. Chinetti was losing his personal, firm grip on NART and the team's poor standards of preparation and race management (especially when Forghieri was not looking after the team's cars) led to silly mistakes and poor reliability. (Ozzie Lyons)

The Ford GT40

Ford first announced their new Prototype in late December 1963, it was revealed to the motoring press at the end of March 1964 and it was first seen in action at the Le Mans Practice Weekend on 18–19 April. It was built in response to Ford's failure to buy Ferrari and formed part of the company's 'Total Performance' package. Ford had made what they regarded as 'a prudent business investment' and gave salient reasons why they should be so deeply involved in motor racing. The motor racing programme was intensive and extensive and apart from the GT40 programme, included backing the Shelby American Cobra challenge in GT racing, sponsoring Lotus with the Lotus-Cortina in saloon car racing and at Indianapolis and, later, underwriting the cost of the Cosworth DFV Grand Prix engine and its Formula 2 counterpart.

The new Ford GT40 seen in the Ford Advanced Vehicles workshops at Slough shortly before its appearance at the 1964 Le Mans Test Weekend. Ford made a major blunder in pressing John Wyer into racing these cars before they were fully developed.

Roy Lunn initiated the project at Dearborn, but during the summer of 1963 Eric Broadley was brought in as consultant and Ford bought his two Lola GT coupés, which had provided the inspiration for the Ford GT40 and were used for test and development work. John Wyer, who had been Technical Director of Aston Martin Lagonda, joined the project in August 1963 and premises were acquired on the industrial estate at Slough, then in Buckinghamshire. Wyer controlled the new company called Ford Advanced Vehicles Ltd; he was responsible for the manufacture of the cars, their preparation and the racing programme. There were conflicts of ideas and practices among those working on the project, and there was too much pressure from Ford to race the cars. When they ran in 1964 they were far from fully developed.

The chassis of the new GT40 was a monocoque constructed from sheet steel with a load-bearing, unitised underbody, the box-side sills of which formed the fuel tanks. The very aerodynamic coupé body had glass-fibre bonnet and boot panels and doors. The front suspension was by double wishbones and coil spring/damper units, while at the rear there were twin-trailing arms, single transverse top links, lower wishbones and coil spring/damper units. The power unit was the 4,181cc (95.5 x 72.9mm) push-rod Ford Indianapolis engine with aluminium-alloy cylinder block and heads, four twin-choke Weber 48mm carburettors and, originally, a power output of 350bhp at 7,200rpm. A four-speed Colotti trans-axle was fitted. For further information about the Ford GT40 project, the reader is referred to the Bibliography.

Le Mans Practice Weekend

The practice weekend revealed just how well sorted were the Ferrari Prototypes and just how much work faced Ford before the GT40 was raceworthy and competitive. Lap times at the Practice Weekend were not necessarily of great significance, but in 1964 they were set in mainly

Above The start of the 1962 Nürburgring 1,000Km race: nearest the camera (No 92) Phil Hill accelerates away with the 246SP that he and Olivier Gendebien drove to a good win. Alongside, No 120, is the 4-litre GTO that Willy Mairesse/Mike Parkes drove into second place. No 96 is the Aston Martin DBR1 of Bruce McLaren/Tony Maggs that finished fifth. Behind the Aston Martin is the Lotus 23 with which Jim Clark snatched the lead on the first lap and stayed in front for the next ten laps. (LAT)

Left Part of the strong Ferrari entry at Le Mans in 1962 was the 4-litre V12 spyder usually described as the Tipo 330TRI. Phil Hill/Olivier Gendebien drove it to a fine victory ahead of two Ferrari 250GTOs. (LAT)

65

The 250P with 3-litre V12 engine was an immensely successful car. Ludovico Scarfiotti/Lorenzo Bandini drove this example to a win at Le Mans in 1963 and another 250P driven by Parkes/Maglioli finished third. (LAT)

Above *In the pit lane at the Nürburgring in 1964 are the Ford GT40 of Phil Hill/ Bruce McLaren on the model's race debut and the Ferrari 250GTO of Peter Clarke, which he co-drove with Dan Margulies.*

Right *Phil Hill was one of the greatest of Ferrari sports car drivers of his era and won Le Mans four times, 1958, 1960, 1961 and 1962, each time with Olivier Gendebien as co-driver. He left Ferrari at the end of 1962 and drove for Ford in 1964–65. Quite what he is eating is best left to the imagination. This photograph was taken at Le Mans in 1965.*

Works Ferrari Prototypes took the first three places at Le Mans in 1964. John Surtees and Lorenzo Bandini drove this 4-litre 330P car into third place behind two other Ferraris. (FotoVantage)

Above *1964 was the year of the Cobra at Le Mans. Dan Gurney and Bob Bondurant took fourth place overall with this Shelby American Daytona coupé and won the 3,001-5,000cc GT class. (FotoVantage)*

Right *Ron Fry, a motor trader in Bristol, scored a vast number of successes in club events with his Ferrari 250LM. Here he is seen at Martin Hairpin at Wiscombe Park hill climb in April 1965. He won his class. (FotoVantage)*

69

Lined up before the start of the 1965 Sebring races are two 330Ps. Graham Hill and Pedro Rodriguez drove the Mecom-entered car on the left and although it retired because of clutch problems, it was classified 37th. On the right is the car driven by Bob Grossman and Skip Hudson, another retirement, but classified 34th. (Ozzie Lyons)

David Piper shared his 250LM with Tony Maggs at Sebring in 1965. They drove a consistent race to finish third behind the 5.4-litre Chaparral of Jim Hall/Hap Sharp and the Ford GT40 of McLaren/Miles. (Ozzie Lyons)

Above *Three Ferraris in formation at Le Mans early in the 1965 race. No 21 nearest the camera is the eventual winner, the NART 250LM driven by Masten Gregory/Jochen Rindt. Lapping it is the 365P of Pedro Rodriguez/ Vaccarella, also entered by NART and behind comes the Scuderia Filipinetti-entered 250LM of Spoerry/Boller.*

Left *All four works Ferraris retired at Le Mans in 1965. John Surtees and Ludovico Scarfiotti shared this 4-litre Tipo 330P and although they led the race for about four hours, they eventually retired after a gearbox failure.*

Above *This 250LM entered by Écurie Francorchamps and driven by Dumay/Gosselin led the 1965 Le Mans race for ten hours after the works Ferraris ran into problems. Some three hours before the finish a rear tyre burst and caused the bodywork damage seen in this photograph. They resumed the race to finish second behind another 250LM entered by NART.*

Right *Le Mans 1965 was the peak of the 250LM's racing career. 250LMs finished first and second and this example driven by Spoerry/Böller and entered by Scuderia Filipinetti took sixth place.*

Above While every endeavour is made to publish only period photographs, this photograph is in fact period, although it was taken in 2000. That claim can be made because it shows David Piper with the last 250LM, chassis number 8165, which he bought in 1966 and has owned ever since. This photograph depicts the 250LM with its original aluminium-alloy body in the Shell Historic Ferrari-Maserati Challenge at Le Mans, 2000.

Left A view of David Piper's 250LM, chassis number 8165, photographed outside his workshop in Surrey in August 2003. The car is wearing its alternative glass-fibre body. This is lighter than the original and permitted under historic racing regulations because two 250LMs were fitted with glass-fibre bodies from new. (Anthony Pritchard)

Above *This view of David Piper's 250LM shows the rear-mounted 3.3-litre V12 engine, with the gearbox behind it. Many drivers consider the 250LM to be the most beautifully balanced of the Ferrari Prototypes and the V12 engine in 3.3-litre form to be superb. (Anthony Pritchard)*

Right *The cockpit of the 250LM is roomy, the instruments well laid-out and relatively few in number. In typical Ferrari fashion, the gear-change operates in an open gate. This is David Piper's car again. (Anthony Pritchard)*

Above *In the mid-1960s Ferrari 250GTOs were just obsolescent competition cars and worth very little money. This slightly tatty example was seen at the Clubmen's Championship meeting at Silverstone in October 1965. The flap covering the cap of the radiator header tank is open. (FotoVantage)*

Left *A contrast in styling: this 250GTO64 was also at the Clubmen's Championship at Silverstone in October 1965. The lines are dramatically different from those of the earlier car. (FotoVantage)*

Above *Seen in practice for the 1966 Monza 1,000Km race is the Ferrari 330P3 berlinetta of John Surtees/Mike Parkes. It was Surtees's first race since his horrific accident in September 1965. The race was run in torrential rain, but despite windscreen wiper problems Surtees/Parkes scored an easy win ahead of two privately entered Ford GT40s. (LAT)*

Right *Bob Bondurant with David Piper's 250LM leads Brian Redman (Lola T70-Chevrolet) in the sports car race at the International Trophy meeting at Silverstone in May 1966. The 250LM was now rather outclassed and Bondurant drove it into tenth place. This was the last 250LM to be built and it can be seen that the frontal treatment is different from that of Ron Fry's car. See Page 125. (T. C. March/FotoVantage)*

Above *At the Spa race* Colonel Ronnie Hoare's Maranello Concessionaires *entered this 2-litre Dino on behalf of* the works. Richard Attwood was partnered by Jean Guichet, but he was not happy with either the car or his co-driver. They did, however, win the 2,000cc Prototype class. (Ford Motor Company)

Above *The Spa 1,000Km race was an addition to the Championship series in 1966 and Parkes/Scarfiotti dominated the race with this 330P3. It was Ferrari's second and last Prototype race win of the year. (Ford Motor Company)*

Right *Rodriguez/Ginther drove this 330P3 spyder at Le Mans in 1966 and although they led for a short while, they retired in the 11th hour because of gearbox failure. It was a disastrous race for Ferrari.*

Above *Part of the line-up for the Le Mans start at Le Mans in 1966 with, from left to right, the Ford Mk II of Sir John Whitmore/Frank Gardner, the winning Mk II Ford of Bruce McLaren/Chris Amon and the Ferrari 330P3 of Pedro Rodriguez/Richie Ginther.*

80 Scarlet Passion

wet weather and emphasised the yawning gap between Ford and Ferrari. Scarfiotti with a 275P lapped fastest in 3min 43.8sec (134.55mph/214.518kph), an unofficial lap record. Other Ferraris driven by Surtees and Parkes were second and third fastest. The two GT40s brought to the circuit had serious aerodynamic problems and they were dangerously unstable at high speed. They also lacked adequate testing. Jo Schlesser achieved the fastest GT40 lap, 13th quickest in pouring rain in 4min 21.8sec and 19.5 sec slower than he achieved with a Cobra.

On the *Mulsanne* Straight Surtees was timed fastest at 193.88mph (312kph). Ford's best speed was again with Schlesser at the wheel, 180.00mph (270kph). During the Saturday Schlesser lost control of the GT40 at the kink on the *Mulsanne* Straight because of aerodynamic instability, crashed heavily and was lucky to escape with only a facial cut. On the Sunday, just after practice started, Roy Salvadori went off with the other Ford GT40 at the approach to *Mulsanne* Corner, an accident initiated by aerodynamic lift and completed by Roy braking too hard. When Eugenio Dragoni reported back to Maranello, the 'Old Man' must have sat at his desk with a self-satisfied smirk on his face.

Nürburgring 1,000Km

Ferrari did not enter the Targa Florio on 26 April and there were several reasons for this: Ferrari needed to concentrate on the preparation of the Formula 1 cars for the Monaco Grand Prix on 9 May, the first World Championship race in the 1964 series; because the Piccolo Madonie circuit was so well-suited to the smaller-capacity works Porsche entries, it was the one race in the Prototype series that Ferrari had only limited prospects of winning; and as the Fords were due to run in the Nürburgring 1,000Km race on 31 May, the team wished to ensure that there was maximum time available for preparation of the Maranello entries for this event. In the Sicilian race Porsche 904s took the first two places, with Alfa Romeo Giulia TZs in third and fourth places.

Three 275Ps ran at the Nürburgring and the smaller-capacity model was favoured because of its superior handling on this difficult circuit. Surtees/Bandini and Scarfiotti/Vaccarella drove works cars proper, while Graham Hill/Innes Ireland had a car

Scarfiotti and Vaccarella with their 3.3-litre Tipo 275P in the 1964 Nürburgring 1,000Km race. They won from Mike Parkes/Jean Guichet with a 250GTO64. The 275P handled better on slower circuits than the 4-litre 330P.

loaned by the works and entered in the name of *Maranello Concessionaires*. Phil Hill/Bruce McLaren drove the single Ford GT40, the stability of which had been much improved by the fitting of spoilers. Surtees/Bandini were fastest in practice, but, surprisingly, the Ford was second fastest. These were also the positions at the end of the first lap, but Surtees was way ahead of the Ford. Phil Hill fell back to fourth place and at the end of lap 11 McLaren took over after the car had been refuelled, holding fourth place for another four laps before a weld in a rear suspension mounting point broke.

After the first round of refuelling stops Graham Hill/Ireland led Surtees/Bandini with Scarfiotti/Vaccarella in third place. Ireland abandoned his 330P out on the circuit because the fuel tank had split. He ran the quarter-mile to the pits, returned to the car with a one-gallon can and rejoined the race, only to be disqualified for infringing the regulation that stated refuelling could only take place in the pits. Surtees/Bandini seemed assured of victory, but at three-quarter distance Surtees was driving when the 250P lost a wheel, but he stayed on the road, slowing the car by running against the hedges. Scarfiotti/Vaccarella won at 86.99mph (139.97kph) from Mike Parkes/Jean Guichet who had driven their 250GTO exceptionally well.

Le Mans 24 Hours, Ford versus Ferrari – Act One, Scene One

This was to be the first real clash between Ferrari and Ford and although the GT40s were to prove unreliable, they did display a very fine turn of speed. The principal Ferrari entries were:

No 14: 330P driven by Bonnier/Graham Hill, entered by *Maranello Concessionaires*. Jackie Stewart was the reserve driver and in his very limited practice with both this car and the team's 250GTO64 lapped faster than the nominated drivers.

No 15: 330P driven by Pedro Rodriguez/Skip Hudson entered by *NART*.

No 19: 330P driven by Lorenzo Bandini/John Surtees; works-entered.

No 20: 275P driven by Jean Guichet/Nino Vaccarella; works-entered.

No 21: 275P driven by Mike Parkes/Ludovico Scarfiotti; works-entered.

No 22: 275P driven by Giancarlo Baghetti/Umberto Maglioli; works-entered.

In addition two 250LM Ferraris ran in this race.

The Ford contingent was made up as follows:

No 10: Phil Hill/Bruce McLaren.

No 11: Richie Ginther/Masten Gregory.

No 12: Richard Attwood/Jo Schlesser.

Another formidable contender, although one unlikely to last the distance, was the Tipo 151/1 Maserati 4,941cc coupé entered by *Maserati-France* and driven by André Simon/Maurice Trintignant. During final practice on the Thursday John Surtees with the 4-litre Ferrari 330P lapped in 3min 42sec, a speed of 135.64mph (218.286kph), significantly faster than his own official lap record of 129.067mph (207.669kph) set in the 1963 race. Richie Ginther achieved the fastest Ford time in 3min 45.3sec, second fastest, and there was reason to believe that John Wyer had instructed his drivers to keep some speed in reserve.

Ferraris held the first three places on the first lap, but on lap two Ginther shot through into the lead with his white and blue Ford. Acting under strict instructions from team-manager Dragoni, the Ferrari drivers made no attempt to challenge the new leader. By 15 laps Ginther had extended his advantage to 40.1sec, but already some of the leading drivers were in trouble. On the first lap Baghetti stopped at Mulsanne Corner because of clutch problems, but eventually made his way back to the pits and after a long time spent working on the car he resumed the race; Parkes had come into the pits for a plug change and Phil Hill was in and out of the pits three times because his Ford's engine was missing on one cylinder – the problem was eventually traced to carburation problems.

When Ginther stopped at the end of the 26th lap to refuel and hand over to Gregory, Surtees, who had already refuelled, moved into the lead. The Ford stop was longer than it should have been because the two fuel tanks had to be filled separately. After two hours' racing Surtees/Bandini had covered 30 laps at 126.14mph (202.96kph) and then came Ginther/Gregory (Ford) and a trio of Ferraris. As the race progressed, Ginther/Gregory continued to chase the Ferraris and Phil Hill/McLaren with their Ford were battling their way back up the leader-board. The first Ford to retire was the Attwood/Schlesser car, which caught fire at about 8pm because of a melted nylon fuel hose.

Not long afterwards the Rodriguez/Hudson 330P retired because of a broken drive-shaft. During the sixth hour Ginther/Gregory dropped out because of transmission problems. The Maserati still battled for third place until it made a long pit stop just before 10pm

Above *Yet another Ferrari victory followed at Le Mans in 1964 and Jean Guichet/Nino Vaccarella won the race with this 275P, ahead of two 330P cars.*

Right *Champagne runs down the windscreen, as Jean Guichet (left) and Nino Vaccarella celebrate their win with their Tipo 275P at Le Mans in 1964. The 3.3-litre cars had a better reliability record than their 4-litre counterparts.*

Prototype Racing, 1964 83

because of ignition trouble. It was shortly after this that Peter Bolton at the wheel of the AC Cars-entered Cobra went off the road between Arnage and White House and was struck by Baghetti whose Ferrari crashed into the ditch. Later the marshals discovered the bodies of three spectators who had been watching the race from a prohibited area.

The Maserati succumbed to electrical problems just before midnight. The surviving Ford of Phil Hill/McLaren moved up to fourth place, but retired at 5.25am when the gearbox failed. Phil Hill had set a new lap record of 131.375mph (211.38kph), but this did little to console the large and over-optimistic contingent from Dearborn. Ferraris were now in the first three places and this was the order until the flag fell and the maroon sounded at 4pm. Guichet/Vaccarella (275P) won at 121.563mph (195.594kph) and also took the Index of Performance. Bonnier/Graham Hill (330P), delayed by various minor problems, finished second and Bandini/Surtees (330P) took third place; the last-named had fallen back because the pipe that picked up the fuel from the bottom of the tank had broken, so only the fuel in the upper part of the tank could be used and they had to make frequent refuelling stops.

Later races in 1964

Although the Prototype Championship was over and settled in Ferrari's favour, there remained a number of minor races. Ferrari withdrew the works Prototypes for the rest of the year and Maranello successes depended on private teams. Ford executives insisted that a full team of GT40s should contest the Reims 12 Hours race, although John Wyer wanted to concentrate on development rather than face another major failure and the ensuing bad publicity. All three Fords again showed an excellent turn of speed, but two retired again due to the failure of the Colotti gearbox and the third broke its crankshaft. Graham Hill/Bonnier (despite the loss of first and second gears) and Surtees/Bandini took the first two places with 250LMs entered by *Maranello Concessionaires* and *NART*.

Maranello Concessionaires entered Graham Hill with their 330P in the 133-mile (214km) Guards Trophy at Brands Hatch on Bank Holiday Monday, 3 August, but it was unsuitable for this winding circuit and Hill drove well to finish fourth behind a trio of much lighter Group Seven sports-racing cars. The Tourist Trophy at Goodwood on 29 August over a distance of 312 miles (502km) was open to sports cars, Prototypes and GT cars. McLaren retired his Cooper-Oldsmobile after leading, then Jim Clark (Lotus 30) went ahead, fell back after a pit stop and rejoined in second place. Graham Hill with the *Maranello Concessionaires*' 330LM, who had climbed back after a spin dropped him to fifth place, now led. The Lotus dropped out of contention because of mechanical problems and Hill won from David Piper (250LM) and Dan Gurney (Cobra).

On 20 September in the USA, *NART* entered a 275P for Pedro Rodriguez and a 330P for Bob Fulp in the division of the Bridgehampton Double 500 race for GT cars over 2,000cc and Prototypes over 1,600cc. Both these cars had simple hoop-type roll-bars in place of the familiar 'bridge-type' structure. Ludovico Scarfiotti also drove a white-painted 330P, which had arrived from the factory only just in time for the race. Walt Hansgen dominated the race with a Scarab-Chevrolet Zerex Special entered by John Mecom and a rather out-gunned Rodriguez finished second, a lap in arrears.

Scarfiotti was in third place near the end of the race when his Ferrari started to lay a long train of heavy smoke. The cause was a loose oil filter. Fulp also retired in this race. Six days later *NART* fielded 330Ps for Pedro Rodriguez and Ludovico Scarfiotti (his was again the white car) in the 250-mile (402km) sports car Grand Prix at Mont Tremblant in Quebec. Bruce McLaren led initially with his new McLaren-Oldsmobile, but dropped back because of mechanical problems and Rodriguez and Scarfiotti went on to take the first two places.

Maranello Concessionaires fielded their 330P for Graham Hill/Joakim Bonnier in the Paris 1,000Km race held on the combined banked track and road circuit on 11 October. In the absence of any serious opposition – apart from the team's own 250LM – they led throughout to win at 95.396mph (153.518kph) from Rodriguez and Schlesser with a 250GTO. The *Maranello Concessionaires*' 330P was the most successful of its type. The race was marred by a bad accident when long-time Jaguar driver Peter Lindner lost control of his 'Lightweight' E-type in the wet and collided with Franco Patria's Abarth that was stationary in the pits. Both drivers and three officials were killed. Rodriguez rounded off his year by driving a *NART* 330P at the Nassau Speed Week, taking third place in the Nassau Trophy and fourth in the Nassau Governor's Trophy.

It had been an exceptionally successful year for Ferrari, for John Surtees also won the Formula 1 Drivers' Championship at the wheel of Maranello's new V8 car. There was some luck in this, for the last race of the year, the Mexican Grand Prix, was a needle-match between Graham Hill (BRM), Surtees and Clark (Lotus), all of whom could still win. Lorenzo Bandini collided with Hill, forcing him to make a pit stop for his exhaust pipes to be cut away and Clark led until he dropped back because of a split oil pipe. Surtees finished second to Dan Gurney (Brabham), good enough for him to win the Championship with 40 points to the 39 of Graham Hill and 32 of Jim Clark. It was obvious that the threat in Prototype racing from Ford would not go away and that the team would bounce back in 1965 with greater speed and, maybe, reliability to match.

Colonel Ronnie Hoare's Maranello Concessionaires' team entered this 330P at Le Mans in 1964 for Joakim Bonnier and Graham Hill and they drove a superb race to finish second. Here Graham Hill is at the wheel. (LAT)

The Ford GT40s failed at Le Mans in 1964, but the American company was expecting good results too quickly. This is the car shared by Phil Hill and Bruce McLaren. They were in fourth place in the 14th hour when the gearbox failed. Following is the privately entered Aston Martin DP214 GT car of Salmon/Sutcliffe.

Prototype
Racing, 1965

In the Targa Florio Porsche was a constant threat to Ferrari and was beginning to beat the Maranello entries on a regular basis. Ferrari made a strong effort in the 1965 race and Nino Vaccarella/ Lorenzo Bandini with this 275P2 won the race from a quartet of Porsche entries. (LAT)

In late 1964 Ferrari extensively tested his latest 1965 4-litre Prototype at Monza and then the new car was revealed to the press at the annual Ferrari Conference held at the Hotel Real-Fini in Modena on 12 December. Although Ferrari provided a great deal of information about his plans for 1965, there was also a great deal left unsaid. He stated that SEFAC Ferrari's expenditure on racing and development during 1964 amounted to 604 million lire (approximately £335,000). In addition to the new 330P2 Prototype, Ferrari also announced that he would be introducing a 1.6-litre V6 GT car, to be known as the *Dino* 166, which would enter production in 1965 and the engine would be used in Formula 2 in 1967.

The P2 Ferrari was a completely new car in most respects and incorporated much of Ferrari's latest Formula 1 technology. The chassis was a semi-monocoque and followed what was to become familiar Ferrari practice of building a steel tubular structure to which aluminium-alloy panels were riveted to form

86 Scarlet Passion

stressed members. The front suspension was largely unchanged, but at the rear there was a new layout incorporating lower wishbones, short transverse top links, twin radius arms each side and the usual combined coil spring/damper units.

The cylinder head and valve gear-design of the engine were derived from those of the 1957 four overhead camshaft V12 Tipo 290MM (See Page 14). The rest of the 330P2 engine design remained as in 1964, late Colombo. Engine capacity of the 330P2 remained 3,967cc (77x 71mm), but power output had risen to a claimed 410bhp at 8,200rpm. No four overhead camshaft 3.3-litre cars appeared initially. Ferrari had evolved the body of the 330P2 in his new, but rather primitive wind-tunnel facility. It was lower and smoother than its predecessor, with spoilers either side on the nose and spot lamps either side of the air intake. There were large air scoops at the front of the rear wings to provide brake cooling. As seen at Modena and raced at Daytona, there was a shallow Plexiglas windscreen and a hoop-type roll-bar. By the European season the usual higher windscreen had been adopted, together with the familiar 'bridge-type' roll-bar.

Daytona

Immediately after the Press Conference, Ferrari painted the first 330P2 Italian racing red and shipped it out to Daytona to compete under *NART*'s name in the 2,000Km race held on 28 February. The race was now a round of the Prototype Championship and was open to sports cars, Prototypes and GT cars. It was held as usual on the 3.81-mile (6.13km) circuit that combined the steeply banked oval and the winding infield road section. Surtees/Rodriguez drove the 330P2 and *NART* also entered a 1964 330P for Walt Hansgen/David Piper and a 275P for Ed Hugus/Bob Grossman. Ford ran two much-modified GT40s, now entered by Carroll Shelby, and these were powered by Ford's V8 4.7-litre cast iron-block production engine and had a Ford-modified Colotti trans-axle. The drivers were Ken Miles/Lloyd Ruby and Richie Ginther/Bob Bondurant.

Surtees with the 330P2 led away from the rolling start; Bondurant passed him and then dropped back when he overshot a corner, and Gurney went ahead with his much-modified, Ford-powered Lotus 19B sports car. Hansgen was holding third place when passing the start/finish line at around 140mph, a rear tyre burst. The Ferrari had run over a con-rod from a Jaguar E-type which had blown up and shed engine components over the track. The 330P spun wildly for over 400yds, bursting another tyre and wrecking the rear suspension. Surtees had handed over to Rodriguez, but on lap 67 the Mexican had a tyre blow out on the infield section of the circuit and as he made his way slowly back to the pits the flailing rubber wrecked the battery. Pedro sprinted to the pits, brought back another battery and motored to the pits.

After two new rear wheels had been fitted and the damaged rear bodywork repaired, Surtees took over from Rodriguez, but there were still problems with the Dunlop tyres; chunks of rubber were flying off them and a vibrating wheel damaged the suspension. So he crawled back to the pits, where the overwrought Italians were screaming at the Dunlop technicians before the car was retired. Hugus/Grossman had worked their way up to third place with the 275P, but retired on lap 99 because of clutch failure. Miles/Ruby went on to win this 327-lap race at 99.94mph (160.80kph) from Schlesser/Keck/Johnson

Although the Dino *166P had retired on the first lap of the 1965 Monza race, it proved both fast and reliable at the Nürburgring. Lorenzo Bandini/Nino Vaccarella drove this* Dino *into fourth place overall. There was no 1,600cc Prototype class and they finished second in the 2,000cc class behind the Porsche of Bonnier/Rindt. (LAT)*

sharing a Cobra Daytona and Ginther/Bondurant with the second GT40. Daytona was not an important race as such, but it had proved a dreadful debacle for Ferrari and made it only too clear that the improved GT40s were likely to provide very serious opposition in 1965.

Sebring 12 Hours

Ferrari had originally planned to enter works cars in this race, but the organisers included Appendix C sports cars, which, subject to their reliability, were likely to leave the Prototypes in the distance; they had larger-capacity engines, albeit of production origin, and more relaxed rules governed their construction. John Mecom entered a 330P for Graham Hill/Rodriguez and *NART* ran a similar car for Maglioli/Baghetti, but for inexplicable reasons the FIA stewards moved the Ferraris from the Prototype class to the sports car category. Shelby entered GT40s for McLaren/Miles and Phil Hill/Ginther. The fastest car in the race, though, was the 5.5-litre Chevrolet-powered Chaparral with three-speed automatic transmission driven by its builders Jim Hall and Hap Sharp.

Richie Ginther led at the end of the first lap, but he dived straight into the pits to check out a braking problem, which the Ford mechanics traced to a stone jamming a disc-brake caliper. Hall/Sharp with the Chaparral then led from Gurney (Lotus 19B). The Graham Hill/Rodriguez Ferrari lost the use of second gear but continued at unabated speed, the Phil Hill/Ginther Ford retired because of a broken spring mounting and Gurney retired the Lotus because of a sheared fuel pump drive.

When a rainstorm inundated the circuit at 5.25pm, the faster cars were reduced to a crawl. Eventually the rain stopped after an hour or so; the circuit rapidly dried out and Hall/Sharp had dropped to three laps behind Hill/Rodriguez and with McLaren/Miles in third place. The Mecom Ferrari was retired with a burnt-out clutch, for which Rodriguez's heavy-footed driving was totally responsible. The Chaparral regained lost ground to win from the surviving GT40, with David Piper's well-driven 250LM shared by Tony Maggs in third place. Maglioli/Baghetti finished eighth with the *NART*-entered 330P.

Le Mans Practice Weekend

At the Sarthe circuit on 10–11 April Ferrari was out in force with a 330P2 and two 275P2s, a model that had not been seen previously. Power output of the new 3.3-litre version was said to be 350bhp at 8,500rpm. The works Ferraris were now fitted with cast magnesium-alloy wheels made to Dunlop patents in Ferrari's own foundry. *Scuderia Filipinetti* appeared with the first of the modified 1964 cars, which Ferrari was supplying to the Ferrari agents who competed regularly and was known as a 365P. This version retained the body of the 1964 330P, while the subsequent 365P2 had bodywork similar to the latest 330P2. There were minor chassis modifications and the main change was an enlarged bore of 81mm, increasing capacity to 4,390cc. Power output was claimed to be 380bhp at 7,200rpm. Tommy Spychiger and Herbert Müller drove the *Filipinetti* car.

The Ferraris set the pace and Surtees was fastest of all in 3min 35.1sec and was *allegedly* timed on the Mulsanne Straight at 205mph (330kph). When organisers issued their final and revised list, it showed both Surtees and Spychiger with the 365P as having been timed at 189.53mph (304.95kph), which seemed slow. Shelby brought along two Ford GT40 coupés, while John Wyer's Ford Advanced Vehicles had a coupé and a new open version. The GT40s were conspicuously slower than the Ferraris, but this was not necessarily of any significance. On the Saturday Lloyd 'Lucky' Casner with the Maserati Tipo 151/1 spun while braking at close to 170 mph as he approached Mulsanne Corner, crashed heavily and suffered injuries to which he succumbed almost immediately.

The *Dino* 166

The *Dino* announced at the press conference in December made its debut on 25 April in the Monza 1,000Km race, another addition to the Prototype Championship series. The engine was the 1961–2 Formula 1 V6 1,593cc (77 x 57mm) unit in 65° form; this had twin overhead camshafts per bank of cylinders, twin-plug ignition with twin distributors mounted at the front of the engine. On a 9.8:1 compression ratio and with three Weber twin-choke 40DCN carburettors, the power output was 180bhp at 9,000rpm. Transmission was by a five-speed trans-axle and the chassis construction and suspension were similar to those of the larger-capacity Prototypes. The *Dino* ran on Campagnolo cast alloy, five-spoke, 13-inch wheels. Coupé bodywork was fitted and it was a handsome little car, although with a very low nose that made the roofline look a little high.

Monza 1,000Km

The race was held on the full 10-km (6.214 mile) banked track and road circuit, with a chicane at the approach to the South Curve to slow the cars. Ferrari fielded a strong team, backed up by private owners, and for the first time in 1965 there was a straight fight between Maranello and Dearborn. There were 330P2s for Surtees/Scarfiotti and Bandini/Vaccarella, Parkes/Guichet drove a 275P2 and the *Dino* 166P was entrusted to Baghetti/Biscaldi. *Scuderia Filipinetti* entered their 365P

Ferrari dominated the results of the 1965 Nürburgring 1,000Km race and took the first two places. Here, on the first lap, John Surtees with the winning 330P2 heads the rest of the field, with Phil Hill (Ford GT40) next in line. (LAT)

for Müller/Spychiger and *Maranello Concessionaires* fielded their 330P for Bonnier/Piper. Shelby entered GT40s for McLaren/Miles and Chris Amon and Italian veteran Umberto Maglioli.

Parkes/Guichet were fastest in practice with the 275P2, followed by the two 330P2s, but there was only a fifth of a second between the three cars, and then came the first of the Fords driven by McLaren/Miles. During practice Bandini crashed heavily with his 330P2, hitting the guard-rail and spinning down to the bottom of the banking. This car had to be rushed back to Maranello for major repairs and arrived back just in time to take its place on the starting grid.

A rolling start was used and the cars were flagged away after a lap behind a course car. Surtees, Bandini and Parkes led initially, but two of the works Ferraris were soon out of the race; Baghetti retired the *Dino* with a blown engine on the first lap, while after only a few laps a rear suspension wishbone broke on Bandini's 330P2 and the Ferrari nearly collided with one of the Fords before grinding to a halt. Surtees suffered tyre failure on the leading Ferrari and by the time he was back in the race he had dropped to seventh place. Bonnier also had a tyre failure on the 330P and this car developed fuel pump trouble. It spent a very long time in the pits before Bonnier rejoined the race, but the 330P was still running badly and was retired without Piper having a drive.

Disaster struck when Spychiger went off at the slow *Parabolica* curve, somersaulted through the trees and was killed instantly. It was believed that the cause of the accident was brake failure. At around half-distance the Amon/Maglioli Ford retired out on the circuit because of collapsed suspension. Parkes/Guichet were still leading and were totally troublefree, while Surtees/Scarfiotti were back in second place, but with no serious prospects of catching the leader. So the race ran out, Parkes/Guichet averaged 125.90mph (202.60kph), finishing nearly two minutes ahead of Surtees/Scarfiotti. McLaren/Miles took third place with their GT40, but they were four laps in arrears and it was obvious that Ford would have to find a lot more speed to beat the latest works Ferraris.

The Targa Florio

Ferrari was out in force at the Sicilian road race on 9 May, partly because Maranello had missed the race in 1964 and more significantly because Ferrari needed to catch up on points in the Prototype Championship after the poor results at Daytona and Sebring. The team entered 275P2s for Vaccarella/Bandini, Scarfiotti/Parkes and Guichet/Baghetti. As usual, the main opposition came from Porsche and there was only a single, open Ford GT40 entered by Ford Advanced Vehicles for Sir John Whitmore/Bob Bondurant.

From the start Vaccarella set a cracking pace; he reduced the lap record to 39min 21sec (68.273mph/109.85kph) on his second lap and by the time he came in to hand over to Bandini at the end of lap three, he had a lead of over five minutes from second-place man Guichet. He received a less than enthusiastic reception from team manager Dragoni who pointed out in very clear terms that the Sicilian teacher was there to help Ferrari win an endurance race and was not on an ego-trip to impress his local supporters. Eugenio Dragoni was a very unpleasant Enzo Ferrari sycophant, but unlike most of his predecessors he did impose team discipline.

Already Scarfiotti had crashed and was out of the race, allowing the well-driven Ford GT40 to move up into third position. However, the Ford ceased to be any threat to the Ferraris after it shed the left front wheel on lap five and this bounced off the road and demolished the overhead cables for the island's main electric railway line. Whitmore put on the spare and was pondering how to make it stay in place, when a local came running up with the hub spinner, which had detached itself half-a-mile up the road. On lap seven the Guichet/Baghetti Ferrari expired out on the circuit because electrical problems had resulted in a flat battery.

As the race progressed, so the state of the circuit deteriorated and much of it was now scattered with loose gravel. The Ford suffered further delays because of fuel pick-up problems and it disappeared out of the race on the last lap when Bondurant lost control on loose gravel, bounced off a wall and completed the destruction of the front suspension on impact with a water trough. Vaccarella/Bandini won at an average of 63.729mph (102.540kph), over four minutes ahead of Colin Davis/Gerhard Mitter with an eight-cylinder Porsche and other Porsche entries took third, fourth and fifth places.

At Le Mans in 1965 Mike Parkes and Jean Guichet drove this 330P2 and were in contention for the lead for much of the race, but fell back before retiring because of cylinder head gasket failure. Here Guichet leads the Ford GT40 of Müller/Bucknum early in the race. (LAT)

Nürburgring 1,000Km
At this stage in the season Ferrari was still – and was to remain for some while – top-dog, while Ford was still very much on a learning curve. The next clash of the titans came in the Nürburgring 1,000Km race on 23 May. The entry from Ferrari consisted of John Surtees/Ludovico Scarfiotti (330P2), Mike Parkes/Jean Guichet (275P2), BRM Formula 1 team-mates Graham Hill/Jackie Stewart (275P2 entered in the name of *Maranello Concessionaires*) and Lorenzo Bandini/Nino Vaccarella (*Dino* 166P). Four Fords were fielded for Bruce McLaren/Phil Hill, Chris Amon/Ronnie Bucknum (both entered by *Shelby American*), Sir John Whitmore/Richard Attwood (open car from John Wyer's Ford Advanced Vehicles) and Maurice Trintignant/Guy Ligier (entered by *Ford France*).

When the flag for the start fell promptly at 9am, Surtees accelerated into a lead that he and Scarfiotti lost only briefly during a routine pit stop and they won at the record speed of 90.66mph (145.87kph). Parkes/Guichet finished second, 44.8sec behind their team-mates, after an equally consistent race. Graham Hill/Stewart retired because of electrical problems. In third place came the flat-eight 2-litre Porsche of Bonnier/Rindt and Bandini/Vaccarella took a fine fourth place with the *Dino*. Three of the Fords retired and the survivor that finished eighth was shared by all four of the Shelby drivers. There were mutterings as to whether the *Dino* had only a 1.6-litre engine, especially as it had beaten several Porsche 2-litre cars and all the Cobras, so Dragoni insisted that the mechanics strip the engine and the organisers arranged for it to be measured.

Two days after the Nürburgring race Ferrari spent a day testing at Monza prior to the Formula 1 Monaco Grand Prix on 30 May and the Le Mans race. In the evening Dragoni allowed his 23-year-old protégé Bruno Deserti to take out a 330P2. Dragoni was a director of *Scuderia Sant' Ambroeus* and Deserti had been driving for him since 1962. He had shared a privately-entered 275GTB with Biscaldi in the 1965 Targa Florio and it seemed that he was being lined up for a works Ferrari sports car drive. At Monza Deserti lost control at the braking point some 300 yards before the *Curva Grande*, crashed and the car caught fire. Deserti was killed in the initial impact and it was believed to be a case of driver error.

It was around this time that Enzo Ferrari, then 67 years' old, decided to shelve some of his responsibilities at SEFAC Ferrari. Although he remained President (and in reality continued to rule the company with a rod of iron), he appointed *Dottore* Piero Gobbato from Fiat as General Manager with overall control, except for the vital area of the company's racing activities; *Cavaliere* Federico Gilberti took over control of racing. Both were members of an executive committee, along with *Ragioniere* Della Casa, the company's accountant. Piero Gobbato, who had previously been with Fiat, was the son of Ubo Gobbato, Alfa Romeo's fascist managing director assassinated on 28 April 1943.

Le Mans 24 Hours – Act One, Scene Two
Although Ferrari was to win the 24 Hours race held on 19–20 June for the eighth time (and it was the marque's sixth successive victory), the race proved a debacle for both Maranello and Ford. The complete works Ferrari team retired and not a single Ford out of the five entered

completed the course. As described in Chapter Nine, private 250LMs finished first and second, while Mairesse/'Beurlys' with a very potent 275GTB entered by *Écurie Francorchamps* took third place.

Ford still seemed unable to learn the importance of a full development programme before racing and their entry included two 7-litre Mk 2 cars powered by the 6,997cc (108 x 96mm) V8 Galaxie engine developing 475bhp at 6,400rpm. One of these cars had completed a 24-hour reliability run at Riverside Raceway, California without problem, but the other had not turned a wheel under its own power before it arrived at Le Mans.

The fate of the Ferrari and Ford Prototypes was as follows:

Ferrari

No 17: Bonnier/Piper (365P2 entered by *Maranello Concessionaires*) ran well initially, rising to third place, but then they dropped back and the car was withdrawn in the ninth hour because of a fractured exhaust manifold.

No 18: Rodriguez/Vaccarella (365P entered by *NART*). This car had clutch and gearbox problems, but eventually finished seventh.

No 19: Surtees/Scarfiotti (works Ferrari 330P2) led from the fourth to the sixth hours, then dropped back because of broken front suspension, rejoined the race and led again in the tenth hour; then cracked brake discs caused further long delays, The car was eventually retired because of a broken gearbox in the 18th hour.

No 20: Guichet/Parkes (works Ferrari 330P2) ran very well and led for three hours before losing time in the pits while the clutch was repaired. This car eventually retired less than two hours from the finish because of a blown cylinder head gasket.

No 22: Bandini/Biscaldi (works Ferrari 275P2) ran steadily, holding second place in the seventh and eighth hours, but the engine went off-tune, the car fell back down the field and it retired because of valve problems in the 18th hour.

No 40: Baghetti/Casoni (works Ferrari *Dino* 166P) retired in the first hour because of engine failure.

Ford

No 1: McLaren/Miles (7-litre Mk. 2 entered by *Shelby American*) set the pace in the early stages of the race and led for the first two hours, but then dropped back because of gearbox problems and retired.

No 2: Phil Hill/Amon (7-litre Mk. 2 entered by *Shelby American*) lay second at the end of the first hour, but was soon in the pits with gearbox problems, fell right down the field and the car was withdrawn in the seventh hour because of gearbox failure. Hill had the consolation of setting a new lap record of 131.375mph (211.382kph).

No 7: Bob Bondurant/Umberto Maglioli (GT40 with enlarged 5.3-litre engine entered nominally in the name of Rob Walker whose proposed *Serenissima* coupé entry failed to materialise). Walker had the final decision as the choice of drivers, but in the event he was not consulted. He took serious exception to Maglioli of whom he did not approve. This car also retired in the third hour because of cylinder-head gasket failure.

No 14: Sir John Whitmore/Innes Ireland (GT40 with standard 4,727cc engine entered by Ford Advanced Vehicles) retired in the sixth hour of the race because of a blown cylinder head gasket.

No 15: Maurice Trintignant/Guy Ligier (open GT40 prepared by Ford Advanced Vehicles with standard 4,727cc engine and entered by *Ford France*) were victims of the ZF trans-axle failure in the second hour of the race.

No 'standard' GT40 was to finish Le Mans until a Wyer-entered car driven by Pedro Rodriguez/Lucien Bianchi won the race in 1968. Of the works Ferrari team, it can be said that its mistakes were forgivable, for it won two of the year's five Championship races and privately entered Ferraris had taken the first three places at Le Mans. With Ford it was different, for to misquote Oscar Wilde, 'To make one mistake is an accident, to make more looks like carelessness.' Ford had simply not taken on board the very obvious message that endurance races could not be won without meticulous testing and equally meticulous preparation. The company had already invested in excess of $6 million on their Prototype programme and while they would dearly liked to have withdrawn from racing, they could not think of a way of doing so without suffering even greater loss of prestige and 'street cred' than they had already suffered.

After Le Mans

There was only a small entry in the Reims 12 Hours, made even smaller by the withdrawal of Ford. Ferrari had not entered and the two most powerful cars in the race were the 365P2s of *NART* driven by Rodriguez/Guichet and *Maranello Concessionaires* whose drivers were Surtees/Parkes. *Maranello Concessionaires* also entered their 330P for Graham Hill/Bonnier. The race started on 3 July at midnight and at the end of the second hour Rodriguez/Guichet made a long pit stop while the clutch was replaced and they dropped from third to 15th place. After this the 365P2 ran faultlessly and steadily worked itself back up the field.

Surtees/Parkes had been leading, but their 365P2 broke a rocker arm, Surtees brought the popping and banging 365P2 back to the pits and it caught fire as he entered the pits road; he was able to put this out with the on-board extinguisher. Surtees/Parkes lost five laps while the rocker was being replaced, but the team's 330P seemed to be firmly in the lead. In fact Hill and Bonnier were struggling with the gearbox, which lost all ratios except second and fifth and retired after ten hours when the gearbox casing broke. Rodriguez/Guichet won by a margin of two laps from Surtees/Parkes, with the *Écurie Francorchamps* 250LM of Mairesse/'Beurlys' in third place.

Maranello Concessionaires entered Mike Parkes with the 365P2 in the 200-mile (322km) Austrian Grand Prix at Zeltweg military airfield on 23 August. The race was open to sports cars, so Hoare's team stripped some of the equipment off the car and fitted a low screen and simple hoop-type roll-bar. Jochen Rindt won the race with a 250LM, but Parkes should have won it despite a pit stop for fuel and tyres. A bolt securing the fuel filter had worked loose, Parkes realised that he was running out of fuel; he completed a slow lap, stopped at the pits a second time for a few extra gallons to be taken on board and rejoined the race to finish 44sec behind the Austrian. Frank Gardner (Lotus 30) took third place.

The mechanics swarm over the 330P2 as Mike Parkes clambers out at Le Mans in 1965. Standing behind the tail of the car are Mauro Forghieri and co-driver Jean Guichet. The 330P2 is about to be retired because of a blown cylinder head gasket.

Lorenzo Bandini and Giampiero Biscaldi drove this works 275P2 at Le Mans in 1965, but although the car ran well for many hours, at one stage holding second place, it developed engine problems and was well down the field when it retired after 17 hours' racing. (FotoVantage)

Prototype Racing, 1965

Another Group Seven sports car race that attracted Ferrari entries was the Guards International Trophy run in two 30-lap 79.5-mile (128km) heats at Brands Hatch on Bank Holiday Monday, 30 August. Parkes drove the *Maranello* 365P2, while Piper had a 365P2 which he had just bought from the works. The Prototypes were heavier and slower than the Group Seven cars. Lola T70s and McLaren's McLaren-Oldsmobile dominated the results. Parkes and Piper finished sixth and seventh on aggregate.

There were two races in North America on 19 September. In the Player's 200 race at Mont Tremblant, Quebec, David Piper brought his 365P2 across the line in second place behind John Surtees's Lola T70-Chevrolet. The same day *NART* ran in the larger-capacity 314.6-mile (506km) race at the Bridgehampton 500 meeting on Long Island. Hap Sharp won with his Chaparral, but Rodriguez took second place, albeit two laps in arrears. Bob Grossman drove the team's 330P and after starting in the dry on rain-tyres, which

94 Scarlet Passion

were changed during his pit stop, he finished fourth.

A week later the Canadian Grand Prix was held at Mosport Park near Toronto. During practice for this race John Surtees crashed heavily when a hub-carrier broke on the Lola he was driving and his injuries were so serious that there were doubts as to whether he would recover. In the race Rodriguez and Piper drove their 365P2s into third and fifth places. Jim Hall won with a Chaparral.

Piper now shipped his 365P2 out to South Africa to run in the Rand Nine Hours race held at Kyalami on 6 November. For the first time his co-driver was Dickie Attwood who tells the story of this event: 'The race was fought out between Peter Sutcliffe's Ford GT40 and David's Ferrari. Peter was very protective of his new car and he had Innes Ireland as co-driver. Innes was a much more exuberant driver than he would have chosen, but whether Ford imposed Innes on him, I don't know. The race started at noon and we led for most of the afternoon until David spun off, tearing off the radiator hoses and we lost 20min in the pits while this was sorted out. Innes and Peter went ahead and built up a lead of four laps, so it was a pretty hopeless situation from our point of view.

'During the last half-hour of the race the Ford slowed right down. Peter was convinced that a wheel bearing was breaking up and, because we were so far behind, he was just keeping going in the hope that the Ford would last the race and win. The pit gave me signs that Peter was in trouble, so I went quicker and quicker and we started to catch the Ford. We passed the GT40 to win in the last ten minutes of the race and for the South Africans it was probably the most exciting race they'd ever seen at the circuit.

'In fact one of the wire wheels on the Ford was breaking up and all that Peter need have done was to stop for a wheel-change. We made the race a real cliff-hanger and we were marginal on fuel, marginal on tyres and we finished the race with a rear tyre that was completely bald and through to the canvas. It was a very good win for us, but also a very lucky win. The 365P2 was a particularly good handling car. It had what I would describe as more power than grip. It was a wonderful car to drive – all those early Ferrari Prototypes were – and it was a classic of its kind. It had the big 4.4-litre engine, the torque just pulled you out of the slow corners at Kyalami and it was cracking in really fast corners. It was a very good, solid, reliable car and ideal for a 24-hour race.'

The European Hill Climb Championship

In 1965 Scarfiotti returned to the European Hill Climb Championship at the wheel of a 206S *Dino* coupé with the 166P engine bored out to 86mm, giving a capacity of 1,986cc. This car was said to have had a compression ratio of 11:1 and with three Weber twin-choke DC40N2 carburettors, power output was 205bhp at 8,800rpm. Scarfiotti proved a superior driver to any of the opposition and the *Dino* was faster and handled better than the Porsche opposition. The Ferrari operation was very low budget, Eugenio Dragoni's *Scuderia Sant' Ambroeus* entered the car and there were only two mechanics in attendance at each event.

The Championship consisted of seven hill climbs, with the results decided on the best five performances. Each competitor had two runs and the times for both were added for classification purposes. Scarfiotti missed the Mont Ventoux and Rossfeld hill climbs and did not run until the third in the series, the 10.75-mile (17.3km) Trento-Bondone event and he set BTD in 11min 56.4sec, smashing Edgar Barth's 1964 record by a margin of 21sec. Second fastest was Hans Herrmann (Abarth) in 12min 2.8sec and Gerhard Mitter, who was holding the lead in the Championship with his Porsche, was relegated to third fastest in 12min 10.6sec.

The next round in the Championship was the 6.84-mile (11km) Cesana-Sestriere event, running from the village of Cesana to the ski resort of Sestriere, on 25 July and here the *Dino* appeared with a very neat *spyder* body. During one of his climbs Scarfiotti glanced against a wall, but his 5min 12.8sec was again BTD and another hill record. Mitter took second place in 5min 19.0sec. The Freiburg hill climb in the Black Forest area of Germany was held on 8 August. Over a distance of 6.96 miles (11.2km) it consisted of the ascent to the Schauinsland Pass, climbing from 1,200ft (366m) to just 4,000ft (488m). Scarfiotti again set BTD and broke the hill record, while Mitter finished second, less than two seconds slower on the aggregate of his two runs.

Scarfiotti won again at Ollon-Villars. With a total of 36 points Scarfiotti could not be beaten in the Championship, but he ran in the last round at the 5.3-mile (8.6km) Gaisberg hill in Austria on 19 September. On the day of the event, torrential rain fell, the course was very slippery and, during the second runs, enveloped for much of its distance in rolling fog. Scarfiotti was very unhappy in these conditions, but he finished fifth behind a quartet of Porsche entries.

Bruce McLaren/Ken Miles drove this Ford Mk II 7-litre car at Le Mans in 1965. After leading for the first two hours, they dropped back because of gearbox problems and retired after the gearbox failed completely. Ford had again made the mistake of racing underdeveloped cars. This photograph was taken in practice.

Prototype Racing, 1966

Mike Parkes/Bob Bondurant shared this 330P3 berlinetta at Sebring in 1966, but failed to finish. Ferrari made the mistake of entering only the one car and at this time the 330P3 was far from fully developed. Parkes towers above the top of the windscreen. Fords took the first three places. The aircraft is a Mooney. (Pete Lyons)

Despite the failure of the works cars at Le Mans, 1965 had proved a very satisfactory season of Prototype racing for the Ferrari team. It was, however, evident that the 7-litre Mk II Ford was a car of immense potential at Le Mans, provided that Dearborn could improve its reliability, but it seemed extremely doubtful whether it would be nimble enough for other circuits. Ferrari contemplated the feasibility of building a car of greater engine capacity and power for the 1966 season but decided before the end of 1965 that it would be preferable to concentrate on the development of an improved version of the 330P2.

The result was the 330P3. Although a multi-tubular chassis was retained, a bonded glass-fibre underbody was moulded round it and this also formed the fuel tanks, while the cockpit area had stressed alloy panels that were riveted on to the small-diameter tubing. Piero Drogo's Carrozzeria Sports Cars built the bodies. The overall height was reduced by 3.7in (94mm) and cars

96 Scarlet Passion

were built with both open and closed bodywork. There was a very large, wide windscreen that curved to blend in with the side windows. The nose was very low and a headlamp and spot lamp were paired each side under Plexiglas covers. The 330P3 was slightly shorter, lighter and wider than its predecessors. Lucas indirect fuel injection replaced the Weber carburettors of the P2; the compression ratio was raised to 10.5:1 and power output was 420bhp at 8,200rpm. Ferrari claimed a maximum speed of 193mph (311kph).

The 330P3 was a works car only and the private teams raced the 365P2/3; this was the 1964 P2 with the single camshaft per bank 4.4-litre engine installed in 1965 and now fitted with 1966 P3-style body and some chassis modifications. Another new model was the *Dino* 206S, with a 1,987cc (86 x 57mm) engine as used in Scarfiotti's 1965 hill climb car. At the beginning of the season three Weber twin-choke 40 DCN2 carburettors were used, but later in the year Ferrari adopted Lucas indirect fuel injection. On a compression ratio of 11:1 both versions developed a claimed power output of 240bhp at 8,800rpm. The real figure, according to insiders at the factory, was just under 220bhp. Carrozzeria Sports Cars were also responsible for the body on this model. The lines were similar to those of the 330P3 and these cars were also built in both open and closed forms.

Daytona 24 Hours

Ferrari missed the Daytona race, now extended to 24 hours, held on 5–6 February and the four Ford Mk II cars proved the epitome of reliability and speed and dominated the results. Both *Shelby American* and engine tuners *Holman & Moody* were now entering these cars in the Prototype class. The original GT40 was homologated for 1966 as a Group Four Competition Sports car and many of these were raced during the year. The 7-litre Fords took the first three places in the order Ken Miles/Lloyd Ruby, Dan Gurney/Jerry Grant and Walt Hansgen/Mark Donohue, while Bruce McLaren/Chris Amon finished fifth.

NART entered two 365P2s and these finished fourth (Pedro Rodriguez/Mario Andretti) and 11th (Jochen Rindt/Bob Bondurant). A new contender making its race debut at Daytona in the hands of Jo Bonnier/Phil Hill was the 5.4-litre Chevrolet-engined Chaparral 2D coupé built to Prototype regulations and still fitted with an automatic three-speed gearbox. Unusual features of this car included a glass-fibre chassis and a large scoop mounted on the roof deflecting air to the carburettors. It had led for the first few laps, before stopping at the pits because of steering problems and dropping right down the field, eventually retired after 14 hours.

Sebring 12 Hours

Ferrari sent a single P3 for Mike Parkes/Bob Bondurant to the Florida airfield race on 25 March, together with a *Dino* 206S for Lorenzo Bandini/Ludovico Scarfiotti. Both cars were fitted with open bodies. *NART* entered a 365P2/3 for Rodriguez/Andretti. There were four Mk II Fords, including an open car driven by Miles/Ruby and one with automatic transmission entrusted to Foyt/Bucknum. The British *Alan Mann Racing* team also ran two GT40s on behalf of the works. Chaparral entered two of the very promising, very fast 2D coupés for Joakim Bonnier/Phil Hill and Jim Hall/Hap Sharp.

Parkes/Bondurant put up a stiff fight, battling for the lead and holding second place at half-distance and on

The experimental Ford 'J' car with honeycomb-aluminium monocoque that appeared at the 1966 Le Mans Test Weekend. It was not raced, but formed the basis of the MkIV that followed in 1967.

the same lap as the leading Ford of Gurney/Grant. The P3 then dropped back to third place, but was still on the same lap as the leaders, and it moved back into second spot again as darkness closed in on the circuit. It imposed too great a burden on both car and drivers to pit one P3 against four Fords and just after the nine-hour mark Bondurant retired out on the circuit due to a seized gearbox. Bondurant sprinted back to the pits to seek the advice of the Ferrari staff, but all he got were grim looks and shaking heads and the Ferrari was abandoned.

The Rodriguez/Andretti 365P2/3 had been running well, it was in fourth place at the halfway mark, but it was not fast enough and too far behind to support the works car. The *NART* entry lost time in the pits when a defective rear light had to be sorted and after the car had been refuelled again Mario Andretti took the wheel. The American-resident Italian apparently selected first gear by mistake as he approached the Webster Turns; the Ferrari spun into the bank and rebounded into a Porsche, which was shoved through the fence lining the circuit. Four spectators, watching from a prohibited area were killed and others injured. Andretti slowly made his back to the pits, with the front of the car severely crumpled and only one headlamp working. While the mechanics were contemplating what, if anything, they could do, the car caught fire and its fate was sealed.

The 1966 Monza 1,000Km race was run in torrential rain and despite wiper failure John Surtees, racing for the first time since his near-fatal accident in 1965, partnered by Mike Parkes, scored a fine victory with their 330P3 berlinetta.

On the last lap the leading Ford of Gurney/Grant with Dan Gurney at the wheel stopped on the circuit because of a broken engine. Gurney began to push the heavy car towards the finish, Ken Miles/Lloyd Ruby passed him with the roadster to win the race, and shortly after Gurney crossed the finishing line his Ford was disqualified for breaching a regulation that prohibited cars from being pushed on the circuit. So Hansgen/Donohue took second place with their Ford 7-litre and Peter Revson/Skip Scott finished third with a 4.7-litre Group Four Ford GT40 entered by the *Essex Wire Corporation*.

Ferrari was not completely out of the results, for Bandini and Scarfiotti with their *Dino* finished in fifth place overall and second in their class. They had led the class-winning Porsche for much of the race, but the *Dino* had dropped back because of gear linkage trouble, costing it several laps in the pits, and collapsing rear suspension that severely slowed its lap times. Both the Chaparrals retired early in the race.

Le Mans Practice Weekend
There were no works Ferraris at the Le Mans Practice Weekend on 2–3 April and while various excuses emanated from Maranello, the real reason was concentration on development of the Formula 1 cars for the new 3,000cc Grand Prix formula that had come into force for 1966. The only Prototype Ferrari to appear was the yellow 365P2/3 belonging to *Écurie Francorchamps*. Ford dominated the weekend and among the cars they brought to the circuit was the experimental J-car with completely new body/chassis structure made from aluminium honeycomb material, sandwiched between two thin sheets of aluminium-alloy and bonded together with exceptionally powerful epoxy resin and riveted in places where the stress was high. This car was fitted with two-speed automatic transmission.

Speeds at the weekend were almost a distraction from the real aims of sorting out the basic questions of fuel consumption, tyre wear and choice of axle ratios, but both McLaren and Amon were reported to have attained 215mph (346kph) with the J-car. During Saturday's practice on a very wet track Ford driver, 46-year-old and vastly experienced, Walt Hansgen, was driving far too fast, lost control at the Dunlop Bridge bend at around 120mph, went up an escape road, hit a sand barrier and rebounded into the retaining wall. Hansgen was grievously injured and had to be cut out of the completely wrecked *Holman & Moody* 7-litre. He died from his injuries five days later in the American hospital in Orléans.

Monza 1,000Km
At Monza *SEFAC Ferrari* entered a single 330P3 with coupé body for Johns Surtees, who had made a remarkable recovery from his near-fatal crash the previous autumn, and Mike Parkes. The only other big Ferrari in the race was the *Écurie Francorchamps* 365P2/3 driven by Lucien Bianchi/'Beurlys'. There were four *Dino* 206S cars: Bandini/Scarfiotti and Vaccarella/Bondurant drove works cars, Ronnie Hoare's *Maranello Concessionaires* team entered a car for Richard Attwood/David Piper and there was a *Scuderia Sant' Ambroeus* entry for Biscaldi/Casoni. Only the Bandini/Scarfiotti car had closed bodywork and this was also fitted with a fuel injection engine. The number of *Dino* runners was reduced to three when Bondurant went off the road in practice with one of the works cars at the *Curva Grande* and wrote it off.

There were no 7-litre Fords entered, the two *Alan Mann Racing* GT40s were withdrawn and so the only Ford runners were five private cars running in the Group 4 Sports class; the fastest drivers of these were Skip Scott/Peter Revson and Masten Gregory/Sir John Whitmore with *Essex Wire Corporation* entries and Innes Ireland/Chris Amon entered by Poole Ford dealer F. English Ltd (which was Ronnie Hoare racing under another hat).

The race was run in torrential rain throughout and Surtees/Parkes stayed in front from start to finish, despite windscreen wiper failure at one-third race distance, which made the dreadful conditions even more difficult. They averaged 103.114mph (165.910kph), a very slow speed for this circuit, and finished ahead of Gregory/Whitmore (*Essex Wire* Ford GT40) and Müller/Mairesse (*Scuderia Filipinetti* GT40). The three *Dino*s also suffered wiper failure – on the works car twice – and Bandini/Scarfiotti took a poor ninth place.

Of this race Richard Attwood, who co-drove the *Maranello Concessionaires*' *Dino* recalls, 'As far as I can remember, I had met Ronnie Hoare at the races and this was my first drive for his team. The Colonel paid his drivers very well, not quite factory prices, but not far off. We always stayed at five-star hotels and ate at the best restaurants. It was an absolute pleasure to drive for the Colonel, because he was such an engaging, charming and charismatic man – he was a wonderful guy to be with. For racing prospects, it wasn't good, because he only had privateer cars and with the P2/3s and the P3/4s we were always a stage behind what the works were racing.

'Monza was a very wet race and before the start Forghieri came up to me and said, "You've got disc brakes, pump them before the first corner because they've got water on them." To me the *Dino* was an uninteresting car to drive because it handled better than the power it could give. It had big tyres, but it didn't have enough power to have any fun with. You drove it as though it was a Formula Junior car, trying to make as clean a line as you could through the corners, scrubbing excess speed off because of the grip you'd got and the power you hadn't got. I didn't enjoy driving it particularly and on the long straights at Monza all the faster cars went streaming past you. After the windscreen wipers failed we dropped to finish 13th and seventh in class. Not a memorable race.'

Interesting cars at the Tourist Trophy

Although an international race, the Tourist Trophy at Oulton Park on 30 April was an event of minor importance. It did however attract three interesting Ferrari entries, only two of which started. Dick Protheroe, 44-year-old former test pilot and Jaguar driver, had completely rebuilt his ex-*Maranello Concessionaires*' 330P and modified the body to P2 style. During unofficial practice on the Thursday before the race the Ferrari's throttle stuck open, the 330P swerved across the infield at Druid's Corner, came out the other side of the corner airborne and landed upside down on the concrete base of a Nissan hut. Protheroe was killed instantly. David Piper, who witnessed the accident, believed that Protheroe tangled his feet in the pedals and jammed the throttle open.

Piper ran his 365P2 in a field consisting mainly of Group Seven two-seater racing cars and finished ninth overall on the aggregate of the two 70-lap 193-mile (311km) heats; apart from starting money and trade bonuses, he won £240 prize money. *Maranello Concessionaires* entered their open red and blue *Dino* for Mike Parkes, but during practice it started to make grinding noises from the rear axle and it was concluded that the differential had failed. Hoare telephoned Maranello and they dispatched a mechanic and replacement differential by air. When the back end of the *Dino* was stripped down, it was discovered that the factory had left insufficient oil flow to the crown wheel and pinion. Hoare decided to race the car on the understanding that Parkes would pull into the pits if the car started to make unpleasant noises, which he was forced to do after just two laps.

Targa Florio

The Sicilian road race on 8 May was a straight fight between Ferrari and Porsche. Maranello sent along a single, open P3 to be driven by Vaccarella/Bandini, two 206S *Dino*s for Scarfiotti/Parkes (their car was on fuel injection) and Guichet/Baghetti (on carburettors), while *Scuderia Sant' Ambroeus* entered a third *Dino* for Biscaldi/Casoni. The works Porsche opposition consisted of a flat-eight 906 Prototype driven by Günther Klass/Colin Davis, two 906 fuel-injected Prototypes for Gerhard Mitter/Joakim Bonnier and Hans Herrmann/Dieter Glemser, together with a Group Four 906 on carburettors for Pucci/Arena. The only GT40 entered was the *Ford France* car driven by Ligier/Greder.

During Friday's practice Parkes lost control of his *Dino* on the fast downhill stretch to Campofelice and in the ensuing crash damaged the front suspension and body. This *Dino* was patched up in time for the race. Vaccarella with the P3 was fastest Ferrari driver in practice in a very quick 39min 7.1sec, but Klass with the 8-cylinder Porsche was even faster with a time of 39min 5.7sec. On the Saturday there was a very heavy storm and torrential rain flooded the roads. The race on the Sunday started in fine, dry weather, but competitors soon found that much of the circuit was coated in mud and littered with stones that had washed down the hillsides. At the end of the first lap Vaccarella led from Mitter, Scarfiotti, Mairesse (*Filipinetti* Porsche 906) and Klass. Rain started to fall while the cars were on their second lap and surface conditions became even more treacherous.

It was on this lap that the Porsche drivers showed that they had the edge over their Maranello rivals. Mitter took the lead from Vaccarella on time and Klass moved up into third place. In these appalling conditions Klass/Davis and Mitter/Bonnier were in the first two places by the end of lap four, the P3 was third and the *Dino*s of Guichet/Baghetti and Scarfiotti/Parkes fifth and sixth. Lap six was full of incidents. Bandini was trying too hard to regain the lead with the P3, misjudged a corner just after Cerda and went off the road; the throttle jammed open on Parkes's *Dino* and he crashed out of the race; Klass and Mitter collided, Mitter went off the road with the six-cylinder 906 and Klass retired the flat-eight Porsche shortly afterwards.

There was now very little interest left in the race and Mairesse/Muller went on to win with the *Filipinetti* 906 at an average of 61.47mph (98.90kph), 8min 29.6sec ahead of the *Dino* driven by Guichet/Baghetti. Biscaldi/Casoni were a poor 12th with the *Scuderia Sant' Ambroeus Dino*. It was a bad day for both Zuffenhausen and Maranello and Ferrari's record in the Prototype series in 1966 was beginning to look more than a little shaky, with only one win in four races and it did not improve much later in 1966.

Spa 1,000Km

A new addition to the Championship series was the Spa 1,000Km race held on the superb Ardennes circuit on 21 May, the same day as the Monaco Grand Prix. This made life especially difficult for Ferrari and Maranello contented itself with sending a single P3 coupé for Parkes/Scarfiotti, while Surtees and Bandini drove the Grand Prix cars at Monaco. A second works Ferrari was a *Dino*, but this was run in the name of *Maranello Concessionaires* who managed the entry driven by Richard Attwood/Jean Guichet. *Écurie Francorchamps* brought along their yellow 365P2/3 for Lucien Bianchi/Jean Blaton and David Piper co-drove his 365P2 with Michael Salmon. A number of 250LMs also ran.

The Ford Prototype opposition consisted of a single 7-litre Mk II car entered by *Alan Mann Racing* and driven by Whitmore/Gardner.

For the race Ferrari decided to switch from Dunlop to Firestone tyres after back-to-back tests with both makes in practice. The Firestones lasted longer and were quicker than the Ford's Goodyears and the Dunlops with which the P3 was originally fitted. Parkes and Scarfiotti built up an unassailable lead to win at 126.43mph (203.43kph). It was Ferrari's second and last win of the year in Prototype Racing. The Whitmore/Gardner Ford took second place, almost a lap in arrears, with Scott/Revson (*Essex Wire Corporation* Ford GT40) third, Sutcliffe/Redman (Sutciffe's private GT40) fourth and Ireland/Amon (*F. English* GT40) fifth. Attwood and Guichet with the *Dino* finished sixth.

In this race Richard Attwood was very unhappy with his co-driver Jean Guichet: 'I was really annoyed with Guichet, he wasn't that fast and, I am only imagining, but he was probably a rich guy and managed to buy his way into a car or two. (*Forghieri describes Guichet as a gentleman driver who later became a very good performer. At this time Guichet was working in the motor trade. He lives in Marseille and runs a large building construction company*.) At Le Mans and races like that he was okay, but the Spa 1,000Km was rather like a sprint and we were up against all the works Porsches. I didn't think that we'd have a chance of beating them with Guichet because he was so much slower than I was. Anyway, I still drove as fast as I could and the Ferrari people were happy enough, although they weren't really interested in the car. I don't know why they did the *Dino*. I think that they saw commercial prospects for it and then lost interest.

'We did win the 2-litre Prototype category and I remember that Hans Herrmann was leading the class with a Porsche. I was going up to *Les Combes* and saw Herrmann parked on the left of the road. His Porsche had shed a wheel and Hans raised a thumb, as if to say, "Fair enough, you're going to win." I thought that I had a very good drive, but in no way rewarding enough with that tin-pot car.'

Piper/Salmon had a miserable race with the former's 365P2, which was down on power; with Piper at the wheel, a tyre burst in practice while running at around 150mph on the Masta Straight and in the race the 365P2 developed gearbox problems. After holding eighth place they retired; the *Écurie Francorchamps* P2/3 holed its radiator and was withdrawn.

Far left *David Piper bought this 365P2 from the works in late 1965. He is seen in the Tourist Trophy at Oulton Park on 30 April 1966. Group Seven sports cars dominated the results and Piper drove a sound race to finish ninth on the aggregate of the two heats.* (T. C. March/FotoVantage)

Left *Giampiero Biscaldi and Mario Casoni drove this Dino 206S spyder entered by* Scuderia Sant' Ambroeus *in the 1966 Targa Florio. They finished a poor 12th. Here the car raises the dust as it scurries through the village of Campofelice.*

Prototype Racing, 1966 101

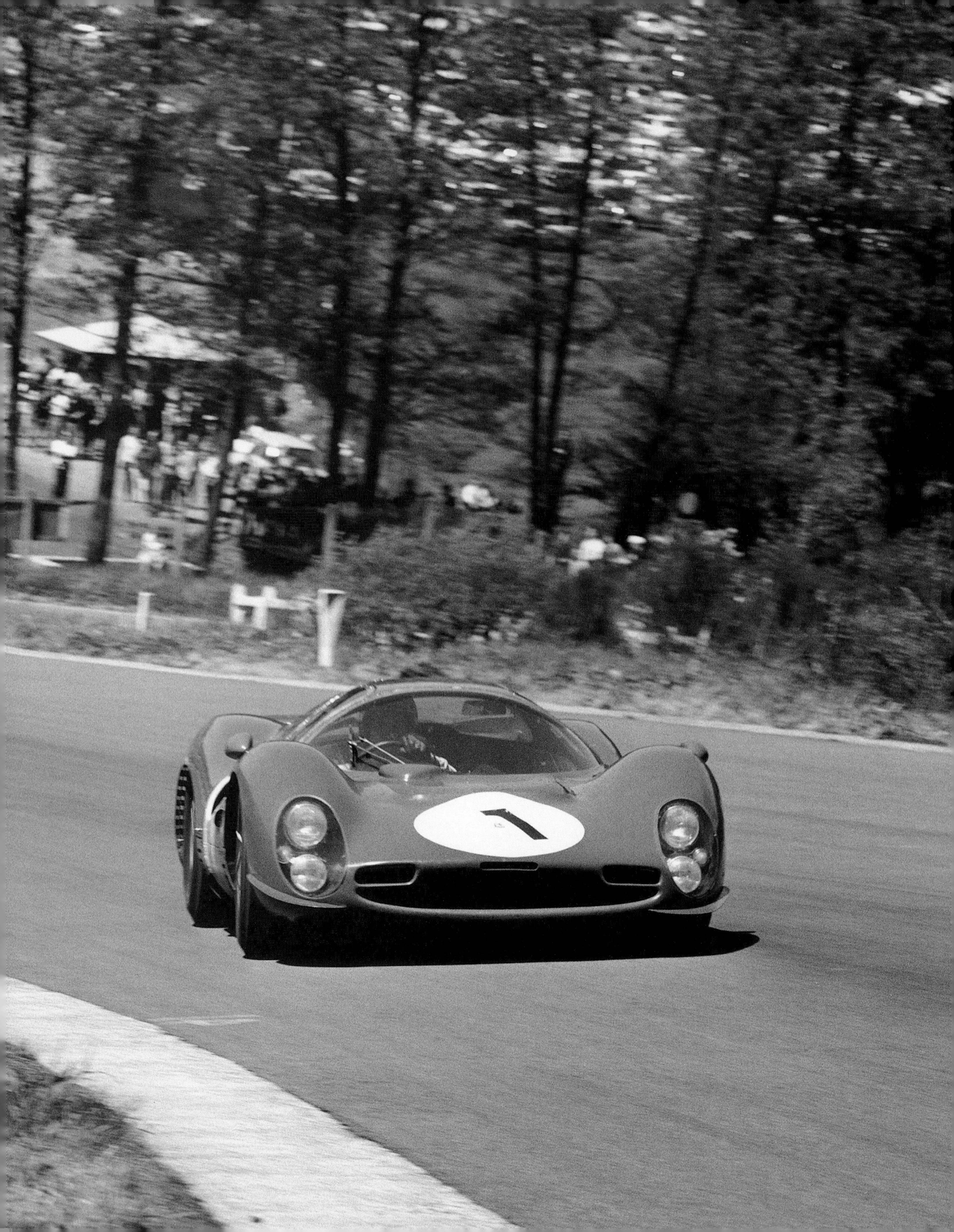
1

Nürburgring 1,000 Km

There were no 7-litre Fords at the German race held on 5 June, which was not a surprise, as the Nürburgring was one of the least suitable circuits on which to race these big Prototypes. There was however an American Prototype appearing in Europe for the first time, the Chaparral 2D, driven by Phil Hill/Joakim Bonnier. Once again Ferrari sent a single open P3 for John Surtees/Mike Parkes, together with a fuel-injected *Dino* driven by Scarfiotti/Bandini. *NART* entered a *Dino* for Ginther/Rodriguez and *Maranello Concessionaires* ran their *Dino* for Attwood/Piper. As usual, there was a strong Porsche entry and a number of Ford GT40s ran in the Sports class. Both works Ferraris were scintillatingly fast in practice and the P3 seemed assured of another outright victory.

Scarfiotti with the works *Dino* was first away from the Le Mans start and at the end of the first lap Surtees led from Scarfiotti and Bonnier. On the second lap Bonnier moved up into second place, while Surtees established a new Nürburgring sports car record of 8min 37sec and began to pull out a lead over the rest of the field. By the end of the fifth lap he had extended his lead to 1min 30sec. After the first hour's racing, the P3's supremacy cracked. Surtees pulled into the pits where after a hurried consultation, the rear of the car was jacked up and a shock absorber changed. By the time this was done and Mike Parkes took the P3 back into the race, the Ferrari had dropped down to 22nd place. Now Bonnier with the Chaparral led, harried by Scarfiotti and Rodriguez with their *Dinos*. Bonnier pulled in to refuel just short of quarter-race distance and for a short while – before Phil Hill repassed them – *Dinos* held the first three places.

Hill extended his lead over the works *Dino* and Parkes had brought the P3 through to eighth place. Surtees then relieved Parkes at the wheel of the P3, but after only a lap he was back in the pits for more attention to the rear suspension. Parkes eventually rejoined the race, but on about the 33rd lap, three-quarters race distance, he was forced to retire because of clutch trouble. Attwood/Piper retired their *Dino* because of gearbox problems. Phil Hill took the last stint at the wheel of the Chaparral and heavy rain began to fall. Hill/Bonnier went on to achieve a completely unexpected win at 89.35mph (143.76kph), while Scarfiotti/Bandini, who won their class, and Rodriguez/Ginther with their *Dinos* took second and third places.

Le Mans 24 Hours – Ford versus Ferrari, Act Two, Scene One

Despite the unreliability of the P3 at several races in 1966, most critics believed that Ferrari was the likely winner at the Le Mans race held on 18–19 June. They also had reservations about the reliability of the 7-litre Fords, although in sheer numbers of potential winners, the advantage was very much on Ford's side. There were also two Chaparrals.

The list of leading contenders was as follows:

Ferrari

No 16: 365P2/3 entered by *Maranello Concessionaires* and driven by Attwood/Piper

No 17: 365P2/3 entered by *Écurie Francorchamps* and driven by 'Beurlys'/Dumay

Left *Ludovico Scarfiotti and Mike Parkes dominated the 1966 Spa 1,000Km race with their 330P3 berlinetta and won easily from the Fords of Whitmore/Gardner and Scott/Revson.* (LAT)

Right *The Ford pit staff push the Mk II of Bucknum/Hutcheson out to the line-up for the start of the 1966 Le Mans race. Ford dominated the results and this car finished third at an average of 121.207mph (195.022kph).*

No 18: 365P2/3 entered by *NART* and driven by Gregory/Bondurant

No 19: 365P2/3 entered by *Scuderia Filipinetti* and driven by Mairesse/Müller

No 20: Works 330P3 driven by Scarfiotti/Parkes

No 21: Works 330P3 driven by Bandini/Guichet

No 22: Works 330P3 entered by *NART* on behalf of the works and driven by Rodriguez/Ginther

In addition to the above there were three *Dino* 206S cars:

No 25: Entered by *SEFAC Ferrari* for Casoni/Vaccarella

No 36: Entered by *Maranello Concessionaires* for Salmon/Hobbs

No 38: Entered by *NART* for Kolb/Follmer

At this point it is necessary to consider the 'Surtees Affair'. There are several versions of what happened. What is said here is the account according to Gozzi in his book *Memoirs of Ferrari's Lieutenant*, but Mauro

Above *The start of the 1966 Le Mans race. The line-up was dominated by the Mk II Fords, but fifth from left is the Ferrari 330P3 of Rodriguez/Ginther.* (FotoVantage)

Right *Early in the 1966 Le Mans race Attwood with the Maranello Concessionaires' 365P2/3 leads the Ford GT40 of Ickx/Neerpasch and the* Scuderia Filipinetti *365P2/3 of Mairesse/Müller in the rush down from the Dunlop Bridge to the Esses. All three of these cars retired.* (LAT)

Forghieri's account, in neutral terms, is set out on Page 197 and John Surtees' own story is on Page 207–209. Since Surtees had joined Ferrari for the 1963 season, Maranello's fortunes had steadily improved.

He was one of the outstanding drivers of his era, and one of the few drivers able to communicate lucidly with the engineering team and play an active role in development. Surtees's near-fatal accident with a Lola Can-Am car in practice for the Canadian Grand Prix in September 1965 had shaken Enzo Ferrari badly. He had come close to losing his number one driver while he was at the wheel of another make of car. In the writer's opinion Ferrari came to see this as a betrayal and his resentment of Surtees grew to unreasonable proportions.

Relations between Eugenio Dragoni ('motor sport director' and Team Manager) and Surtees became

104 Scarlet Passion

impossibly bad and, according to Franco Gozzi, culminated in a public row during practice for the Monaco Grand Prix. Gozzi says that Surtees accused Dragoni of being incompetent and a dictator, while Dragoni responded that Surtees was ill-mannered and untrustworthy. Surtees was summoned to a meeting at Maranello on the Monday following the race and both he and Dragoni gave their explanations for what had happened. The meeting ended on a conciliatory note, but Ferrari had decided that he wanted Surtees out of the team.

A further meeting took place without Surtees being present when Ferrari asked the opinions of general director Piero Gobbato, Gozzi and Dragoni. Dragoni accused Surtees of industrial espionage by passing on details of the 330P3 to Eric Broadley, which enabled him to build 'a Lola sports car that's absolutely identical.' This was a lie for the car concerned, the Lola T70 Mk III GT which appeared for 1967, was based on Broadley's experience that had started with the 1963 Lola GT; it incorporated what he had learned on the Ford GT40 and was a coupé version of the Group Seven car raced in 1965–66.

Ferrari dispatched Gozzi to the Belgian Grand Prix on 12 June and gave him specific instructions to announce after the race that Surtees had been sacked. Surtees won the race and so the announcement was postponed. At Le Mans the following weekend Dragoni informed Surtees that 330P3 No 20 would be driven by Surtees/Parkes with Scarfiotti listed as an additional driver. According to press reports at the time he told Surtees that he did not consider him fit enough to drive with only one co-driver in a 24 hour race. Another argument ensued and Surtees stormed off to see Enzo Ferrari. Inevitably, Ferrari backed Dragoni and Surtees withdrew from the Ferrari team. At Maranello, at least, it was seen as a victory, for Surtees had – in Ferrari's mind – left the team of his own volition.

At Le Mans the *Dino*s were not to provide any challenge to Porsche in the 2-litre Prototype class, for all were in trouble from the start of the race and all three retired during the third hour. The four 365P2/3s were purely makeweight entries. The *NART* 330P3 was a very serious entry, it had been prepared at the works and it was raced under Dragoni's control. Ferrari's biggest weakness was that there were still serious industrial stoppages in Italy and the cars were not prepared to the highest standards. Of the 56 starters, 14 were Ferraris, including three 275GTBs and a 250LM.

Ford
Prototypes
No 1: Ford Mk II entered by *Shelby American* and driven by Hulme/Miles

No 2: Ford Mk II entered by *Shelby American* and driven by McLaren/Amon

No 3: Ford Mk II entered by *Shelby American* and driven by Gurney/Grant

No 4: Ford Mk II entered by *Holman & Moody* and driven by Hawkins/Donohue

No 5: Ford Mk II entered by *Holman & Moody* and driven by Bucknum/Hutcheson

No 6: Ford Mk II entered by *Holman & Moody* and driven by Andretti/Lucien Bianchi

No 7: Ford Mk II entered by *Alan Mann Racing* and driven by Graham Hill/Muir

No 8: Ford Mk II entered by *Alan Mann Racing* and driven by Whitmore/Gardner

Sports Cars
No 12: Ford GT40 entered by *F. A. English Limited* and driven by Ireland/Rindt

No 14: Ford GT40 entered by Peter Sutcliffe and driven by Sutcliffe/Spoerry

No 15: Ford GT40 entered by *Ford France*, prepared by Ford Advanced Vehicles and driven by Ligier/Grossman

No 59: Ford GT40 entered by *Essex Wire Corporation* and driven by Scott/Revson

No 60: Ford GT40 entered by *Essex Wire Corporation* and driven by Ickx/Neerpasch

Controversy also surrounded one of the *Alan Mann Racing* entries because of an incident in practice. On the Thursday before the race Dick Thompson, the original nominated co-driver to Graham Hill, and Bob Holquist (GT40) collided at *Mulsanne* Corner; Holquist's car went off the road and was totally wrecked. Accidents, albeit expensive ones, are commonplace and it was the *Automobile Club de l'Ouest* who caused the problem because Thompson had not, apparently, reported the accident and equally at fault was the entrant, *Alan Mann Racing*. The officials decided that the Ford should be excluded from the race. When this became known, Ford announced that none of their entries would run.

After long discussions, Ford finally agreed that the race regulations had been breached and while their representatives conceded that Thompson would have to be excluded from the race, it was pointed out that this would leave Graham Hill without a co-driver. Alan Mann was fined a nominal dollar and the organisers agreed to close the roads forming the circuit so that a new nominated Ford driver would have an opportunity to qualify in an observed session. Ford chose Australian Brian Muir,

106 Scarlet Passion

Left *The 1966 Le Mans race proved to be a complete debacle for the Ferrari team and, again, not a single works car finished. This is the 330P3 of Scarfiotti/Parkes seen in the Esses during the Saturday afternoon.* (FotoVantage)

Above *Another view of the Scarfiotti/Parkes works 330P3 not long after the 1966 Le Mans race started and with the headlamp patches still in place. Just after midnight Scarfiotti collided with a Matra in the Esses. Following here is the Chaparral 2D of Phil Hill/Joakim Bonnier.*

an exceptionally experienced saloon car racer, who flew from the UK and successfully practised with the 7-litre Ford on the Friday evening before the race.

At the start Rodriguez with the *NART* P3 had difficulty in firing the engine and was almost the last away. A furious battle had started, with Fords in the first three places and the Ferraris chasing them as hard as they could. By the end of the first hour Fords were still in the first three places, Rodriguez had fought his way up the field to fourth place, another Ford was fifth and then came the Ferrari of Parkes/Scarfiotti and the Chaparral of Bonnier/P. Hill. Already Attwood had dropped back with the *Maranello Concessionaires'* 365P2/3 because of overheating. The struggle continued throughout Saturday evening, the Ferraris and Fords seemed very closely matched in terms of sheer speed and while the Fords' main weakness seemed to be higher than expected brake pad wear, the P3s were displaying great reliability at this stage in the race.

Shortly before midnight the Chaparral retired because of electrical problems after holding eighth place. Just after 12.30am the Ferrari team suffered a serious blow when Scarfiotti collided with a Matra-BRM, which Schlesser was reversing back on to the circuit after an off-course excursion. Scarfiotti was injured badly enough to be taken to hospital. The Bandini/Guichet P3 had slipped well down the field and by 1am was in ninth place, but despite overheating the P3 of Rodriguez/ Ginther was still screaming through the summer night and holding on to third place.

Bondurant/Gregory retired the *NART* 365P2/3 after nine hours' racing because of a broken gearbox and a few hours later Mairesse/Müller with the *Filipinetti* car, which had been running well in fifth place, was withdrawn for the same reason. Shortly before 3am the *NART* P3 had to be withdrawn, also because of gearbox trouble. Rodriguez was lamenting that he would never win at Le Mans, but two years later he was to score a fine win with a John Wyer-entered Ford. The *Écurie Francorchamps* 365P2/3 was another victim of gearbox failure and the last vestige of Ferrari hopes evaporated just as dawn was breaking over the circuit when the Bandini/Guichet P3, in 11th place, also succumbed to gearbox trouble. What caused this plague of broken

Prototype Racing, 1966 107

gearboxes is far from clear, save that they were not strong enough to transmit the power of the engine.

So the Fords dominated the race, despite many retirements; with an hour to the finish the surviving trio held the first three places ahead of a hounding pack of Porsche *Carrera* 906s and heavy rain had begun to fall. The most significant Ford retirement had been the leading Gurney/Grant car, which Gurney brought into the pits six hours before the finish with smoke and steam venting from under the engine cover. The cause was cylinder head gasket failure. Earlier Gurney had driven this car to a new outright circuit record in 3min 30.6sec, a speed of 142.979mph (230.053kph).

Ford tried to stage-manage a dead heat and the McLaren/Amon and Miles/Hulme cars, which were on the same lap, lined up abreast to cross the finishing line, with the Bucknum/Hutcheson car, which was a hundred miles behind on distance, formating behind them. The organisers were having none of this and McLaren/Amon were declared the winners because they were the last in the line of the 7-litre Fords at the Le Mans start and were deemed to have covered an additional 20 metres. After three years, myriad mistakes and the expenditure of millions of dollars Ford had finally achieved their goal. There was a small consolation for Ferrari. The *Maranello Concessionaires*-entered 275GTB driven by Piers Courage and Roy Pike, both very successful in Formula 3, crossed the line in eighth place and won the GT category.

As Richard Attwood remembers well, the race was also a disaster for *Maranello Concessionaires*: 'I was driving the Colonel's 365P2/3 with David Piper. The car had been at Ferrari, as the Colonel had asked them to give the car the "once-over" and had given them plenty of time. It arrived on the factory transporter and it looked very nice up there. When it came off the transporter and we looked round it, it became obvious that they had done nothing. They had not prepared it all, but whether they charged him anything, I don't know. The Colonel's mechanics prepared the car for practice and I was driving it when the water pump vee-belt broke just before the end of practice.

'I told everyone, "It's the end of our Le Mans." "What do you mean" they said, "We'll just put another belt on." But I pointed out that we would not be able to run it in – for some reason I knew that with a vee-drive belt, a simple thin belt without teeth, you have to run it in for quite a while, let it stretch normally, not exercising it too stressfully for if you do, it can turn in on itself and then it's a write-off. When you've got that initial stretch, you re-adjust it and then it'll be fine. The others argued, "We can do that, we can run the car up and down."

Left *Bandini/Guichet drove this 330P3 at Le Mans in 1966, but they were never in contention for the lead. They retired on the Sunday morning because of gearbox failure.* (LAT)

Above *Casoni/Vaccarella drove this works 206S Dino coupé in the 1966 Le Mans race, but retired during the third hour because of engine problems. Here the* Dino *leads a 1,300cc ASA and a Ford GT40 through the Esses.*

We had a free day on the Friday and we ran the car as much as we could on the road, then the mechanics re-adjusted the belt.

'They may have made it too tight, but anyway it didn't last and when the water temperature shot up on the first lap, I knew immediately that the belt had come off. We had to complete 25 laps before we could put any oil or water in the car. So I drove round until I'd completed 25 laps, slow enough not to cook the engine, fast enough in the quicker bits so that I could keep out of everybody's way and not be a general pain in the arse. After about two hours, with the 25 laps completed, I came in and a new belt was fitted. I knew it would be a waste of time. I carried on driving, I went really slowly and still the belt came off. So we lost our chance at Le Mans that year on the first lap.'

After Le Mans

Following the Le Mans race Enzo Ferrari and John Surtees had a meeting in the former's private office at the factory and afterwards issued a statement of which the following is a translation that appeared in the British motoring press:

> Today in Maranello, Mr John Surtees, the driver, and Mr. Enzo Ferrari have had a meeting. It appears a situation of uneasiness has arisen in the relationship of technical and sports co-operation now in course, and therefore it has been mutually agreed to give up the continuation of any further relationship.
>
> Signed
>
> JOHN SURTEES   FERRARI
> Maranello, 22nd June 1966

There was very little opportunity for private owners to race their Prototypes after Le Mans, but two did appear in the Kyalami Nine Hours race on 5 November. David Piper shared his 365P2/3 with Richard Attwood and *Écurie Francorchamps* entered their 365P2/3 for Mairesse/'Beurlys'. Initially Roy Pierpoint

Above Écurie Francorchamps entered this 365P2 for 'Beurlys'/Dumay at Le Mans in 1966. After a very slow race it retired because of overheating. It is seen leading the Essex Wire Corporation Ford GT40 driven by Jacky Ickx/Jochen Neerpasch.

Left Throughout the 1966 season the Chaparral showed great potential, but won only the Nürburgring 1,000Km race, which was its European debut. The Chaparral of Phil Hill/Joakim Bonnier is seen at Le Mans where it held eighth place before retiring because of battery trouble.

110 Scarlet Passion

The crowded Le Mans paddock on the Sunday afternoon of the 1966 race. On the top of the Ferrari transporter are the two Maranello Concessionaires' entries, the 365P2/3 driven by Attwood/Piper and the Dino 206S of Salmon/Hobbs. Both cars retired early in the race. (LAT)

led with his Group Seven Lola T70-Chevrolet, but he was soon in the pits to have a broken rocker changed. Then Piper forged ahead and he and Attwood built up a two-lap lead. As the Ford opposition dropped out, so Piper/Attwood increased their lead, easing off as rain started to fall, but at the chequered flag they were still 33 laps ahead of Clarke/Fielding with a Ferrari 250LM. It was Piper's fourth successive win in this race (it was not held in 1964). The *Écurie Francorchamps* P2/3 retired because of engine and brake problems.

Piper stayed in South Africa and later in November competed in the Cape International Three Hours race on the 2.03-mile (3.27km) Killarney circuit. Once again Pierpoint led the race with his Lola T70, but Piper passed the Lola when it made its first refuelling stop and he went on to win by a margin of 10 sec – despite laying a dense trail of blue smoke in the closing laps. In the 252-mile (405km) Nassau Trophy on 27 November, Venezuelan Riodrigo Dorjas appeared at the wheel of what was said to be (but wasn't) a P3 Ferrari. The car had little chance in a field that included the latest Can-Am Lolas, McLarens and a Chaparral 2E; Dorjas somersaulted the Ferrari at the end of the pits straight, it caught fire and the driver was badly burnt.

Overall it had been a very poor year for Ferrari in both Grand Prix and Prototype racing, at least until the Italian Grand Prix. The *SEFAC* had bounced back at the Italian Grand Prix in September with a new version of the V12 3-litre engine, now with three valves per cylinder. Scarfiotti and Parkes took the first two places with the new cars.

Prototype Racing, 1966   111

A soaking wet finish at Le Mans in 1966. Ford stage-managed a dead heat between the Mk II Fords driven by Bruce McLaren/Chris Amon (on the left) and Denis Hulme/ Ken Miles (on the right) and while both cars had averaged the same speed, the organisers determined that because of their positions in the line-up for the start, McLaren/ Amon had covered a slightly greater distance. Following is the Mk II Ford of Bucknum/ Hutcheson, which took third place.

European Hill Climb Championship

The first round of the 1966 Championship was the Rossfeld Alpen-Bergpreis held at Berchtesgaden on 12 June. This was a fast 6-km (3.73-mile) course that rose 500m between start and finish. Scarfiotti defended his 1965 Championship win at the wheel of an open 206S *Dino*, but it soon became obvious that the Ferrari was no match for the latest Porsche flat-eight cars. Gerhard Mitter set fastest combined times for the two runs of 6min 1.72sec, Scarfiotti was just under 5 sec slower and other Porsche entries took the next four places. Mitter's win was despite having to drive with a leg broken in the Spa sports car race just under a month previously and he was wearing a special light plaster cast strengthened by reinforced plastic.

Because of his injuries suffered at Le Mans, Scarfiotti was unable to compete in the second round of the Championship, the French 13.4-mile (21.6km) Mont Ventoux event held on 26 June. Mitter set fastest times, consolidating his Championship lead, and other Porsche drivers took the next five places. On 5 July Ferrari announced that the team would be suspending all racing indefinitely because of the continuing industrial disruptions in Italy. At this time metalworkers in the competition department were working only a three-day week.

However, many critics believed that the real reason was Ferrari's lack of success in both Grand Prix and Prototype racing. The only Grand Prix wins achieved so far in 1966 had been in the non-Championship Siracusa race and in the Belgian Grand Prix and John Surtees had won these events for Maranello before he left the team. As a result there was no *Dino* for Scarfiotti at the Trento-Bondone hill climb and no Ferraris at the British Grand Prix. So once again Mitter was not seriously opposed in the Italian hill climb and won yet again. Edoardo Lualdi with a private *Dino* took sixth place.

Inevitably, Ferrari relented and F1 cars were entered in the Dutch Grand Prix on 24 July and Scarfiotti reappeared the same day with the *Dino* in the Cesana-Sestriere hill climb. He was in sparkling form and was fastest on the aggregate of his two climbs, three seconds faster than Mitter. As Mitter had won the first three of the seven rounds in the Championship, he needed only one more win to clinch victory. This came the following weekend, on 31 July, when he was faster than Scarfiotti by an aggregate of 2.08sec at Freiburg-Schauinsland.

Mauro Forghieri was at Freiburg to supervise operations and the car now had the new Formula 2 engine with three valves per cylinder. Critics commented on the poor turnout and rather battered bodywork of the *Dino*. Scarfiotti won again at Ollon-Villars in Switzerland on 28 August and set a new hill record. Because the Italian Grand Prix was the same weekend, Scarfiotti missed the final round at Gaisberg in Austria where Mitter was the winner from Hans Herrmann.

Prototype Racing, 1967

Night pit stop for the Dino 206S of Rodriguez/Guichet during the 1967 Sebring 12 Hours race. Guichet is at the wheel and Rodriguez is standing by the door. This car retired because of overheating. (Clare Lyons McHenry)

Following the defeat by Ford at Le Mans, there were lengthy discussions at Maranello about a successor to the 330P3. There was a strongly held view that the *SEFAC* should build a car with larger-capacity V12 engine of about six litres for Prototype racing. This would be for use only on the faster circuits such as Daytona, Spa and Le Mans and it would also be possible to use this engine in Ferrari's projected Group Seven Can-Am car. For slower circuits such as the Targa Florio and the Nürburgring the *Dino* with a 2.4-litre V6 engine would be raced. Enzo Ferrari and Technical Director Mauro Forghieri ultimately decided that it would be preferable to race one model that could be used on all circuits and the existing 4-litre capacity would be retained. So the 330P4 was conceived.

Although the P4 was a direct development of the P3, the changes were substantial and significant. As has been mentioned, a 36-valve (two inlet and one exhaust valve per cylinder) development of the 3-litre Formula 1 engine, the work of Franco Rocchi, had appeared at the 1966 Italian Grand Prix. Ferrari claimed that this engine developed 370/380bhp at 10,000rpm and this gave rise to the usual scepticism about Ferrari power output figures. For if Forghieri's claim made earlier in the year that the average power output of the Formula 1 engines was 360bhp was correct, the gain in power was not substantial. In fact the 36-valve V12 was much quicker than its predecessor, as was shown by Ferrari's fine performance at Monza.

The capacity of the 4-litre V12 remained unchanged and there were twin overhead camshafts per bank of cylinders as previously. Lucas fuel injection was retained, but now this fed into air induction tubes located between the camshafts of each bank of cylinders (previously they were located between the cylinder banks). Changes had been made to the cylinder block, which was generally much stronger and featured cross-bolted main bearing caps. Twin Marelli distributors were fitted, there were of course twin plugs per cylinder and on a compression ratio of 10.5:1, Ferrari claimed a power output of 450bhp at 10,000rpm. One of the weaknesses of the 1966 cars had been the five-speed constant-mesh gearbox and this was redesigned for 1967 so that the gears were located on two main shafts. Drive to the rear wheels was by sliding-spline half-shafts.

Although the appearance of the P4 was similar to that of the P3, the chassis had some modifications. It was still a semi-monocoque, with a multi-tubular space-frame stiffened by aluminium-alloy panels and a glass-fibre underbody containing the fuel tanks, but it featured a slightly shorter wheelbase and increased track; these changes were made principally to accommodate the latest wide-tread Firestone tyres. After using Dunlop tyres since 1958, Ferrari had signed an exclusive agreement with the American company. The suspension layout was unchanged. The brakes were Girling ventilated discs and those at the rear had been moved to an outboard position to improve accessibility.

The body featured larger ducts on the nose, slightly more pronounced wings and there were trim tabs on the rear wings. Fifteen-inch, five-spoke, Campagnolo cast magnesium-alloy wheels with knock-off hubs were fitted. These cars were again built in both *spyder* and *berlinetta* forms. Ferrari claimed a weight of 1,950lb (885kg) with oil and water, but without fuel, and a maximum speed of 198mph (319kph). The first car, a *spyder*, was ready by December and was extensively tested at both Monza and Daytona.

An important change was that Ferrari had dispensed with the services of Eugenio Dragoni. Although Dragoni had the toughness that Enzo Ferrari respected, he had lost the services of Surtees (although Ferrari backed him at the time, he later regretted the departure of the British driver) and he was a poor tactician. Journalist Franco Lini took his place. Relations with the press improved, but it seems that he was a pretty clueless team manager. A new recruit to the Ferrari team was Chris Amon, who had co-driven the winning Ford at Le Mans in 1966.

Keith Ballisat of Shell had approached Amon at the United States Grand Prix in October 1966 and asked him if he would go with him to Modena to meet Enzo Ferrari with a view to him driving for the team the following season. They flew out of New York the following day. Chris and Ballisat met Enzo Ferrari and Franco Gozzi and Chris remembers, 'We discussed a contract. I remember there was a basic monthly retainer,

This photograph taken at Maranello shows what was probably the first closed Tipo 330P4 car early in 1967. The P4's combination of performance and style has led to it becoming one of the most highly regarded of competition sports cars (even if they were called Prototypes!). (SEFAC Ferrari SpA)

not a lot; I recall it was about $US1,000 a month, plus a percentage of prize money. The lunch that followed went on a great deal longer than the meeting.' In April 1967 Lini signed up German driver Günther Klass, but he was to make very few appearances for Ferrari.

Chris Amon's first real drive for Ferrari was during the test session at Daytona in December. He recalls, 'I think that we spent close to a week there, it was a great opportunity to get to know the team and the P4. It became clear to me that I needed to establish a presence in the team early on, basically because there were four people competing for two Formula 1 drives. The P4 was a very pleasant car to drive, as it was a great deal more nimble than the Fords I was used to. Although it lacked the ultimate top end pace of the 7-litre Ford, it gave you the feeling that you could drive it to the maximum for the whole race, which really wasn't the case with the Fords, especially the brakes. Daytona with its mix of banking and road circuit was a track that I enjoyed.'

For favoured private owners Ferrari rebuilt the 1966 cars to P4 specification, except that the engines retained two valves per cylinder. They ran on Weber carburettors and were fitted with ZF five-speed gearboxes. At the time this version was known as the 330P3/4, but in recent years it has usually been referred to as the 412P. *NART* also had a 365P2/3 re-bodied by Drogo with long tapering tail and vertical fins, which had holes for mounting an adjustable wing, but this was never used. The *Dinos* were still raced, but had a largely unsuccessful season. Ferrari did complete a *Dino* with a 2,417.3cc engine, basically that used in the 1961–62 246SP competition sports car, but it was entered only once.

Daytona 24 Hours

At the Daytona race held on 4–5 February the Ferraris were beautifully prepared, fully developed and the team was exceptionally well organised, mainly thanks to Mauro Forghieri. Lorenzo Bandini/Chris Amon (with the original *spyder* used for testing) and Mike Parkes/Ludovico Scarfiotti (with a new *berlinetta*) drove the works P4s, while Pedro Rodriguez/Jean Guichet were at the wheel of a *NART*-entered P3/4. *NART* also entered their Drogo-bodied P2/3 for Masten Gregory/Jo Schlesser. It arrived too late for practice and the drivers had to qualify it on race morning. *Écurie Francorchamps* brought along their new yellow-painted P3/4 for Mairesse/'Beurlys' and David Piper ran his 365P2/3 for himself and Richard Attwood.

Ford had entered six modified 7-litre Mk IIs, but the company was repeating the errors of the past and it is believed that none of them had even been tested in their latest form. Chaparral had developed a new Prototype, the 2F, and there were to be two of these cars, rebuilt from the open 2Es with which the team had campaigned the 1966 Can-Am series. They were very smooth coupés, with a tall, strut-mounted aerofoil of the type that within just over a year would be adopted in one form or another by all the Formula 1 teams. Only one of the new cars was ready to race in the two American events and so the team also entered the 1966 2D in modified form. At Daytona Phil Hill/Mike Spence drove the 2F, while Bob Jennings/Bruce Johnson were at the wheel of the older car.

During practice the works drivers were not pressing the P4s, for the team had done more than enough testing to know the cars' capabilities. Scarfiotti had a bad moment during night practice when a much slower car crossed his line through a corner in the infield and the Italian spun wildly, wrecking part of the rear bodywork against the guard-rail. The P4 was very quickly repaired and ran again in Thursday's practice. The fastest times set in practice were A. J. Foyt/Dan Gurney (Ford, 1min 55.1sec), Phil Hill/Mike Spence (Chaparral, 1min 55.35sec, but it is believed that this time was set by Chaparral boss Jim Hall) and Rodriguez/Guichet (1min 55.4sec, set by Rodriguez). In all, nine cars lapped faster than the official lap record.

On the first lap Phil Hill led with the Chaparral and Fords were in second and third places, followed by Bandini and Rodriguez with their Ferraris. Phil Hill still led at the end of the first hour, two of the Fords had already developed transmission problems and it became clear that the Ferraris were being run to target times, regardless of the speeds of other competitors. At the end of the second hour Phil Hill/Spence headed Rodriguez/Guichet, Bandini/Amon and Parkes/Scarfiotti. Just after the end of the third hour Hill spun off on loose gravel as he came off the banking on to the infield section, hit the retaining wall and damaged the rear suspension and bodywork of the Chaparral; he made his way slowly back to the pits, a bent wishbone was changed and although he rejoined the race, he retired after only a few more laps.

Ford transmission problems continued and at quarter-distance the Ferraris held the first four places, the highest-placed Ford of A. J. Foyt/Gurney was fifth behind Rodriguez/Guichet and ahead of Mairesse/'Beurlys' with the Belgian-entered P3/4. Patrick McNally wrote in his report of the race in *Autosport*, 'The Ford pits were now in a frightful shambles with cars in and out every second; conversation was held in short bursts and the tension was like the front line in Vietnam.' The transmission failures were the result of an instruction by Leo Beebe, head of Ford's Special Vehicles Division, that all moving parts were to be renewed for the race.

Ford had fitted new transmission output shafts but these had been incorrectly heat-treated and soon failed. So many gearboxes were changed that it became a routine and the mechanics could change a gearbox in 14 minutes. They changed nine Ford gearboxes and then lost count ... if nothing else, the Ford challenge was doomed because the team was running out of spare gearboxes and it seemed that only the two cars which had been fitted in the pits with older-type gearboxes might survive the 24 hours.

The *Dino* driven by Kolb/Crawford had been running well and battling with the Porsche entries, but the engine seized up on the banking. Piper/Attwood had been driving a consistent race with the 365P2/3, but electrical problems caused it to lose time during the night and it was withdrawn on the Sunday morning because transmission noises indicated imminent failure. The Belgian-entered P3/4 retired because of gearbox problems and the *NART* P2/3 dropped out when it stopped at the pits with water pouring out of the exhausts. The 2D Chaparral retired early on the Sunday morning after its automatic transmission broke as it was passing the pits.

The three leading Ferraris were now in total control of the race. In the closing stages they ran nose-to-tail and they crossed the finishing line at the end of the 24 hours three-abreast. Once the Fords ceased to be a threat, the average speed of the leaders was reduced and Bandini/Amon won at 105.703mph (170.076kph). In second place Parkes/Scarfiotti were three laps in arrears and Rodriguez/Guichet took third place, 29 laps behind the winners. The sole Ford to finish, driven by McLaren, Lucien Bianchi and Dan Gurney took seventh place, 73 laps behind the winner.

Sebring 12 Hours and afterwards

Ferrari decided not to enter the Sebring race on 1 April which seemed a poor tactical move after the great success at Daytona. *NART* also missed the race, so the only Ferraris entered were Piper's 365P2/3 co-driven as usual by Richard Attwood and four *Dino*s; the fastest of these in practice was the *Scuderia Filipinetti*-entered car loaned by the works and driven by Herbert Müller/Günther Klass; Rodriguez/Guichet were at the wheel of the car owned by the Mexican. Kolb's car, fitted with a new engine since Daytona, was again co-driven by Crawford and the fourth *Dino* was shared by Jonathan Williams/Casoni.

Ford entered only two 7-litre cars, a new Mk IV for Andretti/McLaren and a Mk II for A. J. Foyt/Lloyd Ruby and these were first and third fastest in practice. The Mk IV was a development of the J-car seen at the 1966 Le Mans Test Weekend. Mike Spence shared the Chaparral 2F with team boss Jim Hall, because Phil Hill had been admitted to hospital in St Petersburg, west of Tampa, for an operation for acute appendicitis; Johnson and Jennings drove the 2D. *Autodelta*, Alfa Romeo's competition division, entered two of their new Carlo Chiti-designed, Tipo 33 2-litre V8 *spyders* with six-speed gearboxes and although they were very fast, they were to prove very unreliable.

The 2-litre Alfa Romeos led on the first lap, but the Fords soon came through to the front and the Ferrari of Piper/Attwood was running well and provided a greater challenge than expected. On the first lap Kolb's *Dino* expired out on the circuit because of gearbox problems.

An interesting new contender in 1967 was the Lola T70 coupé with Aston Martin engine. This car is seen at that year's Le Mans Test Weekend. The Lola-Aston Martin showed considerable promise, for John Surtees was third fastest overall and fastest in the wet. The engine proved insufficiently reliable for endurance racing.

Both Chaparrals had been delayed by mechanical problems at the start, but soon began to make their way up through the field. By quarter-distance Spence/Hall led narrowly from Andretti/McLaren, Foyt/Ruby and Piper/Attwood. After 65 laps the green Ferrari was retired because of transmission trouble; Rodriguez/Guichet abandoned their *Dino* because of overheating, the Müller/Klass *Dino* was out of the race – as were the Williams/Casoni *Dino* and both Alfa Romeos – and the Chaparrals retired because of mechanical problems.

There was now no challenge to the Fords and they went on to take the first two places – *but* 30 minutes from the finish the Foyt/Ruby car clanked into the pits, a broken camshaft was diagnosed and there the car stayed until the chequered flag fell. Andretti/McLaren won with the Mk IV at 103.133mph (165.940kph), having covered 1,237.6 miles (1,991.3km). The Foyt/Ruby car, 12 laps behind at the finish and still stationary in the pits, was awarded second place even though the Mitter/Patrick 2-litre Porsche had covered the same number of laps. The stewards said that the Ford had covered the greater distance, but it was far from clear how they worked this out.

Le Mans Practice Weekend

A week later, on 8–9 April, the Le Mans Practice Weekend was held. It was dry and cold on the Saturday, but rained for most of the Sunday. Since 1966 the circuit had been resurfaced between Mulsanne Corner and White House with material that gave greater grip in the wet. Ferrari sent along two P4s, a *spyder* and a *berlinetta* and for what little it meant on the Saturday Bandini and Parkes set the fastest times. Bandini lapped in 3min 25.5sec at 146.53mph (235.77kph), while Parkes was 2.1sec slower. Among new cars seen for the first time was the Lola T70 Mk III-Aston Martin GT coupé driven by John Surtees and this was third fastest. The engine was a new Aston Martin V8 four overhead camshaft 5,008cc (98 x 83mm) unit.

John Wyer, who had purchased Ford Advanced Vehicles, now known as J W Automotive Engineering, brought along his latest project, the Gulf Oil-sponsored Mirage. This was a development of the Ford GT40, the production versions of which J W Automotive Engineering still manufactured, but with the upper part of the body and the nose-section made in aluminium-alloy and of much more rounded shape. The two cars at Le Mans had the usual 4.7-litre engine, but Wyer was planning to install engines of just over five litres and later in the year the Mirages ran with 5.7-litre engines developed by Holman & Moody. These cars were painted in powder blue and orange colours, not in fact Gulf's own colours, but those of another company they had recently taken over.

Monza 1,000Km

In the absence of the 7-litre Fords, the Monza race on 25 April proved a straight fight between Ferrari and Chaparral. Maranello entered P4 *berlinettas* for Parkes/Scarfiotti and Amon/Bandini; Rodriguez/Guichet again drove the *NART* P3/4, while Müller/Vaccarella were at the wheel of a *Scuderia Filipinetti*-entered P3/4. The works also entered an elderly *Dino* 206S fitted with the latest three-valve engine and Jonathan Williams and Günther Klass drove this. The main opposition came from the 7-litre Chevrolet-powered Chaparral 2F driven by Mike Spence/Phil Hill. The Mirages, now with special 5-litre engines and typed the M1/500, made their race debut in the hands of Jacky Ickx/Alan Rees and David Piper/Dick Thompson.

Bandini led away from the start, but on the first lap Spence went into the lead and stayed in front until lap ten when Bandini forged ahead again. The Ferraris and the Chaparral stayed in close formation, battling for the lead until Spence regained it on lap ten. Just before the one-hour mark Spence came into the pits because of what he believed to be a flat tyre. A quick check by the mechanics revealed that a universal joint in the suspension was breaking up. Spence took the car out for another slow lap and it was then retired. The works P4s were now unchallenged, apart from Rodriguez with the *NART* P3/4, who was driving furiously and chasing after the leaders following a pit stop to sort out minor problems. In fourth place was the P3/4 of Müller/Vaccarella.

Williams had been driving the *Dino* very hard to stay ahead of the Porsche opposition in the 2-litre Prototype class, but he was passed by Rindt with a works Porsche on lap 13; he stopped at the pits to refuel and hand over to Klass and two laps later the 'baby' Ferrari was out of the race because of overheating. The Mirages were suffering teething problems; Piper spun early in the race because a loose manifold stud had allowed water to spurt on to a rear tyre, which necessitated a pit stop, and later delays were caused by a broken shock absorber and Ickx retired out on the circuit because of ignition problems. Just before half-distance, the Ferrari pit signalled the P4 drivers to ease their pace, but they had not allowed for Rodriguez with the *NART* P3/4 who was still driving furiously after a pit stop to sort out minor problems.

Parkes realised that the Mexican was closing rapidly and he passed Amon. The New Zealander was convinced that the P3/4 was a lap in arrears, so he let Rodriguez go ahead. Rodriguez then tried to pass Parkes into the chicane, but left his braking far too late, took to the grass and hit the guard-rail, wrecking the front of his Ferrari. Not long afterwards Vaccarella spun the *Filipinetti* P3/4 into the guard-rail at the *Curva Grande*, smashing the tail and puncturing both rear tyres. After crawling back to the pits, he rejoined the race in sixth place with two new wheels and the bodywork bashed back roughly into shape. Amon/Bandini won in 5hr 7min 43sec, a speed of 122.375mph (196.934kph), 3min 16.2sec ahead of Scarfiotti/Parkes. Mitter/Rindt with Porsche 910 finished third and won the 2-litre Prototype class, while Müller/Vaccarella had fought their way back to take fourth place, five laps behind the winner. The surviving Mirage of Piper/Thompson was classified ninth.

Of this race Chris Amon says, ' I remember the terrific pounding that we were getting on the bumps on the banking and being thankful that Ferraris had a reputation for strength. Bandini was a great co-driver, he was very helpful to me from the time I joined the team and he was very quick. At the time of his death he was emerging from under the shadow of John Surtees's period with the team when John was very much number one. If it had not been for his fatal accident at Monaco, I believe that Bandini would have gone on to great things.'

Spa 1,000Km

Because only five clear days elapsed between the Monza race and the Spa 1,000Km held on 1 May, poor scheduling left the teams with inadequate time to prepare their cars. Although it was a circuit on which the 7-litre Fords could have performed well, none was entered and it seemed that Ford was now concentrating all its energies on Le Mans. Because Amon and Bandini were

The 1967 Spa 1,000Km race was run in torrential rain and the sole Ferrari entry, this P4 berlinetta driven by Scarfiotti/Parkes, performed badly. The drivers could not match the wet-weather skills of Jacky Ickx and others and finished fifth. (LAT)

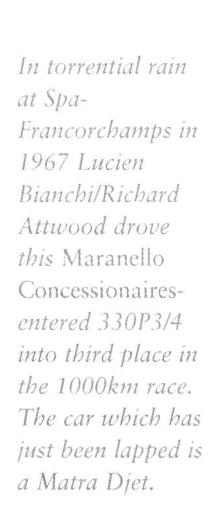

In torrential rain at Spa-Francorchamps in 1967 Lucien Bianchi/Richard Attwood drove this Maranello Concessionaires-entered 330P3/4 into third place in the 1000km race. The car which has just been lapped is a Matra Djet.

Prototype Racing, 1967 119

at Indianapolis, Ferrari entered a single P4 *berlinetta* for Scarfiotti/Parkes. The works car was supported by two P3/4s, entered by *Maranello Concessionaires* for Dickie Attwood/Lucien Bianchi and by *Écurie Francorchamps* for Willy Mairesse/'Beurlys'. There were no *Dinos* entered in this race.

The strongest opposition to the Ferraris should have come from the Chaparral 2F of Phil Hill/Mike Spence. Hill revelled in the very fast curves of Spa-Francorchamps and it was one of his favourite circuits. He set fastest lap in practice and the Chaparral was attaining close to 200mph on the Masta Straight. Wyer's team brought the two Mirages direct from Monza; Jacky Ickx/Alan Rees drove a car fitted with a new Holman & Moody-developed 5.7-litre Ford engine, while Piper/Thompson had a 5.1-litre unit as at Monza. There were two other serious contenders for outright victory, Lola T70 Mk III coupés with 5.9-litre Chevrolet engines; Paul Hawkins/Jackie Epstein drove the latter's car, which had a four-speed Hewland gearbox, and Mike d'Udy/Peter de Klerk were at the wheel of d'Udy's car. During practice d'Udy went off the road and damaged the front suspension and this car non-started.

In contrast to the ideal conditions in which practice took place, race-day dawned to heavy rain and a louring sky with a very low cloud base. It looked as though there would be no respite in the conditions – and there was none. Belgian Jacky Ickx was master at Spa, his home circuit, and a brilliant wet-weather driver, which gave the Mirage team an immense advantage. John Wyer wrote of Ickx's drive: 'the conditions were horrible for everyone else but ideally suited to Jacky Ickx. He swept into the lead at the start and at the end of the first lap, a little over four minutes later, he came down past the pits, over the *Eau Rouge*, up the hill towards *Les Combes* and out of sight before the next car could be heard on the back straight behind the pits.'

But what of the Ferraris? Mairesse, another local driver, held second place with the *Écurie Francorchamps* P3/4, some way behind Ickx, and Parkes was following him closely with the works P4. The *Maranello Concessionaires*' P3/4 was delayed at the start and Richard Attwood explains: 'The start at Spa is downhill and because the car was facing downhill, the pump was not picking up fuel despite a full tank. We'd tried to get some help before the start, but the Ferrari still wouldn't fire up. I decided to start the car by rolling downhill and when I got to the bottom with a bit of a run on level ground, the engine fired after two or three minutes. After that we drove a storming race. We were on new Firestone tyres and they turned out to be fantastic in the wet.'

Phil Hill was in fourth place with the Chaparral, but Paul Hawkins with Epstein's Lola passed him on lap six. A lap later Piper crashed his Mirage at *Malmédy* Corner and careered off the circuit into a ditch. By the three-hour mark Ickx had established a substantial lead and behind him came Mairesse/'Beurlys', Scarfiotti/Parkes, Hawkins/Epstein, Herrmann/Siffert (Porsche 910) and Attwood/Bianchi. The Chaparral had lost over nine minutes during its routine stop when the engine refused to fire up, and Spence was fighting his way back up the field. Wyer wanted Thompson to relieve Ickx, but he could not be found immediately so Ickx lapped for another ten minutes, breaking the race regulation that limited any driver to three hours at the wheel. There were plenty of complaints about this, but no formal protest was made.

The race was soon to lose two of its fastest runners. 'Beurlys' had fallen back while he was at the wheel of the P3/4 and when Mairesse took over again, he tried too hard to make up time on the Mirage. On his first lap he lost control at a fast bend, the Ferrari went off the road and was completely wrecked. The Belgian driver was lucky to escape with minor injuries. Mike Spence set the fastest lap in 4min 3.5sec at 129.54mph (208.46kph), a remarkable speed on a streaming wet track. Shortly afterwards the Chaparral was retired because of what was said to be a seal failure in the automatic transmission. The works P4 dropped to fourth place because of a pit stop while the Ferrari mechanics attended to a loose gear selector rod, which prevented the use of fourth gear.

Ickx/Thompson won at 120.491mph (193.902kph), a clear lap ahead of the Porsche 910 of Herrmann/Siffert, Attwood/Bianchi finished third and on the last lap Hawkins with Epstein's Lola snatched fourth place from the works P4. It was a poor result for Maranello, but the Ferrari drivers had not been able to match the wet-weather skills of Ickx and others. Richard Attwood again: 'Lucien Bianchi was the best co-driver that I have had, he lapped exactly the same speed as I did, he was totally reliable, he never went off and he was the ideal co-driver; he was a wonderfully charming Belgian guy and I got on so well with him. We really gelled and we didn't put a foot wrong that day.'

The weekend after the Spa race, Ferrari suffered a terrible blow. In the F1 Monaco Grand Prix Lorenzo Bandini had set second fastest time in practice with his V12 Ferrari and for 80 laps he contested the lead with Denis Hulme (Brabham). He had dropped back to about 20sec behind Hulme and appeared to have gear-selector problems. On lap 82 of this 100-lap race he lost control at the chicane, clouted the straw bales and the retaining poles on the waterfront. A wheel was torn off the Ferrari, which overturned, trapping Bandini underneath it and caught fire. Helpers righted the car, but the fuel tank exploded and when Bandini was eventually rescued, he was terribly burned. He died after three days of excruciating pain. It is likely that Bandini lost concentration, while struggling with the Ferrari's gearbox.

Targa Florio

The Sicilian road race was held on 14 May and since the 1966 event much of the circuit had been resurfaced and most of the bad bumps eliminated. Ferrari sent along a single P4 *spyder* for Scarfiotti/Vaccarella, the Targa Florio 'ace' who ran a school near Palermo. Müller/Guichet drove the *Scuderia Filipinetti* P3/4 and a 4-litre Ferrari (a 250LM with larger engine) was entered for Walter/Kochert, but non-started. There were three *Dinos*, two of which were works cars on loan, for Ferrari was reluctant to enter these under his own name in view of their continuing failure. Mario Casoni entered a *Dino* with three-valve cylinder heads and fuel injection for himself and Günther Klass, *Scuderia Nettuno* fielded a *Dino* on carburettors for Jonathan Williams/Sicilian driver Vittorio Venturi and Ferdinado Latteri/Ignazio Capuano drove one entered in *NART*'s name.

Once again Ferrari was courting defeat by making only one works entry and the Porsche opposition of three flat-six 2-litre 910 Prototypes and three flat-eight 2.2-litre 910 Prototypes looked pretty unbeatable. *Autodelta* entered four of their so far unsuccessful 2-litre Alfa Romeo 33 Prototypes. Large-capacity contenders were the Chaparral 2F driven by Phil Hill/Hap Sharp (Mike Spence was a BRM Formula 1 driver and was testing the H16 car with the team at Monza) and Epstein's Lola which he was sharing with airline pilot Hugh Dibley. Klass was very fast in practice and, presumably because he was a Ferrari driver, persuaded the organisers that the car should be renumbered from 202; he was given 156 and this enabled him to start ahead of the Porsche opposition.

Vaccarella led on time at the end of the first lap and Klass was heading the 2-litre Prototype class. Behind the Sicilian the order was Mitter and Siffert (both with Porsche 2.2-litre cars), Müller, Phil Hill and Klass. On the second lap Ferrari hopes of a win vanished, as their two leading contenders crashed out of the race. Klass with the *Dino* hit a marker stone and broke a damper. Very soon afterwards Vaccarella made a rare mistake, misjudged his speed into the left-hand hairpin bend in the village of Collesano and slid into a low wall, breaking the front suspension and both right-hand wheels. Mitter went off the road with his Porsche between Caltavuturo and Polizzi, so Müller led with the *Filipinetti* P3/4, but it seemed unlikely that this car would last the distance.

Müller led by 1min 6.6sec when he stopped to hand over to Guichet, who slightly extended the Ferrari's lead on lap four but on the next lap he had gear-selector problems and his lead over the Porsche of Stommelen/Hawkins diminished to a mere 6 seconds. When Guichet came in at the end of lap six to hand over to Müller, there was a great chunk out of one of the front wheels and painful noises from the differential. Müller dropped well back on the next lap and the P3/4 finally retired out

Although the 330P4 was an unsuitable car for the Targa Florio road race in Sicily, Ferrari entered this single car for Vaccarella/Scarfiotti. On the second lap Vaccarella made a rare mistake as he roared into the village of Collesano; he collided with a wall, wrecking the front suspension and damaging both right-hand wheels. (LAT)

at Polizzi when the differential gave up. On the same lap the second-place Tipo 33 Alfa Romeo of de Adamich/Rolland retired because of a broken suspension top link. The Chaparral was now in fourth place, but a lap later it retired too out on the circuit, reportedly because of a puncture. Porsche took the first three places and Williams/Venturi finished fourth with their *Dino*.

Nürburgring 1,000Km

Much of the interest went out of the German race following Ferrari's decision not to enter the P4s but concentrate on preparation for Le Mans. As a token gesture the *SEFAC* sent along a *Dino* with an old 2,417cc V6 engine with the fuel injection induction in the centre of the vee and two valves per cylinder. It has been suggested that this engine powered the Formula 1 car, which Bandini drove to second place in the 1966 Monaco race. There were no P3/4s, but *Scuderia Filipinetti* entered a *Dino* for Müller/Guichet. Neither of these cars started, for during practice the *Dino* with Guichet at the wheel had a carburettor fire that spread to the engine bay. Guichet stopped in the Esses just past the North Turn, but the car was completely burnt out by the time marshals with fire extinguishers arrived on the scene. A piston broke on the works 2.4-litre *Dino* during practice and there was insufficient time for repairs.

Large-capacity Prototypes were limited to the two Mirages, the Chaparral and John Surtees's Lola-Aston Martin making its race debut. In practice Dick Thompson wrote off the 5-litre Mirage he was sharing with David Piper when he took off on one of the bumps, landed badly and spun into a small British Ginetta that had crashed earlier. In sheer numbers, Porsche dominated the entry list with three six-cylinder 2-litre 910s and three eight-cylinder 2.2-litre 910s. They were also ideal cars for this very difficult circuit. The only other competitive Prototypes were three Alfa Romeo Tipo 33s entered by *Autodelta*.

The Lola, which had magneto ignition, fired up at the Le Mans start but stalled and then took some while to restart. On only lap seven a rear suspension wishbone broke, the rear wheels locked up and Surtees had great difficulty in stopping it safely. After a slow start with the Chaparral, Phil Hill took the lead on lap seven, but after 90min he brought it into the pits, with peculiar noises emanating from the automatic transmission. Spence took over, but was forced to abandon the car before he had even completed a lap. Ickx/Attwood with the 5.7-litre Mirage held second place at one stage and closed on the leading Porsche of Mitter/Bianchi, but they fell back to third place and Attwood was forced to retire out on the circuit on lap 30 of this 44-lap race after puncturing both rear tyres on debris lying on the track at Breidscheid. Works Porsche 910s took the first four places, followed across the line by the surviving Alfa Romeo Tipo 33 shared de Adamich/'Nanni Galli'/Bussinello/Zeccoli.

Le Mans 24 Hours – Ford versus Ferrari, Act Two, Scene Two

In an emotional speech made after the 1966 Le Mans victory, Henry Ford II had said, 'We will return.' So he committed Ford to run in the 1967 race, once more at vast cost and when all Ford executives were fervently

122 Scarlet Passion

Left Scuderia Filipinetti *entered this Ferrari P3/4 at Le Mans in 1967 for Jean Guichet/Herbert Müller. Mauro Forghieri, stopwatch in hand, is arguing about tyres with the man from Firestone.*

Above *Seven 7-litre Fords were entered at Le Mans in 1967, but only two finished. This MkIV car driven by Dan Gurney/A. J. Foyt won the race at 135.482mph (217.99kph) from a brace of works Ferrari 330P4s.*

hoping that they could forget about racing and concentrate all the company's efforts on building and selling more and more road cars. Le Mans was also the one race in which Ferrari had no alternative but to respond to Ford's challenge.

Maranello was becoming increasingly bogged down with too many activities: Formula 1 (in which the company was faring badly and failed to win a single Championship race in 1967); the development of V6 Formula 2 cars (one was raced at Rouen only in 1967, but Ferrari was committed to a full season in 1968); Prototype racing (in which the team's record had been indifferent in both 1966 and 1967); the manufacture of the V12 production cars; and the development of the *Dino* 206GT, which appeared at the 1967 Turin Show and entered production in 1968. Financially and administratively *SEFAC Ferrari* was becoming over-extended.

The formidable entry from Ferrari and Ford was made up as follows:

Prototype Racing, 1967

Ferrari

No 19: Works P4 *berlinetta* driven by Gunther Klass/Peter Sutcliffe

No 20: Works P4 *spyder* driven by Chris Amon/Nino Vaccarella

No 21: Works P4 *berlinetta* driven by Ludovico Scarfiotti/Mike Parkes

No 22: P3/4 entered by *Scuderia Filipinetti* and driven by Herbert Müller/Jean Guichet

No 23: P3/4 entered by *Maranello Concessionaires* and driven by Richard Attwood/Piers Courage

No 24: Works P4 *berlinetta* entered in the name of *Écurie Francorchamps* and driven by Willy Mairesse/'Beurlys'

No 25: P3/4 entered by *NART* for Pedro Rodriguez/Giancarlo Baghetti

No 26: P2/3 with Drogo body entered by *NART* for Chuck Parsons/Ricardo Rodriguez (the latter was not related to Pedro and not be confused with his deceased brother)

The works cars now had new gearbox casings that were some 30lb lighter and the P3/4s also had Ferrari

124   Scarlet Passion

gearboxes instead of the original ZF gearboxes. Three *Dino*s were originally entered, but these were withdrawn. Chris Amon told the writer, 'I found Vaccarella to be a very pleasant guy and as far as I can remember, Le Mans 1967 was the only race in which we drove together. I was very keen to win if only for Lorenzo Bandini and his memory. I had a sort of love/hate relationship with Le Mans; I never really looked forward to going there but I usually enjoyed it once I was there.'

Ford

No 1: Mark IV entered by *Shelby American* and driven by Dan Gurney/A. J. Foyt

No 2: Mark IV entered by *Shelby American* and driven by Bruce McLaren/Mark Donohue

No 3: Mark IV entered by *Holman & Moody* and driven by Lucien Bianchi/Mario Andretti

No 4: Mark IV entered by *Holman & Moody* and driven by Denis Hulme/Lloyd Ruby

No 5: Mark IIB entered by *Holman & Moody* and driven by Frank Gardner/Roger McClusky

No 6: Mark IIB prepared by *Holman & Moody*, entered by *Ford France* and driven by Jo Schlesser/Guy Ligier

No 57: Mark IIB entered by *Shelby American* and driven by Paul Hawkins/Ronnie Bucknum

The Mk IIBs were lighter than the 1966 cars; they had new glass-fibre nose and tail sections, repositioned frontal air ducts, 'turbine-styled' magnesium-alloy wheels and the spare wheel alongside the gearbox and removed through the tail.

Evidence of the popularity of Prototype racing was provided by the entry of three other two-car teams:

Chaparral Cars

No 7: 2F-Chevrolet 7-litre driven by Phil Hill/Mike Spence

No 8: 2F-Chevrolet 7-litre driven by Bob Johnson/Bruce Jennings

Lola Racing

No 11: T70 Mk III-5-litre Aston Martin driven by John Surtees/David Hobbs

No 12: T70 MkIII-5-litre Aston Martin driven by Chris Irwin/Peter de Klerk

J W Automotive Engineering Ltd

No 14: Mirage M1-Ford 5.7-litre driven by Jacky Ickx/Brian Muir

No 15: Mirage M1-Ford 5-litre driven by David Piper/Dick Thompson

That Fords were the four fastest cars in practice was largely an irrelevancy, but they set the pace in the race. At the end of the first hour they held the first three places in the order Hawkins, Gurney, McLaren, with Spence fourth after a delayed start with his Chaparral and then came Amon and Rodriguez. Already out of the race was John Surtees who abandoned his Lola after three laps because of a broken piston. The other Lola was also soon in trouble and after two lengthy stops retired in the fourth hour because of engine failure. Spence had led briefly just before coming in to refuel.

Some remarkable speeds were achieved on the Mulsanne straight:

Andretti/Bianchi: 213mph (343kph).
Other Fords were also the next four fastest cars:
Surtees/Hobbs: 205mph (330kph)
Spence/Hill: 199mph (320kph)
Scarfiotti/Parkes: 193mph (310kph).

As John Wyer pointed out, 'On the Mulsanne straight the engine is continually under maximum load for at least 60sec and this happens once each lap for 24 hours. It is this factor which makes Le Mans the supreme test of an engine.' During the early hours of the race Denis Hulme set a new lap record of 147.894mph (237.961kph), a speed later equalled by Mario Andretti.

At the end of three hours Gurney/Foyt with their Mk IV headed Spence/Hill with the Chaparral, Andretti/Bianchi and McLaren/Donohue. The highest placed Ferraris were the P4s of Scarfiotti/Parkes in fifth place and Amon/Vaccarella sixth. All was calm in the Ferrari pit and it was obvious that the P4s were running to a pre-arranged schedule. Ickx/Muir retired their Mirage because of a broken connecting rod in the fourth hour. Phil Hill spent nine minutes in the pits while the mechanics worked on the Chaparral's automatic transmission.

Richard Attwood recalls: 'Ferrari had done a whole batch of P3/4 engines with the wrong piston rings, the piston rings began to drink oil and there was no point in going on.' All the P3/4s retired, the Müller/Guichet car in the seventh hour, the Rodriguez/Baghetti car shortly

Left above
Scarfiotti and Parkes drove this 330P4 into second place at Le Mans in 1967, just over 22 miles (35.4km) behind the winning Ford. It was a close race, but the Fords were just that extra bit quicker.

Left lower
Ludovico Scarfiotti on the bonnet of his 330P4 celebrates his second place at Le Mans in 1967, 32 miles (51.5km) behind the winning Ford.

after the 11-hour mark, and the Attwood/Courage car in the 15th hour after holding eighth place.

In the eighth hour Amon's Ferrari punctured a Firestone and the New Zealander explains the circumstances of the car's retirement: 'Once the tyre had gone completely flat, I had no choice but to change it, as the suspension upright was scraping on the road. I stopped at the side of the Mulsanne Straight, got out the comprehensive kit supplied for such circumstances and then discovered that the torch had flat batteries. So I took out the jack and tried to work by car headlamps; the jack wouldn't work properly, then the head flew off the hammer that I had to use to loosen the spinner.

'I crawled around in the ditch in complete darkness, but I couldn't find the hammer head, so I gave up and tried to drive back to the pits. Shortly afterwards the car caught fire, I aimed it for the ditch, jumped out and ended up in the ditch myself. I'd had enough of it all by then. Of the 11 times that I drove at Le Mans, the only time I finished was in 1966 when I won with Bruce McLaren.'

It was shortly after this incident that Lloyd Ruby abandoned his Mk IV out on the circuit after it shed its sump under-shield during an off-course excursion. In the 11th hour the Chaparral of Jennings/Johnson was withdrawn because of electrical problems after a slow race. Just after midnight three of the Fords were eliminated in one incident and the Ford pit was wondering where the cars had got to when Schlesser came in to retire his car and report that there had been Fords all over the road. Later the full story emerged. Andretti had locked a brake as he entered the Esses and hit the bank, McClusky hit the other bank while trying to avoid him and Schlesser managed to avoid both cars, but hit the bank himself.

At 4am, half-time, when dawn was breaking over the circuit, 37 cars out of 54 starters were still running. Gurney/Foyt led by a comfortable margin from Scarfiotti/Parkes, Hill/Spence with the Chaparral and Mairesse/'Beurlys'. The Ferraris were now being driven flat-out in pursuit of the leading American cars. The Chaparral came into the pits with fluid streaming out of a seal in the transmission system. It would take an estimated two hours to repair the car, the mechanics started work and it rejoined the race in 17th position after nearly three hours. In the 17th hour the transmission failed altogether. It was the last retirement in the race.

McLaren lost the engine cover on his Mark IV, was sent out to recover it and rejoined the race with it patched by masking tape and retained by leather straps. At around this time Hawkins/Bucknum retired their sixth-place Mk II because of engine failure and soon afterwards the fourth-placed Klass/Sutcliffe P4 dropped

out because of a sheared injection pump drive. So with six hours to the finish the order was Ford–Ferrari–Ferrari–Ford; the Ford pit staff just hoping that the leading Mk IV of Gurney/Foyt would stay together and the Ferrari pit were unashamedly praying that something would break.

So the race ran out without further incident and the final finishing positions for the first four cars were:

1st Dan Gurney/A. J. Foyt (Ford Mk IV), 3,251.567 miles (5,231.77km), 135.482mph (216.382kph),

2nd Ludovico Scarfiotti/Mike Parkes (Ferrari 330P4), 3,219.063 miles (5,179.472km), 134.127mph (215.810kph)

3rd Willy Mairesse/'Beurlys' (Ferrari 330P4), 3,159.287 miles (5,083.293km), 131.637mph (211.804kph)

4th Bruce McLaren/Mark Donohue (Ford Mk IV), 3,001.58 miles (4,829.542km), 125.416mph (201.794kph)

In fifth place came Siffert/Herrman with the new 907 Porsche powered by a flat-six engine and they won the 2-litre Prototype class. Other Porsche entries finished sixth and seventh. Steinemann/Spoerry at the wheel of a Ferrari 275GTB took 11th place and won the 5,000cc GT class.

Le Mans was a good victory for Ford, but hardly an overwhelming one as in 1966; it has to be looked at on the light of two years' failures, the remarkable success in 1966 and the fact that only two out of seven entries finished in 1967. All three Ford GT40s running in the Sports class also retired and in four years not a single GT40 had ever finished at Le Mans. For Ferrari it was yet another defeat, but the fact that its cars finished second and third and that 50% of its entry completed the race reduced its significance.

A Controversial Change in the Prototype Rules

On the day following the Le Mans race the *Commission Sportive Internationale*, the rule-making section of the governing body of motor sport, the *Fédération Internationale de l' Automobile*, held a meeting in Paris at which it was decided that there would be a 3-litre capacity limit for Prototypes with effect from 1968. The representatives, who included the Royal Automobile Club's Dean Delamont, had consulted neither race organisers nor constructors. Although it had not yet been publicly announced, it was known that Ford were withdrawing from racing forthwith and there is little doubt that the decision of the *CSI*, which was strongly

French-influenced, was to protect the interests of French constructors, Alpine who were to introduce their 3-litre V8 A-211 Prototype at Montlhéry in October 1967 and Matra who were working on a V12 engine to be used in both Formula 1 and Prototype racing in 1968.

Most constructors, including Porsche, who built smaller-capacity cars, strongly opposed the decision and there was a considerable outcry. When Dean Delamont was questioned about the *CSI* decision, he confessed that the item had appeared on the agenda at the last moment – in itself a good reason to postpone a radical measure that was to come into force in only six months' time. Because the *CSI* also included a class for Group Five Competition Sports Cars (with a theoretical, if not actual, minimum production of 50 cars), the results – by chance, rather than by design – ultimately worked well, especially when the minimum production was reduced to 25 in 1969.

After Le Mans

The Reims 12 Hours race was held on 25 June and the large-capacity Prototype class attracted four Lola T70-Chevrolet coupés, the Ford Mk IIB driven by Hawkins/Bucknum at Le Mans which had been flown to the United States for rebuild, flown back and loaned to *Ford France* for Schlesser/Ligier to drive, together with David Piper's old Ferrari P2/3 which he co-drove with Jo Siffert. Despite problems with a door-catch, which delayed it early in the race, the Ford forged ahead after the retirement of the Lolas and won at 127.296mph (204.854kph). Only 12 minutes from the finish Siffert, in second place, brought the Ferrari into the pits, trailing oil. The engine had thrown a rod and there was a large hole in the cylinder block. Siffert was sent off to cover one slow lap, with the engine clanking away, and then wait at the finish line. So Piper/Siffert took second place behind the Ford, seven laps in arrears. Porsche 2-litre cars occupied the next four places.

Ferrari sent three *Dino*s to the Circuit of Mugello on 23 July, a round in the Group Four Sports Car Championship, to which Prototypes were also admitted. It was held over a distance of 329 miles (528km) on a very difficult 41.13-mile (66.20km) road circuit near Florence and incorporating the famous Futa Pass that had formed part of the Mille Miglia course. Ludovico Scarfiotti/Nino Vaccarella were to drive a car with the four-valve engine, Gunther Klass/Jonathan Williams had a three-valve car and the latest Group Seven 4-valve *Dino* that had appeared in the Trento-Bondone Hill Climb (see below) was brought along for training. Herbert Müller/Mario Casoni drove the *Filipinetti* P3/4. *Ford France* entered the 7-litre Mk IIB Ford for the usual pairing of Schlesser/Ligier; there were three *Autodelta*-entered Alfa Romeo Tipo 33s and a horde of Porsche entries.

In the Reims 12 Hours race in late June David Piper entered his 365P2/3 for himself and Jo Siffert. In the final minutes of the race the engine threw a connecting rod through the cylinder block, but Siffert succeeded in completing a slow lap to retain second place. (LAT)

In practice Ferrari's new protégé Günther Klass crashed the Group Seven *Dino* with fatal results. On a bumpy stretch of road he entered a left-hand corner followed by a right-hand corner too fast, put the two nearside wheels on the grass, tried to correct, slid on to the grass on the right-hand side of the road and slammed into a walnut tree at around 60mph. The car hit the tree with the cockpit and contemporary reports say that it was almost cut in two. There were only two witnesses to the accident, one a child, so the details remain unclear. Although a helicopter arrived on the scene quickly, Klass was terribly injured and died very shortly after being taken on board. Ferrari withdrew his other two entries.

Only four laps from the start Casoni went off the road with the *Filipinetti* P3/4 and returned to the pits to complain that the car was not set up properly and lacked adhesion. Porsche eight-cylinder 910s took the first two places ahead of a Porsche 911R modified production car driven by Vic Elford/Gijs van Lennep. Schlesser/Ligier did well to bring the Mk IIB Ford, a totally unsuitable car for the course, across the line in fourth place, a lap in arrears. All the Alfa Romeo Tipo 33s retired yet again.

A new addition to the Prototype Championship in 1967 was the BOAC '500' race at Brands Hatch on 30 July. Phil Hill/Mike Spence scored a well-deserved win with the 7-litre Chevrolet-powered Chaparral 2F.

BOAC 500

On 30 July the last round in the Prototype Championship, the so-called BOAC 500 race (it was a six-hour event) was held at Brands Hatch. Ferrari was out in force with a view to winning the Prototype Championship and entered P4s for Jackie Stewart/Amon (Stewart was negotiating to drive for Ferrari in 1968), Ludovico Scarfiotti/Peter Sutcliffe and Paul Hawkins/Jonathan Williams. Attwood/Piper drove the *Maranello Concessionaires* P3/4. Mike Parkes was not available to drive, as he had been badly injured in a crash in the Belgian Grand Prix, a week after Le Mans. The Ferraris' most serious opponent was a single Chaparral 2F driven by Hill/Spence, Rodriguez/Thompson drove the 5.7-litre Mirage and there were three Lola-Chevrolets.

The Chaparral was fastest in practice, but initially Surtees's Lola-Chevrolet led, Hawkins went ahead with his P4 on the second lap, two laps later Hulme (Lola) led from Mike Spence, Scarfiotti and Hawkins. Amon then moved ahead of Hawkins. After 40min Hulme slowed right off and pulled into the pits where a broken rocker was changed. When Phil Hill took over from Spence and the car was refuelled, it had dropped back to fourth place. The Chaparral led again at the end of the first hour from Stewart/Amon and Scarfiotti/Sutcliffe, with Hawkins/Williams back in sixth place. By the time the

Ferraris had completed their routine pit stops, the Chaparral had built up a substantial lead, but this was not to last long. Refuelling and pit stops because of punctures on the Chaparral and the Scarfiotti/Sutcliffe P4 meant constant changes of leadership.

Attwood and Piper were in trouble with their P3/4, as Richard explains: 'Brands Hatch was very, very hot, it was a short circuit with no long straights, the car got very hot inside and David and I were suffering badly. The P4s and the Chaparral just ran away with the race, we were also-rans, but that was because of the equipment that we'd got. I remember that David's mechanic "Fax" [Fairfax Dunn] was helping out with the pit crew and the P3/4 had plastic side-screens without frames – "Fax" quite simply took a hammer to them and smashed them to pieces. Then somebody came along and said, "Do you realise that the regulations say that you must have opening and closing windows?" I don't remember what happened then, but it did cure the heat exhaustion from which we suffering. I think that we were overheating more than the engine, but we just kept going.'

By the four hour-mark the Chaparral was back in front, McLaren/Siffert (Porsche) were second, Stewart/Amon third, Elford/Bianchi (Porsche) fourth and Scarfiotti/Sutcliffe fifth. After its final pit stop the Chaparral was still comfortably in the lead, while the Ferraris were left battling with the Porsche entries. The Chaparral went on to win a well-deserved victory, covering 211 laps, 559.15 miles (899.67km) at an average of 93.08mph (149.77kph). Amon/Stewart took second place, a lap in arrears, despite a fuel flap coming open while Amon was at the wheel and gassing him with fumes for the best part of an hour; the result was good enough to secure the Prototype Championship for Ferrari.

Siffert/McLaren (flat-eight Porsche 910) finished third, Herrmann/Neerpasch (flat-eight Porsche 907) took fourth place and then came Scarfiotti/Sutcliffe and Williams/Hawkins with their P4s. Attwood/Piper brought their P3/4 across the line in seventh place. Brands Hatch was not a great race; overtaking was difficult with 36 starters on what was by Continental standards a short circuit; and the circuit itself made a poor comparison with Spa, Monza or Le Mans, but it gave the works Porsche entries the chance to battle on near-enough even terms with the Ferraris.

The final standings in the Group Six Prototype Championship were Ferrari, 34 points; Porsche, 32 points; and Ford, 22 points. When Wyer initiated the Mirage project, he asked Ford whether the name was

Chris Amon and Jackie Stewart drove this P4 spyder in the BOAC '500' race at Brands Hatch in 1967 and took second place behind the Chaparral. It was good enough to clinch Ferrari's win in the Prototype Championship. (LAT)

Left *The 330P4 of Stewart and Amon in the pits at Brands Hatch during the 1967 BOAC '500' race. Stewart is about to accelerate back into the race and Amon has clambered on to the pit counter. At this time Stewart was negotiating with Ferrari to drive for the team in 1968, but instead he raced a Matra-Ford in Formula 1 for Ken Tyrrell.* (LAT)

Right *The 330P4 of Paul Hawkins/Jonathan Williams during a routine pit stop in the BOAC race. The damage to the bodywork was very minor and gave the pit staff no cause for concern. This car finished sixth.* (FotoVantage)

acceptable and they told him that they did not mind what he called these GT40-based cars. After Ickx/Thompson had won at Spa, Ford asked Wyer to see whether the FIA would agree to the Mirages being re-named Fords, so the Spa race would count towards their total. Wyer dutifully did this, was told that the name of a car could not be changed *after* a race, but Ford continued to argue to no avail. If Ford had been able to take over the Mirage's points, they would have had 31 points, but still not enough to wrest second place from Porsche.

The End of the Year

There was an interesting experimental Ferrari *Dino* bodied by Pininfarina and exhibited on this company's stand at the Frankfurt Motor Show in September 1967. It was called the *Dino Berlinetta Competizione Prototipo* and in the words of Peter Easton, who reported the show for *Autosport*, 'One felt it was somewhat of a mixture between a styling exercise, a dream-car and a sports-racer.' It is believed that it was built on a *Dino* 206S chassis and had a very low and aerodynamic, wedge-shaped coupé body with a spoiler projecting from the nose and another at the rear.

Pininfarina claimed that despite the small size of the spoilers, they were very effective because of their relatively distant positioning from the axles. There was an enormous sloping windscreen and upward hinged doors with single curved windows. The steering wheel retracted to facilitate entry and egress. There was to be another Pininfarina-bodied 'Prototype' exhibited before Ferrari returned to racing.

The Paris 1,000Km race at Montlhéry on 15 October was the last European Prototype race in 1967. Although the combined banked track and road circuit was used, speeds were substantially reduced by three chicanes. Torrential rain started to fall after the second hour of the race. Jacky Ickx/Paul Hawkins with the 5.7-litre Mirage won at 85.60mph (137.73kph) from Bianchi/'Beurlys' at

130 Scarlet Passion

the wheel of the *Écurie Francorchamps* P3/4. Schütz/Herrmann took third place with a Porsche 910 and Schlesser/Ligier finished fourth with the *Ford France* 7-litre Mk IIB. Jo Siffert/David Piper had led with Piper's newly acquired, green-painted, ex-*Maranello Concessionaires* P3/4, but it developed a heavy thirst for oil, three plug leads came adrift and it eventually finished fifth.

Piper entered the P3/4 for himself and Dickie Attwood in the Kyalami Nine Hours race on 4 November, but collisions contributed to the car's failure and they eventually finished fifth again, 28 laps behind the winners, Ickx/Redman, with the 5.7-litre Mirage. At the start Piper side-swiped Frank Gardner's Lola and he was in third place when he came into refuel and to hand over to Attwood. Richard takes up the story:

'The pit lane was always very tight, the cars being worked on were on the right and you carried on down the pit lane until you came to a barrier where you were signalled on to the circuit. I was not speeding. I was always quite conscientious about that from the point of view of safety, but there were always risks and I was looking out for them. I saw this guy – he was an Alfa Romeo driver called Fritelli – on my left signalling to his co-driver, he turned, crossed the pit road without looking and walked straight into the front of my car.

'There was no way that I could have avoided him, I was doing 40–45mph, he crashed on to the front of the Ferrari, stoved in the screen and smashed the front of the car; he had hit the screen at the worst possible point so that I had difficulty in seeing anything and the whole of the front of the car was hanging off. I thought that I'd killed him. I couldn't reverse back to the pit, so I had to do a slow lap, following the inside of the circuit. When I reached the pits again, I stepped out of the car and as far as I was concerned the race was finished.

'I thought that there was no point in doing anything, there was too much broken. "Fax" didn't agree and the mechanics set to work on the car. I remember that they fixed a scaffolding pole across the front of the car with wire and then hung the body parts on this, using rope and masking tape. They spent 20 minutes to half-an-hour working on the car. It was a fantastic job – we could still do 170mph on the straight. It looked a right bloody mess, but we finished fifth. But to be honest, I thought that repairing the car was a bit of a waste of time.' A fortnight later Piper drove the P3/4 into second place in the Cape International Three Hours race at Killarney behind Paul Hawkins (Lola-Chevrolet).

The European Hill Climb Championship

Ferrari made no real effort in the Championship in 1967 and did not appear until the Trento-Bondone, the fourth round, on 9 July. Scarfiotti drove a new lightweight Group Seven *Dino* two-seater with four-valve engine, but was beaten into second place by Mitter (Porsche). Günther Klass also drove a works *Dino* and Mario Casoni had a similar car entered by *Scuderia Brescia Corse*. Klass finished fourth, but Casoni was out of the first six. Ferrari missed the Cesana-Sestriere event the following weekend when Casoni drove the *Brescia Corse* car into fifth place. Ferrari withdrew from the Freiburg hill climb on 30 July and there were no private *Dinos* entered. The works cars were not seen again, but Casoni took third place at Montseny in Spain and fifth at Cesana-Sestriere. Mitter (Porsche) won the Championship for the second year in succession.

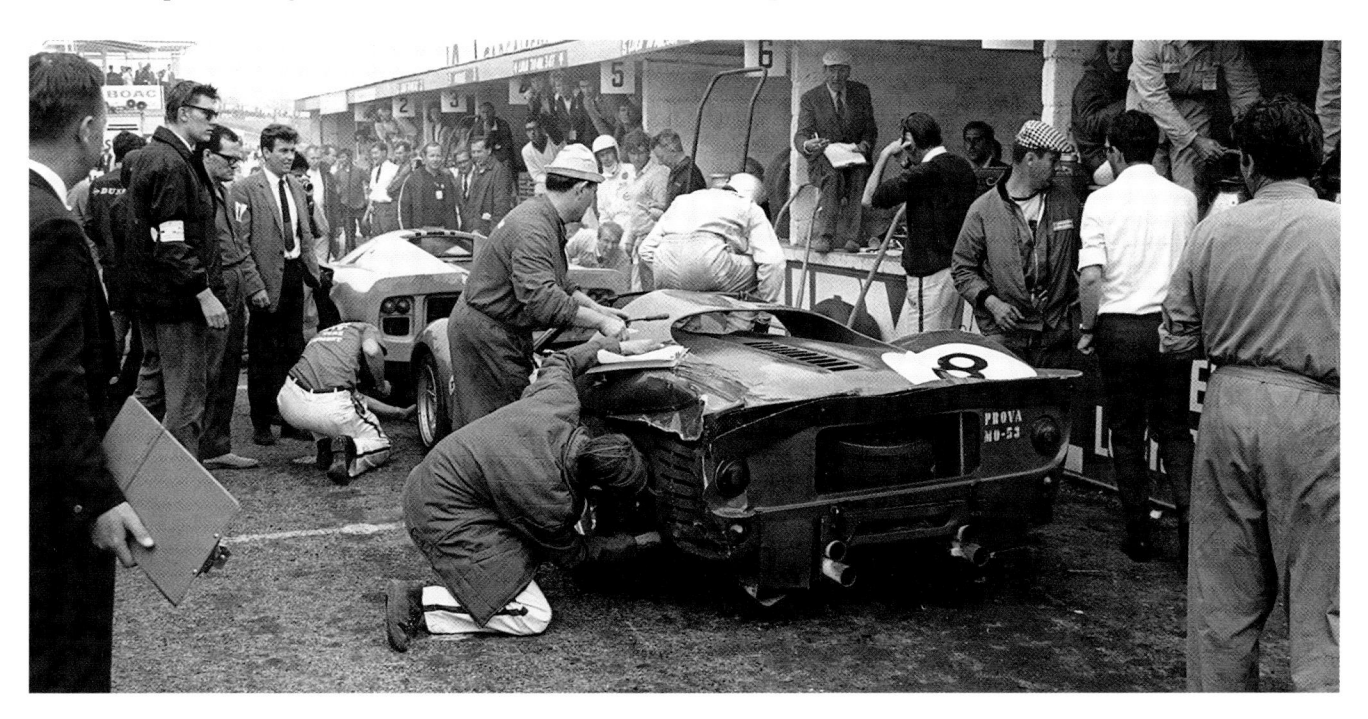

The 250LM
1963–68

Well crunched – the 250LM entered by Écurie Francorchamps for Dumay/van Ophem at Le Mans in 1966. Dumay caused the damage when he spun on the first lap, but after a troubled race the 250LM finished 16th. (LAT)

Following the overwhelming success of the long line of front-engined GT cars culminating in the 250GTO, Ferrari was determined to consolidate his position with a new model capable of beating any foreseeable opposition. The result was the 250 *Le Mans Berlinetta* (or 250LM for short), in essence the 250P GT Prototype in closed form and with slight chassis modifications. By developing a production car from a Prototype Ferrari was doing exactly what the Prototype regulations intended, but Ferrari's plans went seriously wrong.

The chassis of the 250LM was constructed of heavier-section steel tubing than that of the 250P, mainly because of the weight of the doors, and four of the main chassis members acted as water and oil lines to the radiator, the oil cooler and the oil tank, which were mounted at the front of the car to achieve the best distribution of weight. The fuel capacity was 130 litres in two 65-litre tanks mounted on each side ahead of the rear wheels.

132 Scarlet Passion

The familiar Colombo-type 60° V12 2,953cc engine was to exactly the same specification as that of the 250P and developed 300bhp at 7,500rpm. As on the 250P there was a five-speed, non-synchromesh gearbox in unit with the final drive with the gearlever operating in an open gate. The body, styled by Pininfarina, closely followed the lines of the 250P, but many cars were fully trimmed out with a comprehensive instrument panel and cloth-upholstered, well-padded seats. Only the body of the first car was built in the Pininfarina works and thereafter Scaglietti undertook construction. All the cars had aluminium-alloy bodies, except for two with glass-fibre bodies, and all except three had right-hand drive.

After the first car had been exhibited at the Paris Salon, it was then displayed at the Turin, London and Brussels shows. All subsequent 250LMs had a 3,286cc (77 x 58.8mm) engine developing 320bhp at 7,500rpm, although the model designation remained unchanged. References to 275LM are generally regarded as incorrect. At the Le Mans Practice Weekend on 18–19 April 1964 Ferrari ran a 250LM with streamlined rear bodywork intended to increase the maximum speed, but this left the driver with almost no rear vision and was abandoned.

The final specification of the 250LM was settled by May 1964. In its original form the car had a spoiler integral with the roof, but this was deleted. The air intakes for cooling the rear brakes and feeding the carburettors, which were originally on the sides of the rear wings, were now larger, fed air only to the brakes and were mounted on top of the wings. Originally, there were twin exhaust tailpipes passing through the rear panel, but these were replaced by four tailpipes passing under the panel. There were also modifications to the air intake at the front, the position of the headlamps and to the dashboard.

In April Ferrari had applied to the *CSI* for homologation of the 250LM as a Grand Touring car, which meant that 100 examples had to be built. By 100 examples, what was meant was at least 100 of the basic design, so that the homologation of such cars as the Ferrari 250GTO, the Aston Martin DB4GT and the 'Lightweight' Jaguar E-type included the standard production models. Ferrari lied about 250LM production. While the *CSI* was considering homologation, Ferrari development engineer Mike Parkes told a journalist that production was already close to 100 cars and in an interview Ferrari claimed that 42 examples had been dispatched to the United States. Other constructors, notably Carroll Shelby, made representations to the *CSI* that the 250LM should not be homologated and in July homologation was refused.

Although Ferrari's protests were vociferous, he did not suffer as a result of the *CSI*'s decision. The 250GTOs in their latest form won the 1964 GT Championship, Italian race organisers included a special class for 250LMs and in any event, the cars were potent enough to hold their own in Prototype racing against everything except Ferrari's own Prototypes and the unreliable Ford GT40s. Maranello built a total of 32 of these cars and this was a satisfactory figure for a car of such limited application. The works initially loaned 250LMs to selected entrants (with an option to buy the cars at the end of the season) and they were destined to gain a remarkable number of successes.

1964

Luigi Chinetti bought the prototype 250LM and it first appeared with Pedro Rodriguez at the wheel in the Challenge Cup at Daytona on 15 February. Rodriguez retired in this race because of a broken fuel line. The car

This view of the first 250LM was taken at Maranello just before Ferrari exhibited it at the 1963 Paris Salon. The standard of workmanship on the first of the breed was very high indeed. (SEFAC Ferrari SpA)

had been entered for the Daytona Continental 2,000Km race for GT cars the following day, more than a little premature, as application for homologation had not even been made at this stage. After Daytona a 3.3-litre engine was fitted. *NART* next entered the car for Buck Fulp in a SCCA race at Augusta, Georgia on 1 March and he finished a poor eighth.

Charlie Kolb and Tom O'Brien drove the 250LM in the Sebring 12 Hours race on 21 March, but they were a very early retirement. On only the fourth lap a stone shattered the windscreen, a piece of glass entered O'Brien's eye and he was forced to come into the pits to hand over to Kolb. While the Ferrari's fuel was being topped up, Kolb jumped into the car, knocking the ignition switch with his foot causing a short-circuit; the 250LM caught fire and was burnt out.

Two 250LMs were entered at the Nürburgring 1,000Km race on 31 May. The Belgian *Écurie Francorchamps* team entered a car loaned by the works and painted red for Pierre Dumay/'Beurlys' – his 'real' name was Jean Blaton – and *NART* fielded a car for Umberto Maglioli/Jochen Rindt. The Belgian-entered car retired after only seven laps because of problems with the front suspension, while Maglioli/Rindt finished at the tail of the field after spinning off in the wet. The same two 250LMs ran at Le Mans on 20–21 June. Jochen Rindt/David Piper were to drive the *NART* car, but it blew an oil filter at the start. The engine had not been fully warmed up and the oil pressure was too high. Gerald Langlois and Pierre Dumay drove the Belgian entry; Langlois spun off on the first lap, badly damaging the nose of the 250LM and they carried on to finish well down the field in 16th place.

The 250LMs dominated the Reims 12 Hours race in 1964. Bonnier/Graham Hill won with the car entered by Maranello Concessionaires and John Surtees/Lorenzo Bandini drove this NART 250LM into second place. (LAT)

The next endurance race was the Reims 12 Hours event on 5 July and apart from three works GT40s there was little serious opposition to the three 250LMs entered. Once again the new Fords failed and Graham Hill/Joakim Bonnier with a 250LM entered by *Maranello Concessionaires* won at 126.81mph (204.04kph) despite the loss of first and second gears. The similar car entered by *NART* and driven by John Surtees/Lorenzo Bandini took second place, less than eight kilometres behind on distance. Langlois/'Beurlys' drove the *Écurie Francorchamps* car, but retired because of electrical problems.

A fortnight after the Reims race Roy Salvadori with the *Maranello Concessionaires* 250LM won the 100-mile Scott-Brown Memorial Trophy from Mike Salmon (Aston Martin DB4GT). The race was for GT cars, so the organisers, the Snetterton MRC, clearly took a very relaxed view about such matters as homologation. The same day Lucien Bianchi with a 250LM entered by *Écurie Francorchamps* won the 131-mile (210.8km) Limburg Grand Prix at Zolder from Peter Sutcliffe ('Lightweight' Jaguar E-type). Both this and the forthcoming Goodwood race were open to Prototypes and GT cars. David Piper made his debut with his new green-painted 250LM in the three-hour Tourist Trophy at Goodwood on 29 August and finished second to Graham Hill (*Maranello Concessionaires* 330P).

Ludovico Scarfiotti with a *Scuderia Filipinetti* 250LM set fastest time at the Swiss Sierre-Montana-Crans hill climb on 30 August. A week later the Coppa Inter-Europa was held as two races before the Italian Grand Prix. There was a three-hour race for GT cars up to 2,000cc and a one-hour race for GT cars and Prototypes over 2,000cc. In the event for larger-capacity cars there was a race-long battle between Roy Salvadori (*Maranello Concessionaires* 250LM) and Nino Vaccarella (*Filipinetti* 250LM) which the Italian won by a narrow margin. After pit stops to change plugs Piper finished third with his 250LM. A week later Walt Hansgen with John Mecom Jnr's 250LM won the Road America 500-mile race at Elkhart Lake in Wisconsin and Pedro Rodriguez with a *NART* 250LM took first place in the inaugural race at the Mont Tremblant circuit in Quebec.

On 20 September Bob Grossman with a 250LM finished third in the class for GT cars over 2,000cc and Prototypes over 1,500cc in the Bridgehampton Double 500 race held on Long Island. Walt Hansgen (Scarab-Chevrolet Zerex Special) and Pedro Rodriguez (Ferrari 275P) took the first two places. The following weekend at Snetterton David Piper crashed his 250LM heavily. The car had to be rebuilt with a new chassis frame. Several 250LMs were entered in the Paris 1,000Km race held at Montlhéry on 11 October, but none performed as well as expected. Graham Hill/Joakim Bonnier won the race with a 330P entered by *Maranello Concessionaires*. In second place for the first third of the race were Jackie Stewart/Ludovico Scarfiotti with the 250LM belonging to the same entrant, but they dropped back to seventh after a steering link came adrift.

Heavy rain began to fall and although Stewart was lapping faster than anyone in these conditions, the 250LM dropped further back when the young Scot went off the road in avoiding another, spinning competitor and time was lost while the mechanics bashed the bodywork clear of the left rear wheel. By the end of the race Stewart and Scarfiotti were still back in tenth place, nine laps behind the winner. The only other 250LM to finish was the *Écurie Francorchamps* entry driven by Annie Soisbault/Guy Ligier. They had risen to fourth place at one stage, but in the heavy rain the ignition system had become waterlogged and they finished 18th.

David Piper had won the Kyalami Nine Hours race with his 250GTO in both 1962 and 1963 and he entered the 1964 race held on 31 October with a 250LM loaned by *Maranello Concessionaires* with South African Tony Maggs as co-driver – Maggs had been his co-driver in 1963. They won easily from John Love/Peter de Klerk who were at the wheel of Piper's 250GTO. Peter Sutcliffe/Dickie Stoop finished third with the former's 'Lightweight' Jaguar E-type.

Écurie Francorchamps had shipped their two 250LMs out to Luanda to compete in the Angolan Grand Prix on 29 November. At this time Luanda was a calm, peaceful seaside town basking in the warmth of the African sun, where the local Portuguese were very rich and the local blacks were very poor. It all changed when the Portuguese fled Angola in 1975 and the country was ripped apart by civil war. In this 300-km (186 mile) race Willy Mairesse and Lucien Bianchi drove the 250LMs into the first two places ahead of a brace of Porsche 904GTS cars.

The same day Walt Hansgen, Bob Grossman and Pedro Rodriguez finished second, third and sixth with 250LMs in the 252-mile (405km) Nassau Tourist Trophy, the main event of the Bahamas Speed Week. Although the 250LMs had performed badly in the early part of the year, as the season progressed they had gained the reliability to match their speed and 1965 was to prove even more successful.

1965

At the Geneva Salon in March 1965 a road-going version of the 250LM painted white with a central blue stripe running from front to rear was exhibited on the Pininfarina stand. It had supplementary gull-wing door flaps above the conventional doors, a sweeping tail with large Plexiglas rear window and grilles that covered the air intakes in the rear wings. The interior was fully trimmed and upholstered in leather, there were electric windows but, rather oddly, no speedometer. It was very much a one-off show car and no further examples were built.

There were no works Ferraris at the Sebring 12 Hours race on 27 March, but the total of nine private entries included two 250LMs. The strongest contenders were the factory Ford GT40s and the Chaparrals with 5.4-litre engines and automatic transmission. These cars, built by Jim Hall and clandestinely supported by General Motors, were Group C sports cars and not eligible for points in the Prototype Championship. The race started in oppressively hot conditions but the sky became blacker and blacker until 5.25pm when, after over seven hours' racing, a torrential downpour inundated the circuit. This rainstorm lasted for an hour during which the faster cars had to crawl round.

Once the rain stopped, the circuit soon dried out, but the lead of seven laps held by the Chaparral of Hall/Hap Sharp became a deficit of three laps to the Ferrari 330P, entered by John Mecom Jnr for Graham Hill/Pedro Rodriguez. After this Ferrari retired because of a burnt-out clutch, the Chaparral was uncatchable and won by four laps from the surviving Ford GT40 of Bruce McLaren/Ken Miles. David Piper partnered by Tony Maggs, and both driving superbly, finished third with his 250LM. This was Piper's original car that had been crashed at Snetterton in 1964, rebuilt with an unnumbered chassis from the factory. Mecom had entered the other 250LM and Walt Hansgen/Mark

136 Scarlet Passion

Donohue drove it into 11th place after it had lost time through mechanical problems.

Works Ferraris took the first two places ahead of a Ford GT40 in the Monza 1,000Km race but the 250LMs had a miserable race. Innes Ireland and Michael Salmon drove the *Maranello Concessionaires* 250LM very well, but were delayed by a tyre failure and finished sixth. Oddone Sighala and Luigi Taramazzo with their 250LM entered by *Scuderia Sant' Ambroeus*, were sixth at one stage, but fell back to take tenth place. The Tourist Trophy was held at Oulton Park on 1 May with the results decided on the aggregate of two two-hour races, with a 90min interval between them. Sports cars, Prototypes and GT cars were admitted and Denis Hulme with Sid Taylor's 2-litre Brabham BT8-Climax won from David Hobbs (4.7-litre Lola T70-Ford) and David Piper with his familiar green 250LM.

Vaccarella/Bandini with a 275P2 won the Targa Florio on 9 May from a quartet of Porsche entries. Bill Gavin commented in his report on the race in *Autosport*, 'The 250LM Ferrari is presumably homologated in Italy (if nowhere else), for the Targa organizers had a special national GT class for four pairs of Italian drivers in LMs.' Taramazzo/Sighala with a *Scuderia Sant' Ambroeus* 250LM won this class and took eighth place. The 500-km (311 mile) Spa race was held on 16 May. Mike Parkes led with the *Maranello Concessionaires* 330P Ferrari until it developed fuel pump problems and then Willy Mairesse with a yellow 250LM entered by *Écurie Francorchamps* took the lead to win at 125.74mph (202.32kph) from David Piper's 250LM.

Five 250LMs ran in the Nürburgring 1,000Km race on 23 May, but were out of luck and the highest placed was that of Piper/Maggs which finished 16th. On 6 June the Circuit of Mugello, first held in 1920, was revived after ten years (and the 1955 race was the first since 1929). The course was near Florence and had a length of 66.2 kilometres (41.14 miles). It was said to have the greatest height variations of any circuit in the world; at the start the height was 205m (673ft), it climbed to 879m (2,885ft) at the Giogo Pass, dropped to 422m (1,385ft) at Firezuola and climbed again to 903m (2,964ft) at the Futa Pass. The race was run over eight laps, a total of 328.72 miles (529km) and in the absence of works teams, 250LMs took first three places in the order Tonino Nicodemi/Mario Casoni, Maurizio Grana /Cesare Toppetti and Oddone Sighala/Luigi Taramazzo. Enrico Pinto (Alfa Romeo Giulia TI saloon) was fourth.

The Ferrari 250LM had been proving itself an ideal car for private entrants, very successful in minor events, but not achieving wins in major events which were, after all, the bailiwick of the works team. This was all to change in the Le Mans 24 Hours race held on 19–20 June. A total of five 250LMs were entered:

Maranello Concessionaires: Lucien Bianchi/Mike Salmon (chassis number 6023)
NART: Masten Gregory/Jochen Rindt (chassis number 5893)
Écurie Francorchamps: Langlois van Ophem/'Elde' (chassis number 6023)
Écurie Francorchamps: Pierre Dumay/Gerald Gosselin (chassis number 6313)
Scuderia Filipinetti: Armand Bohler/Dieter Spoerry (chassis number 6119)

It was a disappointing race for both Ferrari and Ford. All the cars of both works teams retired, albeit the much delayed 330P2 of Guichet/Parkes not until the 23rd hour when it succumbed to a blown cylinder head gasket. In the 11th hour the 250LM of Dumay/Gosselin assumed the lead from the 275GTB of Mairesse/'Beurlys' and the 250LM of Gregory/Rindt. Within the next hour Gregory/Rindt moved up into second place. The Belgian-entered Ferrari remained in the lead until just after midday on the Sunday when Dumay burst the right rear tyre on some object in the road on the Mulsanne Straight.

Dumay drove back to the pits on the rim, the bodywork of the Ferrari badly damaged. The wheel was changed, but the officials would not allow the car to rejoin the race without attention to the body. With a spade a mechanic bashed the wing back into something approximating to its original shape, but by the time the yellow 250LM roared back into the race, it had lost the lead to Gregory/Rindt and was five laps in arrears. Gregory/Rindt went on to win at 121.09mph (194.83kph) from Dumay/Gosselin, Mairesse/'Beurlys' (275GTB), a brace of Porsche entries and Bohler/Spoerry with the *Filipinetti* 250LM. It had been a magnificent performance by two private Ferraris, even though they were in receipt of works support.

David Piper with his 250LM in the Tourist Trophy race held at Oulton Park on 1 May 1965. He finished third on the aggregate of the two heats behind Denis Hulme (2-litre Brabham BT8) and David Hobbs (Lola T70-Ford). Piper is leading Chris Amon's Elva-BMW. (T. C. March/FotoVantage)

The 1965 Prototype Championship series was over and the remainder of the year's Prototype racing was fought out between private owners in less-important events. Guichet/Rodriguez with a *NART* 365P won the Reims 12 Hours race on 4 July from Surtees/Parkes with a similar car entered by *Maranello Concessionaires*. Mairesse/'Beurlys' with an *Écurie Francorchamps* 250LM finished third ahead of Piper/Attwood with the former's 250LM, which had been slowed by a broken brake pipe and the loss of all gears except top. The 500-km (311 mile) City of Enna Cup race was held on a very fast 4.7-km (2.9 mile) Pergusa circuit on 8 August and was a round in the GT Championship, although 250LMs were allowed to run under Italian national rules. Mario Casoni (250LM) won at

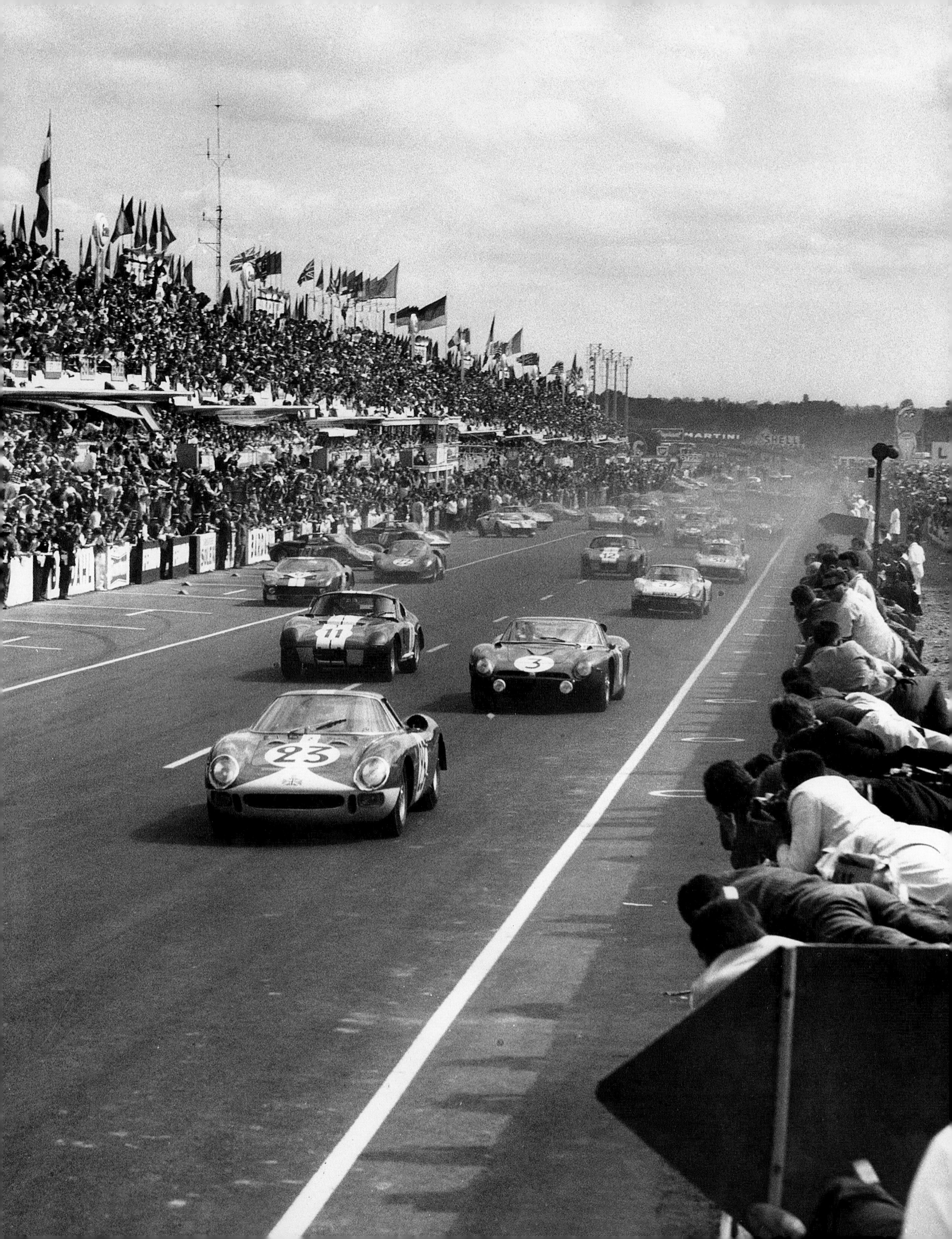
MARTINI
SHELL

Left *The start of the 1965 Le Mans race; some of the fastest runners are already away; Lucien Bianchi (Maranello Concessionaires 250LM) heads de Mortemart (Iso Grifo No 3) and Jack Sears (Shelby American Cobra No 11).*

Above *After first the Fords and then the Ferrari Prototypes dropped by the wayside, 250LMs moved up into the lead at Le Mans in 1965. Masten Gregory/Jochen Rindt drove this NART-entered 250LM to a win at 121.92 mph (196.17kph). This car is now in the Indianapolis Motor Speedway Museum.*

126.07mph (202.85kph) from David Piper with his 250LM and *Shelby American* Cobras in third and fourth places.

Piper and his 250LM then trekked to Austria to compete on 22 August at Zeltweg in the 200-mile (322km) Austrian Sports Car Grand Prix. Mike Parkes set the pace with the *Maranello Concessionaires* 365P Ferrari, but had to make two pit stops, the first of which included a change of tyres. Jochen Rindt slipped into the lead with a 250LM entered by Viennese jeweller Gottfried Kochert and he won from Parkes and Frank Gardner (Lotus 30 sports car). Piper was fastest in practice, but retired because of steering problems. The following weekend Piper finished seventh on aggregate in the two 80-mile (128km) heats of the Guards Trophy at Brands Hatch. The results were dominated by Group Seven sports cars.

David Piper/Richard Attwood won the Kyalami Nine Hours race on 6 November at the wheel of Piper's newly acquired 365P2, but Jackie Epstein/Paul Hawkins and John Love/Mike Spence (with Piper's car) took third and sixth places with 250LMs. Another African race was the

The 250LM, 1963–68 139

300km (186 mile) Angolan Grand Prix on 28 November. The street circuit had a length of approximately 1.98 miles (3.19km) and was a mixture of tarmac and cobbles. David Piper with his 365P2 won the race, but with 250LMs Herbert Müller (*Scuderia Filipinetti*), Pierre Dumay (*Écurie Francorchamps*) and Vic Wilson (*Team Chamaco Collect*) took second, third and fourth places. The 250LMs' year ended with the 3-hour Roy Hesketh race at Pietermaritzburg on 27 December and here Jackie Epstein with his 250LM finished second behind Peter Sutcliffe (Ford GT40).

During 1965 some owners had enjoyed prolific success with 250LMs in minor events. In sheer numbers no one could match the success of Bristol motor trader Ron Fry who bought his car from *Maranello Concessionaires* in September 1964 and over a two-year period won more than 50 awards, mainly in sprints and hill climbs. For 1967 he switched to a Ford GT40. In Italy Edoardo Lualdi-Gabardi won out 11 out of 12 events entered in 1965, mainly hill climbs, with the 250LM belonging to *Scuderia Sant' Ambroeus*; as mentioned, this car was also successfully raced by Taramazzo and Sighala. Another very successful 250LM was that owned by David McKay in Australia and which Spencer Martin drove in 1965. Martin entered 15 races, won eight, finished second in four and third in two.

1966

On 19 February 1966 the *CSI* homologated the Ferrari 250LM and the Ford GT40 in the new Sports class. Strictly speaking Ferrari should have built 50 of these cars to ensure homologation, but the governing body of motor sport was no longer being so pernickety. In international racing this meant that owners had to fit a luggage compartment, in some cases this was neatly installed within the tail, but cars were also seen with the compartment secured externally on the back of the tail.

During 1966–7 Richard Attwood raced David Piper's 250LMs on many occasions. He comments: 'the 250LM was my favourite engine and most of the reason why it was so good was because it was in 3.3-litre form, as opposed to the original 3-litre. It just went on and on and on, it sounded fantastic and had absolutely the right amount of power. The Porsche 917 was a good engine, we used to rev it to 8,000rpm, at 8,200 or 8,400rpm it still gave very good power, but at 8,600rpm it was gone – it'd blown.

'With the 250LM it didn't really matter, you could rev over the 7,500rpm limit that we gave ourselves by a substantial margin and it would still be fine. I've seen these engines with the 'tell-tale' showing that they'd been over 9,000rpm and they were still in one piece. It was a really wonderful engine – 12-cylinder engines have still got to be the best, haven't they?'

Eight 250LMs were entered in the Daytona 24 Hours race held on 5–6 February. There were no works Ferraris and the latest 7-litre Mk II Fords took the first three places, followed across the line by the *NART*-entered 365P2 of Rodriguez/Andretti. The 250LMs performed dismally and only three finished, driven by Rindt/Bondurant (*NART*) ninth, Peter Clarke with Koenig and Hurt (ex-*Maranello* car, chassis number 5895) 13th and Piper/Attwood 15th.

The 250LMs also failed at Sebring on 26 March and out of four 250LMs entered in the Monza 1,000Km event on 25 April the sole finisher was the ex-*Filipinetti* (6119) which de Siebenthal/Peixnho drove into eighth place. This pattern of poor results continued in the Targa Florio in which there were four 250LM starters and two finishers, Ravetto/Starabba and Nicodemi/Lessona in 13th and 14th places. The Spa 1,000Km race on 22 May was a new addition to the Prototype Championship and on the Ardennes circuit Epstein/Hawkins and Gosselin/de Keyn (*Écurie Francorchamps* entry) took seventh and eighth places.

Three 250LMs ran at the Nürburgring on 5 June and Mairesse/Müller drove the last 250LM to be built for *Scuderia Filipinetti*. This was chassis number 8165, with modified bodywork and other changes, and they took ninth place. This car, loaned by Ferrari, was sold to David Piper who raced it, modified it over a long period and still owns it today. The sole 250LM to run at Le Mans was an *Écurie Francorchamps* entry for Gosselin/de Keyn and they were in 13th place when the engine failed in the 18th hour of the race.

On 26 June Piper raced both his 250LM and his 365 P2 in the Circuit d'Auvergne at Clermont-Ferrand. Richard Attwood drove the 250LM and tells the story: 'I adored Clermont-Ferrand; a five-mile road circuit built round a mountain with features of the Nürburgring and other great European circuits such as Rouen and Spa. I had broken the lap record there twice in the past and in practice for this race I was almost as quick as David with the P2. Beltoise drove a Matra-BRM and he was on pole. We were chatting to Beltoise on the grid and he said to me, "Ah, Richard, you 'ave this race *dans la poche*." I said, "Hang on, you've got a works Prototype, you're going to be much quicker." He thought I was going to win, maybe he thought that I was holding back.

'I took the 250LM off the line and I was just getting to peak revs in first gear, the rear wheels had stopped spinning, a wonderful start, and suddenly at about 7,000rpm, it flew out of first gear and the rev counter went to about 9,500rpm. "Oh shit," I thought, "That's it." I put it into second and the engine had definitely lost its edge. It kept going, as those engines did, maybe it had bent a valve on a couple of cylinders, it had lost compression and it no longer had any real go. Even so,

Below *Bob Bondurant drove David Piper's 250LM in the sports car race at the International Trophy meeting at Silverstone in May 1966 and finished tenth overall. Following is the Group Seven Attila sports car of Julian Sutton. (T. C. March/ FotoVantage)*

Right *Ron Fry's 250LM proved outstandingly successful in British club events in 1965–6. Here Fry's car is in the paddock at Wiscombe Park hill climb in Dorset on 16 May 1965. This angle shows off the 250LM at its very best. (Guy Griffiths)*

The 250LM, 1963–68   141

David and I both passed Beltoise, who retired with electrical trouble, and I took second place behind David. After that, whenever I started a race with a 250LM, I held it in first gear just as a precaution.'

At Crystal Palace on 6 August David Piper raced his new 250LM for the first time and won the 10-lap GT race in very wet conditions from a Chevron and a Lotus Elan. The Surfer's Paradise 12 Hours race was held on this new circuit in Queensland, Australia on 21 August and attracted several British entries. Jackie Stewart and New Zealander Andy Buchanan drove the 250LM entered by David McKay's *Scuderia Veloce*. The 250LM lost eight minutes in the pits because of a jammed starter and the timekeepers lost the plot. They initially credited

Above *Écurie Francorchamps entered this 250LM for Gosselin/de Keyn at Le Mans in 1966, but it retired because of engine failure. It was the only 250LM to run in the race.*

Above right *David Piper with his 250LM at the Gold Cup meeting at Oulton Park in September 1966. He scored an easy win in the* Autosport *race for Special GT cars from Mike d'Udy (Porsche 906). (T. C. March/FotoVantage)*

Right *Richard Attwood frequently drove David Piper's Ferraris, especially the 250LMs, and was also regularly entered by Maranello Concessionaires. This photograph was taken in 1970 when he drove for the works Porsche team.*

142 Scarlet Passion

victory to Sutcliffe/Matich (Ford GT40) with 488 laps completed to the 484 of the Ferrari. Corrected results were subsequently issued and this listed Stewart/Buchanan as winners with 493 laps completed to the 492 of the Ford drivers.

On 29 August Piper was in action with his new 250LM at Brands Hatch and he won the 20-lap British Eagle International Trophy from Mike Salmon with a Ford GT40. The Kyalami Nine Hours race was held on 5 November and attracted a strong field which included David Piper with his Ferrari 365P2/3 and several 250LMs. With Richard Attwood as co-driver Piper won the race for the fourth successive time and Peter Clarke took second place with his 250LM, which he co-drove with Viscount Rollo Fielding. Heavy rain fell in the closing stages of the race and dramatically lowered lap speeds. Jacky Ickx/'Elde' were at the wheel of a 250LM entered by *Écurie Francorchamps*, but retired because of persistent overheating.

1967–69

Throughout 1967–68 Piper continued to race his 250LM with considerable success. His best performance during 1967 was at the International Trophy meeting at Silverstone in April. He won the 20-lap *Autosport Trophy* for Group Four sports cars from Denis Hulme with a Ford GT40. Piper took part in the *Autosport Trophy* series all season and ultimately finished second in his class to Paul Hawkins (Ford GT40), the overall winner. In the Reims 12 Hours race on 24 June, Attwood and Lucien Bianchi drove Piper's 250LM (8165) and ran in the Group Four class. Richard tells the story again: 'The 250LM was going so well at the Le Mans start that I was first driver away, which was quite pleasing. It was a typical endurance race, a lot of cars dropped out mainly because several of the much faster, but far less reliable, Lola T70-Chevrolets ran into problems. We were in second place after three hours behind the surviving Lola of Hulme/Gardner.

'At half-distance we were still in second place behind the *Ford France*-entered 7-litre Ford driven by Schlesser/ Ligier. It was getting light in the morning and I was driving. I was coming up the back straight to *Thillois* corner, you go up a hill and down a big swoop, when the car suddenly veered violently to the right. I caught it, but my heart was pounding, I backed off a lot and as I went further down the straight, I realised that the more

Above *Richard Attwood at the wheel of the Maranello Concessionaires 250LM in the race for Group Four sports cars at the 1967 British Grand Prix meeting at Silverstone. He won the race after the retire-ment of the faster and more power-ful Ford GT40s of Paul Hawkins and Charles Lucas. (T. C. March/ FotoVantage)*

Right *David Piper acquired the last 250LM to be built and he entered it in the BOAC '500' race at Brands Hatch on 7 April 1968 for Pedro Rodriguez and Roy Pierpoint. They drove a good race to finish fifth overall. (FotoVantage)*

throttle I put on, the more the Ferrari turned to the right and if I came off the throttle, it went near-enough straight or slightly to the left. Something had broken inside the differential, it was effectively driving to one rear wheel only, we couldn't go on like that and we retired.'

The 250LM's most important success in 1967 was the win for the second year in succession by David McKay's 250LM in the Surfers Paradise 12 Hours race on 3 September. Gerry Cusack and Bill Brown were the drivers and at the finish they were 22 laps ahead of Jackie Epstein/Paul Hawkins whose Lola T70 Mk III-Chevrolet had been slowed by overheating.

Because of strikes in France the 1968 Le Mans race was postponed from its usual date in June to 28–29 September. At Le Mans Piper drove his 250LM partnered by Richard Attwood. As a private owner, David was particularly keen to finish the race, despite time lost when a stone became jammed between a brake calliper and the wheel and also problems caused by the battery being overcharged by a faulty regulator. In contrast co-driver Attwood thought, 'we're not going to finish in the first six or three or whatever. I don't need to finish way down the field. David's car was on wire wheels, but *NART* had entered a 250LM for Masten Gregory/Kolb and this was running on smaller disc wheels.

'They were much faster than us down the straight, their 250LM was cleaner through the air, and then we would pass them again through the corners because we had better grip. We didn't need the wide tyres at Le Mans – we just needed top speed. It was so frustrating and then in the middle of the night it began to rain heavily.' Richard would cheerfully have retired the car and had virtually to be dragged out of bed for his stint early on the Sunday morning. They finished seventh at 105.124mph (169.145kph).

At Le Mans in 1969 *NART* wheeled out their much-travelled 250LM that won the race in 1965. Theo Zeccoli/Sam Posey drove it to eighth place at 115.540mph (185.904kph), slower than its 1965 winning speed but the addition of the Ford chicane at the 1968 race had reduced Le Mans lap speeds.

The 250LM would have been a great GT car surpassing the fame of the 250GTO. Instead it became a secondary runner in the Prototype class and even in its heyday could only win major events when faster works cars retired or were not entered.

The Can-Am Cars 1967–72

None of the Ferrari contenders in Can-Am racing proved successful. This is the rebuilt NART P3/4 spyder driven in a couple of races in the 1967 series by Ludovico Scarfiotti seen on the right of the photograph with his helmet under his arm. The race is at Bridgehampton where Scarfiotti qualified 17th, but finished a fairly respectable seventh.
(Pete Lyons)

During the 1960s races Group Seven sport cars in the United States and Canada grew in popularity, and also had a strong following in the UK. The *CSI* suggested a series with events held in both Europe and North America, but nothing came of the idea as proposed. Instead United States and Canadian race organisers collaborated in promoting the annual Can-Am series of races for these cars and the first Can-Am Championship was held in 1966. The British McLaren team dominated the series although other contestants included Chaparral and Lola. The annual series attracted big publicity and good money and Ferrari was pressurised by Luigi Chinetti to build cars to compete. Although Ferrari built cars for Can-Am racing between 1967 and 1969, they were not treated at Maranello as important and not surprisingly they were consistently unsuccessful. The main problems were lack of development and lack of sufficient power to be compteitive.

146 Scarlet Passion

1967

The first Ferrari Can-Am car was commissioned by Chinetti and was a rebuild of the 330P3/4 that *NART* had entered in races earlier in 1967. Chinetti had the work carried out at Maranello and in its rebuilt form there was a low, *spyder* body with single headlamps, a much lower Plexiglas windscreen, no spare wheel, and no luggage space as required on Prototypes, a large duct in the bonnet, a NACA-type air inlet on the right of the bonnet and a simple, tubular roll-bar.

Chinetti's car, which retained the same designation in rebuilt form, ran in only two races and in both it was driven by Ludovico Scarfiotti. He appeared with the car at the second race in the series, the Chevron Grand Prix at Bridgehampton on Long Island on 17 September. Scarfiotti qualified 16th, about mid-field, and finished seventh in this 199.5-mile (321km) race, two laps in arrears. The works McLarens took the first two places. The Ferrari was substantially underpowered compared to most of the opposition, so it was a creditable performance. Scarfiotti and the P3/4 then ran in the Player's 200 race at Mosport Park, Ontario on 23 September. He qualified 12th and retired from the race after puncturing a tyre due to debris on the track.

Back at Maranello Ferrari had been rebuilding two of the 1967 P4s as Can-Am cars. These were factory project number 218 and were typed the *350 Can-Am*. In many respects these cars resembled that built for Chinetti, but there were a number of significant differences. On the Tipo 350s there was a monocoque centre-section with glass-fibre skinning (on the *NART* car this was aluminium-alloy) and engine capacity had been increased to 4,176cc (79 x 71mm); on an 11:1 compression ratio Ferrari claimed 480bhp at 8,500rpm. It should be stressed that the factory cars were of course 36-valve and fuel-injected, whereas the *NART* car retained the 24 valves and carburettors as raced in Prototype form.

The body was glass-fibre (that of the *NART* car was aluminium-alloy), it was much neater, with no headlamps and an even lower windscreen. The large intakes for the fuel injection, splayed outwards, were mounted on the rear decking. Bill Harrah, Ferrari distributor for the West Coast of the United States, entered the cars, although they had full factory support including the presence of Mauro Forghieri, and the drivers were Chris Amon and Jonathan Williams. By the time the 350s arrived in the United States, there were only three races left in the 1967 Can-Am series.

Their first race was the 204-mile (328km) Monterey Grand Prix at Laguna Seca on 15 October. Like *NART*'s 330P3/4 they lacked the power and torque to be competitive; Amon and Williams qualified 16th and 20th and in this very hot race Amon finished fifth (four laps in arrears) and Williams was placed eighth. At the 203.5-mile (327.43km) *Los Angeles Times* Grand Prix at Riverside Raceway, California on 29 October the cars were again slow in qualifying and the race; Amon took fifth place, three laps in arrears, while Williams finished eighth. The final round was the 210-mile (338km) Stardust Grand Prix held at Las Vegas on 12 November. On the first lap Williams's Ferrari collected, through its air intake, sand and stones thrown on to the track during a multi-car crash; the throttle slide plates became jammed and he was forced to retire. Amon survived until the last lap and was within 100yds of the finish when he was involved in a collision with a Lola-Chevrolet and ricocheted into the abutment of a bridge, wrecking his Ferrari.

The engine bay of the Tipo 350 Can-Am car driven by Jonathan Williams at Las Vegas in 1967. With 4.2-litre engines these cars were simply not quick enough to beat the Chevrolet-powered McLaren opposition. (Pete Lyons)

A chastened Forghieri and Ferrari team returned to Italy, in the knowledge that a great deal more power – and thus a much larger-capacity engine – was needed if Maranello was to succeed in Can-Am racing. As Pete Lyons commented in his article on the technical aspects of the series in *Autosport*, 'There is nothing wrong with the lightened Group Four P4 that about another litre wouldn't cure. Jonathan Williams describes a great deal of activity in Maranello as the *Commendatore* bestirs himself to put down that brash tractor manufacturer [Lamborghini] and Mr Harrah wants to sell a lot of cars.'

1968

It was known that there would be a new Can-Am Ferrari, but at the first race of the 1968 series, the 200-mile (322km) Road America event at Elkhart Lake on 1 September, there was no sign of it. Instead *NART* entered a Tipo 350, apparently a spare car built in 1967, and Pedro Rodriguez drove this. Rodriguez qualified tenth fastest, the race started in rain and water shorted the ignition. He lost ten minutes in the pits while this was sorted out; he rejoined the race to finish 13th, five laps in arrears, but even so he won $700. A fortnight later Rodriguez and the Tipo 350 ran in the 200-mile (322km) Bridgehampton race. The Mexican qualified 11th fastest and in the race had a close fight with Sam Posey (Lola), but they collided on the eighth lap, the Ferrari broke a wheel and shot through the sand and over a bank. This Ferrari failed to appear in any further races in the series.

The new works Ferrari finally appeared at the sixth and final round, the 210-mile (338km) Stardust Grand Prix at Las Vegas on 10 November. This, project number 228, was typed the 612P (sometimes also referred to as the 612 *Can-Am*) and had a 6,221cc (92 x 78mm) V12 engine with Lucas fuel injection, Marelli *Dino*plex ignition, 10.5:1 compression ratio and a claimed power output of 620bhp at 7,000rpm. Transmission was by a four-speed gearbox in unit with the final drive. The engine can be described as a prototype for the 5-litre unit used in the 1970 *Tipo* 512S, while the chassis was a derivative of that of the P4 and a similar design was followed on the 1969 312P.

The glass-fibre body was of very low construction with low wide air intake, two ducts on top of the bonnet on either side close to the wings fed air to the oil coolers behind the doors and this exited through outlets on top of the rear wings. There was a large aerofoil mounted immediately behind the cockpit, adjustable through hydraulic pressure from the engine and controlled by the driver using a button on the steering wheel; there were brake flaps on the wing operated by another hydraulic circuit and a third hydraulic circuit operated a small air brake between the front wings. The Plexiglas windscreen was very low and extended round the cockpit. The weight was said to be 1,750lb (794kg), which meant that the 612P was 670lb (304kg) heavier than the rival McLaren-Chevrolet M8As.

The Ferrari team was out in force at Las Vegas, with Franco Gozzi running the team, Mauro Forghieri looking after the mechanical side and four Italian mechanics. The car had not been extensively tested and it was known to have unresolved handling and braking problems. Amon qualified ninth, but dust from a multi-car collision at the start, clogged the 612P's throttle slides and the car was out of the race. Once again Ferrari returned to Maranello with its tail between its corporate legs.

1969

Ferrari was determined to continue with the Can-Am programme, primarily to keep Chinetti and Harrah happy, and by the time that the 612P reappeared in 1969 it had been extensively developed; both the chassis and the body were lighter and the new bodywork was wider, with neither aerofoil nor front brake flap. There was also a spoiler running across the tail. The suspension was much less affected by camber changes and the spring rates were stiffer. Because Ferrari was now so heavily committed in European racing, the car was run by a private venture based in Detroit; Chris Amon remained the driver, Bill Gavin was team manager and Roger Bailey looked after the mechanical aspects of the car.

Of the 1969 Can-Am programme, Chris Amon told the writer, 'Quite a lot of pre-season development work was done in Italy, but the one big question mark prior to the first race was whether we would have enough effective aerodynamic downforce, compared to, say, the McLarens that were running with large suspension-mounted wings. Ferrari refused to consider these for any formula, which had put us at a disadvantage in Formula 1 after Lotus had introduced them in 1968. The "Old Man" maintained that these wings were too dangerous for structural reasons and ultimately, of course, he had been proved right.

'I argued for them strongly for the Can-Am car and managed to get a concession from him that if we found after the first race that we needed one, then we were free to have one built and fitted – but Ferrari would accept no responsibility in the event of a failure.' [*In races to international rules movable aerodynamic devices had been banned since the 1969 Monaco Grand Prix, but this did not affect Can-Am racing. Author's Note.*]

The 612P arrived late for its first race, the 203-mile (327km) Watkins Glen event on 13 July, the third race in the extended 1969 series, and ran in only the final qualifying session. Amon qualified third fastest and in the race he finished third behind the McLaren M8Bs of Bruce McLaren and Denis Hulme. In the 200-mile (322km) Klondike race at Edmonton Speedway Park Alberta on 27 July, Amon again qualified third, chased the McLarens hard and finished second to Hulme after McLaren retired.

The next round was the Buckeye Can-Am at Lexington, Ohio on 17 August and here the Ferrari appeared with a high-mounted wing designed by Paul Lamar. It was not properly braced and was flopping about, so there was no alternative but to remove it. During practice the Ferrari's engine broke a piston and Amon qualified well down the field in 13th place. In this 192-mile (309km) race he drove superbly with a rebuilt engine that was down on power and took third place, a lap in arrears.

By the 200-mile (322km) race at Elkhart Lake on 31 August, the Lamar wing was securely mounted. Amon qualified seventh and was in third place behind the works McLarens when the oil pump failed. Next came the Bridgehampton race on 14 September. The team had rebuilt the engine and it was reckoned to be developing about 630bhp. Support from the factory seemed conspicuous by its absence and team manager Bill Gavin commented, 'what we seem to be doing is running a development programme for the 512S at our expense. And you may quote me.' Amon qualified third fastest, but he retired after only three laps because of oil pump failure.

Chris Amon comments, 'From this point onwards I considered that the 612 was a superior-handling car to the McLarens and in comparison I was quite disappointed with the McLaren when I drove one at Laguna Seca; the McLaren, however, more than made up for any handling deficiencies with its acceleration, and the straight-line top speeds of the two cars were reasonably well-matched. Oil-related problems ruined the whole season. The engines were sent back after each race for rebuilding at Maranello and it was noticed that the bearings were showing signs of very high oil temperatures to the point that we were only just completing races.

'I was seeing very high oil temperatures, around 120°C from memory and on the factory's advice we had fitted a larger, aircraft-specification oil cooler at Elkhart Lake. This had resulted in an immediate 10° to 15° drop in oil temperature and so we assumed that we were on a winner. When I retired at Elkhart Lake, we assumed that the cause was oil pump failure and, basically, these problems continued for the rest of the season.'

The two Tipo 350 Can-Am cars based on Tipo 330P4s seen at Las Vegas in 1967. Although they had full factory support, they were entered in the name of Bill Harrah, United States West Coast Ferrari distributor. Ferrari mechanic Giulio Borsari stands at the rear of car No 27. Looking into the cockpit is photographer Pete Lyons's sister, Claire. Drivers Jonathan Williams (in helmet with back to the camera) and Chris Amon (smoking a cigarette) are behind the car. (Pete Lyons)

Next came the 195-mile (314km) race at Michigan International Speedway. During qualifying the engine lost its oil pressure, Amon slowed off as quickly as possible, but the engine had suffered internal damage and despite the fact that he had been fastest prior to this, there was no alternative but for the Ferrari to non-start. Then at the Castrol-Monterey Grand Prix at Laguna Seca the Ferrari lost its oil pressure – again during qualifying – despite an engine rebuild, so Amon drove a McLaren in the race.

By the *Los Angeles Times* Grand Prix at Riverside Raceway on 26 October the team had received a new supposedly 6.9-litre engine from Maranello. Mauro Forghieri told the author that he recalls the cylinder dimensions as being 92 x 85mm (6,781cc) and commented 'It was a unique prototype with very short development.' This engine peaked at the lower speed of 7,500rpm and the only distinguishing feature was the longer inlet trumpets for the fuel injection. The car, now known as the 712P, was still plagued by what seemed to be oil pump problems, but Amon set third fastest qualifying time behind the two works McLarens. When the cars were lined up on the grid, the Ferrari's engine refused to fire up, so the team push-started it. Inevitably, on the third lap the officials black-flagged Amon and in the pits he was told that the car could only be started by an on-board system.

He now had to switch off the engine, fire it up again and then he was able to rejoin the race. Despite the team's protests that it had been started on the starter motor, the Ferrari was again black-flagged and Amon pulled in to retire. The team was funded by Amon, but it had earned so little money during the series that it was in dire financial trouble. During qualifying at the last round in the series, held at the Texas International Speedway, the 6.9-litre engine had piston trouble in practice and so the 6.2-litre engine was substituted. Amon qualified fourth fastest, but he retired in the race because of engine problems.

Of the season Chris commented, 'In hindsight it is easy to look back and say we should have been able to identify the problem, but the messages coming back from the factory were not entirely clear as to what was causing the failures Was it an oil supply temperature problem or a supply problem such as insufficient pump capacity? At the end of the season, in desperation really, we cut this top-specification oil cooler in two and found that it had a major internal restriction caused by a manufacturing fault. For me, one of the sad factors about the series was that we could have given the McLarens a good run, especially when we had the larger engine, and this influenced my decision to leave the team, which proved a huge mistake in the long run.'

Chris Amon at the wheel of the 6-litre Tipo 612 Can-Am car at 'Thunder Valley' at Elkhart Lake in 1969. This was the first occasion on which the 612P was raced with the Paul Lamar-built rear wing. Amon failed to finish in this race. (Pete Lyons)

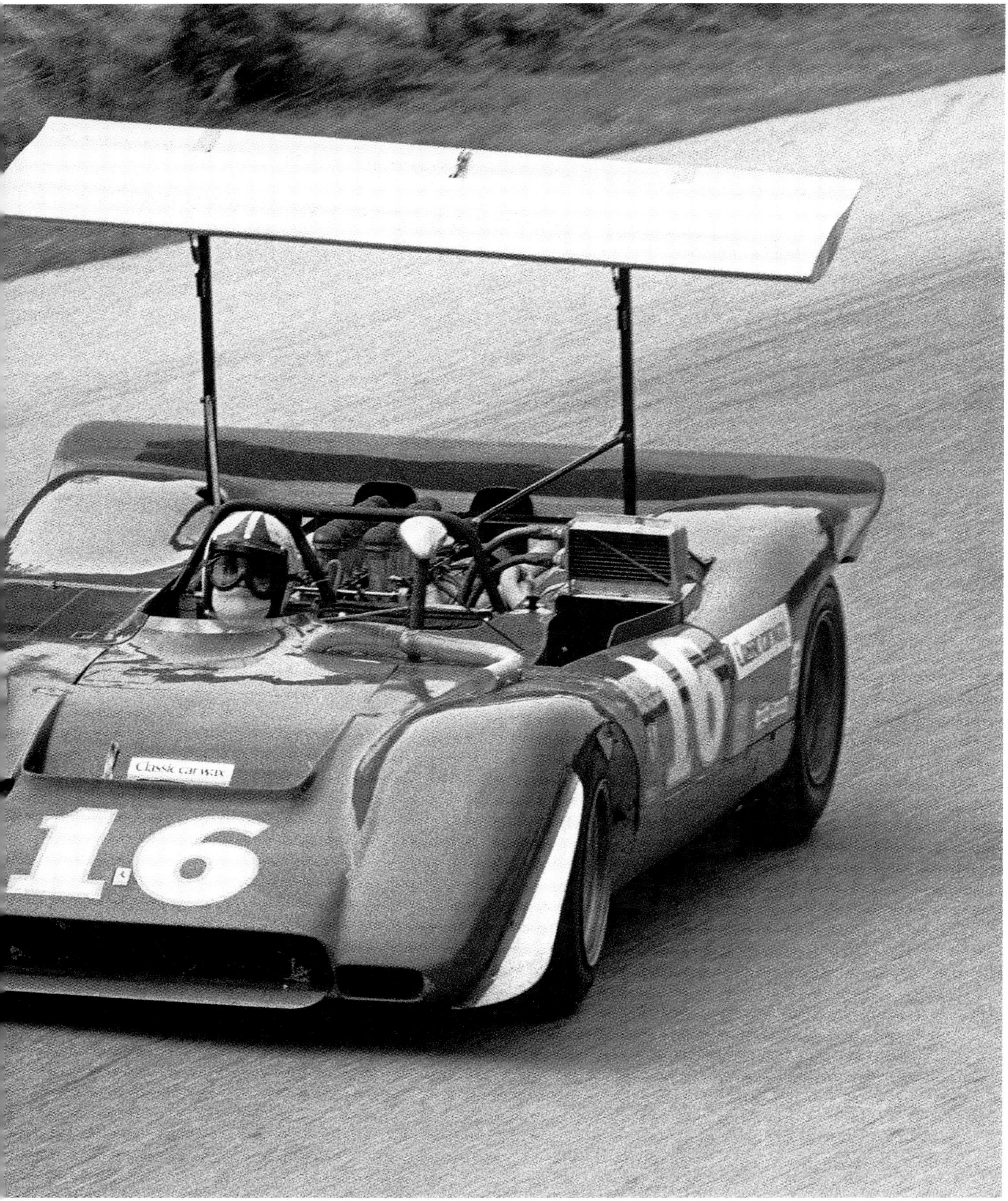
Classic car wax
16

1970

The 612P reappeared at the 210-mile *Minneapolis Tribune* Can-Am race at Donneybrooke International Speedway on 27 September 1970 – except that it was no longer the 612P. Two Californians, Steve Earle and Chris Cord, who wanted to become Ferrari agents, had acquired the car but Maranello, it was said, would not be able to supply 6.2/6.9-litre engines until 1971. So the car had a 5-litre engine and there were modifications to the body that included a large fixed wing running across the tail. In this form it was generally known as the 512P. Jim Adams was nominated driver and at Minneapolis he qualified sixth and finished fourth. At Laguna Seca on 18 October, fuel system problems plagued the Ferrari and Adams was forced to retire; at Riverside Raceway the Ferrari was involved in a multi-car accident and retired because of front-end damage.

1971

Before the start of the 1971 Can-Am season chief mechanic Spencer rebuilt the 512P, although there were limitations as to what modifications he could make, for Earle and Cord were anxious to do nothing that would offend Maranello. By the end of the 1970 season the weld-points of the chassis were badly cracked, so Spencer rebuilt the chassis with fewer, larger-section tubes. At the first race at Mosport Park on 13 June, Adams had trouble with the Ferrari's fuel system and finished eighth. Adams and the Ferrari missed the Ste Jovite race, but reappeared at Road Atlanta, Georgia on 11 July. Adams was ninth fastest qualifier and finished tenth in the race.

The 612P stripped down in the pits at Bridgehampton in 1969 to reveal the massive 6-litre V12 engine. Note the brackets on the rear suspension uprights for mounting the wing. (Pete Lyons)

At the fourth race in the series at Watkins Glen on 25 July there was a surprise debutant, a new Ferrari 712P, which Mario Andretti drove. This was based on what was said to be 'an experimental 512 frame with somewhat altered front and rear suspension geometry.' The power unit was a supposedly 6.9-litre unit with a specially cast, aluminium-alloy block. When Peter Lyons asked Andretti about the engine dimensions, he said, 'Oh, there are four different combinations, I don't quite know which this is.'

The body was rather like an enlarged version of the 312PB, with small tail-fins and a spoiler running across the tail of the car. Originally there was an aerofoil on stalks mounted above the engine bay; but after this collapsed, it was removed and Andretti found that the handling was better without it. He qualified fifth and finished fourth. Adams had missed Watkins Glen and neither he nor Andretti ran at the Mid-Ohio Can-Am race at Lexington. The 712P was absent because it had been dispatched back to Italy for more development work and failed to reappear during the series.

Adams reappeared with the old 512P at Edmonton on 26 September. It had a new 512M engine and Spencer had modified the body by removing the rear spoiler and substituting two small wings. Adams qualified well in sixth place, but he retired in the race because of final drive failure. At Laguna Seca on 17 October Adams qualified tenth fastest and finished eighth. He ran again in the last race, the *Los Angeles Times* Grand Prix at Riverside Raceway, qualifying 14th, but retired because of brake problems. Andretti did appear again with the 712P, in the 168-mile (270km) STP Challenge Trophy, a Formule Libre race, held at Kindley Field, Bermuda on 19 December. He qualified eighth in a very mixed field, but the Ferrari's throttle stuck open at the first corner on the first lap and he collided with Motschenbacher (McLaren M8D Can-Am car), putting both cars out of the race.

1972

There was no sign of the 712P at the start of the 1972 Can-Am series, but *NART* brought it along to the third round, the Watkins Glen race on 23 July. After the 712P had been returned to the factory in 1971, little work had been carried out and a cracked front steering member had not been replaced, which may well have accounted for its handling problems. Sam Posey was due to drive it at Watkins Glen, but after a couple of practice laps he came back into the pits complaining, 'It feels like a combination of chassis flex and bump-steer' (quoted by *Autosport*'s US correspondent Pete Lyons). Jean-Pierre Jarier, who co-drove *NART*'s class-winning Ferrari *Daytona* in the Six Hours race, took it over and first drove it in the 25-minute warm-up before the race. He started from the back of the grid, as he had recorded no practice time, and finished tenth.

Jarier volunteered to drive the 712P again and reappeared with it at the Road American Can-Am at Elkhart Lake, Wisconsin on 27 August. After qualifying tenth, he drove a good race to take fourth place, partly because of the high level of retirements. However, the Ferrari missed the remaining rounds of the Can-Am series.

After McLaren had dominated the Can-Am series for five years, the winner in 1972 was George Follmer at the wheel of a turbocharged Porsche 917 *spyder* entered by the Penske team. Apart from the sheer strength of the opposition, Ferrari's persistent failure in Can-Am racing was mainly the result of lack of commitment. The *SEFAC* was content to cobble together cars to meet the demands of those selling production Ferraris in the United States, but because of its commitments in Formula 1 and sports car racing, it lacked the finance, the interest or the time to undertake serious development work.

The Can-Am Cars, 1967–69 153

The 312 Prototypes
1969–71

At Sebring in 1969 the 312P made its debut in the hands of Amon/Andretti. Here Andretti leads Mark Donohue in the Roger Penske-entered Lola T70 Mk IIIB-Chevrolet. Despite problems Amon/Andretti drove a stirring race to finish second.
(Pete Lyons)

Following the introduction of the 3,000cc capacity limit for what had become Sports Prototypes, Ferrari withdrew from sports car racing at the end of 1967. Some experimental work on a 3-litre car was carried out and one result was exhibited on Pininfarina's stand at the 1968 Geneva Salon. This car, designated the P5, had a chassis similar to that of the Formula 1 cars, but widened, and powered by the 3-litre 48-valve V12 Formula 1 engine and five-speed gearbox. The body was very low, with smooth lines, the windscreen, side-windows, roof and engine cover were all made of Plexiglas, with most of the support coming from a slender roll-over bar. Gull-wing doors were hinged at the roof centre-line and a single headlamp unit consisting of eight iodine-vapour elements in a strip across the top of the air intake. An unfortunate feature was the louvres running across the tail, something seen on latter-day Ferrari road cars.

154 Scarlet Passion

The overall length was 13ft 5in (4,090mm) and the height was only 3ft 2in (965mm). The weight was given as 1,465lb (664kg). The P5 was in effect a motor show 'special' built on a Prototype chassis. When Ferrari returned to Prototype racing in 1969 with cars of stunning appearance, the new cars had close similarity in chassis design to the P5. The 1968 Sports Prototype regulations favoured the construction of coupés, but for 1969 the regulations were relaxed and there was no longer a minimum weight limit, minimum ground clearance or minimum windscreen height and it was no longer necessary for a spare wheel to be carried.

The 312P in detail

Since the introduction of the 3,000cc Grand Prix formula in 1966, Ferrari had been racing the Tipo 312 V12 car, albeit with mixed fortunes, but by 1969 was well advanced with plans for a new flat-12 Grand Prix car. The 312P Prototype was a direct development of the existing V12 Formula 1 car and in appearance and general layout resembled the 612P *Can-Am* car that was raced once in 1968. These cars were largely the work of *Ing.* Gaicomo Caliri. It would be two years before a Ferrari Sports Prototype with the flat-12 engine appeared.

The power unit of the 312P was the familiar 60° V12 2,997cc (77.1 x 53.5mm) Formula 1 engine. This had twin overhead camshafts per bank of cylinders chain-driven from the nose of the crankshaft, four valves per cylinder, Lucas fuel injection, single-plug ignition, outside exhausts and it was of light alloy construction throughout. In sports form the engine was slightly detuned in the interests of reliability and on an 11:1 compression ratio it developed 420bhp at 9,800rpm (compared with the 436bhp at 11,000rpm of the Formula 1 engine). Transmission was by a twin-plate clutch and the usual Ferrari-built five-speed and reverse gearbox in unit with the final drive.

The chassis, in accordance with what had become usual Ferrari practice, was a multi-tubular structure of welded steel tubing with stressed light alloy panels riveted to it to increase strength and rigidity. The double wishbone and coil spring front suspension differed from the Formula 1 car and the springs were mounted outboard because of the full-width body. At the rear the suspension was the same as on the Formula 1 car, single top links, reversed lower wishbones, twin radius arms each side and coil spring/damper units. Girling disc brakes were fitted, initially inboard at the rear, but later moved outboard, and there were beautifully cast Campagnolo 15-inch alloy wheels secured by three-ear hub caps at the front and by central locking nuts at the rear. The fuel load was carried in side pontoons. The steering was right-hand.

The open body was a smooth, wedge-shaped design originally constructed in aluminium-alloy, but by the start of the European season glass-fibre construction had been substituted. The aim had been to create aerodynamic down-thrust at all speeds. There was a large air-box on the engine cover to draw in air to the fuel injection inlets, trim tabs on the front wings had been fitted for the Brands Hatch race, and there was a spoiler on the tail. A very low Plexiglas windscreen was fitted and the doors, which extended inwards to partially enclose the cockpit, were hinged on the top leading edge. Initially only one car, chassis 0868, was built and it was painted the usual Ferrari red with gold wheels.

The 312P V12 Prototype made its second race appearance in the BOAC '500' race held on 13 April 1969. Chris Amon, seen here at the wheel, co-drove with Pedro Rodriguez. At this stage in its development the 312P lacked the speed of the Porsche 908s and after problems at Brands Hatch it finished fourth.

The Opposition

During 1968 sports car racing had been fought out between Porsche and the Gulf-sponsored Group Four Ford GT40 cars developed and prepared by John Wyer's J W Automotive Engineering company at Slough. Initially Porsche raced the flat-eight, air-cooled 2.2-litre 907 coupés, but early in the season Zuffenhausen introduced the very much quicker 3-litre 908s and these were raced in *Normal* and *Lang* coupé forms. Both the Fords and the Porsche entries achieved a good measure of success, but overall the Fords were more successful and won that year's Championnat International des Marques.

By 1969 intensive development work had made the 908s both faster and more reliable and Porsche had also developed a *spyder* version, which was to prove the year's most successful car. The 908 *Spyder* (350bhp at 8,400rpm) was less powerful than the 312P, but it was lighter and shorter. John Wyer's Ford GT40s were no longer competitive, but won at Sebring in 1969 because of Porsche unreliability and for this reason, coupled with Wyer's superb preparation and tactics, a Gulf GT40 won at Le Mans for the second year in succession. All the other 3-litre Sports Prototypes, which included cars from Alfa Romeo, Alpine, Ford (built by Alan Mann Racing) and Matra could be discounted as serious opposition.

Daytona 24 Hours

The new Ferrari was not ready in time to compete in the first round of the Championship, the Daytona 24 Hours at the beginning of February, the Porsche 908s and the Ford GT40s ran into problems and the race was won by the Roger Penske-entered Lola T70 Mk IIIB-Chevrolet coupé of Mark Donohue/Chuck Parsons. This car had lost 40 laps in the pits while the exhaust system was rebuilt and when it took the lead on the Sunday morning

Left *The V12 engine of the 312P with the inlet ports for the Lucas fuel injection in the vee and the exhausts on the outside – not a layout personally favoured by Mauro Forghieri.* (Pete Lyons)

Right *Ferrari Dinos were still being raced and in the 1969 BOAC 500 Miles race at Brands Hatch Tony Beeson and Alain de Cadenet drove this car. They finished in 15th place.*

after the retirement of the Ford GT40 of Ickx/Oliver, it was still way behind the distance covered by the Wyer entry and it was another 90 minutes before it had exceeded that. It was the only Championship event to be won by a Lola in five seasons of racing.

Sebring 12 Hours

Ferrari had intended to enter two 312Ps at the Sebring race on 23 March, but only the one car was ready in time. Chris Amon and Mario Andretti were the drivers and director of the racing department Franco Gozzi was in charge of operations. The 312P was superbly turned out, it was shatteringly fast in practice; it recorded best time in 2min 40.14sec, a speed of 116.39mph (187.27kph) and it needed almost no attention from the mechanics. It looked and behaved like a winner. Amon made a poor start in the race, but he soon climbed through the field to hold fourth place. When the leading Porsche 908s made their routine pit stops, the Ferrari went into the lead. Not long afterwards Amon spun to avoid a marker cone thrown up by another competitor.

The Ferrari was still in second position shortly after half-distance, but then it sucked into its air intake a large chunk of glass-fibre from a Chevron tail-section that had blown off and disintegrated. By the time it reached the pits, the 312P was overheating badly. Time was lost while the inlet duct was repaired, and topping up the radiator caused air locks which the mechanics tried unsuccessfully to cure later in the race. But while the Ferrari lapped at reduced speed, throwing out clouds of white smoke on the over-run, the Porsche 908s were also running into mechanical problems.

Then the 312P started to run well again and moved back into the lead. However, another ten minutes were lost while the mechanics struggled again to clear air locks but once it was back in the race again the Ferrari lapped slower and slower. Eventually Ickx/Oliver with their *Gulf* GT40 took the lead and at the end of the race they were a lap ahead of the 312P, with the surviving Porsche 908 *Spyders* third, fourth and fifth.

BOAC 500

Once again two Ferraris had been entered for the race at Brands Hatch on 7 April, but only a single 312P appeared; a new car with chassis number 0870, driven by Chris Amon/Pedro Rodriguez. They were second fastest in practice in 1min 30.0sec at 106.00mph (170.55 kph), 1.2 seconds slower than Siffert/Redman with their Porsche 908 *Spyder*. Amon led away at the start, but the Ferrari punctured a tyre after 38 miles of racing and following a pit stop for the wheel to be changed, it rejoined the race in seventh place. The Ferrari drivers steadily climbed back through the field to second place, but then lost a place during their last refuelling stop. Amon was still driving at his hardest, but the throttle cable stretched and by the finish the Ferrari had dropped back to fourth behind a trio of Porsche 908 *Spyders*.

Monza 1,000Km

Because of the importance to Ferrari of races on Italian soil, the team entered two cars in the Monza race held on 25 April (Liberation Day, a bank holiday in Italy). The race was run on the full combined road and banked track, 6.214-mile (10km) circuit, but the organisers erected chicanes before each banking to reduce the speed of the cars. This was a precautionary measure because of the poor state of the concrete surfacing. Even so, the fastest cars were attaining speeds of around 170mph as they passed the pits on the outer section of the banking.

Very experienced engineer and driver Mike Parkes joined Gozzi to help him manage the team. Chris Amon/Mario Andretti drove 0870, which was said to have a slightly more powerful engine and with more anti-dive built into the front suspension. Pedro Rodriguez and Peter Schetty were at the wheel of 0868. Schetty usually drove the 212E *Montagna* car in the European Hill Climb Championship. Since Brands Hatch the trim tabs at the front had been removed from the 312Ps.

The race proved an exciting high-speed battle between Ferrari and Porsche. The Ferraris had speed enough to beat the main opposition, a four-strong team of Porsche 908 *Lang* coupés, but they were plagued by failures of their Firestone tyres. During the second day's practice Schetty had a tyre burst as he came out of *Ascari* Corner at about 160mph (260kph). The flailing tread damaged the rear suspension, tore apart the rear bodywork and smashed the oil tank. The mechanics faced a frantic rush to repair the car in time for the start of the race. Amon was fastest in practice in 2min 48.2sec, a speed of 134.453mph (216.334kph), half a second faster than Siffert/Redman's 908.

The Ferraris led away at the start, chased hard by Siffert, and the Swiss driver was in second place at the end of the first lap. The three leading cars were closely slipstreaming each other, exiting the banking nose-to-tail and weaving through the slower cars that they were soon starting to lap. Siffert out-braked Rodriguez into one of the chicanes on lap 12 and then Andretti slowed right off, as he crawled back to the pits because of a punctured Firestone. He rejoined the race in sixth place. Within a couple of laps Rodriguez was back in the lead. At the first refuelling stops, just after quarter-distance, Rodriguez handed over to Schetty and Brian Redman took over from Siffert. Schetty was faster than Redman and began to extend the Ferrari's lead, while Andretti had passed Elford's 908 to retake third place.

It began to look as though Ferrari would win, but then Maranello's prospects of victory began to slip away. Schetty with the leading 312P had a puncture on lap 37 and pulled into the pits for a wheel-change. The V12 engine was reluctant to fire up so it was push-started by the mechanics and then, in accordance with the race regulations, the engine was switched off and Schetty restarted it on the starter motor. By the time he was back in the race he was in fourth place, a lap in arrears. Andretti now took the lead and stayed in front for just one lap before he came in to refuel.

Amon took over from Andretti, rejoining the race in fourth place, but within half a lap the engine blew up. Chris, by now becoming completely disenchanted with everything Ferrari, strode back to the pits and shouted at Forghieri, 'Why can't you build me an engine that lasts!' Schetty had steadily been closing the gap on the 908s and was within 45sec of the leading car of Siffert/Redman when he came in to refuel on lap 60 of this 100-lap race. It was a slow pit stop, lasting 1min 55sec; Rodriguez took over and started a fast and very skilful chase of the 908s.

Three laps after he had rejoined the race, Pedro spun at the *Parabolica* while avoiding a slower car, hit the guard-rail, shattered both nose and tail of the 312P, punctured a rear tyre and then pulled into the pits. Once a new wheel had been fitted, Rodriguez roared back into the race, without bothering to explain to Mike Parkes what had happened. The Mexican began to close up on the second-place 908 of Herrmann/Ahrens, but three laps later, as he passed the pits on the outside straight at about 170mph, a piece of glass-fibre damaged in the earlier accident broke off, allowing the airflow to lift the tail-section, which started to disintegrate and the 312P spun out of control. The Ferrari slammed backwards into the guard-rail, the rear suspension was wrecked and the car then hurtled on down the straight, eventually stopping after 200 yards (182.3m). Rodriguez was badly shaken, but unhurt.

The Porsche 908s went on to take the first two places. It had been a hopelessly unsuccessful race for Ferrari, but it was the most exciting of the year witnessing the 312Ps at their most competitive and it heralded the Ferrari-Porsche battles of 1970. The Ferrari team was forced to miss the Targa Florio on 4 May because the Spanish Grand Prix was held the same day. Porsche 908 *Spyders* took the first three places in Sicily.

Spa 1,000Km

Sports car racing was concentrated early in the season and the Spa race was held only a week after the Targa Florio. There had been insufficient time to rebuild 0868 since its Monza shunt and so only 0870 was entered. Chris Amon should have partnered Pedro Rodriguez, but he was unwell and for this race David Piper was brought into the team. Porsche brought along two examples of their Group Five 917 4.5-litre car, which had first been exhibited at the Geneva Salon in March. These cars were far from fully sorted, only one ran, and the main thrust of the Porsche onslaught was three 908 *Lang* coupés.

In 1969 the Spa-Francorchamps circuit, perhaps the finest road circuit in Europe, had been black-listed on safety grounds by the Grand Prix Drivers' Association, so the Belgian Grand Prix was not held that year. The same considerations did not apply to sports car racing and in fact most sports car drivers revelled in Spa's high-speed, sweeping curves. Again Rodriguez battled with Siffert (908) for the lead, but made an early pit stop to have the bodywork checked after a collision with a Porsche 907. At half-distance Rodriguez was in second place, but when Piper took the wheel he steadily lost ground. Rodriguez resumed at the wheel, but at the

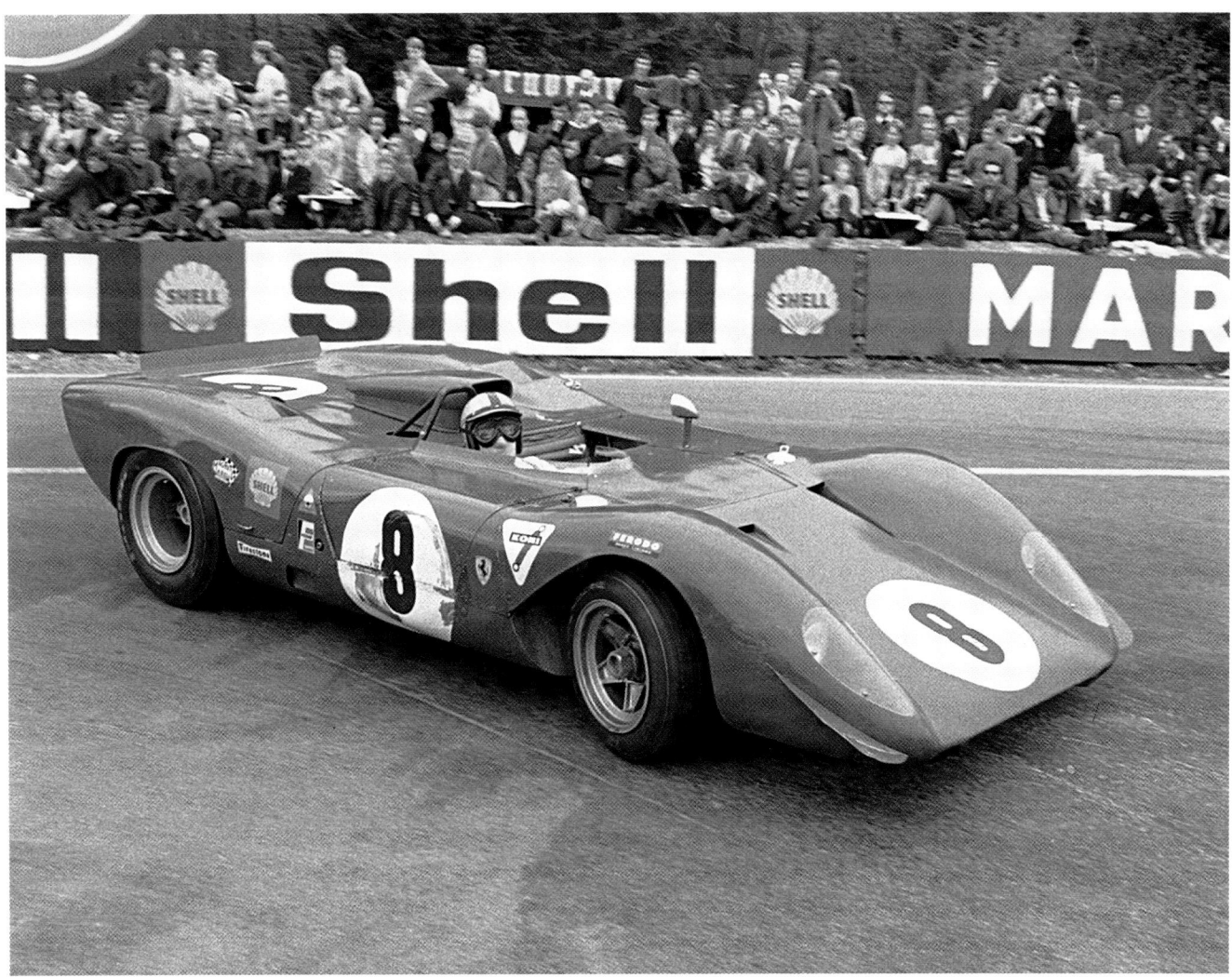

Above *Pedro Rodriguez at the wheel of the 312P in the 1969 Spa 1,000Km race. In this race his co-driver was David Piper because Amon was ill. They finished second behind the Porsche 908 of Siffert/Redman.*

Right *Pedro Rodriguez, who drove Ferrari sports-racing cars and Prototypes for many years. He joined the Gulf-Porsche team in 1970 and was killed when he crashed a Ferrari 512S in an Interserie race in 1971.*

The 312 Prototypes, 1969–71

finish he was a little over 2½ minutes behind the winning 908 of Siffert/Redman. In this race the 312P simply lacked the speed of the 908s through the curves.

Nürburgring 1,000Km

Once again, only a single 312P, 0870, was entered in the German race on 1 June for Amon/Rodriguez. After the Spa race Rodriguez had tested the 312P at the Nürburgring, now set up with a higher ride height and Ferrari had carried out fuel system modifications, fitting a new reservoir to prevent fuel surge when the tanks were low. Already it was common knowledge that chassis 0868 had been rebuilt as a coupé for Le Mans later in June. As usual the principal opposition came from Porsche, with a strong team of 908 *Spyders*. Amon with the 312P was second fastest in practice behind Siffert.

There was a rolling start at this race and Amon was slow away, in sixth place but up to third by the end of the first 14.17-mile (22.8km) lap. He soon passed Mitter (908 *Spyder*) and as he chased after Siffert with the leading 908, both drivers were repeatedly breaking the sports car record, despite the fact that rain was falling on the northern side of the circuit. When Amon made his routine pit stop, it proved another example of poor Ferrari pit-work. Rodriguez took over and he had dropped to 35sec behind the leading Porsche, now with Redman at the wheel. Rodriguez was not on top form

Top left *Chris Amon was a highly talented and very able driver who was a member of the Ferrari Formula 1 team in 1967–69. He left Ferrari at the end of 1969 and his career went into a downhill spiral with, first, the March team and then, the French Matra concern.*

Left *David Piper was one of the great privateers of the 1960s, almost always at the wheel of Ferraris. He raced a Porsche 917 in 1970, but his serious racing career came to an end when he crashed badly during the making of Steve McQueen's Le Mans film and had to have his right leg amputated due to an infection he caught in a French hospital. He still appears with his 250LM at historic events.*

Right *The second race appearance of the 4.5-litre Porsche 917 came in the 1969 Nürburgring 1,000Km race. The works drivers refused to race the 917 at this early stage in its development, so David Piper and Frank Gardner were brought into the team. They drove steadily to finish eighth. The 917 was still far from fully sorted, especially so far as the aerodynamics were concerned.*

that day and was steadily losing ground. At half-distance the leading cars made their routine stops when two wheels had to be changed on the Ferrari and Amon rejoined the race in fourth place, 2min 30sec behind the leader.

By the time that Amon was back in the race, he was angry and wound up. He passed Elford (908) to take third place, but he came into the pits at the end of lap 26 because of a bad front-end vibration and the other front wheel was changed. On lap 28 Amon set a new outright circuit record of 8min 3.3sec, a speed of 106.70mph (171.68kph), but on only the next lap the Ferrari stopped out on the circuit because of electrical trouble. Amon lifted the bonnet and succeeded in restarting the engine but had covered only a short distance before it cut out again and he abandoned the car. With the retirement of the Ferrari, the race had lost all interest and Porsche 908s took the first five places.

Le Mans 24 Hours

By the Le Mans race on 14–15 June both 312Ps had been rebuilt with coupé bodies. Testing at Modena and Monza with 0868 had established a distinct aerodynamic advantage in this form. Other changes included the deletion of the anti-dive in the front suspension, which necessitated modifications to the front of the chassis, and the installation of the heavier and stronger gearboxes used in the 1967 P4 Prototypes. The cars were to be driven by Rodriguez/Piper (0870) and Amon/Schetty (0868). For Schetty it would have been his first Le Mans. It was unlikely that the Ferraris would last the 24 hours, but one of the 312Ps was to be eliminated by an accident on the first lap.

Porsche had entered two 917 4.5-litre cars and a third was a private entry driven by the very enthusiastic, but inexperienced John Woolfe, partnered by veteran works Porsche driver, Herbert Linge. Largely because of the unstable aerodynamics of the 917, Woolfe lost control on the first lap through the curves leading to *White House* corner and crashed with fatal results. Amon, who was close behind, cannoned into the blazing fuel tank of the Porsche and this wedged under the nose of the Ferrari. Amon pulled off the road, pressed the fire extinguisher and abandoned the 312P, which was not too badly damaged.

Rodriguez, at the wheel of 0870, was still struggling to do up his seat harness on the Mulsanne Straight and was well down the field. He and Piper worked their way up to ninth place, but were then delayed by gearbox problems. They climbed back to eighth place, but retired at 5.20 on the Sunday morning because the gearbox was tightening up and the V12 engine had developed an ever-increasing thirst for oil. Ickx/Oliver with a *Gulf*-entered Ford GT40 won from Herrmann/Larrousse (works

Porsche 908 *Lang*). In the closing laps of the race Ickx and Herrmann battled closely for the lead and the young Belgian crossed the line a mere 100yds (91.5m) ahead of his German rival.

Postscript by Chris Amon

Of his 1969 season Chris Amon says, 'The 312P was a car that promised much, but really didn't ever quite deliver. I think that as much as anything it was a victim of the chaos that was Ferrari at the time – the F1 programme was a disaster along with the Can-Am. In comparison to the Porsche 908 I felt that the Ferrari was the better car, but it lacked power. I think we were also quite unlucky in 1969; there is no question that Mario and I would have won at Sebring, had it not been for the problem with the debris.

'Equally, I think that we could have won at Monza had the engine stayed together. The same could be said of the two races that I did with Pedro Rodriguez – I think that we were in a position to win both had it not been for the problems that intervened. As it was unlikely that the 917s would last the distance at Le Mans, I think that we had the pace to win; the accident was very unfortunate, for my engine had been reluctant to start, I got away well down the field and I was just in the wrong place at the wrong time.

'Franco Gozzi did a competent job, mostly the logistical side of things and Mike Parkes was really in charge of the race team as such. I don't think that the lack of success could be blamed on the people in the field. I found Mario Andretti to be a great team-mate and co-driver; obviously, he was very quick and totally reliable, and also a great guy to get along with and a pleasure to be around. I also enjoyed co-driving with Pedro Rodriguez, he could sometimes be erratic in F1, but I think that few have been his equal in long-distance sports car races.

'Mauro Forghieri was the finest engineer that I ever worked with; he was brilliant at communicating with a driver and acting on what he said; he was capable of engineering the whole car, including the engine and gearbox, something that few others have ever done. I feel that I can best sum up Mauro by saying that if one looks at the period from the early 1960s into the 1990s, Ferrari enjoyed their best times when he was at the engineering helm. I left Ferrari because of complete frustration at the whole 1969 season. I felt that I was going nowhere and that time was passing. It was probably the most unsettled time in Ferrari history, with the partial sell-out to Fiat taking place, and 1969 was one of Italy's worst years for industrial problems and these impacted on Ferrari's race efforts.'

Left *For Le Mans in 1969 Ferrari prepared two 312Ps with very stylish coupé bodies. Pedro Rodriguez and David Piper drove this car. It retired because of gearbox failure.*

Right *This view of the Rodriguez/Piper 312P during a routine pit stop at Le Mans shows the elegant tail treatment to good advantage.*

Schetty in the 1969 European Hill Championship, 1969

During the years 1966–68 Porsche and their driver Gerhard Mitter had dominated the European Hill Climb Championship and won it three years in succession. In passing it should be mentioned that Mitter crashed fatally with a Formula 2 BMW in practice for the 1969 German Grand Prix at the Nürburgring. Both Porsche and BMW abstained from running in the 1969 Championship and Ferrari faced opposition only from Abarth.

Ferrari built a special Group Seven car, the development of which was entrusted to Stefano Jacoponi who in 1969 was also responsible for the engineering aspects of the Formula 1 cars. This new Ferrari was typed the 212E (*Esperimentale* or, more usually *Sperimentale*, 'Experimental') and the engine was a horizontally opposed flat-12 derived from that of the Tipo 1512 Grand Prix unit, but substantially different (see Mauro Forghieri's comments on Page 199); the capacity was 1,991cc (65 x 50mm), compared with the 1,487cc (56 x 50.4mm) of the earlier engine. This engine had Lucas fuel injection and on a compression ratio of 11:1 power output was 280bhp at 11,000rpm.

The chassis generally followed that of the *Dino* 206S and as usual there was a five-speed gearbox in unit with the final drive. Right-hand drive was fitted. The body was a very neat low *spyder*, rather like a smaller version of the 1967 Tipo 350 *Can-Am* cars and it featured a low, wrap-round Plexiglas windscreen, tubular roll-bar and spoiler running across the edge of the tail.

Former Abarth driver Peter Schetty drove the 212E and the main opposition came from Arturo Merzario with a 2-litre Abarth, but Schetty persistently beat him and consistently broke Mitter's existing hill records. There were seven events in the series, Montseny, Rossfeld, Mont Ventoux, Trento-Bondone, Freiburg, Cesana-Sestriere and Ollon-Villars and Schetty won them all. It was the last time that Ferrari competed in the Championship.

The 312P and NART, 1969–71

The works team did not race the 312Ps again after Le Mans in 1969 and missed the final rounds of the Championship at Watkins Glen and the Österreichring. Maranello was preoccupied with final testing of the new 312B flat-12 Formula 1 car, scheduled to run in the Italian Grand Prix on 7 September. The team was not satisfied with the car and it was not raced until 1970, so only an old V12 was entered at Monza for Rodriguez. This was the final straw for Amon and he left the team, frustrated by racing uncompetitive Grand Prix cars. The two 312Ps were refurbished and sold to *NART*. One of the cars ran in a couple of Can-Am races, but, inevitably, it was outclassed.

Both 312Ps were entered by *NART* in the 1970 Daytona 24 Hours race held that year on 31 January–1 February. They displayed astonishing reliability and both had a trouble-free race. Parkes/Posey and Piper/Adamowicz drove them into fourth and fifth places and took the first two places in the Prototype category. The fourth-place 0868 had a bulge in the roof to accommodate the very tall Mike Parkes. On 21 March *NART* entered the two cars in the Sebring 12 Hours race and Mike Parkes/Chuck Parsons drove 0868 into sixth place overall, but only fourth in the Prototype category because so many of the faster Competition Sports Cars had retired, and the Prototypes entered by other teams were now performing rather more reliably. The other

In the 1970 Sebring race Mike Parkes/Chuck Parsons with one of the NART 312Ps leads the Alfa Romeo 33/3 of Piers Courage/Andrea de Adamich through the Green Park chicane. It is a very American scene with Spanish moss hanging from the pine tree and Florida Highway Patrol cars in the background. What seems to be a wooden fence behind the Alfa Romeo is fabric netting used to arrest jets on aircraft carriers. The bulge in the roof of the 312P was to clear the head of the very tall Parkes. Parkes/Parsons finished sixth. (Pete Lyons)

164 Scarlet Passion

312P shared by Luigi Chinetti Jnr/Adamowicz retired because of fuel pump failure.

Nothing more was seen of the 312Ps until the Le Mans race in June. Adamowicz and Parsons drove a steady race with 0868, but lost time through a stop to change the fuel pump. Later Parsons spun on a wet track, damaging both front and rear bodywork. The 312P was repaired, using parts from the second car that the team had entered and brought to the circuit, but not raced. The 312P was in sixth place when it developed an incurable engine misfire, it was very difficult to start after pit stops and while it could barely drag itself up the hill from the pits, it was running on most, if not all, cylinders on the Mulsanne Straight. Although it finished tenth on the road, it was too far behind to be classified.

For 1971 NART re-bodied one of these cars in *spyder* form. Luigi Chinetti Jnr/Garcia Veiga drove it at Daytona on 30–31 January, finishing fifth overall and winning the Prototype class in which there were a large number of retirements. At Sebring Chinetti Jnr/George Eaton brought it across the line in eighth place.

Above *Chinetti's NART acquired the two 312Ps after the 1969 Le Mans race. This is a view of the cockpit of one of these cars at the Inver-House Scotch Can-Am race at Bridge-hampton in September 1969. Pedro Rodriguez drove it into fifth place.* (Pete Lyons)

Right NART *entered Tony Adamowicz and Chuck Parsons with this 312P at Le Mans in 1970. After many problems that included an accident, fuel pump trouble and an engine misfire, it was still running – just about – at the finish, but was too far behind to be classified.*

The 312 Prototypes, 1969–71   165

The 512S and 512M Competition Sports Cars, 1970–71

Mario Andretti with his 512S Spyder at Turn Two at Sebring in 1970. He and Jacky Ickx won the race after the Gulf-Porsche 917s ran into problems. It was Ferrari's only Championship race win that year. (Pete Lyons)

When the *Commission Sportive Internationale* incorporated in the sports car regulations for 1968 onwards a category for Group Four Competition Sports Cars of up to 5,000cc, it was intended as an interim measure to allow owners of existing cars such as the Ferrari 250LM, the Ford GT40 and the Lola T70 Mark III to continue racing. It was not anticipated that these would be raced for more than a couple of years and then disappear from the racing scene as they became increasingly obsolete. For 1969 the minimum number of cars built to be eligible for homologation in Group Four was reduced to 25, a change intended to assist manufacturers such as Alfa Romeo who had built quite a number of their 2-litre Tipo 33/2 cars and wanted to see them raced in this class.

During 1969 Porsche completely upset the intentions of the *CSI* by introducing their 4.5-litre 917 model, which was based on the existing 3-litre eight-cylinder 908 Prototype with four cylinders added. To satisfy the

166 Scarlet Passion

homologation requirements Porsche had to set up a line of 25 cars for official inspection. Porsche spent much of the 917's first season struggling to resolve handling and aerodynamic problems with these cars, but the 917s displayed remarkable speed – if not reliability – at Le Mans that year.

What was not publicly known until later in the year was that Ferrari was also developing a Competition Sports Car, as an answer to the 917. The new 512S was first shown to the press in November 1969 and it made its racing debut at Daytona at the end of January 1970. The battle between Ferrari and Porsche in 1970 completely overshadowed the 3-litre Prototypes in all the year's races except the Targa Florio and the Nürburgring. Both Porsche and Ferrari incurred enormous cost in building 25 Group Four cars that were of such high performance that they could only be handled competently by a limited number of drivers and, inevitably, a number of both 917s and 512S cars remained unsold.

The 512S in Detail

The new Ferrari, typed the 512S (five litres, 12 cylinders, *Sport*) was powered by a development of the 60° V12 engine used in the 1967 P4 cars and the 1969 6.2-litre Can-Am car. The capacity of the new engine was 4,994cc (87 x 70mm) and it was mounted ahead of the rear axle. In accordance with usual Ferrari design practice there were twin overhead camshafts per bank of cylinders and these were chain-driven from the nose of the crankshaft. Each bank of cylinders had a single camshaft cover. The inlet ports were in the vee of the engine with the exhausts on the outside. The cylinder heads incorporated four valves per cylinder.

Lucas high-pressure fuel injection was fitted and a Marelli *Dinoplex* transistor pack, driven from the rear of the inlet camshaft of the left-hand cylinder block, fired the single plugs per cylinder. Lubrication was dry sump and there were cooling systems for each cylinder block with the radiators mounted behind the firewall on either side of the engine. Paired individual exhaust pipes for each cylinder fed into twin pipes for each bank of cylinders and the lower of these stopped short of the upper. In its original form the engine developed 550bhp at 8,500rpm.

Transmission was by a dry triple-plate clutch and a five-speed ZF gearbox in unit with a final drive that incorporated a limited slip differential. The multi-tubular space-frame was constructed in mild steel and it extended to the rear of the car. The front of the engine was attached to cross-tubes immediately behind the cockpit firewall and the rear of the engine was mounted by a chassis extension, which also located the rear suspension. The centre-section of the body, which formed the cockpit and incorporated the fuel tanks within the sills, was a stressed alloy structure that stiffened the chassis.

At the front there was the usual Ferrari arrangement of unequal-length wishbones and combined coil springs and Koni dampers together with an anti-roll bar. Single upper arms, lower reversed wishbones, coil springs/Koni damper units and an anti-roll bar were used for the rear suspension. The Girling cast-iron ventilated disc brakes were hub-mounted and there were the usual superb-looking, 15-inch Campagnolo centre-lock, five-spoke, cast-magnesium wheels. Steering was rack-and-pinion and right-hand drive was fitted.

The body followed the style of the 312P, but the delicacy of line had been lost and the 512S looked big, brutal and formidable. The nose and tail-sections of the

The 512S made its debut in the Daytona 24 Hours race at the end of January 1970. This is the car that Ickx/Andretti drove into third place behind two Gulf-Porsche 917s. It is seen here during a typical, confused Ferrari pit stop. Mauro Forghieri can be seen at the right side of the tail and Jacky Ickx is standing alongside him. (Pete Lyons)

body, together with the doors, were constructed in glass-fibre by Cigala and Bertinetti in Turin and were taken from aluminium-alloy master panels formed at Maranello. A coupé body was used originally, with a swept-up tail-section featuring stabilising fins; at the front of the nose there was a slit air intake and two square spotlights were mounted in the centre of the nose. The twin fillers for the water radiators were on either side at the rear of the roof, the fuel fillers were mounted either side just ahead of the windscreen and the oil tank filler was behind the left radiator. The spare wheel was mounted horizontally in the nose. Aerodynamic problems were only partially resolved as the season progressed.

Although the 512S and the Porsche 917 were closely matched in performance and they were both evolved from existing designs, each was a typical product from a factory with distinct and individual design practices. Despite the fact that air-cooled engines are inherently less powerful than their water-cooled counterparts, the 917 matched the power output of the 512S and at about 1,970lb (894kg) dry it was about 120lb (54.4kg) heavier. For 1970 Porsche entrusted preparation and entry of the works 917s to John Wyer's *Gulf* team based at Slough. The pale blue and orange *Gulf* cars were consistently better prepared and more reliable than their Maranello rivals. The *Gulf* team also had the advantage of the two fastest sports car drivers in the world, Jo Siffert and Pedro Rodriguez, and rarely could even Jacky Ickx of Ferrari match their speed.

Mauro Forghieri, who had great affection for the 512S, frequently commented: 'It is heavy, it is slow, but it is reliable.' Unfortunately, the last of these comments was far from true. John Wyer highlighted another problem faced by the Ferrari team in his autobiography, *The Certain Sound*, 'No team however well-endowed with engineers and mechanics can support two major formulae and expect to win them both.' The effort and energy expended on sports car racing sapped the competitiveness of the Ferrari Formula 1 team and it was only after the sports car racing year had substantially ended that Jacky Ickx and the new flat-12 Tipo 312B began to challenge Grand Prix supremacy of Lotus. The 512S was announced at a press conference at the Gatto Verde restaurant near Maranello in November 1969 and it was stated that cars not required by the works team would be available for sale to private owners at a price of 24,000,000 lire. Originally, Ferrari planned that the 512S would make its debut in the Kyalami Nine Hours race in November 1969 with David Piper as one of the drivers. Ferrari then scratched the entry, so Piper accepted an offer from Porsche to sell him a 917 on favourable terms and with Richard Attwood as co-driver they won the race.

Apart from the great Jacky Ickx, Ferrari had a fairly strong team of drivers that included Ignazio Giunti, Arturo Merzario, Peter Schetty and Nino Vaccarella. A number of other drivers were brought into the team during the year. Mario Andretti could only drive for Ferrari occasionally because of his USAC commitments, although they would have liked him to drive for the team on a regular basis. John Surtees (who had been asked by Enzo Ferrari to prepare a report on the 512S), Chris Amon, Derek Bell and Ronnie Peterson all drove works 512S entries on occasion. Forghieri's workload was far too great, for at races he was responsible for both team management and engineering. Franco Gozzi remained racing manager, although Forghieri seemed to be left to do all the work, and there was of course a strong team of mechanics.

The 1970 Racing Season

There were ten rounds in the 1970 Sports Car Manufacturers' Championship. In addition to these, the Buenos Aires 1,000Km race had been restored to the calendar and was held on 11 January. It was to be a round in the Championship the following year. Neither Ferrari nor the *Gulf* team competed in this race. The two V8 3-litre Alfa Romeo 33/3 Prototypes ran into mechanical problems and Jean-Pierre Beltoise partnered by Henri Pescarolo won with a Matra MS630/650 V12 3-litre Prototype. A week later a second race of two 100-mile (161km) heats was run at Buenos Aires and Piers Courage/Andrea de Adamich won this with their Alfa Romeo 33/3.

Daytona 24 Hours

Because of bad weather in Italy Ferrari had been unable to carry out a full test programme with the 512S and the team lacked the confidence that the cars would last 24 hours. All the 512S entries had coupé bodies. Jacky Ickx/Peter Schetty, Mario Andretti/Arturo Merzario and Nino Vaccarella/Ignazio Giunti were the works driver pairings. In addition *NART* fielded a car for Dan Gurney/Chuck Parsons (this 512S was distinguished by a bulge in the roof to clear Gurney's lanky frame) and *Scuderia Piccho Rosso* entered their 512S for Gianpiero Moretti/Corrado Manfredini. The Italian privateers were pathetically slow in practice – and the race – and many held the view that they should not have been allowed to start.

Wyer's *Gulf-Porsche* team was also uncertain about the reliability of their 917s, as these had only been delivered three weeks before the race, and both Wyer and racing manager David Yorke considered that there had been insufficient time to prepare them to their exacting standards. Jo Siffert/Brian Redman and Pedro Rodriguez/Leo Kinnunen drove the *Gulf* cars, the team's usual pairings in 1970. Porsche's Austrian subsidiary, *Porsche Konstruktionen* KG of Salzburg also ran a 917 for Kurt Ahrens/Vic Elford.

Another view of the 512S of Ickx/Andretti in the Sebring 12 Hours race.

Andretti was fastest in practice and he and Siffert accelerated away from the rolling start side-by-side, but by the end of the first lap Siffert and Rodriguez were in the first two places ahead of Andretti and Gurney. Giunti, running in fifth place after an hour and a half's racing, had a tyre fail as he came off the banking on to the road section, the 512S slewed into the retaining wall, shattering the bodywork and damaging the rear suspension uprights. For nearly two hours the Ferrari mechanics struggled to repair the damage, but eventually they decided that it was hopeless. Very soon after the mechanics had abandoned this thankless task, Ickx, who had been driving a steady cautious race and was holding 11th place, had a tyre fail on the banking. Ickx lost control, hit the retaining wall and another Ferrari was out of the race due to damaged rear suspension.

Forghieri switched Ickx to co-drive with Andretti and by the Sunday morning the race had settled down into a procession with Rodriguez/Kinnunen leading Andretti/Ickx and the second 917 of Siffert/Redman trailing badly after an 80-minute pit stop for the clutch to be replaced. At about 9am Ickx brought the second-place Ferrari in to report handling problems. The rear chassis member supporting the gearbox had broken, but the 512S was so far ahead of Rodriguez/Kinnunen that Forghieri decided that this should be welded.

The stop lasted 45 minutes and when the Ferrari rejoined the race, it was back in second place behind Rodriguez/Kinnunen and was still handling atrociously. Ickx returned to the pits where the mechanics worked on the car for a further 32 minutes. Because one rear wheel was out of alignment Ickx lapped at reduced speed and Siffert/Redman had now closed within five laps. Just before 1pm the Porsche moved into second place but Andretti went ahead again when the 917 spent five minutes in the pits having damaged bodywork taped up. Then Siffert resumed at the wheel, rapidly closed the gap on the ailing Ferrari and moved back into second place two laps before the finish.

Sebring 12 Hours

Maranello was not too disappointed with the outcome of the Daytona race, but extensive development was carried out in the seven weeks before the Sebring race held on 21 March. Ferrari made suspension modifications to cure the excessive tyre wear that had caused punctures at Daytona. Power output was increased to 575bhp. The chassis was lightened, a new, squarer nose was fitted and two of the cars in the 12 Hours race had lighter open bodywork. The *spyder* version proved to have better front-end adhesion. The drivers, as always, disliked the claustrophobia and high noise level of a coupé and were much happier with the new bodywork. Andretti/Merzario and Ickx/Schetty drove the open cars, while Giunti/Vaccarella had one of the coupés raced at Daytona. *NART* also entered their coupé for Sam Posey/Ronnie Bucknum. In addition to the *Gulf* 917 entries, *Porsche Salzburg* entered two 917s for Elford/Ahrens and Herrmann/Lins.

It was to prove another race of attrition, although on this one occasion in 1970 the outcome favoured Maranello. In the interests of safety a rolling start was used at Sebring for the first time. Andretti led Siffert until the first round of routine pit stops, then the Swiss *Gulf* driver forged ahead. Mainly because of circuit characteristics, broken wheel bearings on the right front suspension upright plagued the 917s and these failures, coupled with other Porsche problems, allowed the Ferraris to move up into the first three places in the order Andretti/Merzario, Ickx/Schetty and Giunti/Vaccarella. The 512S

The 512S and 512M Competition Sports Cars, 1970–71 169

works cars pounded round the Florida circuit, apparently invincible, but it was not to last.

As the darkness of the warm evening closed in on the circuit, the Ickx/Schetty car stopped out on the circuit. The engine was red-hot, but the cause was not investigated until after the race and was traced to cylinder head gasket failure. Four hours from the finish the Giunti/Vaccarella car went off the road at the hairpin and punctured a tyre. By the time that Giunti had driven back to the pits on the rim, the suspension was damaged. The mechanics changed the unit in 24 minutes and this car rejoined the race in second place.

Only 80 minutes before the finish Merzario suddenly slowed with the leading 512S, the gearbox had jammed in one gear and shortly afterwards when the transmission seized up, Merzario trekked back to the pits to report the bad news. Andretti switched to the surviving 512S and this car went on to win from the Porsche 908/02 of film actor Steve McQueen/Peter Revson. Masten Gregory/Hezemans with a works Alfa Romeo 33/3 were third and the *Gulf-Porsche* 917 shared by Rodriguez, Kinnunen and Siffert took fourth place, four laps in arrears.

In the 1970 BOAC 1,000Km race Chris Amon co-drove this works 512S with Arturo Merzario. Amon leads the winning Gulf-Porsche 917 of Rodriguez/ Kinnunen and a privately entered Porsche 910. Amon/Merzario were badly delayed in this wet race because of fuel starvation and finished in fifth place. (Guy Griffiths)

Brands Hatch and the Le Mans Practice Weekend

Because of an organisational blunder, the Brands Hatch 1,000Km race and the Le Mans Practice session were held the same weekend. On the Saturday 11 April, Ickx flew to Le Mans where he drove a 512S, which he tried with different nose and tail sections and then flew back the same day to compete at Brands Hatch on the Sunday. Giunti and Schetty drove the 512S at Le Mans on the Sunday, but high winds and rain squalls prevented any good times from being set.

Originally Ferrari had entered three cars at Brands Hatch, but then decided that this was stretching the organisation too far and so only two cars arrived at the circuit, both with open bodywork. The drivers were Jacky Ickx/Jackie Oliver (the latter deputising for Andretti who was racing at a USAC meeting) and Chris Amon/Arturo Merzario. *Scuderia Filipinetti* entered their Daytona-style coupé for Herbert Müller/Mike Parkes. The team had set the car up for the diminutive Müller and although a hole had been cut in the roof to clear the helmet of the very tall Parkes, he was uncomfortable throughout the race.

George Loos and Jonathan Williams were to drive Loos' *Gelo Racing* car, but after a poor showing in practice, it non-started. The team said that once it was known that the race would be run in the wet, there was insufficient time to fit rain tyres as they were the last in the queue for a set of wet-weather Firestones. Although the *Gelo* team had tested this 512S, they had not raced it before and it seems that in any event Loos was unwilling to risk it in the wet in its first race.

Brands Hatch was a very much a Porsche race, both Rodriguez and Siffert drove with spectacular speed on the streaming wet track and the Ferrari drivers had a thoroughly miserable time. Only Ickx could approach the speed of the leading *Gulf* drivers but Ferrari pit work was vastly inferior to that of the Wyer team and both cars were delayed by minor problems and collisions. Redman crashed the 917 that he shared with Siffert, but Rodriguez/Kinnunen scored a brilliant win, followed by the *Porsche Salzburg* 917s of Elford/Hulme and Attwood/Herrmann and with the 908 *Spyder* of van Lennep/Laine in fourth place. Amon/Merzario, slowed by fuel-feed trouble, finished fifth and Ickx/Oliver were eventually eighth after problems with the windscreen wipers and wet electrics.

Monza 1,000Km

The fourth round of the Championship took place at Monza on 25 April and was now run on the road circuit only because of the dilapidated state of the banking. Since their last outing Ferrari had made only minor changes to the 512S cars. There were three works entries, Amon/Merzario and John Surtees/Schetty with coupés and Giunti/Vaccarella with a *spyder*. Jacky Ickx was out of racing because of burns that he had suffered in a bad crash in the F1 Spanish Grand Prix. Parkes/Müller drove the *Filipinetti* car and *Scuderia Picchio Rosso* entered a car for Moretti/Manfredini. As was becoming usual, the Porsche 917 opposition came in the form of two cars each from the *Gulf* and *Porsche Salzburg* teams (one of the latter's cars had a 5-litre engine). There were also three private 917s.

In practice the Ferraris were under-steering badly and they were again suffering from excessive tyre wear. On the Friday Merzario lost control of his 512S through the *Lesmo* curves and battered the Ferrari against the guard-rails. Practice was stopped while the shattered Ferrari was recovered and work could start on its repair. Remarkably, the Ferrari mechanics had completed the work by the end of the four-hour practice session. As John Wyer wryly commented, 'It's the usual principle; if Ferrari can't practice, no one else is allowed to either.' Ferrari's consumption of Firestone tyres was so heavy that if they had fitted the usual compound, the cars would have had to stop to change the front tyres every 37 laps of this 174-lap race. After experimenting with different trim tabs and various compounds of tyres, the team settled for a harder compound than normal, but it had not located the cause of the problem.

Although the 917s set the pace, with the 5-litre

Salzburg car of Elford/Ahrens out in front, the Ferraris ran steadily and swiftly, if not quite swiftly enough. In any event poor pit work destroyed Maranello's prospects of success. On lap 67 the left rear tyre failed on the 5-litre Porsche, flailing rubber smashed the bodywork, wrecked the rear suspension and holed the oil tank. Ahrens was forced to abandon the car out on the circuit. Rodriguez/Kinnunen now led for *Gulf*, but Giunti slipped ahead just before Kinnunen made a routine pit stop. Now Ferrari threw away all chances of victory; for the second time in this race all three cars had been called into the pits to refuel at the same time. With Rodriguez back at the wheel of the *Gulf* 917, Maranello's hopes of victory had evaporated.

When Giunti made his last refuelling stop, Forghieri decided that Amon should relieve him. Fuel beneath the Ferrari ignited as Amon fired up the 512S and by the time that the fire had been extinguished and the windscreen cleared of foam, Amon rejoined the race over a lap in arrears. For the remainder of the race Amon sat on Rodriguez's tail, hoping that the Mexican would make a mistake. Surtees/Schetty took third place, despite a puncture in the closing laps, and Amon/Merzario finished fourth, both cars three laps in arrears but two laps ahead of the Matras, which finished first and second in the Group 6 category.

Sicilian Road Race

On 3 May the Targa Florio was held over 11 laps of the winding, badly surfaced, treacherous 44.7-mile (72km) Sicilian *Piccolo Madonie* circuit. Ferrari was in a very difficult position as he had only the 512S, a totally

The 512S and 512M Competition Sports Cars, 1970–71 171

unsuitable car, while Porsche had built a team of 3-litre 908/03 *Spyder* Prototypes specifically for this race and the Nürburgring 1,000Km event. Ferrari solved his dilemma by entering a single 512S for local hero Nino Vaccarella partnered by Ignazio Giunti.

A note from Ferrari was inserted in the programme, with greetings to the *tifosi*, saying that the team did not expect to win with the 5-litre car, but Ferrari had entered it because he had promised Vaccarella a chance in the race that he had won previously. There was also a note from the Sicilian, commenting that when Ferrari entered its new 3-litre Prototype in 1971, the Porsche team would be under real pressure. In the event, Ferrari did not enter the next year's race. *Scuderia Filipinetti* ran their 512S for Müller/Parkes.

Above *In the absence of any suitable car for the race Ferrari entered a single 512S spyder in the 1970 Targa Florio and had a note of apology to the tifosi entered in the race programme. Nino Vaccarella and Ignazio Giunti drove a brilliant race to finish third behind the Gulf-entered Porsche 908/03s of Siffert/Redman and Rodriguez/ Kinnunen.* (LAT)

Right *In the 1970 Spa 1,000Km race the 512S Ferraris were unable to match the speed of the Gulf-Porsche 917s. Jacky Ickx (seen here at the wheel), partnered by John Surtees, drove a good race to finish second, on the same lap as the winners.* (LAT)

172 Scarlet Passion

Race-day was wet and depressing with the roads mud-covered and slippery. The start was delayed by traffic congestion that had prevented many of the officials from arriving on time. The first cars to leave were the Ferraris of Vaccarella and Müller and both drivers were handling their cars with great caution, but throwing up blankets of muddy spray. A further handicap faced by the 5-litre cars was the necessity to refuel every two laps. The most serious opposition to the Porsche 908/03s should have come from the Alfa Romeo Tipo 33/3 Prototypes, but the Milan team's challenge soon faded and Vaccarella and Giunti put up a much stiffer fight than expected.

An unexpectedly quick pit stop at the end of lap four enabled Vaccarella to rejoin the race sandwiched on time between the 908/03s of Siffert/Redman and Rodriguez/Kinnunen. The circuit had dried out and two laps later Vaccarella had taken the lead and the Sicilian was flicking the 512S lithely through the bends in a manner that seemed impossible for such a big and bulky car. The Porsche drivers started to turn on the pressure and in the closing laps, while the slower Giunti was at the wheel of the 512S, they had made up sufficient time to push the Ferrari back to third place. Müller and Parkes drove their 512S into sixth place, a lap in arrears.

Spa 1,000Km

A fortnight later, on 17 May, the sports car scene switched to the gentle pine-clad slopes hills of the Ardennes and Spa-Francorchamps, the fastest and the most beautiful road circuit in Europe. Ferrari entered three 512S coupés, a new car driven by Jacky Ickx/John Surtees and two of the Monza cars for Merzario/Schetty and Giunti/Vaccarella. Amon was not available because of qualifying at Indianapolis. The single private 512S was another brand-new car, the yellow-painted *Écurie Francorchamps* coupé driven by Derek Bell/Hughes de Fierlandt. Since their last appearance the Ferraris had been modified by the adoption of a small lip running across the bottom of the nose to improve high-speed stability. The main opposition consisted of the two-car entries each from *Gulf-Porsche* and *Porsche Salzburg*, three of which had 5-litre engines.

The *Gulf-Porsche* 917s overshadowed the entire opposition on this circuit and the mastery of Rodriguez in particular through the fast curves was breathtakingly impressive. Despite the retirement of the Rodriguez/ Kinnunen 917, the Ferrari team threw away its prospects of winning the race through Ferrari politics. Just before the start there was an only too typical Ardennes rain shower and although it was driven away by the warm sunshine, the track was still wet when the cars went out for an exploratory lap. On the grid some of the cars were fitted with intermediate tyres and in clear breach of the race regulations Forghieri went from Ferrari to Ferrari, topping the fuel tanks to the brim.

Early in the race Ickx was up with the *Gulf* 917s on the 200mph Masta Straight and held second place briefly. Ferrari had misunderstood the race regulations and believing that gravity hoses were banned, refuelled the cars from churns. Even so, the Ferrari pit stops were swift and after the first round of stops Ickx was still in second place behind Rodriguez; the Belgian took the lead when Rodriguez made an unscheduled pit stop because a rear tyre was throwing chunks of tread. At the next

Above *Derek Bell and Hughes de Fierlandt shared this yellow-painted 512S entered at Spa by Écurie Francorchamps. Despite a fire during a refuelling stop, they finished eighth.* (LAT)

Right *The NART Ferrari 512S of Sam Posey/Ron Bucknum swoops through the Esses early in the 1970 Le Mans race. Following is the NART-entered 312P driven by Tony Adamowicz and Chuck Parsons. Posey/ Bucknum in fourth place were the highest-placed Ferrari finishers.* (Guy Griffiths)

refuelling stop Ickx handed over to Surtees who lost ground and fell back to second place. When Surtees came into refuel, instead of replacing him with Ickx, who was as fast as any driver in the race, Forghieri sent out Surtees again and sealed Ferrari's defeat. Maybe he had little choice about this because of the report on the 512S that Surtees was preparing for Enzo Ferrari.

There was also drama in the *Écurie Francorchamps* pit after petrol was spilt during a refuelling stop. Bell fired the engine, there was a tremendous whoosh and in seconds the car was engulfed in flames and photographers and pit staff fled as fuel running down the pit road ignited. The interior door wire had broken and Bell was trapped in the car until the fire had been brought under control. It was all over in less than a minute and Bell jumped out unharmed apart from singed eyebrows. The car was wiped down, the windscreen cleared and Bell rejoined the race. At the end of this 71-lap event Siffert and Redman won at the astonishingly high speed, including stops, of 149.42mph (240.42kph) and Ickx/Surtees finished second, just under three minutes in arrears. Giunti/Vaccarella took fourth place, Merzario/Schetty were seventh and Bell/Fierlandt eighth.

Nürburgring 1,000Km

This race on 31 May was another in which, in the face of the Porsche 908/03s, Ferrari stood little chance of success. Maranello entered three 512S *spyders* to be driven by Ickx/Giunti, Surtees/Schetty and Vaccarella/Merzario. The Ferrari entry was soon reduced to two cars when Ickx arrived at the circuit with a sprained wrist, having added to his Spanish Grand Prix woes by falling downstairs at home, and he was clearly not able to race. The question of a substitute driver resolved itself during Friday's practice. Schetty spun at around 120mph in the wet on the fast stretch of the circuit after the *Adenau* Bridge, disappeared into the trees and the car was wrecked. Ferrari then switched the driver pairings to Surtees/Vaccarella and Giunti/Merzario. *Scuderia Filipinetti* entered their 512S for Parkes/Müller.

On the first lap Rodriguez (908/03) took the lead from Siffert with a similar car, but Giunti forced his big red Ferrari ahead of the Swiss driver and set up a moving road-block until Siffert scrambled past again on the second lap. On only the next lap this Ferrari retired out on the circuit because of fuel metering unit failure. Surtees was in fourth place, but stopped at the pits at the end of lap seven because the steering wheel had broken. After this had been replaced and the car refuelled Vaccarella took over but he was back again after two laps complaining about the car's handling. All four wheels were changed and Vaccarella rejoined the race to fight his way back up the field. Both Gulf 908/03 entries retired, so the *Salzburg* 908/03s of Elford/Ahrens and Herrmann/Attwood took the first two places ahead of the 512S of Surtees/Vaccarella, which was a lap behind. The *Filipinetti* car of Parkes/Müller finished fourth, two laps in arrears.

Le Mans

The 512S Ferraris and the Porsche 917s were out in force for the 24 hours' race held on 13–14 June. Ferrari had been carrying out steady development work to improve the reliability of the 512S and there were detail changes to the camshaft profiles, injection trumpets and exhaust manifolding. The team had reverted to the original, more rounded noses, all the works cars had coupé bodywork, there were ventilation louvres in the front wings and the long tails, tried at the Practice Weekend, were fitted, still with small, white-painted fins. Amon was heavily engaged with development of the March 707 Can-Am car and was unable to drive for Ferrari, while Surtees had declined an invitation.

So the driver pairings were Ickx/Schetty (No 5), Vaccarella/Giunti (No 6), Derek Bell/Ronnie Peterson (No 7) and Merzario/Clay Regazzoni (No 8). Ickx was still in pain from the petrol burns suffered in April, and walking with a limp and his left hand was badly scarred. During practice the Ferraris were weaving on the straights and there were obviously as yet unsolved aerodynamic problems. Forghieri was concerned about the reliability of the gearboxes because slowing the cars from very high speeds for Mulsanne corner meant heavy use of the gearbox as well as the brakes. Special parts were sent from Maranello and on the Wednesday evening before the race the mechanics built up a gearbox with stronger bearings for the car to be driven by Ickx/Schetty.

The tachometer cable broke on the Bell/Peterson car before Wednesday's practice session and then the replacement broke. Peterson was turning in some very fast laps, but his practice came to an end when a connecting rod went through the side of the cylinder block. It seems that the tachometer cable had broken yet again and Ronnie had inadvertently over-revved the engine.

In addition to the works cars there were seven private 512S entries, which can be summarised as follows:

No 9: Jose Juncadella/Juan Fernandez entered by *Escuderia Montjuich*, an early ex-works car, with short tail and large louvres in the rear wings

No 10: Helmut Kelleners/Georg Loos with the usual *Gelo Racing* car, still with short tail and entered in this race by *Scuderia Filipinetti*

No 11: Sam Posey/Ronnie Bucknum entered by *NART*, with the team's original car still with a bulge in the roof on the driver's side, rebuilt at the works and fitted with long tail

Ferrari mechanics clean the bugs off the windscreen of the 512S driven by Ickx/Schetty in the 1970 Six Hours race at Watkins Glen. In a very crowded pit scene Maurio Forghieri (in glasses and dark jacket) supervises operations. Ickx/Schetty finished fifth. (Pete Lyons)

No 12: Hughes de Fierlandt/Alistair Walker entered by *Écurie Francorchamps* with the car first seen at Spa, now rebuilt at the works and fitted with a long tail

No 14: Joakim Bonnier/Reine Wisell entered by *Scuderia Filipinetti* with an early car loaned by the works, fitted with long tail and prepared by the team itself

No 15: Mike Parkes/Herbert Müller entered by *Scuderia Filipinetti* with the team's usual car, prepared by the works and fitted with a long tail

No 16: Corrado Manfredini/Gianpiero Moretti entered by *Scuderia Filipinetti* with their *Scuderia Pichio Rosso* car, short tail and large louvres in the rear wings.

Both the *Gulf* team and *Porsche Salzburg* entered three 917s and there were also two private 917s. Once again the 917s dominated the race. During the first hour Merzario briefly held second place behind Rodriguez, but dropped back after stopping at the pits for the suspension to be checked. Bell lost time because of a puncture and Vaccarella crawled into the pits to retire because of a con-rod through the side of the cylinder block. Ickx had agreed with Forghieri to avoid the flat-out sprint of the early laps and was running steadily in sixth place. It was at this time that light rain began to fall.

After two and a half hours' racing Ferrari's hopes of a win diminished in a four-car accident. Wisell had eased off in his *Filipinetti* 512S because he was having difficulty seeing through his oil-smeared windscreen. As he approached *White House*, the battling trio of Bell, Regazzoni and Parkes caught up with him. Bell swerved round the *Filipinetti* car, Regazzoni rammed it about 150mph, Wisell's car was pushed into a crash barrier and rebounded to the centre of the track where it and Regazzoni's car were both rammed by Parkes. Parkes's car caught fire and he was lucky to escape with only leg burns. In the confusion Bell missed a gear and, unaware of the havoc behind him, crawled back to the pits to retire with a broken engine.

Only Ickx and Schetty with the surviving works car were left to challenge the 917s. They were now fourth but dropped back because of minor problems and then began to make up ground again as the rain intensified. By 10pm Ickx, still not fit after his accident in Spain, had worked his way back to third place, although he was becoming desperately tired. Ahead of him were Siffert/Redman and Elford/Ahrens (*Porsche Salzburg* 917) and when Elford came into the pits to investigate a handling problem, Ickx moved up to second. The Ferrari then dropped again to fifth place while Schetty was at the wheel.

At just after 1.35am Siffert and Ickx were approaching the *Ford* chicane together when the young Belgian lost control of the 512S under braking, spun over a sandbank and killed a marshal. It was never known whether a brake caliper had locked up or Ickx had made an error. What was very obvious was that Ickx was deeply distressed by this accident. The 512S caught fire, but Ickx escaped unhurt. Just over half an hour later Siffert with the leading 917 missed a gear-change and broke the engine of the leading 917. The race was to all intents and purposes over and the 917s of Attwood/Herrmann (*Porsche Salzburg*) and Larrousse/Kauhsen (*Martini* team) finished first and second ahead of the 908/02 *Spyder* of Lins/Marko. The Ferraris 512S cars of Posey/Bucknum and de Fierlandt/Walker took fourth and fifth places.

A Poor End to the Season

There were two more Championship races in 1970 and on 11 July the Watkins Glen Six Hours was held. The two principal Porsche teams made strong entries, but Ferrari sent only two short-tail *spyders* for Ickx/Schetty and Andretti/Giunti. *Gelo Racing* also entered their 512S for Loos/Pesch. The *Gulf* 917s of Rodriguez/Kinnunen and Siffert/Redman dominated the race, although the Ferraris put up a fight in the opening laps.

Andretti/Giunti lost time because of a vapour-lock in the fuel system, but finished third, three laps behind the winners. The Salzburg-entered Porsche 917 of Hulme/Elford, which had been plagued by tyre trouble, took fourth place. Ickx/Schetty were fifth, after being delayed early in the race because of brake problems and then losing more ground when Schetty made a pit stop to change to wet-weather tyres in the heavy rain that fell in the last hour of the race.

The following day Ickx and Andretti drove the works 512S cars in the 200-mile (322km) Can-Am race on the same circuit. Inevitably, the big-capacity Group Seven sports cars dominated the entry and Denis Hulme won with his 8-litre Chevrolet-powered McLaren. Porsche 917 drivers filled the next three places and Andretti finished fifth – despite a spin on the third lap which dropped him to 23rd place while he waited for the traffic to pass. Ickx was eliminated by an accident early in the race.

The *Scuderia Piccho Rosso* 512S was shipped out to Japan where it won a race on the Mount Fuji circuit and was then shipped back to Europe to compete in the Imola 500Km race on 13 September. It joined an ex-Nürburgring works *spyder* driven by Giunti/Merzario and the *Escuderia Montjuich* 512S of Juncadella/Schetty. Merzario led for the first 12 laps, but then Rodriguez (Gulf 917) squeezed past but Redman (*Gulf* 917) overtook the Ferrari on lap 17 and three laps later

Merzario pulled into the pits because he had strained his wrist coping with a difficult gear-change. Giunti took over and rejoined in eighth place, but the Ferrari later retired because of fuel pump problems and a leaking fuel line. Juncadella retired his 512S because of a broken differential and Manfredini/Moretti finished sixth.

On 11 October the last round of the Championship, the Austrian 1,000Km race, took place at the Österreichring. Ferrari entered a modified 512S that was the prototype of the 1971 512M. This car, driven by Ickx/Giunti, had new and lighter nose and tail sections, together with small, fixed, rear flaps, and had been tested at both Imola and Modena. Loos/Pesch with their *Gelo Racing* car were the only other 512S drivers. There were the usual two-car entries from *Gulf-Porsche* and *Porsche Salzburg*. Ickx took the lead at the start and extended this lap after lap until 49 of this 170-lap race when the Ferrari expired out on the circuit. He walked back to the pits and then returned to the car with two mechanics lugging a replacement battery.

After the car had been started up, Ickx pulled into the pits for it to be checked and for Giunti to take over. Giunti covered only four laps before he was back in the pits because the new battery had flattened itself, the result of a loose earth wire. The car was now so far behind that it was retired, but Ickx had the small consolation of having set a new circuit record of 132.34mph (212.94kph). The *Gulf-Porsche* 917 of Siffert/Redman won the race from a 3-litre Alfa Romeo 33/3 driven by de Adamich/Pescarolo that was stationary in the pits with a broken engine when the flag fell. Loos/Pesch were hopelessly uncompetitive with their 512S and finished seventh.

A week after the Austrian race the private 512S cars of *Escuderia Montjuich* driven by Juncadella/Jabouille and *Gelo Racing* with its usual drivers, ran in the Paris 1,000Km race held on the combined banked track and road circuit at Montlhéry. Juncadella/Jabouille finished a good second behind Jack Brabham/François Cevert with a works 3-litre Matra Prototype. The Loos/Pesch car retired out on the circuit because of broken transmission.

Next, on 25 October, came the Madrid Six Hours race at Jarama. Only a single 512S ran, the *Escuderia Montjuich* car of Juncadella partnered by Merzario, but after two slow laps the Ferrari retired because of gearbox trouble. The final race for Ferrari in 1970 was the

Left *At the 1970 Austrian 1,000Km race Ferrari entered this car for Ickx (seen here) and Giunti. It was the prototype of the 1971 512M and although it displayed tremendous speed, it was plagued by electrical problems and eventually retired.* (LAT)

Above *Pedro Rodriguez drove this NART-entered 512S in the Road America Can-Am race at Elkhart Lake on 30 August 1970. The car ran badly in practice, he qualified a poor 20th and then drove a storming race. He shattered the body against a Lola-Chevrolet that he was trying to pass, stopped at the pits for repairs and rejoined the race to finish seventh.* (Pete Lyons)

Kyalami Nine Hours held on 7 November. It was the first race in the six-round Springbok series and the only one that accepted Group Four Competition Sports Cars. Ickx/Giunti with the latest works 512M led almost throughout the race to win at 104.83 mph (168.67 kph) from the *Martini*-entered Porsche 917 of Siffert/Ahrens. Bell/de Fierlandt with the *Écurie Francorchamps* 512S finished sixth.

The 512M

Despite Porsche's domination of the year's racing, the 512S had shown considerable promise and the efforts of the works team had been thwarted only too often by poor team management or minor mechanical problems. Mainly because 1971 was to be the last year in which five-litre cars would be admitted to Championship racing, Ferrari decided to concentrate on development of his new flat-12 3-litre Prototype. So only private teams raced the 5-litre Group Four cars in 1971.

A substantial number of privately owned 512S cars were rebuilt at Maranello to the definitive 512M specification. Apart from the changes to the body, there was a much lighter chassis with fewer tubes and slimmer main front cross-member and larger rear brakes were fitted. The engine now had chromed-alloy cylinder liners, improved fuel injection, improved inlet and exhaust manifolding and was claimed to develop over 600bhp. The principal entrants of 512Ms were *NART*, *Scuderia Filipinetti*, *Herbert Müller Racing*, *Escuderia Montjuich* – and the *Roger Penske Racing Team*.

The Sunoco-Ferrari

This car started life as a 512S and Jim Adams ran it in a few 1970 Can-Am races. After this it was sold to Kirk White of Philadelphia who entrusted its preparation to the *Roger Penske Racing Team*. Penske stripped the Ferrari down to the bare chassis, replaced many of the chassis components and made changes to the steering geometry. The team removed the original riveted aluminium-alloy panelling and fitted the car with a 512M-type body. At the rear there was a full-width aerofoil.

The chassis was treated with epoxy paint and many special features were added. To save time during pit stops there was a special pressurised fuel refilling system, the oil and water reservoirs were filled by compressed air and a vacuum device on the brake master cylinders drew the fluid back from the brakes and pulled the pistons back into the callipers to speed up brake pad changes. Another effort to save time at pit stops was to fit seat belt buckles strapped to the driver's waist. Penske sent two Ferrari 5-litre engines to Traco, the Chevrolet engine development specialists, who rebuilt them and incorporated modifications that increased power output to 600bhp. This Ferrari was painted metallic blue with yellow wheels and polished rims. Mark Donohue and David Hobbs were the usual drivers, but more than a fair share of misfortune plagued the car.

The 1971 races in South and North America

The first round of the 1971 Championship was the Buenos Aires 1,000Km race held on 10 January on a 3.79-mile (6km) circuit at the Buenos Aires Autodrome. Four Group Four Ferraris ran in this race; a 512M which Parkes/Bonnier drove for *Scuderia Filipinetti*, together with 512S cars for de Fierlandt/Gosselin (*Écurie Francorchamps*), Posey/Veiga/di Palma (*NART*) and Juncadella/Pairetti (*Escuderia Montjuich*). None was ever a serious contender and after Giunti's fatal crash with the leading Ferrari Prototype, Porsche 917s took the first two places ahead of two Alfa Romeo 33/3s. The 5-litre Ferraris finished in the next three places in the order Juncadella/Pairetti, Parkes/Bonnier and Posey/Veiga/di Palma.

Three weeks later on 30–31 January the overlong and very boring Daytona Continental 24 Hours race took place. The Sunoco-Ferrari made its debut and there were also five other 5-litre Ferraris entered. Donohue/Hobbs battled for the lead with the *Gulf* Porsche of Rodriguez/Jackie Oliver until the Sunoco-Ferrari was delayed by electrical troubles and dropped back to third place. Just after midnight a Porsche 911 collided with the Sunoco car and well over an hour was lost while the body was patched-up.

When the leading Porsche 917 jammed in top gear, it was so far ahead that the *Gulf* team decided to rebuild the gearbox. The *NART* 512S of Bucknum/Adamowicz assumed the lead after an hour and Donohue/Hobbs with the Sunoco-Ferrari moved into second place. After over 1½ hours spent in the pits and 45 minutes' resumption of racing, the 917 retook the lead and at the finish was a lap ahead of the *NART* car with the Sunoco-Ferrari in third place. The other 5-litre Ferraris retired.

By the Sebring 12 Hours race on 20 March the Sunoco-Ferrari had a new body made in California and featured a much larger rear wing. The Sunoco team was in trouble before it left Philadelphia, for the better of the team's engines had blown up during testing and Donohue had sprained his ankle. There were doubts as to whether he would be able to drive, but after resting he decided that he was fit enough. *NART* entered a 512M for Revson/Savage, together with 512S cars for Bucknum/Posey and Parsons/David Weir who owned the car. In his report of the race in *Autosport* Pete Lyons commented, 'All three machines were in frankly ragged condition, and arrived with far too few mechanics to service them properly.' Greg Young's *Young American* team entered a 512M with a Traco-developed engine for Young and Masten Gregory.

Elford/Larrousse with their *Martini*-entered 917 won the race from a brace of works Alfa Romeo 33/3s and the two *Gulf* 917s, which had been plagued by problems. Once again Donohue and Hobbs battled for the lead, but Donohue and Rodriguez (*Gulf* 917) collided while they were lapping a slower car. Both cars were badly damaged, Penske entered protests generally about the *Gulf* team (which were rejected) and the Ferrari lost 19 laps while a breathing orifice for the pressurised refuelling system was repaired and tested. Donohue/Hobbs rejoined the race to finish sixth, 16 laps behind the winners. All the other 5-litre Ferraris retired.

The first races of the European Season

The BOAC 1,000Km race at Brands Hatch on 4 April was the first European round of the Championship. Two 512Ms were entered, the newly rebuilt *Escuderia Montjuich* car of José Juncadella partnered by David Hobbs and Herbert Müller's ex-Steve McQueen and Solar Productions film car brought up to 512M specification, which he shared with René Herzog. There was a high rate of attrition amongst the 917s and the first three places went to de Adamich/Pescarolo with one of the much improved Alfa Romeo 33/3s, Ickx/

Regazzoni with the Ferrari 312PB and the first of the 917s driven by Siffert/Bell. Müller/Herzog and Hobbs/Juncadella took fourth and fifth places.

At the Le Mans Practice Weekend held on 17–18 April a three-hour race was held on the Sunday. The field included the *Escuderia Montjuich* 512M driven by Juncadella/David Hobbs and the *Gelo Racing* car handled as usual by Loos/Pesch. Juncadella was left on the line at the start because of a flat battery, while the *Gelo* car was leading on the last lap when it ran out of fuel. The race had a very weak entry and the winner was the Porsche 908/02 of Ballot-Lena/Chasseuil.

The entry of 5-litre Ferraris in the Monza 1,000Km race on 24 April was strong in numbers if not quality. *Scuderia Filipinetti* sent a 512S for Parkes/Bonnier and Manfredini's own 512M, which he shared with Gagliardi. Juncadella/Merzario drove the *Escuderia Montjuich* 512M and *Herbert Müller Racing* entered three 512S cars, but certain of the drivers were hopelessly inexperienced and only nominated because they were helping to underwrite the cost of the entries. Under pressure from the organisers one car was scratched and Müller/Herzog and Moretti/Zeccoli drove the other two. Merzario with the *Montjuich* car was eliminated in a multi-car accident triggered off by Meier with a Porsche 907 who had pulled across the front of the Ferrari at the *Ascari* curve. The highest placed Ferrari finishers were Müller/Herzog in sixth place.

The Interserie Championship had been inaugurated in 1970 and was intended as a European version of Can-Am racing and was open to Group Four Competition Sports Cars, Group Six Prototypes and Group Seven two-seater racing cars without any engine capacity limit for the last of these categories. The first Interserie race in 1971 was the Shell Cup at Imola on 2 May and here Ferrari entered a very special, lightweight version of the 512M rumoured to be powered by a 7-litre engine as a try-out for the Can-Am series. Mauro Forghieri cannot remember whether this was the case, but there seems little doubt that the engine was the 6.7-litre unit installed in the car that Andretti drove in the United States later in the year. The Imola race was run in two 30-lap heats and Merzario with the works 512M won them both. Juncadella and Loos with 512Ms finished fifth and seventh.

At the Spa 1,000Km race on 9 May, *Scuderia Filipinetti* entered Manfredini's 512M for him and Gagliardi, while *Herbert Müller Racing* fielded a 512M for Müller/Herzog and a 512S for Wisendanger/Kocher, a very inexperienced pair. Kocher was unable to persuade the 512S to fire up and it never left the start, which was perhaps just as well. The Müller/Herzog 512M blew its engine when in sixth place and the Manfredini/Gagliardi car put a rod through the block. The *Gulf-Porsche* 917s took the first two places.

No 5-litre Ferraris ran in the Targa Florio, but three appeared at the Nürburgring on 30 May. These were the *Herbert Müller Racing* cars of Müller/Herzog (512M) and Wisendanger/Kocher (512S), together with the *Gelo Racing* 512M of Loss/Pesch. Only Loos/Pesch finished, in ninth place. Italian driver 'Pam' (Marsilio Pasotti) drove a 512M in the Interserie race at Zolder in Belgium on 6 June, but finished well down the field in eighth place.

For the 1971 Le Mans race Mike Parkes developed this special version of the 512M for Scuderia Filipinetti. It had a lower and narrower cockpit, the driver sat closer to the centre of the car and it had a much larger rear aerofoil. Early on the Sunday morning Parkes spun it into the barrier at White House and then crawled back to the pits to retire. (LAT)

Le Mans

There was a strong entry of 5-litre Ferraris at the Sarthe circuit for the 24 hours' race held on 12–13 June, but only the Sunoco car was able to present a serious challenge to the Porsche 917s. Penske had been intending to rebuild this Ferrari for Can-Am racing, but he had abandoned the idea and took the place of one of the *NART* entries. Donohue/Hobbs drove it as usual and it was fourth fastest in practice.

Of the two *Filipinetti* cars, the more interesting was a version developed by Mike Parkes and informally designated the 512F. The cockpit was two inches lower than standard (but retained a bulge to clear Parkes' head) and five inches narrower. The driver sat nearer the centre of the car and the windscreen, which was more steeply raked, came from a Porsche 917. A single fuel tank was mounted on the right side and the battery, oil tanks and oil pump on the left balanced this. There was a larger rear aerofoil and lighter aluminium-alloy radiators. Parkes/Pescarolo drove this car and *Filipinetti* also entered Manfredini's 512M in which he was partnered by Gagliardi. *NART* entered a 512M

Above Escuderia Montjuich *entered this 512M at Le Mans in 1971 for José Juncadella/ Nino Vaccarella. They drove well and led the race early on the Sunday morning, but the car retired out on the circuit. Following are a Porsche 911T and a Chevrolet Corvette.* (LAT)

Right *The engine installation of the Sunoco 512M Ferrari. Penske had the 5-litre engines rebuilt by Chevrolet specialist Traco. He also modified the car in many other respects and although there were some rather specialist modifications, it represented what the factory should have produced in the first place. This photograph was taken at Watkins Glen in 1971.* (Pete Lyons)

for Posey/Adamowicz and an old 512S *spyder* for Gregory/Eaton. Other 512Ms were driven by de Fierlandt/de Cadenet (*Écurie Francorchamps*), Loos/Pesch (*Gelo Racing*), Juncadella/Vaccarella (*Escuderia Montjuich*) and Weir/Craft (entered in David Piper's name).

Although all these cars were privately entered, some of them performed remarkably well in the face of the three-car 917 entries from *Gulf-Porsche* and the *International Martini Racing Team*. Others performed abysmally and the two *NART* entries were scruffily turned out, bringing little credit to the factory with which Chinetti was so closely associated. While Vaccarella and Donohue were fourth and fifth in the opening laps, Gregory/Eaton had not left the start and Posey had stopped because of low oil pressure on his 512M. Gregory eventually joined the race after half-an-hour completing only a single lap. Three hours were then lost while the mechanics struggled to sort out a fuel blockage and this Ferrari retired after completing only seven laps.

Later the Posey/Adamowicz 512M, still suffering from low oil pressure, ran out of petrol twice and flattened its battery – but stayed in the race. Both the *Filipinetti* entries had problems. The Parkes/Pescarolo entry developed a worrying engine knock and had stopped for the fan belt-drive to be changed. The Manfredini/Gagliardi 512M lost 2½ hours while the clutch was replaced and rejoined the race in full health, but totally out of contention. Just as darkness was enveloping the circuit, Donohue – then in second place – crawled into the pits to report that the engine had

The 512S and 512M Competition Sports Cars, 1970–71 183

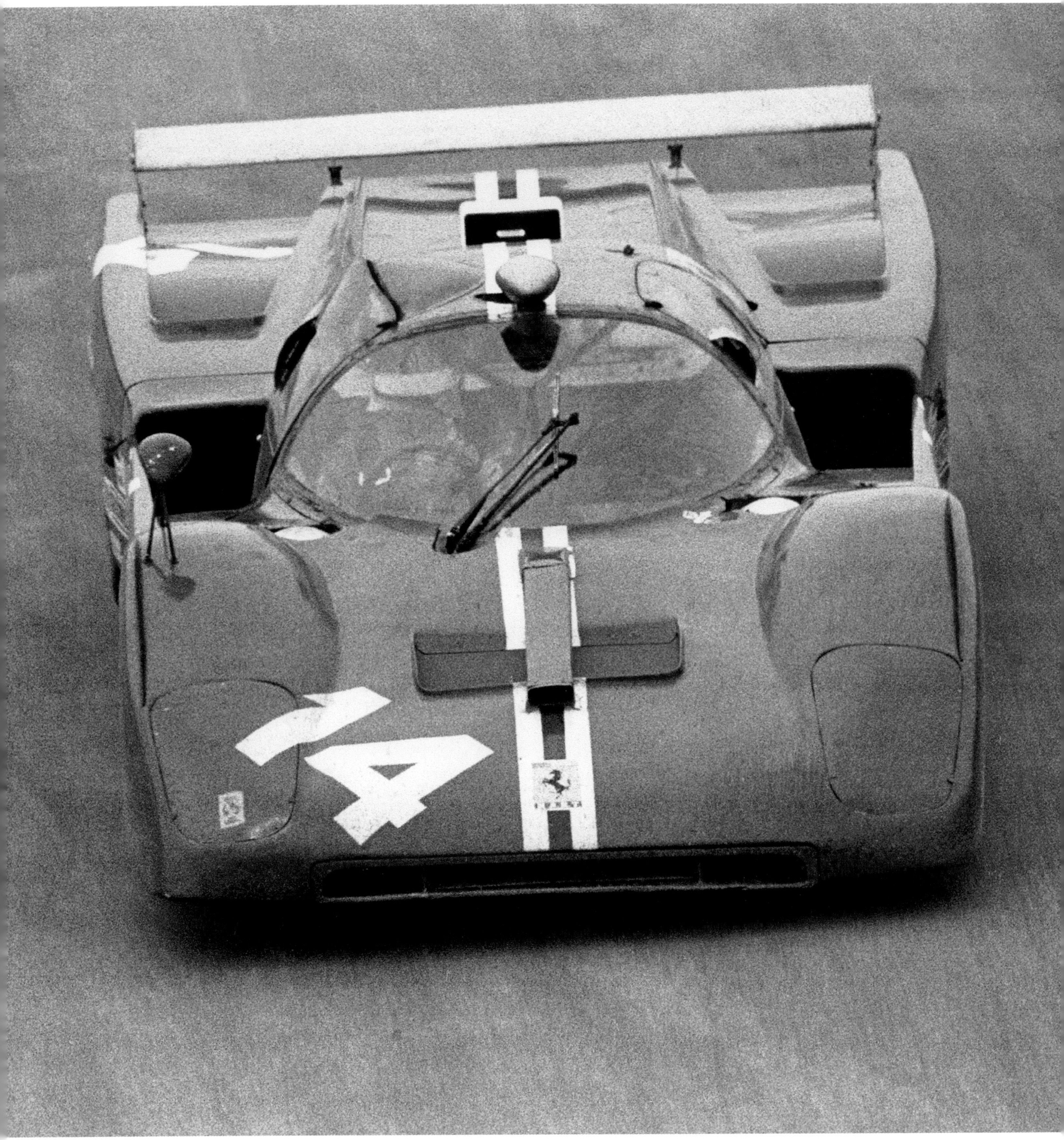
14

tightened up badly. Penske tried to start the car again, but the engine refused to fire and the car was out of the race.

At 1am on the Sunday morning Parkes spun the 512F at *White House*, wrecking the front and rear bodywork and damaging the wheels and suspension. He crawled back to the pits and retirement. When the two leading 917s developed mechanical problems, the Juncadella/Vaccarella 512M took the lead, but then lost time while the clutch was adjusted and soon afterwards expired out on the circuit because of a broken gearbox. The same problem had eliminated Manfredini/Gagliardi a little earlier. Porsche 917s took the first two places ahead of Posey/Adamowicz, whose car had survived against the odds, 257 miles behind the winner, with Weir/Craft fourth. Of the 13 cars to finish, seven were Porsche 911s in the GT category.

Later 1971 Races

The next round in the Championship was the Austrian 1,000Km race on 27 June. Four 512Ms were entered, but the sole finisher was the *Scuderia Brescia Corse* entry driven by 'Pam'/Casoni which took fourth place behind a Porsche 917 and two Alfa Romeo 33/3s. On 4 July René Herzog drove a *Müller* 512M in the Vila Real Grand Prix in Portugal and was leading the race when he spun into a guard-rail because of a deflating rear tyre.

An Interserie race was held at the Norisring the following weekend. In this race the great Pedro Rodriguez drove one of Herbert Müller's 512Ms. He was leading in the first heat; he braked late for a sharp right-hand bend and lost control, the tail of the Ferrari hit the guard-rail, the car rebounded across the track into a wall and back on to the other side of the track. It caught fire immediately and although Rodriguez was rescued after several minutes, he was terribly burned and died later the same day in Nürnberg hospital. The Mexican, who had been closely associated with the works Ferrari team up until the end of 1969, was a great loss to motor racing.

Sam Posey with this NART 512M took sixth place, three laps in arrears, in the Can-Am race at Watkins Glen in 1971. This photograph taken from the starter's bridge shows the Ferrari entering the old Turn One and highlights the powerfully brutal styling of these cars. (Pete Lyons)

Five 512Ms ran at Watkins Glen, the last round in the 1971 Championship held on 24 July. Donohue/Hobbs were again at the wheel of the Sunoco car and Donohue set the pace, leading until lap 53 when he went off the road. The cause was a broken steering tie-rod bolt, attributed to the bumpy corners of the Watkins Glen circuit. An Alfa Romeo Tipo 33/3 driven by Peterson/de Adamich won the race from two *Gulf-Porsche* 917s. Alain de Cadenet/Lothar Motschenbacher with the ex-*Écurie Francorchamps* car now owned by *Écurie Evergreen* took fourth place. This had become another Ferrari with a bulge in the roof, because of Motschenbacher's height. In the Can-Am race the following day Sam Posey finished sixth with a *NART* car. Donohue drove the Sunoco-Ferrari, but it retired in its last race because of a broken piston.

The 512Ms continued to be raced with some success in 1971. On 22 August Müller drove a 512M into fourth place, four laps in arrears, in the Mid-Ohio Can-Am race at Lexington and the following weekend he finished eighth at Elkhart Lake. Three 512Ms ran in the Interserie race at Imola, but the only finisher was the *Scuderia Brescia Corse* car driven into seventh place by Pasotti. Pesch finished sixth with the *Gelo* 512M in the Interserie race at Hockenheim on 3 October. There were no 512Ms in the Barcelona 1,000Km race on the Montjuich Park circuit and all three 512Ms retired in the Paris 1,000Km event at Montlhéry. Herbert Müller entered a 512M in the Kyalami Nine Hours race, but failed to arrive at the circuit.

Sadly, the 5-litre Ferraris had not proved a match for the better-driven Porsche 917s. Any real prospects of them being competitive in 1971 were destroyed when Ferrari opted to concentrate on the 3-litre Prototype. The ban on 5-litre cars in Championship events after 1971 and the complete lack of interest in the cars by the factory resulted in their rapid disappearance from the racing circuits.

There is an amusing sequel to the 512M story. In 1972 a young Los Angeles interior decorator bought the much-modified, ex-*Scuderia Filipinetti* 512F that had been developed by Mike Parkes. In the grip of enthusiasm he entered it in the last of the 1972 Can-Am races at Riverside Raceway on 29 October 1972. He wanted Parkes to drive it and so wired him and sent first class air tickets. Parkes flew over and drove the car to tenth place in the face of overwhelming opposition. Delighted by the performance of the car, the young owner took it on the track crowded with spectators and did a couple of fast, if erratic laps. Inevitably, the organisers took a dim view of this breach of the race regulations and disqualified Parkes from the race.

The 312PB 1971–73

The second race appearance of the 312PB was in the 1971 Sebring 12 Hours race. The Ferrari ran well until it developed transmission problems. Here Andretti is seen at the hairpin. (Pete Lyons)

In 1970 the *FIA* had announced new Sports Car Regulations for 1972 which imposed a maximum engine capacity limit of three litres for all except GT cars, whereupon Ferrari implemented the construction of a new 3-litre model designated the 312PB and derived from the 312B Grand Prix car. The intention was to use 1971 as a development year and field a full team of 3-litre cars in 1972 when the opposition would be limited to cars of similar capacity. Ferrari had developed the 312B with flat-12 engine during 1969 and the aim had been that it should make its debut in the Italian Grand Prix in September.

During testing with Chris Amon at the wheel, the engine proved dismally unreliable and in the words of Amon, 'every time I drove that flat-12, the thing flew to pieces ... it was either blowing pistons or breaking its crankshaft.' Immediately prior to Monza the new Ferrari had another crankshaft breakage and the 312B's debut was postponed until 1970. This was the final straw for

186 Scarlet Passion

Chris Amon, who had been struggling with the old V12s all year, and he decided to quit the team.

By 1970 the 312B was a much-improved car, but it suffered teething troubles early in the season. Later in the year Ickx was second in the German Grand Prix at Hockenheim and won the Canadian, United States and Mexican races, while Regazzoni was the winner at Monza. In the Drivers' World Championship Ickx and Regazzoni took second and third places behind the posthumous Champion, Jochen Rindt, who had crashed at Monza with fatal results in practice for the Italian Grand Prix.

The 312PB in detail

The 312PB was powered by a horizontally opposed 12-cylinder engine of 2,991cc, with the revised cylinder dimensions of the Formula 1 car adopted for 1971 (78.5 x 51.5mm). The flat-12 design featured twin overhead camshafts per bank of cylinders running on needle rollers, four valves per cylinder and the inlet ports situated between the camshafts and with the exhaust ports beneath them. There were twin plugs per cylinder and Lucas fuel injection. Power output was 440bhp at 10,800rpm (compared with 470bhp at 12,600rpm for the 1971 version of the 312B Grand Prix car).

The five-speed gearbox was at the rear of the car in accordance with the team's Formula 1 practice and had a short gear-change, which moved in a small gate situated on the right-hand side of the driving-seat (right-hand drive was fitted). The reverse gear was forward on the left, with a catch operated by a separate lever to prevent accidental engagement. First gear was to the left and down and the remaining four gears were in the usual H-pattern.

Chassis design followed conventional Ferrari practice and there was a multi-tubular space-frame to which aluminium-alloy sheets were riveted to provide stiffening. Behind the cockpit there was a tubular structure over the engine. At the front Ferrari used the usual arrangement of outboard double wishbones and combined coil spring/damper units. The cast-alloy hub carriers extended towards the rear to form the steering arms. The rear suspension was by lower wishbones, single upper transverse links, twin radius rods each side and coil spring/damper units. At the front the cast-alloy hub carriers extended backwards to form the steering arms and also carried the disc brake calipers. At the rear the hub carriers incorporated the brake calipers.

There were wide sponsons each side of the cockpit, the one on the left containing a 120-litre fuel tank (the maximum capacity permitted by the regulations). This counterbalanced the weight of the driver and the sponson on the right was empty. The large fuel filler was positioned at the front of the right-hand sponson and from this a pipe ran down and across the cockpit floor to the fuel tank. Twin water radiators were mounted each side at the rear of the sponsons.

The oil tank was behind the left-hand radiator and the oil cooler was mounted on top of the clutch housing. The wedge-shaped body was constructed in glass-fibre in two sections; the front section consisted of the nose, cockpit sides and doors and was hinged on pivots by the lower front wishbone mountings; the rear section formed the tail and was hinged behind the cockpit by the roll-over bar. Both body sections were painted the usual Ferrari red, but the sponsons were left unpainted. One of the remarkable features of the car was its very compact size.

Night pit stop for the Ferrari 312PB in the 1971 Sebring 12 Hours race. Ickx is at the wheel. (Pete Lyons)

1971

Buenos Aires 1,000Km

Ferrari sent two 312PBs (chassis numbers 0880 and 0882) to the Buenos Aires Autodrome on 10 January, but only the one car, 0882, driven by Ignazio Giunti/Arturo Merzario was raced. It was a familiar venue, but a different circuit from that used for the last World Sports Car Championship race held in 1961. In practice the Ferrari drivers were second fastest to the *Gulf-Porsche* 917 of Rodriguez/Oliver. Giunti led initially, both Siffert and Rodriguez passed him with their Porsche 917s, but when the blue and orange 917s stopped for the first time to refuel, Giunti went ahead again. On lap 37 of this race Jean-Pierre Beltoise (Matra MS660) ran out of fuel a few hundred yards short of the pits and started to push his car, keeping to the left side of the track. Beltoise then began to push the Matra across the track to the entrance to the pits.

The marshals should have stopped Beltoise, but they did nothing. The other drivers had lapped the Matra several times and so had a pretty good idea where he was on the circuit. Giunti, who was driving in the slipstream of Parkes's *Scuderia Filipinetti* 512M, pulled out to lap him and collided with the Matra, which was straddled across the road, directly in his path. The Italian could not avoid the Matra; he hit it almost flat-out, the impact catapulting the 312PB some two hundred yards down the road and it burst into flames. The marshals seemed incapable of acting; Merzario sprinted from the pits and dragged Giunti from the car. Giunti was terribly burned, he had suffered serious head injuries and was dead on arrival at hospital.

In the ensuing chaos the official timekeeping and lap-keeping went awry. The cars filed past the wreck in single file and eventually the organisers tried to stop the race by waving the red flag. Some drivers ignored the flag and drove past it, so the flag was withdrawn and the race continued. Beltoise's racing licence was suspended and in the Argentine he was charged with manslaughter. Although he left the country on bail, the charge was never pursued. It was a terrible blow for Ferrari and Italy, made all the sadder because Giunti was engaged to be married a few weeks after the race. Siffert/Bell and Rodriguez/Oliver took the first two places with their *Gulf-Porsche* 917s.

Sebring 12 Hours

The 1971 Daytona race was held on 30–31 January, but Ferrari did not send a car and the other serious 3-litre Prototype entrants, *Autodelta* and Matra both gave the race a miss. Rodriguez/Oliver won with their Porsche 917 from the *NART*-entered 512S of Bucknum/Adamowicz. The Ferrari team reappeared with 0880 at Sebring on 20 March and this car was raced for most of the year. Ickx/Andretti were the drivers and were second fastest in practice. In the early stages of the race Andretti held fifth place, but as the 312PB covered more laps between refuelling stops (30 to the 26 of the *Gulf-Porsche* 917s and 20 of the Sunoco-Ferrari), it built up a lead of three minutes by the third hour, but retired because the Formula 1 gearbox could not take the strain. Elford/Larrousse (*Martini* 917) won from Stommelen/Galli and Vaccarella/de Adamich/Pescarolo (Alfa Romeo Tipo 33/3s).

BOAC 1,000Km

At Brands Hatch on 4 April Ickx/Regazzoni drove the 312PB, running in lighter form without headlamps and other lighting components. Fastest in practice, Ickx led away from Pedro Rodriguez (*Gulf-Porsche* 917). Conditions were poor with light rain at the start and Ickx ran on wet-weather tyres. On lap five he was about to lap McGovern's slow Dulon Prototype when the driver lost control at Westfield Bend. Ickx swerved to avoid the British car, spun onto the grass, wrecked the nose against the guard-rail and punctured a rear tyre. He made his way slowly back to the pits where a new nose-section was fitted and the right front wheel was changed, but he was eight laps down by the time he rejoined the race.

Ickx and Regazzoni spent the rest of the race driving their hardest to make up lost ground. While the Swiss driver was at the wheel, his visor blew off his helmet but he carried on, tucked down into the cockpit as much as possible. At the 100-lap mark the Ferrari was in fifth place, Regazzoni stopped on lap 114, handed over to Ickx and then went to the medical centre for attention to his badly cut and bruised face. Ickx lost over four minutes in the pits while the mechanics worked on a jammed starter solenoid. Still the Ferrari drivers fought on, the *Gulf-Porsche* 917s had run into problems and Alfa Romeos held the first two places.

The leading Alfa Romeo of Stommelen/Hezemans retired in a cloud of white smoke, so de Adamich/Pescarolo led with their Tipo 33/3 and the Ferrari was now up into second place. Regazzoni, trying too hard, spun at *Druids* and collided with Siffert's 917. At the chequered flag the winners were de Adamich/Pescarolo, with Ickx/Regazzoni second, still three laps in arrears, and Siffert/Bell third. The Ferrari was not only very quick, but it seemed unburstable and, apparently, destined to win a race very soon.

Monza 1,000Km

Ickx/Regazzoni drove the 312PB at the Monza race – held on the road circuit only – on 25 April and now with two small fins on the trailing edge of the rear decking. Both days' practice were held in heavy rain, but despite this many of the drivers were trying very hard and Ickx/Regazzoni were second fastest. Race day was fine and initially Ickx held fifth place. On lap 12 Meier's Porsche 910 took Merzario's line at Lesmo and Ickx was unable to avoid the spinning 512M. The 312PB was too badly damaged to continue. Rodriguez/Oliver and Siffert/Bell took the first two places with their *Gulf-Porsche* 917s.

Spa 1,000Km and the Targa Florio

There were only 28 starters at Spa-Francorchamps on 9 May, but it was a quality entry that included two *Gulf-Porsche* 917s, two *Martini* 917s, several 512M Ferraris, a brace of Alfa Romeo 33/3s – and Ickx/Regazzoni with the 312B. On this fast circuit the flat-12 Ferrari was outpaced by the 917s, but Ickx/Regazzoni were fifth fastest, 4.9sec quicker than the first of the Alfa Romeos. In the race the 312PB lapped steadily and was in third place and all set to win the Prototype category when the Dulon caused its downfall again.

On lap 55 of this 71-lap race Ridelagh with the Porsche-engined Dulon pulled across the front of the Ferrari just before *Stavelot*, Regazzoni ran up the back

At the start of the 1971 BOAC 1,000Km race at Brands Hatch, Jacky Ickx with the 312PB leads away and almost alongside is the Alfa Romeo Tipo 33/3 of Rolf Stommelen/Toine Hezemans. The Alfa Romeo retired while leading the race and Ickx, partnered by Regazzoni, finished second behind the other Tipo 33/3 driven by de Adamich/Pescarolo. (Guy Griffiths)

The 312PB, 1971–73 189

of the British car and both skittered along the road for about 300yds before crumpling themselves against the guard-rail. Rodriguez/Oliver and Siffert/Bell with the *Gulf-Porsche* 917s took the first two places ahead of Pescarolo/de Adamich (Alfa Romeo 33/3). Although a shattered wreck out on the circuit, the 312PB was classified eighth.

Legislation in Italy had now banned all races and hill climbs on public roads, with the saving clause that events that had been held for more than 30 years were excluded. So the Targa Florio took place on 16 May, though its days were numbered, and without Ferrari who had decided to miss the race. The race was a battle between three Porsche 908/03s and three of *Autodelta*'s much-improved Alfa Romeo Tipo 33/3s. Two of the 908/03s were eliminated on the first lap by accidents – as was one of the Alfa Romeos – and the third 908/03 retired because of collapsed suspension. Vaccarella/Hezemans and de Adamich/van Lennep took the first two places for Alfa Romeo ahead of the 1.8-litre Lola of Bonnier/Attwood.

Nürburgring 1,000Km

Many changes had been made to the Nürburgring following the refusal of members of the Grand Prix Drivers' Association to compete there in 1970 and then the transfer of the German Grand Prix to Hockenheim. The organisers had removed thousands of trees, miles of crash-barriers had been installed and the 'yumps' had been levelled off. Porsche ran four of their 908/03s, two in the name of *Gulf-Porsche* and two in the name of *International Martini Racing Team*, while *Autodelta* entered three Tipo 33/3s and Jacky Ickx/Clay Regazzoni drove the rebuilt 312PB. There was no comparison between lap times on the circuit in old form and 1971, but Ickx/Regazzoni were fastest in 7min 36.1sec, heading Stommelen/Nanni Galli (33/3) and the Porsche 908/03 drivers.

The Ferrari was conspicuously quicker than the other 3-litre Prototypes, Ickx leading away from the start, and by the end of the fourth lap he had pulled out a lead of 27.1sec and on his next lap he set fastest lap of the race and a new circuit record in 7min 40.8sec at 110.86mph (178.37kph). Ickx pulled into the pits at the end of the next lap because the 312PB was overheating merrily, there was clearly a leak, but the mechanics could not trace it, so the water was topped up, more fuel added and Ickx screamed back into the race, now in fourth place.

By lap 12 Ickx was back in the lead and at the end of lap 13 had extended this to 25.5sec. Ickx stopped at the end of lap 15, Regazzoni took over with a lead reduced by the pit stop to 18.5sec, but the engine started to overheat again and the Ferrari was laying a plume of blue smoke, so he pulled into the pits at the end of lap 21. Water was poured in, but it ran straight out of the exhaust pipes and the Ferrari was out of the race. The cause was the failure of a cylinder sealing ring. Larrousse/Elford, Rodriguez/Siffert and Marko/van Lennep took the first three places with Porsche 908/03s and then came two Alfa Romeo 33/3s.

After Le Mans

Neither Ferrari nor *Autodelta* entered the 24 Hours race on 12–13 June. The 312PB reappeared at the Austrian 1,000Km race on 27 June and Ickx/Regazzoni were second fastest in practice. Slight rain was falling at the start of the race and initially Ickx held second place. When Rodriguez made a long pit stop with his *Gulf* 917 on lap 30, Ickx took the lead; Regazzoni dropped behind the 917 of Marko/Larrousse following the Ferrari's first pit stop, then heavy rain began to fall and once he was back at the wheel Ickx went ahead and extended the Ferrari's lead.

On lap 132 of this 170-lap race Regazzoni resumed at the wheel of the Ferrari, still firmly in the lead, and the Maranello entry seemed all set to win its first race. Only 22 laps from the finish Regazzoni lost control under braking and slammed the Ferrari into a guard-rail and out of the race. It seems likely that something in the front suspension had broken. Rodriguez/Attwood (*Gulf-Porsche* 917) won the race from Hezemans/Vaccarella and Stommelen/Galli with Alfa Romeo 33/3s.

So the sole 312PB had to be rebuilt yet again for the last round in the Championship series, the Watkins Glen Six Hours race held on 24 July where extensive work was in progress to upgrade the circuit. It had been widened to a uniform 36 feet throughout, most of it had been resurfaced, the former Fast Bend was replaced by a chicane and the final corner was much tighter and banked. The circuit length had been increased slightly from 2.35 miles (3.78km) to 2.428 miles (3.907km), but by the United States Grand Prix in October, on completion of the works, the length was 3.377 miles (5.434km).

Ickx shared the 312PB with Andretti and in practice they were third fastest and timed on the straight at 165mph (265kph). Donohue/Hobbs (Sunoco-Ferrari) were fastest and timed at 185mph (298kph). There were two paced laps and then the race started. Ickx held second place, moving into the lead briefly while the Sunoco-Ferrari was refuelled and then became the leader when the 5-litre car went off the road. On lap 56 Ickx brought the 312P in to refuel, but the engine refused to fire up; the starting motor had jammed at the beginning of the race and burnt out. The Ferrari mechanics worked on the car for 14 minutes, but it was a waste of effort and it was pushed into retirement. Ronnie Peterson/de Adamich (Alfa Romeo Tipo 33/3) won the race from the two *Gulf-Porsche* 917s, both of which had mechanical problems.

Jacky Ickx at the wheel of the 312PB he shared with Clay Regazzoni at the Nürburgring in 1971. It was the fastest car in the race, but retired because of engine failure. (LAT)

The 312PB was tested at Imola in September and the team stayed at the circuit for Regazzoni to drive the car in the Interserie race, consisting of two 93.5-mile (150.54km) qualifying heats and a short 31.2-mile (50.2km) final. It was cut short because heavy rain had made the heats last much longer than expected and the organisers feared that, if they ran it to the same distance as the heats, darkness would fall before racing finished. The conditions were quite appalling and in the first heat Alfa Romeo 33/3 driver Klaus Reisch aquaplaned into a wall, the car burst into flames hurling the driver on to the track. He was fatally injured and died shortly after arrival at hospital. Regazzoni lapped the rest of the field and averaged 92.88mph. Brian Redman (Can-Am BRM-Chevrolet) won both the second heat (a lap ahead of the rest of the field) and the final (in which Regazzoni retired on the first lap because of fuel-pump failure). This win was to have important repercussions for both Redman and Ferrari.

Ferrari had built a new 312PB and entered both cars in the Kyalami Nine Hours race on 6 November. The new car had a more compact body, cockpit modifications to comply with the 1972 regulations and low-profile wheels. Jacky Ickx/Mario Andretti drove this car, chassis number 0884, while Clay Regazzoni/Brian Redman had the earlier model. The main opposition

Above Belgian driver Jacky Ickx who was a member of the Ferrari team between 1970 and 1973. He was immensely successful during these years, but achieved even greater success in the last years of his racing career when he drove Porsche works cars in endurance racing.

Above right Another outstanding Ferrari driver of the 1970s was Swiss Clay Regazzoni. His racing career came to an end when a bad crash, with an Ensign Formula 1 car at Long Beach in 1980, left him paralysed from the waist down.

came from two Porsche 917s entered by David Piper. The Ferraris took the first two places, but were not without their problems and only won because the 917s had even more problems.

Regazzoni took the lead at the start, but the engine of Andretti's car cut out and he was badly delayed while he tried to fire it up again. During the second hour Regazzoni collided with the Piper-entered Porsche driven by Adamowicz and spent three minutes in the pits while a new nose-section was fitted and the car refuelled. Regazzoni/Redman were penalised two laps because more than the permitted number of mechanics had worked on the car. Andretti now led, but shortly afterwards his Ferrari coasted to a halt out on the circuit.

The Ferrari mechanics went out to work on the car and by the time it had been fired up, driven to the pits, refuelled, a new battery fitted and Ickx had taken over,

45min had been lost. Regazzoni/Redman went on to win the race at 100.58mph (161.83kph) and Ickx/Andretti fought their way back to finish second, all of 15 laps in arrears. Howden Ganley/Paddy Driver/Mike Hailwood were third with a 1.8-litre Chevron B19-Cosworth FVC and Adamowicz/Casoni (917), who had been holding second place until a flat battery caused an engine misfire, took fourth place.

1972

For 1972 there was a new championship, known as the World Championship for Makes, for what were now known as Group Five sports cars up to 3,000cc and Group Four Special Touring Cars of unlimited capacity. The events were the same 11 as in 1971, but (with the exception of Sebring and Le Mans) no event should last more than about six hours, so the Daytona race was shortened accordingly – for which everyone was thankful as it was the most tedious of the year's races.

With what amounted to a full season of testing behind it, the 312PB's prospects of success were strong and Ferrari dominated almost the whole of the year's racing. Ferrari built six cars to the specification of the revised model seen at Kyalami. Peter Schetty was now team manager and the team drivers were Ferrari's Formula 1 regulars, Jacky Ickx, Clay Regazzoni and Mario Andretti, together with Brian Redman, Ronnie Peterson and Tim Schenken. Ferrari brought other drivers into the team during the year. Former Gulf chief mechanic Ermanno Cuoghi joined Ferrari as joint chief mechanic.

For identification purposes the cars had blue, green, white and yellow stripes on the bonnet, tail-fins, rear

Pedro Rodriguez entered this Dino 206S for himself and Jean Guichet at Sebring in 1967. This car, seen here in the Webster Turns, retired because of overheating. (Claire Lyons McHenry)

A group of cars stream down from the Dunlop Bridge towards Tertre Rouge in the Le Mans 1967 24 Hours race. No 30 is the Matra-BRM of Jaussaud/Pescarolo which is being lapped by the Ferrari 330P4 of Günther Klass/Peter Sutcliffe. Immediately behind is the Scuderia Filipinetti-entered 330P3/4 of Jean Guichet/Herbert Müller and the Ford GT40-based Mirage of David Piper/Dick Thompson.

Another view of the 1967 Le Mans race taken from the same point on the circuit. Irwin/de Klerk with their Lola T70 Mark 3-Aston Martin lead the Ferrari 330P3/4 of Guichet and Müller. Both the Lolas retired early in the race and this 330P3/4 was eliminated by an oil leak.

Dan Gurney and A J Foyt drove this 7-litre Ford Mk IV entered by Shelby American to win the Le Mans race at 135.482 mph (127.991mph). It was one of only two Fords to finish.

Chris Amon at the wheel of one of the Tipo 350 4.2-litre spyders based on rebuilt 330P4s at Las Vegas in the 1967 Can-Am series. He qualified 13th, but finished a satisfactory fifth with a car that was substantially down on power compared to its American-engined rivals. (Pete Lyons)

Ferrari returned to Can-Am racing in 1968 with the 6.2-litre Tipo 612 Can-Am. Chris Amon is seen during qualifying at Las Vegas where he crashed at the first corner of the first lap of the race. Note the adjustable aerofoil and the air brake across the front of the car's nose. (Pete Lyons)

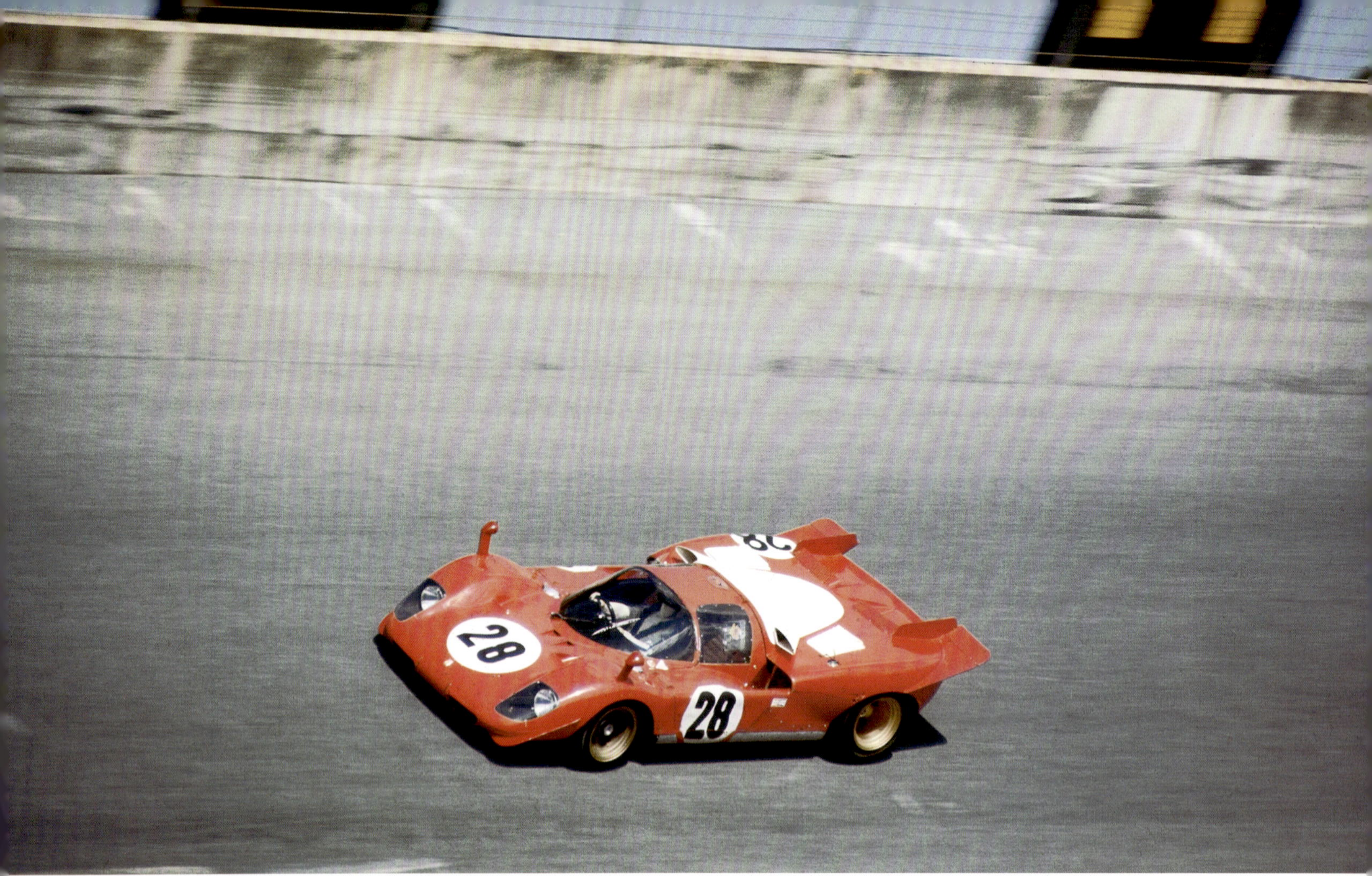
28
28

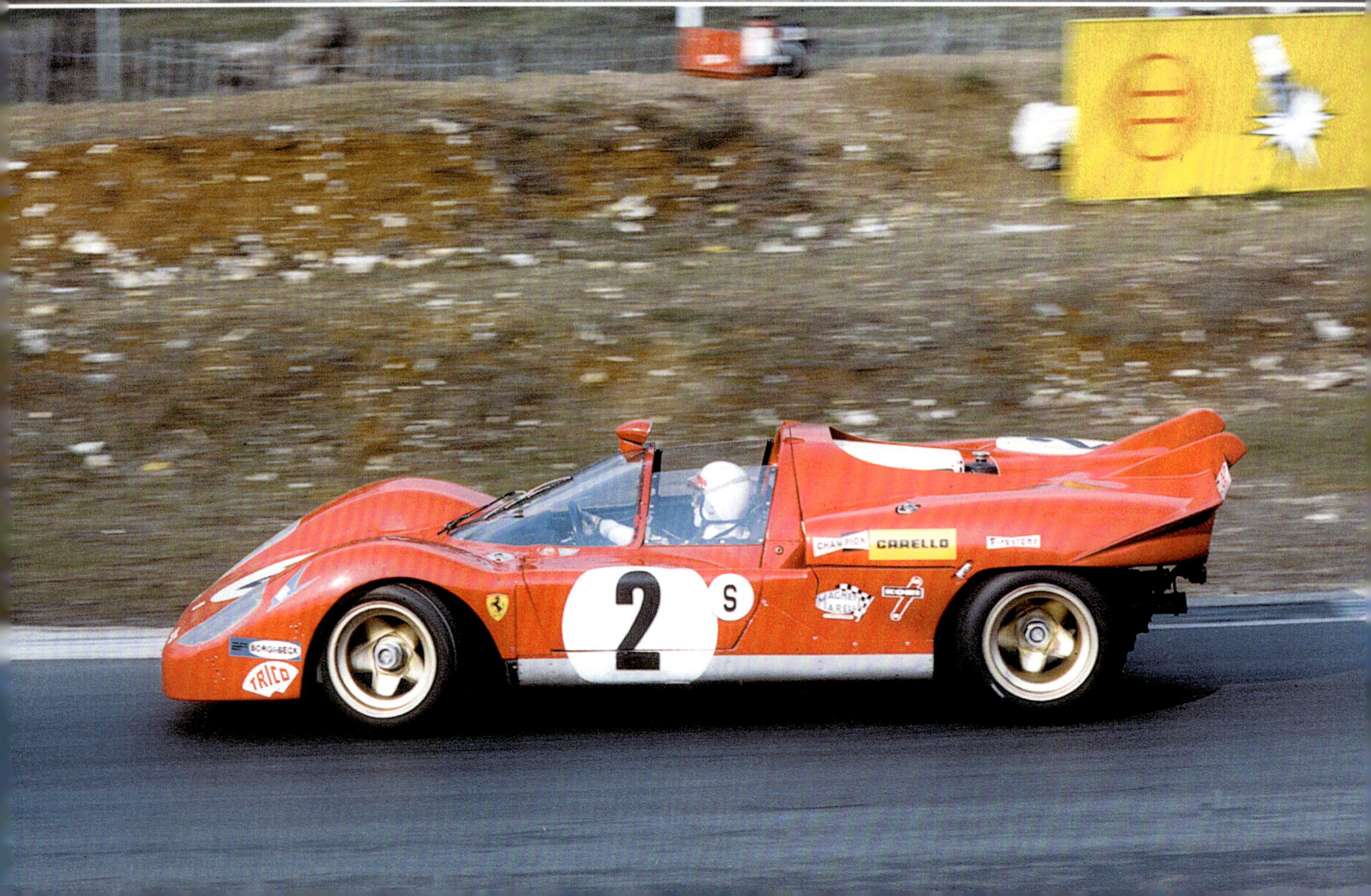
2
S
CHAMPION
CARELLO
TRICO

Above left *On the banking in the 1970 Daytona 24 Hours' race is the works Tipo 512S Ferrari shared by Mario Andretti, Jacky Ickx and Arturo Merzario. They finished third behind the two Gulf-Porsche 917s.*

Left *Throughout 1970 the works 512S cars were no match for the Porsche 917 opposition. In the BOAC 1,000Km race at Brands Hatch in April, Chris Amon/ Arturo Merzario drove this car to a poor fifth place. They were the highest-placed Ferrari finishers. (Guy Griffiths)*

Above *Baron Hughes de Fierlandt/Alistair Walker shared this works-prepared Écurie Francorchamps 512S with long-tail body at Le Mans in 1970. They drove a good race to finish fifth. (Guy Griffiths)*

Right *Tony Adamowicz/Chuck Parsons appeared with this old 1969 312P entered by NART at Le Mans in 1970. They had a far from trouble-free race and although they finished, they were too far behind to be classified. (Guy Griffiths)*

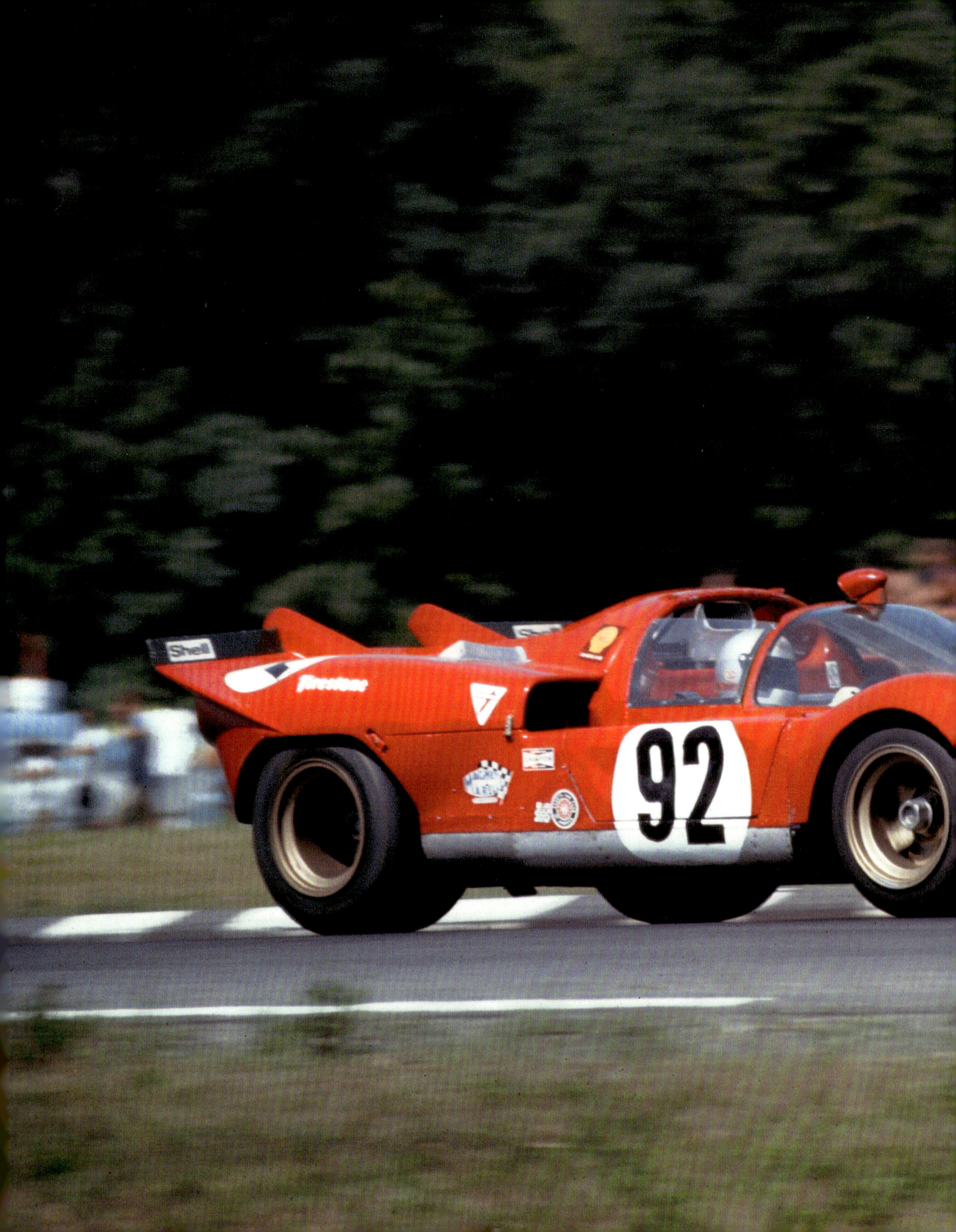
Shell
Firestone
92

Ignazio Giunti at the wheel of the 512S he shared with Mario Andretti in the Watkins Glen Six Hours race in 1970. Although they could not match the speed of the Gulf-Porsche 917s and were delayed by vapour locks in the fuel-feed system, they did well to finish third. (Pete Lyons)

Above *At Daytona in 1971 the Sunoco-Ferrari driven by Mark Donohue powers past the re-bodied Ferrari 312P entered by NART for Luigi Chinetti Jnr and Garcia Veiga. The NART entry finished fifth and won the Prototype category. (Pete Lyons)*

Right *To quote the photographer, 'Warrior at dawn – daylight reveals the scars of the Penske 512M's night-time misadventures.' In the 1971 Daytona race a Porsche 911 had collided with the Sunoco-Ferrari just before midnight and when the 512M rejoined the race it was 53 laps in arrears. Donohue/Hobbs eventually finished third, 14 laps behind the winning Gulf-Porsche. (Pete Lyons)*

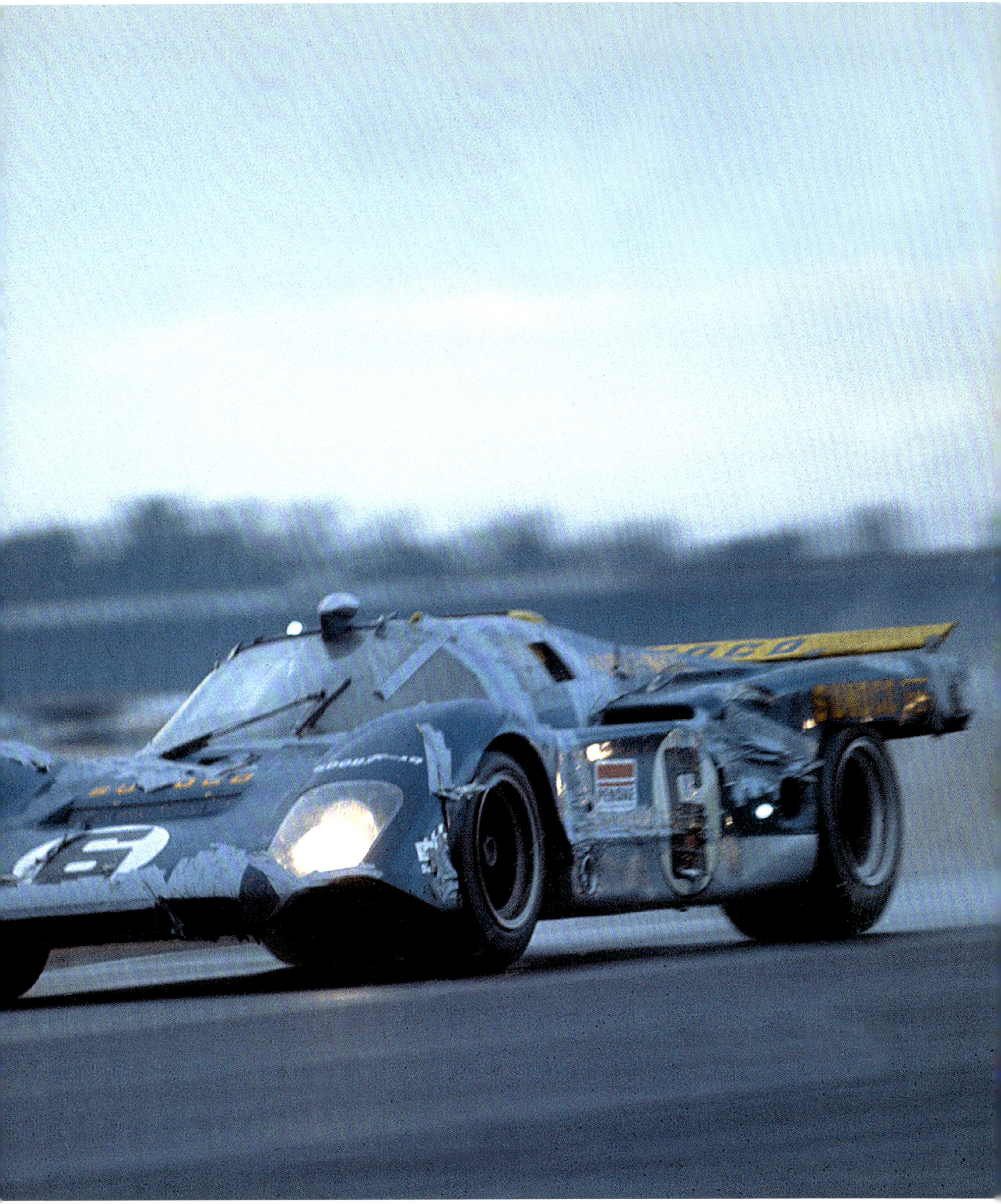

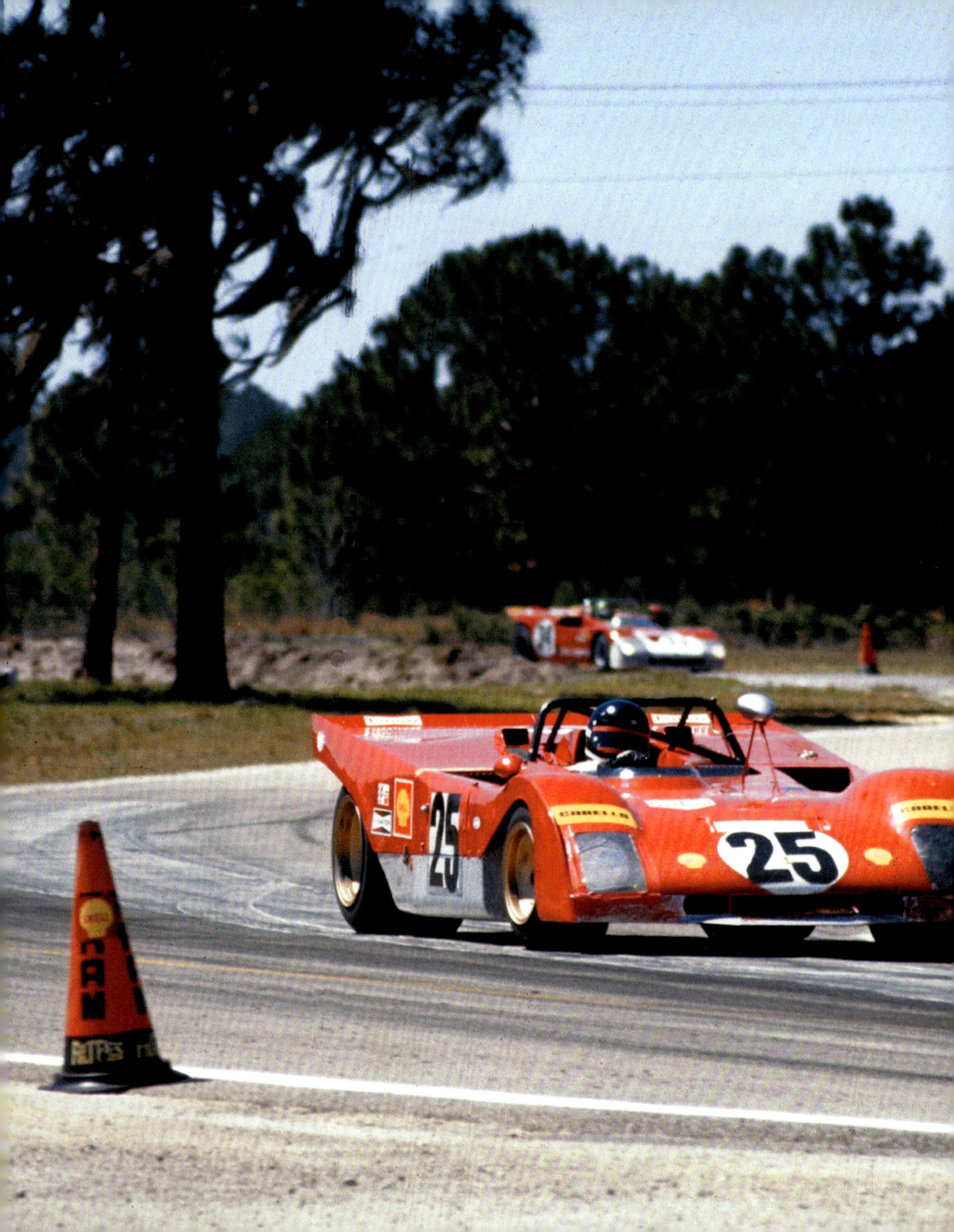
25
25

Jacky Ickx speeds through the Esses (proper name the Green Park Chicane) at Sebring in 1971. The 312PB ran well, but retired because of transmission problems. (Pete Lyons)

Above *Jacky Ickx and Clay Regazzoni drove this 312PB in the 1971 BOAC 1,000Km race at Brands Hatch. The Ferrari was delayed by a collision with another car, but the pair drove a good race to finish second behind an Alfa Romeo Tipo 33/3. (Guy Griffiths)*

Right *Mario Andretti at the wheel of the 6.9-litre Tipo 712 Can-Am Ferrari with distinctive wedge-shaped body in the 1971 Watkins Glen race. Andretti described it as, 'One of the worst cars I ever drove.' Andretti finished fourth behind Revson and Hulme with 8-litre McLaren-Chevrolets and Siffert at the wheel of a 5-litre Porsche 917 Spyder. (Pete Lyons)*

204

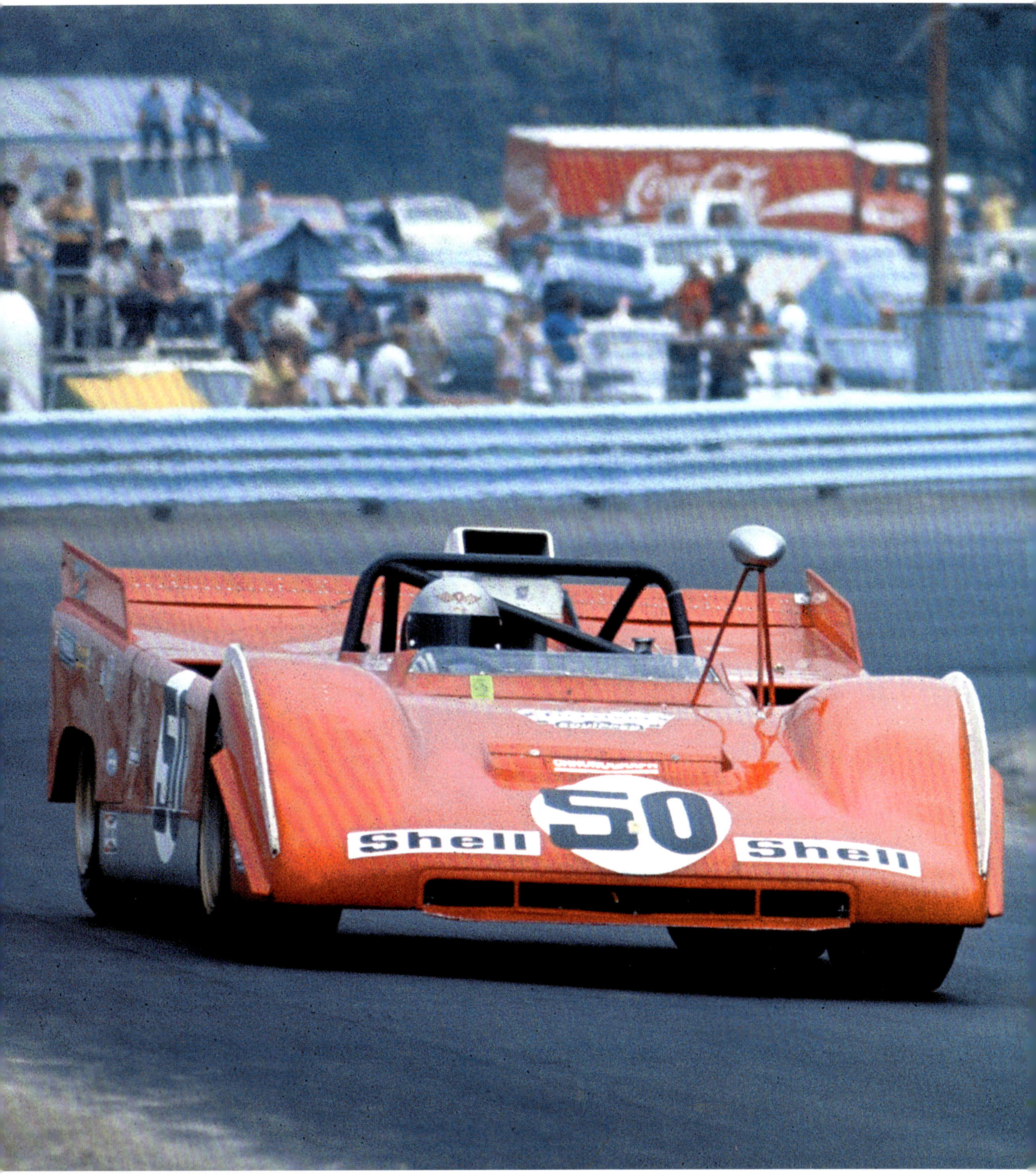
Shell
50
Shell

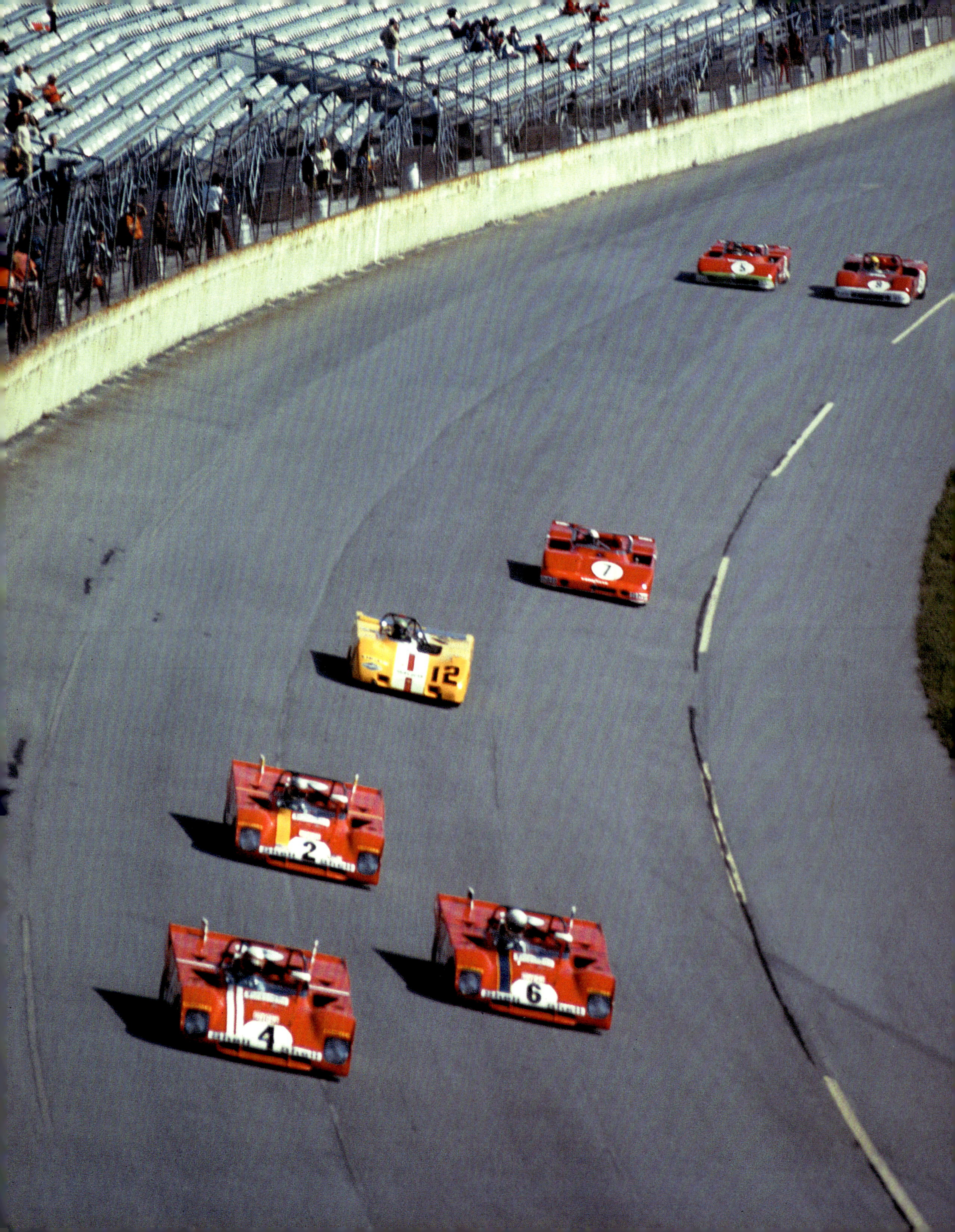

Left *In front of a very sparse audience at Daytona in 1972 the three works 312PBs stream by in the order Regazzoni, Peterson and Andretti. Behind them comes the Lola T280 of Bonnier/Wisell and the Alfa Romeo 33TT3 of Stommelen/Revson. Although it is the start of the race, the other two works Alfa Romeos are already beginning to drop back. (Pete Lyons)*

Above *In the 1972 Daytona race Jacky Ickx crosses the start/finish line with the winning 312PB which he shared with Mario Andretti. (Pete Lyons)*

Above *The 312PB of Ickx/Andretti at Sebring in 1972. Andretti is hurtling through the U-bend just before the pits. They moved back into the lead after the Regazzoni/Redman car caught fire and won from team-mates Peterson/ Schenken. (Pete Lyons)*

spoiler, air-intake cowl and rear-view mirror. The team entered three cars in every race except the Targa Florio. As raced in 1972, the 312PBs had increased power output of 460bhp at 10,800rpm and to comply with the 1972 regulations the cars were a little wider and about 40lb (18kg) heavier.

The real problem throughout the years of the 3-litre Championship was an inadequate number of competitive cars. *Autodelta*, the Alfa Romeo works team, was still racing a development of the Tipo 33/3 V8 car that had first appeared at Sebring in 1969. During 1971 they had won three rounds in the Championship when the Porsche opposition failed. A 33/3 was included in the *Autodelta* entry at the first two races, but otherwise the team relied on the newer Tipo 33TT3. *Autodelta* had developed a flat-12 3-litre engine, but this was not ready to race in 1972 and throughout the year the V8 engine was used.

As for the rest of the opposition, it amounted to very little. Porsche had now withdrawn from racing, although 908/03s were seen in the hands of private owners. Matra had introduced its own V12 engine in 1968 and used this in both Grand Prix and sports cars. The 1972 Prototype was known as the MS670, but Matra decided to restrict their sports programme to a four-car entry at Le Mans. Matra won Le Mans, but it could have been a different story if Ferrari had run. The *SEFAC* entered the race, ran cars at the Practice Weekend, one of which had a very long tail and four tail-fins bridged by two adjustable spoilers, but withdrew shortly before claiming that 'the 312PB's engine was not designed to run for such long periods of time.'

Joakim Bonnier's *Écurie Bonnier* ran two Lola T280 cars powered by the latest Cosworth DFV Grand Prix engines, but the team was short of finance, leading to inadequate preparation of the cars and unreliability. Bonnier was killed when he crashed one of these cars at Le Mans and although the team took delivery of the first of the improved 1973 T282 cars late in the year, efforts following Bonnier's death were half-hearted. John Wyer's *Gulf* team built the Cosworth-powered Mirage M6 designed by Len Bailey, but development was slow and the team failed to achieve any success during the year.

Buenos Aires 1,000Km, 9 January

Following the death of Giunti in the 1971 race, the organisers made changes to the circuit, which had been widened in places, and there were chicanes on the main straight, on the back part of the circuit and before the cars reached the pits. Very great care was taken over fire precautions and signalling lights had replaced marshals' flags.

The 312PBs had cut-off fuel fillers to take petrol under gravity from 10ft-refuelling towers, the maximum height permitted under the regulations, but the organisers appeared ignorant of these and banned this set-up. Under pressure from the *CSI* representative, the organisers relented and *Autodelta* hastily adopted the same arrangement. *Autodelta* entered three 33TT3 cars and a 33/3. Two of the Ferraris had older-type gearboxes with one-piece casings, but the Regazzoni/Redman car (0084) had a new gearbox with a split casing that facilitated changes of ratios. Ickx/Andretti had a new car to replace that destroyed a year ago, but still carrying the chassis number 0882. Because of an error made at the factory, two Ferraris had wrong gearbox ratios and these had to be changed.

Ickx/Andretti led initially, but Andretti pitted twice because the engine was cutting out, the problem was traced to a battery isolator switch and this was changed. They climbed back through the field to fifth, but when Ickx stopped to refuel and hand over to Andretti, inspection revealed that the starter motor bracket had sheared off and cut through the cable. Ten laps were lost before the car rejoined the race and Ickx/Andretti took tenth place. Regazzoni/Redman had moved well into the lead, but a puncture dropped them behind Peterson/Schenken (0886) who won at 108.05mph (173.85kph). The highest placed Alfa Romeo was the works 33/3 loaned to Alberti who shared it with Facetti/de Adamich and they finished third.

Daytona Continental Six Hours, 6 February

After the race at Buenos Aires, the 312PBs raced there were flown back to the factory and prepared for Sebring, while three new cars were flown out for this race. Ickx/Andretti were fastest in practice in 1min 44.2sec at 131.61mph (211.76kph). Wisell (Lola) led briefly, Ickx/Andretti passed Regazzoni (0890) to lead, fell back behind Stommelen/Revson (Alfa Romeo) during a refuelling stop, went ahead again and at the finish won by two laps. They averaged 124.72mph (200.67kph).

Regazzoni had led in the early stages, but on lap 27 a tyre punctured as he came off the banking, the 312PB spun wildly, and the rear body-section detached itself and was hit by Wisell's Lola. Clay abandoned the car, which was towed to a safer position by a rescue truck, and went back to the pits to discuss the situation with Peter Schetty; he returned to the car and drove it back slowly with a shredded rear tyre. About fifteen minutes after the crash Regazzoni rejoined the race with a new tail-section and right rear wheel. The car climbed back to fifth place, but Redman then spun as he came off the banking and wrecked the 312PB's tail. Another tail was fitted and Regazzoni/Redman finished fourth. Peterson/Schenken (0892) enjoyed a largely troublefree race, leading briefly and the only problem was a punctured front tyre near the end. At the chequered flag they were second, two laps behind Ickx/Andretti.

Sebring 12 Hours, 25 March

The three Ferraris were the Buenos Aires entries, rebuilt at the works and fitted with the new split-casing gearboxes (which enabled the ratios to be changed quickly) and larger rear brake calipers of the same size as those on the front. As was becoming usual, there was no opposition to the Ferraris apart from the Alfa Romeos. *Autodelta* had entered three Tipo 33TT3 cars, but they would never prove competitive in the absence of the flat-12 engine. The new Mirage M6 powered by the Ford-Cosworth engine made its race debut driven by Derek Bell/Gijs van Lennep, but it was lacking development and this Len Bailey-designed car would only show its potential later in the season.

Ickx/Andretti were fastest in practice and after three paced laps (because of spectators on the course)

Above *On the pits straight at Daytona in 1972 the 312PBs of Peterson/Schenken and Regazzoni/Redman stream past the sparsely filled stand. Car No 4 shows the scars from Regazzoni's spin on the banking.* (Pete Lyons)

Above right *The winning 312PB in the pits at the 1972 Sebring race. As the mechanics refuel and top up the water, Andretti exits the left of the car, as Ickx gets back in on the right. Ferrari pit work could be very slick, as on this occasion, but on others it verged on the incompetent.* (Pete Lyons)

Right *In this wonderfully evocative night shot Mario Andretti with his 312PB hurtles through Sebring's U-bend at night. Ickx/Andretti won the 1972 12 Hours race convincingly.* (Pete Lyons)

210 Scarlet Passion

SPARK PLUGS
SHELL
SHELL
Shell
Firestone
2
Shell
Shell

JACKY ICKX
MARIO ANDRETTI
2

Andretti took an immediate lead. Like the other Ferraris, this car developed an engine oil leak and it dropped back to second place during the fourth hour after Ickx came into the pits complaining that 'the car was weaving all over the road.' With new front tyres Ickx lapped at undiminished speed and took the lead again when the Regazzoni/Redman 312PB burnt through a battery lead. The Swiss driver had passed the pits with the tail blazing furiously, he abandoned the car out on the circuit and it was burnt out before the fire fighters arrived.

Lack of oil pressure meant Ickx/Andretti were slowing in the closing laps of the race – as well as avoiding the need for a final refuelling stop – and the team reckoned that if the engine were to be switched off, it would fail to fire up again. They won at an average of 111.51mph (179.42kph). Peterson was lying third in the third hour when he ran out of fuel on the circuit because the pumps were not drawing the last of it from the tanks. He ran to the pits for a can of petrol and back to the car. Schenken soon had the car up to fourth place, but just after four hours' racing he came into the pits because of a burst front brake pipe. Despite fuel mixture problems, which necessitated extra refuelling stops, they finished second. Schenken set fastest lap in 2min 33.80sec, a speed of 121.72mph (195.85kph).

BOAC 1,000Km

There was a very small entry at Brands Hatch on 16 April, mainly because the organisers would not accept GT cars. The entry was further reduced by two cars because of the CSI's rule that required all drivers of each car to qualify at a speed calculated by the time of the fastest qualifier plus 23%. Another two cars failed to start because of mechanical problems and so only 23 runners made the grid.

At this race all three Ferraris had longer tails. Regazzoni/Redman had the same car as at Daytona. Because Regazzoni thought that the engine was down on power, it was changed before the race. Regazzoni/Redman were fastest in practice and Regazzoni led until passed by Ickx. This car had developed a bad oil leak from the differential and during the last hour it started to misfire and throw out clouds of smoke. Regazzoni made two unscheduled pit stops, the second of which lasted 15 minutes during which a new coil was fitted.

Regazzoni joined the race in seventh place, crossed the line sixth and was elevated to fifth – behind two Alfa Romeos – after the disqualification of the fifth place Chevron because it was underweight. Regazzoni, Ickx and Peterson shared fastest lap of 1min 27.4sec at 109.15mph (175.62kph), a new sports car record. Ickx/Andretti enjoyed a troublefree race and after Ickx had passed Redman, they remained in front to win at 105.12mph (169.14kph). Peterson/Schenken had a new car (0894) but it was plagued by oversteer problems in practice and to a lesser extent during the race. Despite running low in fuel towards the end of the race they finished second, a lap behind the winners.

Monza 1,000Km

Both Alfa Romeo and John Wyer's *Mirage* team missed this race held on 25 April, the National holiday celebrating Italy's liberation from the Third Reich in 1944. At the start of practice the drivers were soon back in the pits complaining about their gearboxes – by error these had been assembled with fifth where there should have been fourth, and fourth where there should have been fifth! Under the draconian 123% qualifying rules, what had been a large entry was whittled down to 23. The organisers wanted to allow 40 cars to start, but Peter Schetty made it clear that if they did this, he would withdraw the 312PBs. The reason was quite simply the speed differential between the Ferraris and slower runners. Eventually, there were only 21 starters after two cars went off the road during the familiarisation session on race morning.

Race day dawned to torrential rain which failed to slacken throughout the day. Because of the conditions, a little over half-an-hour before the 11.30am start the drivers were allowed out on to the circuit to familiarise themselves with the terrible conditions. Peterson slid off at the *Parabolica* curve, damaging the nose of his Ferrari and Peter Schetty persuaded the organisers to postpone the start while the nose-section was changed. In the absence of the Alfa Romeos, which were at less of a disadvantage in these conditions and *maybe* could have put up a stiff challenge to the Ferraris, the 312PBs were unopposed. There were only seven finishers.

Ickx led initially throwing up clouds of spray and like all the other drivers of open cars, he was soaking wet, as the electrics of the Ferrari soon became. The Belgian dropped back and at the end of lap 12 stopped at the pits where the mechanics tried to dry out the electrics. During the stop the alternator caught fire, but after the fire had been put out and a new alternator fitted, Regazzoni joined the race eight laps in arrears. He stopped again after a single lap to change his visor, but then this Ferrari started to make its way back up through the field.

On lap 73 Regazzoni snatched the lead from the Porsche 908/03 of Jöst/Schüller, but came into the pits four laps later with a recurrence of the electrical problems. Regazzoni rejoined the race a minute behind the Porsche, but within six laps Regazzoni was in front again and at the end of this 178-lap race this Ferrari led by four laps. Despite a spin by Peterson at the *Curva Del Vialone* and a long pit stop while the 312B was repaired, Peterson/Schenken took third place behind the Jöst/Schüller Porsche 908/03. Redman, co-driving with Merzario, also spun at the *Curva Del Vialone* and hit the barrier so hard that he had to abandon the car.

Spa 1,000Km

Once again there was a very poor entry and *Autodelta* had decided to miss the race, held on 7 May, to concentrate on preparation for the Targa Florio two weeks later. The Grand Prix Drivers' Association had banned Spa-Francorchamps for Formula 1 racing and at Sebring Jackie Stewart had circulated a petition urging sports car drivers not to race there. Fortunately most

Left 'Light as air' – at Clearways in the 1972 BOAC 1000Km race Jacky Ickx lifts the inside front wheel of the winning 312PB he shared with Mario Andretti. It was a year of complete domination for Ferrari. Melaware was a heavily promoted brand of plastic tableware that achieved popularity in the 1970s. (Pete Lyons)

Right The 1972 Spa 1,000Km race: Tim Schenken at the wheel of the 312PB that he regularly shared with Ronnie Peterson in 1972. In the closing stages of the race rain began to fall near the start/finish area, Peterson failed to appreciate that Les Combes *corner was wet and crashed. The other team Ferraris took the first two places. (Pete Lyons)

sports car drivers were unmoved by the caution of the GPDA, but an exception was Joakim Bonnier, president of the GPDA, who declined to enter his Lolas, although one driven by Larrousse/de Fierlandt ran as a private entry.

All three Ferraris had the longer tails to improve their aerodynamic advantage on this very fast circuit. Ickx/Regazzoni were fastest in practice – and fastest in the race – but dropped to second place because of sheer bad luck. Ickx had built up a substantial lead early in the race, and when he stopped to refuel, the left rear tyre was changed; Regazzoni took over, but was back in the pits after only a lap for a loose wheel nut to be tightened. At half-distance Ickx was in the lead again and after the third and final routine pit stop, lasting 66sec because all four wheels were changed, Regazzoni took over and still with an advantage of over a lap.

On his first lap a rear tyre punctured at *La Source* hairpin just before the pits but he only became aware of this after he had passed the pits and reached the top of the hill from *Eau Rouge*. He had to complete nearly a full lap and by the time that he reached the pits, a flying tread had damaged the rear bodywork and the oil tank. After the mechanics had fitted a new tail and repaired the oil tank, Ickx took over and eventually brought this Ferrari across the line in second place. Ickx set a new 3-litre sports car lap record in 3min 20.7sec, a speed of 157.15mph (252.85kph).

Ferrari sent only a single 312PB for Arturo Merzario and rally driver Sandro Munari to the 1972 Targa Florio. They faced a strong team of four Alfa Romeos, but the Ferrari won by a narrow margin. Here Merzario with the 312PB storms through the village of Bivio Polizzi. (Pete Lyons)

Redman/Merzario held second place, but took the lead after the first pit stops; Merzario disliked the circuit and was around 12sec a lap slower than his team-mate. While the Italian was at the wheel Ickx regained the lead, but Redman and Merzario went ahead again when the fastest Ferrari ran into more problems. Late in the race Redman was leading Peterson at *Les Combes* when he noticed that there was movement among the spectators, he second-guessed that they were putting on their coats because it had started to rain, so eased off and scrabbled round the corner. Peterson noticed nothing amiss, entered the corner at undiminished speed and crashed. As heavy rain swept across the circuit, Redman/Merzario won at 145.05mph (233.39kph).

Targa Florio

There were only five 3-litre sports cars entered in the 491.7-mile (791.15km) Sicilian road race held on 21 May, four Alfa Romeos and a Ferrari. There had been anxiety that Ferrari would miss the race, but instead Maranello prepared a single, special car. This was chassis number 0884, the car which had caught fire while leading at Sebring, and it had the right side of the front

The 312PB, 1971–73 215

of the monocoque removed so that a spare wheel could be accommodated. There was the softest possible suspension and large exhausts as fitted to the Formula 1 cars at Monaco. The engine had been tuned to give as smooth a power range as possible from 5,000rpm through to its peak of 11,800rpm. The team brought along 0882 as the *muletto*. The drivers were Merzario and rally exponent Sandro Munari.

Autodelta, who had not raced since Brands Hatch, brought along four 33TT3 cars, plus a spare. However well the Alfa Romeos performed, they were on a hiding to nothing, for if *Autodelta* won the race, everyone would say, 'so they should' and if the single Ferrari won, Alfa Romeo would be humiliated. Because of a firemen's strike, practice was postponed from the Thursday before the race to the Saturday. Two official practice laps were compulsory, but most drivers were allowed no more to save the cars and so flogged round and round the course in touring cars to learn it as best they could.

The pace lap at the 1972 Watkins Glen Six Hours race. On the front row are Peterson (No 86, fastest in practice) and Mario Andretti with their 312PBs. On the left in the second row is Derek Bell with the Mirage M6-Ford and Brian Redman with his Tipo 312PB. Ickx/Andretti and Peterson/Schenken took the first two places for Ferrari. (Pete Lyons)

Lots were drawn for the start and the 3-litre cars departed at one-minute intervals from 9am. Elford (Alfa Romeo) started first, ahead of de Adamich (Alfa Romeo), Merzario, Galli (Alfa Romeo) and Vaccarella (Alfa Romeo). Merzario screamed past the pits first, with a lead of 42sec. By the end of the second lap Merzario had extended his lead to 70sec, even though he had stopped to top up the fuel at the Ferrari outpost at Bivio Polizzi. At the end of lap three Merzario stopped at the pits to hand over to Munari, almost overshot and an over-excited Munari nearly drove off after the mechanics had changed the rear wheels, but not those at the front. The stop lasted 1min 45sec, enough to lose the lead to 'Nanni Galli'/Marko with their 33TT3. At the end of his second lap at the wheel Munari misread an *Autodelta* pit signal for Hezemans and stopped a lap earlier than intended.

It was probably for the best, for Munari was significantly the slower of the two Ferrari drivers. Peter Schetty had now decided that drivers should cover only two laps before handing over. By the end of his first lap back at the wheel Merzario led again by a margin of 19sec and he stopped at the end of lap seven. It was another chaotic pit stop, for he collided with the Italian driver Bonetto (presumably no relation to the great Felice), breaking a headlamp cover and 1min 40sec were lost before Munari could leave the pits refuelled and with new tyres. On lap eight the race swung in Ferrari's favour. 'Nanni Galli', leading on time, but following Munari on the road, was chasing the Ferrari driver hard; near Collesano Munari passed a Lancia Fulvia, which promptly spun, and 'Nanni Galli' also spun to avoid a collision; the Alfa Romeo stalled and it took two minutes to induce the very hot V8 to fire up.

Munari stopped to refuel and hand over to Merzario at the end of lap nine and the little Italian was away in 28sec. Merzario was feeling unwell, as he had consumed too many iced drinks while waiting in the pits, and also his hands were badly blistered. He took it easy on lap ten and made an all-out effort on the last lap. Marko, however, was driving his 33TT3 like a man possessed; he closed to within 28sec of the Ferrari on lap ten and at the finish on lap 11 he was only 16.9sec behind. Merzario was so exhausted that he had to be lifted out of the car. Ferrari's record of race wins in 1972 remained unbroken, it was a great Targa Florio and the most exciting race in what was proving a rather predictable and boring season.

Nürburgring 1,000Km
Race day, 28 May, was bitterly cold and heavy rain fell before the start. As usual Ferrari entered three 312PBs, there were three 33TT3s from *Autodelta* (but Carlo Chiti ran only two in the race), a Porsche 908/03 and the much-improved Mirage M6 driven by Bell/van Lennep. Joakim Bonnier did not enter his 3-litre Lolas, as he was concentrating on preparation of these for Le Mans. All three Ferraris had the longer tails first seen at Monza and both Ferrari and Alfa Romeo started the race on wet-weather tyres. Ickx/Regazzoni's 312PB ran badly in practice and they were only ninth fastest. By the second lap Ickx had recovered from his poor starting position on the fifth row of the grid and took the lead. The track had been drying rapidly and on lap 17 Regazzoni, still on wet-weather tyres, lost control at *Hohe Acht*, about nine miles from the start, and crashed into the guard-rail near-enough head-on.

Redman was suffering from a viral infection, was far from well and slower than usual. Merzario started the race, led briefly on the fourth lap and they finished second. Although Peterson was the faster driver, Schenken started the race. He held second place until the Mirage passed him on lap 17 and this pair assumed the lead when the Mirage made a very slow pit stop at the end of lap 18. A lead of three minutes dropped to two minutes when Schenken had a front tyre puncture and stopped for both wheels to be changed. They went on to win at 103.59mph (166.67kph). Andrea de Adamich/Helmut Marko took third place, a lap in arrears, with their Alfa Romeo Tipo 33TT3 and although it was not running at the finish the Mirage was classified fourth.

Le Mans 24 Hours
After Ferrari decided to miss the race, held on 10–11 June, and John Wyer withdrew the Mirage because he did not consider the Ford engine reliable enough to last 24 hours, the serious 3-litre entry consisted of four

Matras (it was the French company's only sports car race in 1972), three Alfa Romeos, the two Bonnier Lolas and an ostensibly private, four-year-old Porsche 908 *Lang* coupé prepared at the factory and looked after by factory mechanics.

In the first French victory at Le Mans since 1950 Pescarolo/Graham Hill and Cevert/Ganley took the first two places ahead of the Porsche 908 driven by Jöst/Weber/Casoni and the surviving Alfa Romeo of de Adamich/Vaccarella. The race was marred by Bonnier's fatal accident when he collided with a Ferrari *Daytona* at *White House* and his Lola rebounded over the guard-rail into the trees. Bonnier died almost immediately and it was a sad end for a driver who had been racing for nearly 20 years.

Österreichring 1,000Km

With the Championship in the bag, for this race on 25 June, Ferrari entered four cars all with long 'Monza' tails, and, as Alfa Romeo had withdrawn from Championship racing until 1973, they were almost completely unopposed. The only car likely to provide any sort of opposition was the *Gulf* M6 driven by Bell/van Lennep. The M6 was fastest in practice and the *Écurie Bonnier* Lola driven by Larrousse/Elford was second fastest.

It was difficult enough to find eight drivers capable of handling these cars, but Peter Schetty had more problems when Regazzoni slipped while playing football in the paddock during testing on the Wednesday before the race and broke a bone in his left wrist. He brought into the team Austrian Helmut Marko who was usually a member of the *Autodelta* squad. During Friday's practice Ickx drove a 312PB fitted with a full Formula 1 engine developing about 470bhp, but the chances of measuring its performances were lost because of heavy rain that flooded the track in places. There were only 24 starters.

The Belgian was very quick away from the start and led the other three Ferraris with Bell (Mirage) in fifth place. He and Redman stayed in front throughout, except when Marko briefly went ahead during the first round of refuelling stops and when Redman stopped to take on extra fuel because an air-lock had prevented the team from fully topping up the tanks at the first stop. Ickx set fastest lap at 129.71mph (208.71kph) and Ickx/Redman averaged 125.42mph (201.80kph). Helmut Marko/Carlos Pace drove well as newcomers to the team. Marko collided with a Porsche 908 that he was lapping and Pace lost time complaining in the pits that the car was weaving. They drove well to finish second, with Peterson/Schenken third and Merzario/Munari took fourth place despite throttle and battery problems.

Watkins Glen Six Hours

This race on 22 July was held for the first time on the full and lengthened Watkins Glen circuit. The only major teams to run were Ferrari and *Gulf Research Racing* with two Mirage M6s and, after qualifying had eliminated some of the entries, the number of starters was 31. Ickx/Andretti drove a 312PB with modified rear suspension to eliminate the model's bump-steering tendencies. Instead of the triangular struts that normally located the bottoms of the wishbones, there were wide-based parallel lower struts and single top links. It also had the rear wing raised by about three inches and this enabled the car to pull another 200rpm along the straights. Initially Andretti held second place behind Peterson, but the fuel-metering unit slipped out of adjustment so that the engine gave very little power below 8,000rpm and he fell back. The heavier fuel consumption meant that they had to refuel every 35 laps instead of 42 laps for the other cars.

Despite these problems and despite signals from the pits, Ickx fought hard to catch the race leader in the closing laps of the race and ten laps from the finish he went ahead of Peterson to win by 13.9sec. Ickx/Andretti averaged 109.39mph (176.01kph), having covered 658.515 miles (1059.55km), and Ickx won US$1,000 for setting fastest lap at 113.41mph (182.48kph). Peterson/Schenken led for much of the race and the only incident was when Schenken spun and damaged a headlamp cover when the brakes began to fade towards the end of the race, allowing the dynamic Ickx to catch and pass them shortly before the finish.

Into Eau Rouge at the 1973 Spa 1,000Km race, the 312PB of Pace/Merzario leads the Matra shared by Pescarolo/Larrousse/Amon and the Mirage of Bell/Hailwood. In this race Pace/Merzario finished fourth, but British Mirages took the first two places. (LAT)

Third place went to Bell/Pace with the Mirage M6 who had another problem race and were 14 laps in arrears. Redman/Merzario drove a steady race, holding second place after the Ickx/Andretti car developed its fuel-metering trouble, but then dropping back to third place. Their race ended on lap 137 of this 195-lap event when their Ferrari broke its crankshaft. Ferrari did not run in the following day's Can-Am race. This was because the organisers told Peter Schetty that Ickx would have to start from the back of the grid because the car had not qualified with fully legal Group Seven bodywork.

On 17 September Ferrari entered two 312PBs in the Imola 500Km (311-mile race) held at the *Dino Ferrari Autodromo*. Merzario won with his 1972 312PB from Ickx whose car was to semi-1973 specification. Following their success in the 1971 event, Ferrari shipped out two cars to compete in the Kyalami Nine Hours race on 4 November. Both had increased front track and longer wheelbase and power output had risen to 470bhp at 11,000rpm. They were running on Goodyear tyres following Firestone's uncertainty as to whether they would be racing in 1973. Ickx/Redman and Merzario/Regazzoni were the drivers and as they started practice a week before the race, it was clear that it was being used as a test session.

The Nine Hours was an immensely popular race and it was estimated that there were 75,000 spectators at the circuit. Ickx took the lead from Regazzoni on lap eight and this was the situation until shortly before half-distance when the leading Ferrari's engine expired in a cloud of blue smoke. Merzario/Regazzoni went on to win the race at 103.8mph (167.0kph), six laps ahead of Jochen Mass/Gerry Birrell with a 2-litre Hart-powered Chevron B25.

No team has ever enjoyed a more successful year in sports car racing than that of Ferrari in 1972. The team was manifestly superior but in most races the cars were not stretched to the full, so a greater level of reliability could have been expected.

1973

Although Ferrari announced major cutbacks in its racing programme for 1973, these seemed to have little effect on the sports car programme and three 312PBs were entered in most races. Peter Schetty had relinquished the post of Racing Manager to return to the family textile business in Switzerland and *Ing.* Gaicomo Caliri acted as both technical director for the sports car team and racing manager. Caliri lacked the experience to lift the team through the downturns of the year and, perhaps, if he had possessed greater experience he could have exerted the pressure needed to improve both speed and reliability.

Ferrari faced only one serious opponent in 1973, *Matra Sports* managed by Gérard Ducarouge. He was a fine and talented engineer, but he was also a man full of enthusiasm, a great communicator and talker and with all the qualities necessary to build team spirit. There had always seemed to be something slightly messy about the Matra team; the cars never looked quite right, the mechanics always seemed just a trifle muddled-headed and there were constant minor changes in specification. Ducarouge had now swept up all the potential and enthusiasm of the team into a tight, well-organised effort and the benefits were reaped in 1973–74.

Matra Sports was running a full season of sports car racing in 1973 and their MS670 had improved handling and increased power. At Daytona and Le Mans power output was about 450bhp, but in the shorter events with the engines in full Formula 1 tune they developed around 475bhp at 11,200rpm. And did they scream – for anyone who attended races at this time the tortured penetrating, high-pitched note of the Matra V12 engine is unforgettable.

Maranello made substantial changes to the 312PB for 1973. The cars were rebuilt versions of the 1972 cars with the longer wheelbase and wider front track seen at Kyalami the previous year. The maximum rev limit had risen to 11,600rpm, power output was slightly higher and there was a new exhaust system intended to improve

The 312PB, 1971–73 **219**

engine torque. The bodywork was much smoother, there was an air-box mounted between the struts of the roll-over bar and the rear wing was integral with the body. Later twin air-scoops were substituted. The Formula 1 gearbox was now used and the brakes were larger and had ventilated discs. At many races inboard-mounted rear brakes were fitted and this necessitated a change in the rear suspension from triangular wishbones to parallel rods.

Ferrari tested the cars exhaustively and as late as mid-February was still testing with Brian Redman at the wheel at the very modern French Paul Ricard circuit – ideal for winter testing because of the Mediterranean warmth. Argentinian Carlos Reutemann (who drove Brabhams in Formula 1) and Brazilian Carlos Pace (a member of the Surtees Formula 1 team) joined the Ferrari sports car team on a regular basis. Despite all the work put into developing the 312PB, its handling was still very unpredictable, with a tendency to switch rapidly from oversteer to understeer and the power output of the flat-12 engine remained slightly lower than that of Matra's V12.

Both Ferrari and Alfa Romeo missed the first round of the 1973 World Championship for Makes, the Daytona 24 Hours at the beginning of February. After the retirement of the sole Matra, Peter Gregg/Hurley Haywood won the race with a Porsche 911 *Carrera*. The Sebring 12 Hours and the BOAC race at Brands Hatch had both been cancelled and there were new rounds of the championship at Vallelunga near Rome and at Dijon.

The Merzario/Pace 312PB stands in front of the Ferrari pit during practice for the 1973 Spa 1,000Km race. Pace is standing at the tail of the car with his hand resting on the rear wing. Fourth from left, back to the camera, is Alfa Romeo racing boss Carlo Chiti and Ferrari team-member Carlos Reutemann in dark sweater is standing on the pit counter to the right. (Pete Lyons)

Vallelunga Six Hours

This addition to the Championship series took place on 25 March and was primarily to enable Romans to see a Ferrari victory, but in this they were to be disappointed. Vallelunga was not popular amongst the teams, as it was a tight 'mickey-mouse' circuit that was very hard on the drivers' neck muscles and arms and made concentration difficult as they tried to put 450-plus bhp through the back wheels in a smooth and quick manner. Ferrari was now running on Goodyear tyres and in practice they were chunking and wearing very quickly. After practice Ferrari carried out modifications that caused excessive understeer. Throughout the race the cars were in and out of the pits for wheel changes, harder compounds were fitted but the cars still handled badly and Ferrari had lost the race before it started.

Cevert was leading with the Matra he was sharing with Beltoise when the engine lost its oil pressure and expired in a cloud of blue smoke. He then took over the second Matra entered for Pescarolo/Larrousse and this trio went on to win by a margin of a little over two kilometres. The outclassed Ferraris had to settle for second, third and fourth places. Schenken/Reutemann finished second. Ickx drove his heart out in the early laps of the race, hotly pursued by Cevert (Matra), but on lap 14 Ferrari tyre problems started. At his second stop, the mechanics loosened off the front roll bar to reduce the understeer and fitted a new tail section with flatter aerofoil angle. Redman took over to drive a 312PB that was now oversteering excessively. Ickx/Redman eventually finished third and Merzario/Pace took fourth place.

Dijon 1,000 Km

New to the calendar, the Dijon race on 15 April was on another slow, difficult circuit with a length of only 1.994 miles (3.208km) and the fastest 3-litre cars lapping in just over a minute. The entry was small, partly because the organising club could not afford to offer starting money and there were only 19 cars on the grid. There were still metalworkers' strikes in Italy and this reduced the Ferrari entry to two cars for Ickx/Redman and Merzario/Pace. Both 312PBs were running on larger, 15-inch wheels, which necessitated minor suspension modifications. Enzo Ferrari was so concerned about the ability of the team to beat the Matras that he telephoned Peter Schetty in Basle and asked him to act as manager at this race. Matra entered the same cars seen at Vallelunga, but with minor engine and exhaust modifications the team was claiming 485bhp.

Because of the difficulties at the factory, Ickx/Redman drove the car handled by Merzario/Pace at Vallelunga while Merzario/Pace had a new car. After practice Ferrari fitted this car with a deeper nose-section in an attempt to reduce understeer, but under braking the front of the new nose ground itself away against the track. Ickx battled with the Mirages in the opening laps of the race, but the Ferrari was delayed by problems; the nose-section had to be changed and Redman had a rear tyre puncture in front of the pits – which meant completing a full lap at very slow speed before the wheel could be changed.

Both Ickx and Redman charged hard in the later stages of the race, trying to get to grips with the leading Matra of Pescarolo/Larrousse, but they finished second, nearly a lap and a half behind at the finish. Merzario battled with the Mirages until they ran into problems and towards the end of the race this Ferrari slowed off because of engine overheating. Merzario/Pace finished fourth behind the Matra of Cevert/Beltoise, but ahead of the well-driven *Gulf* Mirage M6 of Hailwood/Schuppan.

Monza 1,000Km

The very fast Monza course in Milan's Royal Park was as close as Ferrari could get to having a 'home circuit' and the team always made a special effort in this race,

220 Scarlet Passion

held annually on 25 April, an Italian Bank Holiday. Alfa Romeo was still not ready to race the new Tipo 33TT12 cars, but *Autodelta* were there to support a private entrant and their driver Rolf Stommelen told journalists that the 33TT12 was as fast as the Matras, which gave hopes of closer and better racing in the future. Although the Matras failed at Monza, they were faster than the Ferraris while they were still running and on this circuit the Mirages were outpaced.

Despite the labour problems in Italy, Ferrari ran three cars prepared and turned-out to a very high standard. As Monza was a power circuit, the team had reverted to the Formula 1 exhaust arrangement and power output was reckoned to be around 470bhp. Long tails were used and these allowed the cars to pull another 300rpm on the straights, but they understeered a little more through the curves. The cars also practised with short tails, as the team had no spare long tails. All three cars had inboard rear brakes. During practice Ferrari experimented with mounting the battery at the front of the car to improve weight distribution and handling, but it was restored to its normal position in the tail for the race. Instead, there was ballast in the form of 30lb (13.6kg) of lead in the nose-section of each car to reduce understeer.

Ickx/Redman were second fastest in practice, unable to match the speed of the Matra of Cevert/Beltoise. Ickx led initially and then Beltoise went ahead on lap five. Ickx stayed in the car after the first refuelling stop, charging as hard as possible, but still losing ground. Cevert lost a lot of time when he took over from Beltoise, trying to leave the pits in reverse gear, stalling and needing the help of a mechanic to find a forward ratio! By the time he screamed away, slipping the clutch in third gear, Ickx was back in the lead. Cevert took the lead from Redman shortly before stopping to refuel again, but after several pit stops he retired because of a bad vibration caused by a broken left front stub-axle. Ickx/Redman were able to cruise to the finish, averaging 150.67mph (242.43kph).

Reutemann/Schenken were in third place after the second Matra driven by Pescarolo/Larrousse lost 11 laps while the broken left front stub-axle was changed. This

The 312PB, 1971–73 221

Ferrari started to overheat in the closing stages of the race, but Reutemann ignored this and continued to drive as hard as possible. They finished second, three laps behind the winners and seven laps ahead of Pescarolo/Larrousse. Merzario pulled off at *Lesmo* with the car he was to share with Schenken after only ten laps and walked back to the pits to report that the car was vibrating badly and he thought that either the engine or gearbox was about to seize up. Ferrari won through the failure of Matra, but it was not a success repeated during the remainder of the year and the team was to receive two surprise defeats.

Spa 1,000Km
Ferrari contented himself with two entries in the fastest European race, held this year on 6 May; both cars had long 'Monza' tails and the batteries at the front. There were two Matras, two Mirages and the Alfa Romeo T33T12 was entered on its intended race debut for de Adamich/Stommelen. Originally it was thought that there would be only the one Matra, as both Cevert and Beltoise were members of the Grand Prix Drivers' Association and toed the party line by not competing at Spa-Francorchamps; the French team however brought in Graham Hill and Chris Amon to drive the second car. After the Alfa Romeo chunked a tyre tread during practice, hurling itself and de Adamich backwards into the guard-rail at the exit to *Stavelot*, *Autodelta* loaded up their transporter and returned to Settimo Milanese.

Ickx was fastest in practice, but Pescarolo led away with his Matra at the start. Redman took the lead ahead of the Bell/Hailwood Mirage after a tyre chunked on the leading Matra, damaging the bodywork. With Ickx back at the wheel, this Ferrari continued to head the field until just before half-distance when it rolled to a halt at *La Source*. An oil union had become detached from the gearbox oil cooler, most of the oil was pumped out, the gearbox had seized up and Ickx could not select any of the lower ratios. Bell/Hailwood took the lead and won from Mirage team-mates Schuppan/Ganley. It was a surprise result that injected a new level of interest in sports car racing.

Pace/Merzario were completely at odds as to how they liked their car set up. Pace preferred a fraction of oversteer, while the mercurial Merzario liked massive understeer that enabled him to slide the car through corners dramatically (at the expense of heavy tyre wear). Merzario shouted and waved his arms, while the Brazilian maintained an aloof, tight-lipped silence. After the retirement of Ickx/Redman, Pace struggled to close the gap on the leading Mirage, but soon charged back into the pits with the oil pipe dangling from the oil cooler and the rear of the car coated in oil. Although the gearbox was damaged, he was able to rejoin the race with some of the ratios still operative. Pace, who did most of the driving in this race, rejoined in third place. After Merzario had relieved Pace, Chris Amon, who had taken over the Pescarolo/Larrousse Matra, passed the little Italian and the Ferrari finished fourth.

Targa Florio

As was usual, sports car races were succeeding each other in quick succession, and this inevitably damaged Ferrari's Formula 1 efforts. The Sicilian race, on 13 May, was run over ten laps of the 44.7-mile *Piccolo Madonie* circuit, but complied with the Championship rules – despite its short, but arduous distance – because it lasted a little more than six hours. Opposition to the Targa Florio had grown because of the dangers of this road circuit and the impossibility of marshalling it adequately; despite strong local support, this proved to be the last race. Ferrari and Alfa Romeo each fielded two cars and the *International Martini Racing Team* entered three Porsche *Carreras* that ran in the Group Five class.

The race proved a debacle for both Ferrari and Alfa Romeo. One Alfa Romeo failed to start after Clay Regazzoni spun and rolled it in practice. In the race Stommelen set fastest lap in 34min 13sec. 78.451mph (126.228kph), but his partner de Adamich crashed his 33TT12 out of the race when he collided on lap four with a slower competitor. At this time the Alfa Romeo was leading the Ferraris. Of the latest flat-12 Alfa Romeo, Regazzoni said that he considered that it had more precise handling than the 312PB, but that the engine's spread of useable power was narrower and its brakes were inferior.

The Ferraris had been extensively modified with a spare wheel on the driver's side of the chassis and this formed a bulge in the bodywork; there were single-rate coil springs (providing maximum suspension deflection on the very bumpy roads) and a longer exhaust system. Ferrari was also using a two-way radio system between the driver and the pits and an aerial was mounted on the roll-bar. Ickx went well initially, even if slower than the 33TT12, but he disappeared off the road on lap two and the car was out of the race without Redman having a drive.

Merzario (co-driving with Vaccarella) started the race, but a rear tyre deflated on the second lap when, instead of stopping at the Ferrari out-station at Collesano, he drove all the way back to the pits. This cost a lot of time and shortly after he rejoined the race, a drive-shaft failed. After the retirement of the fastest cars, van Lennep/Müller with a Porsche *Carrera RSR* won at 71.266mph (114.667kph) from Munari/Andruet (Lancia Stratos). The consistent success of the Porsche *Carreras* in 1973–74 was ultimately to lead to the adoption in 1976 of the Group Five World Championship for Makes for production-based cars

Nürburgring 1,000Km

After Le Mans, the 1,000Km event on 27 May in the Eifel Mountains was the most prestigious of the year's races. Ferrari, Alfa Romeo and Matra all made two-car entries. The main opposition to the Ferraris was reduced early in the race. On the first lap Pescarolo retired the Matra that he was sharing with Larrousse because of a blown engine and only a lap later Regazzoni slowed off with the 33TT12 that Carlo Facetti was due to co-drive; the Alfa was trailing blue smoke and a broken valve was suspected. Ickx/Redman drove a standard short-tail car. Ickx trailed Cevert (Matra MS670), gradually losing ground, but on lap 13 of this 44-lap the Cevert/Beltoise Matra retired because of engine failure out at *Wippermann* and Ickx/Redman went on to win at 111.190mph (178.905kph).

Merzario/Pace drove an experimental car, built in an effort to close the performance gap between the Ferrari and the Matras. The tail now had a lowered centre-section between the wheels and there was a large Formula 1-style air-box. The lowering of the tail necessitated mounting the oil coolers lower, just in front of the right rear wheel, with a cooling duct in the sill of the chassis in place of the two normally positioned on top of the tail. The pick-up points for the bottom rear suspension links were mounted lower to reduce the height of the car, but neither driver was convinced that there was any improvement in handling. Merzario/Pace ran third ahead of the de Adamich/Stommelen Alfa Romeo, which retired with a variety of mechanical problems on lap 11, then moved up to second after the Cevert/Pescarolo Matra blew its engine and stayed there to the finish.

Jacky Ickx was due to drive this 312PB with Brian Redman in the 1973 Targa Florio, but on the second lap he went off the road and down the side of ravine. (LAT)

During the final quarter of the race Merzario struggled to wrest the lead from Ickx, who could not pull away from him because his rev limiter cut-out had developed a fault and was coming in too early. Three times the Ferrari pit hung out the 'Come In' signal to Merzario and three times he ignored it. When Merzario did eventually come in, he had to be prised out of the car and he stormed out of the Ferrari pit. Pace finished the race according to orders, but closed on Ickx so that they could cross the line almost side-by-side, but with Ickx finishing one-tenth of a second ahead on official timing. Merzario failed to show up at the prize-giving after the race. Enzo Ferrari wanted to drop Merzario from the team at Le Mans, but driver shortages made this impossible.

Le Mans 24 Hours

After missing the 1972 race, Maranello ran a strong team in the 1973 race on 9–10 June. Part of the reason for the entry was that if Ferrari could win, defeating the

Spot lights ablaze, Carlos Pace with his 312PB chases after the Matras at Le Mans in 1973. Despite a leaking fuel tank and clutch problems Pace/Merzario took second place behind the Matra of Pescarolo/ Graham Hill.

Matras, then it would have the Sports Car Championship in the bag. Matra entered four cars; three of them were completely new and to a modified MS670B specification. There were two *Gulf* Mirage M6s, a single Lola T282 and a privately entered Alfa Romeo 33TT3. *Autodelta* works team missed the race because there was no hope of a 33TT12 lasting 24 hours.

The Ferrari team ran three of the usual cars with slight modifications and for this race Ferrari reverted to outboard rear brakes. There were long tails that sloped down at the rear and with an adjustable lip on the trailing edge of the tail, the space behind the rear wheels was boxed in to reduce turbulence and the nose had been modified so that four headlamps could be fitted. Ferrari sources were claiming a power output of 450bhp at 10,500rpm, exactly as were Matra for their V12s.

The cars formated two-by-two for a rolling start after the warm-up lap. Redman started the race and drove steadily, holding ninth place at the end of the first hour, then this car gradually moved up through the field and it took second place during the eighth hour. Following the retirement of the leading Ferrari of Reutemann/ Schenken, Ickx/Redman assumed the lead in the 11th hour and although it was still going strongly as dawn broke, this Ferrari sounded flatter and flatter as the morning moved on. Just after 9am, shortly after he had relieved Ickx, Redman came back into the pits.

While the mechanics replaced a broken exhaust pipe and fitted a new tail-section (because one of the hinges on the original had broken), the Matra of Pescarolo/Larrousse had taken the lead. Later Ickx lost 25 minutes when he brought his Ferrari back into the pits because of a leaking auxiliary fuel tank. The leading Matra then lost 20 minutes after its starter motor jammed during a routine pit stop. Ickx and Redman chased the Matra hard, two hours from the finish they were only a lap behind, but Ickx came into the pits 30 minutes later to retire because of engine failure.

Merzario started the race, driving hard and acting as the hare; he stopped on lap 12 for fuel, lost the lead to the Cevert/Beltoise Matra, but was soon back in front. Merzario handed over to Pace, but the Brazilian was straight back into the pits, throwing out the seat cushion and jumping after it. The auxiliary fuel tank was leaking, just as that on the Ickx/Redman car was to do later in the race. Six laps were lost before this car rejoined the race and started a chase up through the field. Merzario/Pace eventually finished second, six laps behind the winning Matra. Reutemann/Schenken drove a fast race, moving up the field to lead before the end of the sixth hour from the Matra of Pescarolo/Larrousse. This Ferrari stayed in front until 2.35am on the Sunday morning when the engine gave up, despite normal oil and water temperature levels.

Österreichring 1,000Km

Ferrari still led the Championship, but the outcome was very uncertain. Only 19 cars turned up to compete in the Austrian race, but these included two of the older MS670 Matras, two *Gulf* Mirage M6s, a single 12-cylinder Alfa Romeo for Stommelen and Regazzoni, together with two works Ferraris. Ickx/Redman drove a 312PB which was generally in the same configuration as at Le Mans, save for extra lights in the centre of the nose. The Matras simply ran away from the Ferraris in this race and Ickx/Redman held third place almost

224 Scarlet Passion

throughout, rising briefly to second when Beltoise/Cevert were delayed by fuel pump problems. They finished third, a lap in arrears, and Ferrari still led the Championship with 122 points to the 104 of Matra.

Pace/Merzario had the modified car seen at the Nürburgring, but it now featured a nose rather imitative of the 33TT12 Alfa Romeo, sloping smoothly upwards without any vertical surface. Early in the race Pace moved up into fourth place, but on lap nine the front left tyre threw a tread, making a hole in the front wheel arch. He made his way back to the pits, the wheel was changed, the brakes were bled and this Ferrari then rejoined the race four laps in arrears. After another six laps Pace was back in the pits because the nose-section had started to break up round the hole, a new nose-section was fitted and this car eventually finished sixth.

Watkins Glen Six Hours

The race held on 21 July, as usual, proved a straight fight between Ferrari and Matra, with the Matras having the advantage in terms of speed. There were no *Autodelta* Alfa Romeos, but *Gulf* sent two M6 Mirages as usual. It was to prove another Matra-dominated race and the image of the all-conquering Ferrari team seen in 1972 had disappeared forever. Ickx/Redman drove a car featuring a new nose design with a lightweight, slatted grille that was intended to improve handling by releasing air pressure that had built up under the nose. In simple terms, it did not work, but Ferrari persevered and used it in the race. All three Ferraris at this race had outboard rear brakes.

The faster cars had problems lapping slower-moving traffic and Ickx, in third place, was forced to brake hard when he was cut up by a slower car that he was trying to lap. Cevert with the fastest of the Matra entries rammed the back of the Ferrari, and although the 312PB suffered bent exhaust pipes, the Matra's nose was shattered and Cevert was forced to stop for this to be taped up. The Ferrari's pipes were banged back into shape as far as possible during the car's next routine stop and seemed to have suffered no harm from the constant bottoming prior to the stop. Despite the loss of power caused by the damaged exhausts, Ickx/Redman held a steady third place, moving up to second when team-mates Reutemann/Schenken retired shortly before the finish when the belt driving the distributor broke.

Merzario/Pace were the fastest of the Ferrari drivers in practice. At the rolling start Merzario accelerated into the lead and he stayed in front of the Matras until lap 16 when Gérard Larrousse with his MS670 Matra passed him. Larrousse/Pescarolo stayed in front for the remaining 5½ hours of the race. The Ferrari lost second place when the front brake pads were changed; Merzario rejoined the race, but was back after six laps complaining that the handling was so bad that he was exhausted. Pace took over but returned after a lap, insisting that the left rear tyre be changed. The Ferrari mechanics changed all four wheels and after Pace had left the pits, it was noticed that the left rear tyre that he had been insistent about had a slow puncture and was gently deflating. Pace/Merzario finished third.

In the Championship both Ferrari and Matra had to shed points and rely on their best results in the permitted number of qualifying rounds. At this stage Ferrari had a net 115 points compared with a net 124 of Matra. When Ferrari announced that the team would not be competing in the last round of the Championship at Buenos Aires, Matra automatically became the winner. The Buenos Aires race was ultimately cancelled. Matra continued to compete in sports car racing in 1974 and after failing in their first race of the season, the Monza 1000Km, won the following nine races entered, including Le Mans for the third year in succession.

Ferrari Postscript

It had been one of the least successful seasons in Ferrari's history and by the end of 1972 Fiat was pressuring Enzo Ferrari to cut back on racing expenditure. However, it was decided that the team would defend its title in the Sports Car Championship, which proved a tactical and financial error, for the 312PBs proved a poor match for the latest Matras. To run the team drained resources and there were no funds for major development work. Another problem faced by Ferrari at this time was industrial unrest in Italy and this had caused major problems for both the Formula 1 and sports car programmes. No works Ferrari ever again ran in a sports car race. In Chapter 14 Mauro Forghieri tells the story of the failure of the 1973 Grand Prix cars. Luca di Montezemolo became team chief and by concentrating on Formula 1 and using Fiat money, Ferrari regained eminence.

With his new 1973 Formula 1 car Forghieri laid down the design principles which were to lead to a generation of much more successful cars. In 1974 Regazzoni and Niki Lauda took second and fourth places in the Drivers' Championship; Lauda won the Championship in 1975 the year in which the 312T with transversely-mounted gearbox appeared; he was second in 1976 (despite his near-fatal crash in the German race) and won again in 1977. Jody Scheckter won the Drivers' Championship in 1979, but a year later the final version of the flat-12 Ferrari, the 312T5 was so uncompetitive that Scheckter failed to qualify as a starter at the Canadian Grand Prix. After winning the Constructors' Championship in 1979, the team dropped to tenth in 1980. It was a blip in an otherwise outstandingly consistent racing history. Another era had ended and in 1981 the first Ferrari turbocharged cars appeared, yet again the work of Mauro Forghieri.

An interview with Mauro Forghieri
Formerly Technical Director of Ferrari Sport

Mauro Forghieri in conversation with Jody Scheckter. The photograph was taken in 1979, Scheckter's World Championship year with the 312T4.

Mauro Forghieri was born in Modena on 13 January 1935. He studied mechanical engineering at Bologna University and graduated in 1959 as a doctor of engineering, but in Italian academic terms, he does not have a doctorate as such. He taught for a short while, but joined Ferrari in 1960. This chapter is based on an interview that took place in Baggiovara, Modena on 29 May 2003. The material used has been checked and approved by Ing. Forghieri.

In my young years I was a lover of gas-turbine engines and aeroplanes. Originally I had an ambition to move to the United States and work for a company, such as Northrop, that built gas-turbine engines. At that time aero-engine companies in Italy had connections with American gas-turbine makers, but there were none that made them. I did not fulfil my ambition because when I finished studying, family circumstances made it impossible for me to move to the United States immediately. Before the Second World War my father, Reclus, had worked with Enzo Ferrari in the machine department on the first Alfa Romeo *Alfetta* 158. The story of my family is quite difficult to explain. The family were deeply involved in politics and belonged to the Socialist party. They lived much of the time out of Italy, but even so my father had a close relationship with Enzo Ferrari.

Enzo Ferrari telephoned me and I told him of my ambition and that I was waiting to go to the United States. He said, 'Waiting! Come here and work with me!' So I went to Ferrari and it was many years before I moved. I started doing testing work in the engine department. Gianpaolo Dallara joined the company soon afterwards and Carlo Chiti, the chief of the Technical Department, put him in charge of chassis and gearbox development. Ferrari was a small company at this time. Dallara, who was around 27, and I were both of a 'young school' of engineers and we did not like the way in which Ferrari tackled technical questions – that was normal enough for young men. So I was close to leaving, but Dallara left before me and almost immediately started working for Lamborghini.

At the end of 1961 there was a revolution, a fight between the managers and the President Enzo Ferrari and his family. I don't know the reasons, I was too busy working and I did not follow the politics. After they had left, I was the only engineer in the factory. Ferrari called me in and I told him, 'Listen, I'm leaving.' The Old Man said to me, 'You cannot leave because you will leave me alone – I need you. I will give you responsibility for the racing department.' I was shocked, I thought that he was crazy, and I said, 'I don't have enough experience.' But he told me, 'You look after the technical side and I will look after the political side. You will never have political problems. You will tell me what you would like to do and I will tell you if you can do it for economic reasons.' When I became head of the racing department, I started going to races regularly.

At this time Ferrari had no help from outside the factory. We achieved a great deal, even if we did not win as much as we would have liked. The company was divided into sections: the first was the production section and this gave Ferrari the opportunity to sell cars; from the money that the Old Man gained from selling cars we were able to do Formula 1, Formula 2 and hill climbing; after that another section was sports car and GT racing; the fourth section was racing in the United States, mainly California and Can-Am racing, and other countries such as South Africa. With one exception the cars that we ran in Can-Am racing were modified Prototypes and Competition Sports Cars, which had very little development.

When I took responsibility for the racing department, I was lucky because in the department there were two men: Franco Rocchi, who was a good engine man and Walter Salvarani who was good with gearboxes; both had chassis knowledge, but mainly with front-engined chassis. Both were very good draughtsmen and both had worked at *Officine Meccaniche Italiane Reggiane*, near Modena, a company that during the war had built some very successful fighters. After the war the Americans took all the drawings for the last design, the RE 2005 *Sagittario*, to the United States. Together we learned everything we could about rear-engined cars. They designed the first Ferrari monocoque chassis built in 1963–64.

In 1962 we did not have the time or the resources to make new cars; in Prototype racing we used mainly the 246SP, a 1961 car, which was fast and had acceptable

Mauro Forghieri in his office at Oral Engineering in Modena.

handling. When you have a car that is very reliable for long-distance endurance events, you have to make comprises on power, on handling, on everything. If a car has exceptionally good handling, you are going to use more tyres, more brakes. Remember, the main sports car event of the year for us was Le Mans where reliability is of the greatest importance. At Le Mans in 1962 we won with the front-engined 330TRI driven by Phil Hill and Olivier Gendebien.

Ferrari had only very limited experience of building rear-engined cars and those that he had built had been the responsibility of Chiti. I was not initially in a position to design such a car. I believe that Stirling Moss had an agreement with the Old Man for 1962, but of course this came to nothing after Moss's crash at Goodwood and so there was no help in that direction. I had developed a close relationship with the *UDT-Laystall Racing Team*. They were very nice people, the chief engineer, the head mechanic and the mechanics and they helped me as much as they could. We also loaned one of our Formula 1 cars to them for the 1962 International Trophy at Silverstone and Innes Ireland drove this. After the race he told me that he thought that the engine was good, the gearbox was good, but the handling was poor. I spent a lot of time in England, learning from this team.

I was in trouble at the beginning of 1962 and I was very lucky to have Innes Ireland and the *UDT-Laystall* team to convince me that I was not wrong and doing the right things. The Ferrari Formula 1 drivers at this time were Phil Hill and Baghetti, together with Willy Mairesse. Mairesse was a Belgian driver, a very strong character, a very brave guy with tremendous courage. The car we raced in 1962 was, of course, the work of Chiti and had won in 1961 mainly because it had about 40bhp more than the opposition. The drivers had no need to push the cars over the limit and so they were easy to handle. They pulled away from the opposition on the straight.

In the meantime BRM and Coventry Climax had brought out their V8 engines with as much or even more power than we had and BRM and Lotus immediately started to beat us. In 1962 the Ferrari drivers had to push the cars into corners at the same speed as the British cars and the shortcomings of the chassis revealed themselves. Innes Ireland had already told us this, he'd said, 'The stiffness of the chassis is not enough.' Phil Hill and Baghetti were convinced that it was my fault and only Mairesse thought otherwise and told me, 'Mauro, it's not your fault because now we have only the same horsepower as the others, but not such good handling.' They told me that I was a young engineer and I'd got things wrong. I understood how they felt because the previous year they were winning and one year later they were losing everything.

This convinced me that everything in Ferrari had to be changed; it was too close to the practices of the old days. It was not just the chassis, but the gearbox, the engine, the suspension. Back in Italy in late 1962 we started an intensive development programme with the help of John Surtees who had signed up to drive for our team. In 1962 Lotus had brought out the Lotus 25, the leading car of the time with monocoque construction. We were not immediately in a position to design a car like that. With two draughtsmen I designed a car with a multi-tubular space-frame, quite rigid, a little bit heavier than it should have been, and I used the existing V6 engine as a stressed member. The chassis was very much like that of the Lotus 24 and the Lola.

It was quick enough for Surtees to set fastest race lap at Monaco and win the German Grand Prix. Later that year we designed our first monocoque car. When I saw Surtees fighting Jim Clark – in my opinion the best driver in the world – at the wheel of the Lotus, a very impressive car, I knew that the new Ferrari was good and I began to believe in myself again.

In Prototype racing in 1963 we introduced the 12-cylinder 250P. Someone at Ferrari – I do not remember who it was – said that it was impossible to make a rear-engined car with a very bulky engine like a 12-cylinder. I did not understand the reasoning, so we took a 246SP and installed a 12-cylinder engine and John Surtees tested it at Monza in late 1962, consistently beating the lap record. After testing we changed the car completely and we removed the twin-nostril nose because, aerodynamically speaking, it had no advantage. We had carried out a lot of aerodynamic development and we developed a 'Targa' device, it was both a roll-bar and an aerodynamic device that increased the downforce and the negative lift, especially at the back of the car.

We knew that Ford was coming into racing and Broadley had run the very promising Lola GT with Ford 4.7-litre engine at Le Mans in 1963. The engine had a lot more torque than our 3-litre car, so for 1964 the aim was to increase the power and we built cars with 4-litre engines, the 330P and the cars that followed in 1965–67. The problem we found in increasing the power and the speed was the brake performance. We were using Dunlop brakes, but in the meanwhile we started to work in 1964 with Girling on ventilated disc brakes and I was going to Birmingham regularly. The performance of the ventilated disc brakes was amazing, but we had a shortage of funds and we couldn't do a 24-hour test like everybody does today. So we were testing over 1,000 kilometres and there were no problems in tests or during

The Chiti-designed rear-engined Grand Prix car with which Forghieri and the drivers had to struggle in 1962. Ferrari loaned this 65° V6 car to UDT-Laystall Racing Team for Innes Ireland to drive in the International Trophy race at Silverstone in May 1962. He finished fourth behind Graham Hill (V8 BRM), Jim Clark (V8 Lotus) and John Surtees (four-cylinder Lola-Climax).
(T. C. March/FotoVantage)

228 SCARLET PASSION

races like the Targa Florio and Monza held only in the daytime.

When we first used ventilated disc brakes at Le Mans in 1965 on the factory 330P2 Prototypes, we had tremendous problems with distortion of the discs and cracking during the low temperatures at night. At 1am in the morning I realised that my ventilated discs were cracking and the big question was what we could do about it. The private 250LM of Rindt/Gregory was leading, but we had to keep our 330P2s in the race to provide back-up. So the chief mechanic from the customer side of the company and I went to the car parking area. We found a 275GTB, which had solid discs the same size as those of the ventilated discs of our Prototypes. We disassembled the discs from the customer's car; we left a piece of paper saying that we would return the discs at the end of the race, and put them on our cars.

At the beginning my relationship with Surtees was very good and very close. Later I went to Canada to visit him after his accident in September 1965. At this stage there was already some misunderstanding between Ferrari and Surtees. This was because he was working for us on sports cars and at the same time he was working for Lola. Enzo Ferrari was a very jealous man about the drivers who worked for him. I discussed the situation with Ferrari after the working day was over. Ferrari said, 'Why is John working for other people? If he learns something at Ferrari, he will transmit it to other people.' I said, 'That's normal.' This is what disturbed Ferrari.

Ferrari loved John; he had tremendous respect for him, because he reminded him of Nuvolari, a bike rider and a car driver, like John. When friction starts, it is difficult to stop it. There was talk in the team about Surtees and that was not good. John was a good friend, but I had to be on the side of the factory. John didn't like this much, but I don't think that he really understood my position. I could not be on John's side when he was fighting with the factory.

When the final conflict with Dragoni happened at Le Mans in 1966, you can believe me when I say that it was not Dragoni who took the decision to send away John Surtees, it was, of course, Enzo Ferrari. No one could take such a high-level decision without the okay or suggestion of Ferrari. Ferrari was in charge of his factory 100%. I had the maximum freedom from a technical point of view, but I informed him what I was doing and it was the right course of action, because I was not spending my money, I was spending his money. The best that I could do was to advise him and try to convince him that what I was trying to do was right.

Dragoni came to Ferrari at the time the managers walked out. It was a time when Ferrari was weak from an economic point of view. He ran the *Scuderia Sant' Ambroeus* in Milan and was entering young Italian drivers. Both he and Ferrari were keen to run Italian drivers: Bandini, Scarfiotti and Patria [*who was killed at the wheel of an Abarth at Montlhéry in 1964*], they had all been part of the *Sant' Ambroeus* team. He became sports director of Ferrari and he was very close with Enzo Ferrari. He was so close to Ferrari that every wish of Ferrari was for him the law. He helped Ferrari a lot, especially on the competition side. I liked Dragoni very much; he was almost like a father to me, for he was already an old man.

Dragoni was a small man, but very strong, and a little hard on everybody. On the track he was the long arm of Ferrari. He was not an easy man to deal with, especially for journalists. He was not dependent on Ferrari, because he was a rich man and he had a very successful factory making cosmetics and perfume. He was not paid by Ferrari and met his own expenses. Dragoni also had problems with John Surtees, for the same reason, that he was racing a sports car for Lola. Even when Ferrari was forced to get rid of him, Dragoni still followed the team and he came to the testing with the P4 at Daytona just before Christmas in 1966. He was in the pits helping and he did not leave the team completely until the beginning of 1967.

By the time of the Daytona tests the sports director was Franco Lini, a journalist who worked for *L'Equipe* and *Auto Italiano*. He was a nice person, but I have to say that controlling a team was not his job. He had good relations with the press, which Enzo Ferrari wanted after the Dragoni era. By the time that Dragoni left, Italian journalists were against the team a lot. Unfortunately, Lini lasted only a year and then Franco Gozzi took his place. Gozzi was close with Ferrari and he also had very good relations with the press. He took over the race management because there was no one else to do it at this time. I still attended all the races and took responsibility for the cars during practice and the race.

When we built the 1966 Ferrari V12 Formula 1 car, we built the chassis with plating riveted to it. It was not a pure monocoque like the 1964 V8 car, because monocoques were very expensive for us. Apart from other considerations, we had to teach the mechanics how to build a monocoque. I believe that a chassis is good when it is light and rigid and the ratio of the rigidity to the weight is as high as possible. I would remind you that a very successful British Formula 2 car, the Protos, was made in wood. It was a very good-handling car, although maybe it was not so good from the point of view of safety! So we had found a way to make chassis at low cost and they were especially easy to repair. We adopted this method of chassis construction for both Prototypes and the 512S competition sports car. During 1966-67 I changed almost all the mechanics and took on new and younger guys.

We produced a family of Prototypes. After the 275P and 330P in 1964, we built the more powerful 275P2 and 330P2 with four overhead camshafts for 1965. Then came the 330P3 in 1966, which was even more powerful and had better torque. That year we had a lot of problems with our own gearboxes and we needed to improve the reliability. We did this, but it was still not enough. During 1966 Ford produced the 'J' car with the 7-litre engine already raced, but with a new and advanced chassis, and I knew that we would be in trouble in 1967; so I went back to the Old Man and discussed it with him.

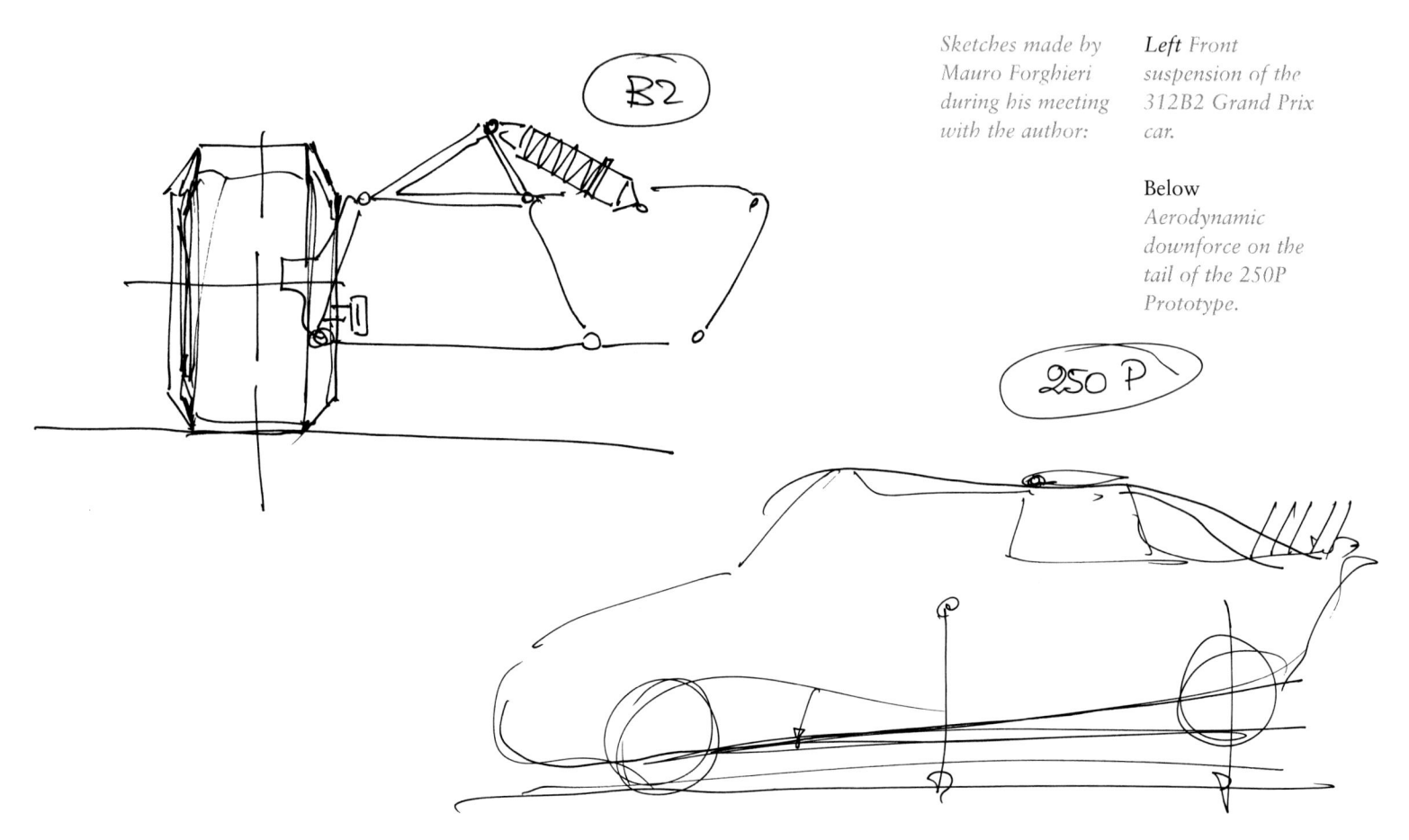

Sketches made by Mauro Forghieri during his meeting with the author:

Left *Front suspension of the 312B2 Grand Prix car.*

Below *Aerodynamic downforce on the tail of the 250P Prototype.*

The result was the P4, which was a completely new car in most respects, with new gearbox, new engine and new, aluminium-alloy, triangulated chassis, stiffened wherever possible. We also used a new system of ventilated disc brake, which, to be honest, was not our idea. Ford were not able to solve the cracking problem with their Kelsey ventilated discs, so they made quick-changeable ventilated discs and calipers – and we did almost the same thing. We were able to change the disc more quickly than the Americans, we had to do it during the night and we could do it in less than 40 seconds. The wheel and brake were assembled in a particular way, to enable us to do this. After the Daytona tests we were well prepared for the 1967 season.

We were very close with the teams that ran our cars privately, especially Ronnie Hoare of *Maranello Concessionaires*, Jacques Swaters of *Écurie Francorchamps* and Luigi Chinetti. Ronnie Hoare was a close friend and it was through him that I was able to take Mike Parkes on to the staff at Maranello. I remember that after the 1962 German Grand Prix, I flew to England with Colin Chapman and the other British team leaders. We went to an American air base and the aircraft was a Webbair Douglas DC-3. We landed at Gatwick, on a grass runway, at 6am and Ronnie Hoare was there to meet me. The following day Ronnie took me to see the racing at Brands Hatch. *Maranello Concessionaires* were running a GTO and the driver was Mike Parkes.

When I got back to Italy I talked to the Old Man about Parkes. I told him, 'He's a driver and an engineer; he's a quick driver with a knowledge of cars. We must have him to work on the development of production cars.' Ordinary racing drivers are not the men to develop production cars because they are too racing-orientated. The man who is going to develop a production car must have the knowledge to solve noise problems, comfort and safety. Ferrari agreed that we should engage Parkes and this was thanks to Ronnie Hoare.

We helped all the private teams as much as possible and sometimes we preferred not to win, provided that the winner was a Ferrari customer. For us the difficulty in the 1960s was that the racing budget was very small. For example, in 1962 the successes of customer drivers with 250GTOs meant sales for Ferrari. It is important to remember that during these years Ferrari was not building thousands of cars, but hundreds and the prices were a lot lower than now.

After Ferrari's withdrawal from Prototype racing, we devoted some resources to Can-Am racing. It was mainly because of Chris Amon's wishes that we ran in Can-Am racing. We modified two of the P4s at the end of the 1967 Prototype season, re-bodying them and making them a little lighter. Chinetti organised the entries and it was good publicity for the Can-Am organisers. We soon learned that even with Chris Amon driving the capacity of the Ferrari engines was too small for us to be competitive and that we could achieve only lower places.

So we took the decision to build a special car for Can-Am racing in 1968 and we used aerodynamic brakes and a special device on the rear end of the car to increase downforce. The car was not ready until the last race of the series and I was there to supervise its running. It was important to see whether we could run a competitive programme in 1969. Ferrari did not like to race too far away, because he couldn't have immediate information about the progress of the cars. It was only thanks to Chinetti that we were there at all. Our efforts in Can-Am racing never represented a serious programme.

In 1969 Ferrari raced the 312P V12 3-litre Prototypes and these had an engine developed from the Formula 1 engine. In 1967 I had redesigned the V12 engine so that the exhausts were in the vee. I love central exhaust systems because of the excellent heat dissipation. A revised version appeared at Monza in 1968 and this had new cylinder heads, modified combustion chambers and the exhaust system on the outside of the engine. This engine was used in the 312P. I had nothing to do with the 312P, as I was fully engaged at Modena on the new flat-12 Grand Prix project and I had already started work on the layout of the 312T with transversely mounted gearbox.

Another car that we built in 1969 was the 212E for Peter Schetty to drive in the European Hill Climb Championship. I gave the responsibility for the design of the engine to Jacoponi. It was built before the 312B and was inspired by the 1965 Tipo 1512 1.5-litre Formula 1 engine, but it was completely different and a much more modern design. The 1512 had the cylinder bores evenly spaced, but the 212E engine had the centre-bore distances changed so that there was uneven spacing between alternate bores. It was much more reliable in this form. Both this engine and the 312B were flat-12s, but they were completely different in terms of philosophy and structure.

When I was considering leaving Ferrari in 1969, I put Caliri, who worked for me, in charge of the new sports car project, the 512S Group Five Competition Sports Car. It was designed and built in a very short time in response to the Porsche 917 that had appeared in 1969. We designed it on the drawing board and with the use of a simple computer, but there was no aerodynamic development. We built the required 25 cars, 12 to 15 assembled and the others still in component form. I told the Old Man that it was going to be very difficult for us to develop such a car, because we were at the same time developing the new Formula 1 engine which I designed in 1969, the 180° flat-12. People call it a 'boxer', but it was not a 'boxer' because a 'boxer' is an engine in which the pistons on both sides of the cylinder block move in the same direction at the same time.

Only a few young people in the factory collaborated on the 512S. We fought quite well against the Porsche 917s and we won at Sebring in 1970, but usually we could not win because our cars were being driven on the limit every lap. In the meanwhile we were developing a new 5-litre car, the 512M. This came out at the end of the 1970 season, but we were running in Formula 1, Formula 2 and sports car racing and our resources were stretched to the limit. I was at races every weekend and it was really too much for me. Remember that Ferrari had signed a contract with Agnelli of Fiat before the start of the 1970 season and the Old Man told me, 'Forghieri, you are not going to have any more economic problems. Do your best.' During 1969–70 Ferrari as a company changed completely the way it worked.

I had developed the 512M, a much improved car and in late 1970 and this had led the Austrian 1,000Km race and won the Kyalami Nine Hours. In September the Old Man decided not to race the 5-litre cars any longer against Porsche. I do not know his reasons, for the 512M was a very competitive car and better than the Porsche 917. We discussed developing a 3-litre Prototype with the flat-12 engine. Ferrari knew that 5-litre cars would be banned at the end of 1971 and he wanted us to develop a car that would win races in 1972.

Mark Donohue and his entrant Roger Penske came to Italy and they were planning to run the car that became the Sunoco-Ferrari. With the help of Luigi Chinetti I asked Enzo Ferrari if I could give all the drawings for the 512M to Donohue and he agreed. I told the Old Man, 'Mark Donohue is a good driver, he is a good engineer, and they can do a 512M even better than ours.' It was a miracle that Ferrari agreed! They bought a 512S, rebuilt it to 512M specification and then added all the special features, quick-refuelling system, special, lighter body, etc. After he first drove it, Mark Donohue told me, 'It is really a very enjoyable car, Mauro.'

We designed the 312PB in a very short time, using the Formula 1 flat-12 engine just as it was. The American aero-engine manufacturer Franklin originated the engine when it came to Ferrari to ask us to develop an engine for installation within the wing. All the ancillaries, injection, ignition were in line with the engine. It was an acceptable configuration for Formula 1, but it was not acceptable in a sports car; there had to be access to change the alternator and many other components during races. We built a car that was an exact copy of the Formula 1 car apart from the bodywork and before Christmas 1970 we took it for testing at Kyalami and, if I remember rightly, we spent two weeks in South Africa.

When we came back, we redesigned the car and built the definitive 312PB. We modified the engine completely, including moving the ancillaries at the front of the engine to the top. Originally we raced only one car in 1971 because there was a limit on the resources available. Our first race in 1971 was at Buenos Aires. Ignazio Giunti was killed and the car destroyed. Beltoise was pushing his car back to the pits and this was forbidden by the rules. Giunti was one of the few very promising Italian drivers at the time and his death was a big shock to Enzo Ferrari. Racing is dangerous, but when a driver is killed because of something stupid like this, it is not acceptable. I remember especially the drive of Jacky Ickx and Clay Regazzoni at Brands Hatch where they had a tremendous race. I developed the 1972 version of the 312PB intended for Le Mans before I resigned from Ferrari yet again.

We had a lot of tyre vibration, which the tyre manufacturer could not cure. So I tried to solve the problem by using a special damping device, but I was unsuccessful. Because of the tyre vibration problem we were severely criticised in the Italian press. The journalists were writing that Forghieri likes to introduce new developments; he doesn't like to race the older cars although they are without problems. Also Jacky Ickx was getting himself involved in the politics of the company. So I resigned from Ferrari in July 1972 and went to my design study centre at Modena to design the 'snowplough' car, which later became the second version of the 312B3. I had nothing to do with the 1973 312PB sports cars, which proved no match for the Matras, apart from designing a long tail which Colombo asked me to do. I believe that my research office is now used as a gymnasium by Michael Schumacher!

In 1972 a new guy, Sandro Colombo, came to Ferrari from Fiat to work on a Formula 1 car. He was only the organiser and he gave the design work of the original 312B3 to Rocchi and Salvarini. Colombo had the monocoque chassis made by Thompson in England and it was not successful. I have no complaints about Thompson, he did well what he was told to do. In my opinion Ferrari should not have commissioned construction of the chassis or other major components outside of the factory. In the meantime I was developing a different idea. I was lucky enough to have tested a lot of sports cars in the wind tunnel at Stuttgart, which at that time belonged to the university and a very high-level aerodynamicist was helping me to develop my ideas.

Ferrari sports cars had a lot more downforce than the Formula 1 cars. The reason was the surface area of the sports cars was five times more than the Formula 1 cars. At that time all Formula 1 cars had a very slim profile, so I designed a car with a wide, flat body to improve

Among Forghieri's most successful designs was the 312B flat-12 formula 1 car. One of Enzo Ferrari's favourite drivers, Mario Andretti, is at the wheel in the 1971 Spanish Grand Prix. He ran well until the fuel-pump casing cracked and the fuel was ignited by the car's own electrical system.

downforce and British journalists called this 'the snowplough'. It was purely an experimental car. At this time I almost resigned from Ferrari, for the Old Man was sick, but he told me, 'Don't move Mauro, wait!' So I moved to Modena to design the 'T' car. They called me back to Maranello because the Thompson-built car was unsuccessful during the 1973 season, it had very poor handling and Jacky Ickx complained about it.

The Old Man asked me how long it would take to modify the car. He said, 'Do you believe that you can modify the car so that it is quicker than the B3 that we are racing?' I said, 'Of course, but it will take a month.' So I modified the Thompson car in the way in which I was designing the 'T' car. I designed side pontoons, I moved the radiator forward to increase weight at the front, I developed a high air intake and I improved the rear wing. I changed both the weight distribution and the aerodynamics, following what I had learned in Stuttgart. Within three weeks I had built a car with which Merzario beat the lap record on the Fiorano test track by almost two seconds and Merzario, certainly, was not better than Jacky Ickx.

Colombo left, the young engineer Ferrari left and so we had gaps in the team. We raced this version of the 312B3 during the remainder of 1973. Ferrari had recovered from his sickness. He had feared that he was dying, but he was not, he only had a problem with the medicine that he was taking. Ferrari had previously discussed with me big changes in the team and these were now put in hand. Jacky Ickx left the team at the end of the year because Ferrari no longer wanted him. The reason was that Ickx was becoming political.

Montezemolo came from Fiat with the support of Gianni Agnelli and he took over the responsibility for competition and press relations. Although Fiat influence was becoming stronger, this did not affect me and I had very good relations with Fiat. Now that I was in the racing department again I continued developing the 'T' car. I decided against using it in 1974 because in my opinion it required further development. We did not race the 312T until 1975.

Mauro Forghieri resigned from the racing department of Ferrari at the end of 1984, but became responsible for the advanced engineering department of Ferrari Automobili SpA. *Fiat would not permit him to leave Ferrari for a period of two years. In 1986 he became Technical Director of the newly created* Ferrari Engineering *division and designed and developed a very advanced Ferrari four-wheel-drive car. During 1984–86 he also worked in Turin for Ghidella, who was Chairman of Fiat. In 1986 he went to see Enzo Ferrari and told him, 'I can leave now.'*

He signed a contract with Iacocca, the President of Chrysler, in 1987 and he founded Lamborghini Engineering. Forghieri was Technical Director of Lamborghini until December 1991. He designed a Formula 1 engine which was used by Lotus in 1990, but unfortunately Chrysler had financial problems during Forghieri's time with Lamborghini. Ayrton Senna tested the Lamborghini-powered Lotus and was very impressed with the engine. Later Forghieri designed a concept electric minivan for the Italian National Electricity Board and he was Technical Director of Bugatti Automobili SpA *from May 1993 until December 1994. He now runs* Oral Engineering, *based in Modena and which undertakes research and development projects for various motor manufacturers.*

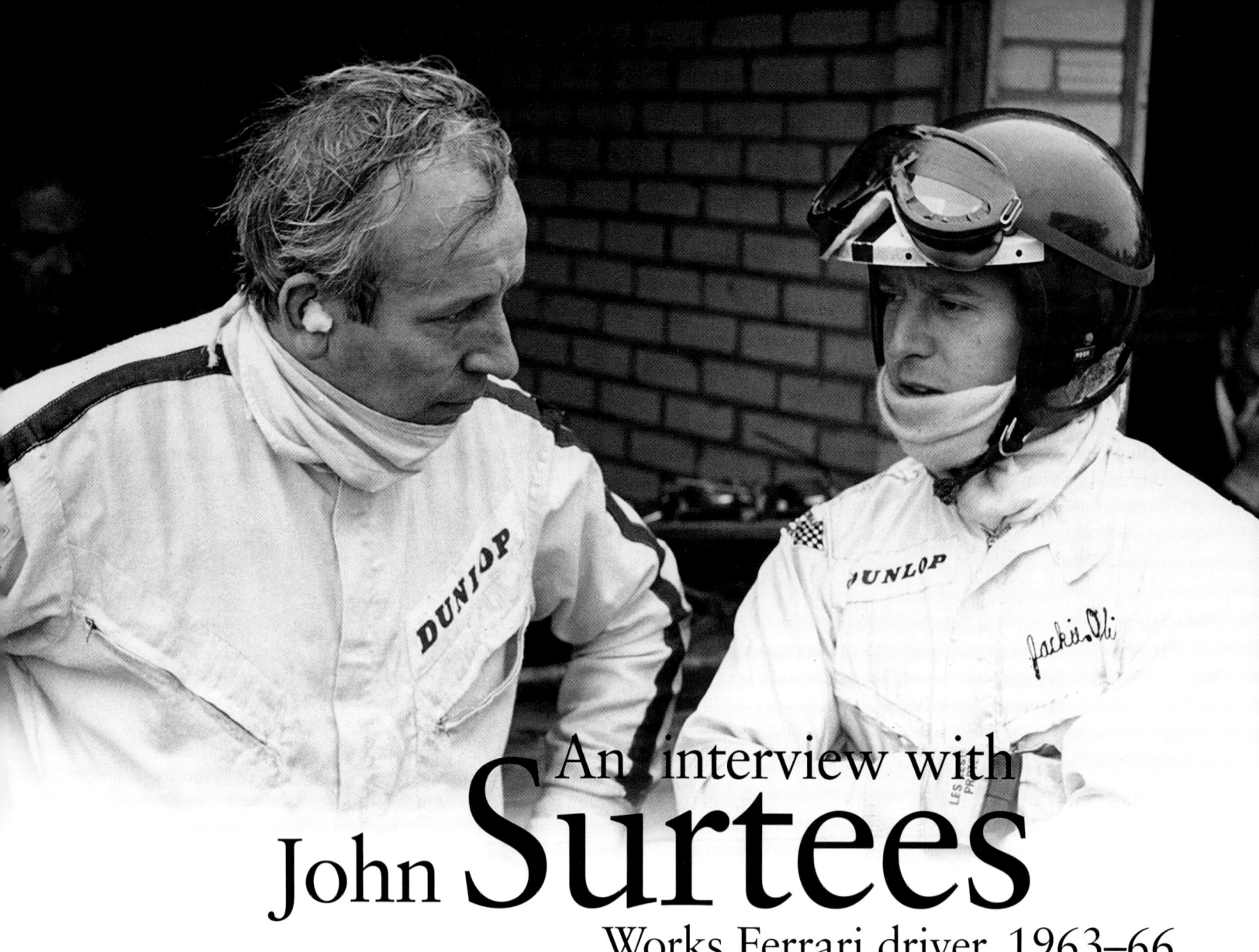

An interview with
John Surtees
Works Ferrari driver, 1963–66

John Surtees had been a Ferrari team member between 1963 and 1966, and drove twice for the team in 1970 to enable him to make a report on the 512S for Enzo Ferrari. Surtees is seen with Jackie Oliver, when they were both BRM team members in 1969. Oliver also drove a works 512S in the BOAC race at Brands Hatch in 1970.

Born in 1934, John Surtees is the son of renowned motorcycle sidecar racer Jack Surtees. He started motorcycle racing in 1951, becoming a member of the works Norton team in 1955. For 1956 he joined MV Agusta and won his first World Championship in the 500cc class. The 1957 season was not so successful because of mechanical problems. Thereafter MV Agusta enjoyed much greater success and Surtees with his MVs won the 350cc and 500cc Motorcycle World Championships in three successive years, 1958, 1959 and 1960. He retired from motorcycle racing at the end of 1960 to concentrate on car racing. This chapter is based on an interview that took place at Edenbridge, Kent on 19 June 2003. The material used has been checked and approved by Mr Surtees.

Before I started car racing I had only driven two competition cars, the sports-racing Aston Martin DBR1 with which Stirling Moss had won the 1959

Nürburgring 1,000Km race and a Vanwall. I drove them during the same week in 1959. The first car race I ever saw was at Goodwood in 1960 and I saw it from the cockpit of a Formula Junior car. During that year I drove Lotus cars for Colin Chapman at certain races that didn't interfere with my motorcycle racing. My second and third races were with Formula 2 cars for Chapman and my fourth race was the Formula 1 International Trophy at Silverstone. So it was quite a speedy transition. After that I drove for Chapman in a number of Grands Prix and my best performance was second place in the British Grand Prix.

I had intended to stay with Colin Chapman for the 1961 season; he had offered me a number one position in the team, but at the end of 1960 I was asked to go out to see Enzo Ferrari. I was told about all the team's plans for 1961, I saw the line-up of drivers and I thought, 'Where do I fit in here? There are too many people about.' I said 'No, I'll come back when I have more experience.' Someone then said, 'No, we don't ask twice.' After that I shot myself in the foot somewhat by walking away from the Lotus deal. There were problems with Innes Ireland and frankly I didn't want to get involved in controversy. *[Innes Ireland left Lotus at the end of 1961 because the combination of Jim Clark and Innes was unworkable as a team. Innes joined UDT-Laystall for 1962.]*

So that is why I walked away and joined *Yeoman Credit*, as it was then. Reg Parnell was after all a very experienced team manager, it was quite good from that point of view, but we didn't get the cars that we were supposed to have had and ended up with customer cars – private Coopers. This was why I suggested the Lola and so the Lola T4 was built. I instigated that programme and in fact I signed the contract and passed it over to *Bowmaker Racing*, as the team became known for 1962. It probably had the best first-year results of any team there was. We nearly won Grands Prix, but not quite, it wasn't a bad car and then Coventry Climax said that they couldn't continue supplying us with engines.

Ferrari again asked me to join them and I thought, frankly, they'd had a dreadful year in 1962, they were a shambles, what better time to join them? I went out again to Maranello, this time they didn't list all the things they wanted; they said, 'You'll be team leader, you'll be number one.' I told them, 'Forget that, I'll be number one by being fastest.' This was, of course, always my attitude; if I wasn't fastest, that was it. Their whole attitude quite excited me; I liked the Italian scene, it was a newish team, but not that new; when you actually looked at the scene, you found that Chiti had done very little, he had largely been a front-man, and the power behind things lay with people like Rocchi and Salvarani.

Mauro Forghieri was a young man in the middle of things; he was the link-man. There was no 'This is the project for next year.' As in most teams, it was a question of continuous bits of development. There was one of the original V6-engined cars (the 246SP) and this was going to be the basis of the car for the new Prototype class. The tubular chassis was cut off at the back, a *Testa Rossa* engine installed and I was given the job of doing all the testing. To start with the chassis was rather flexible and you'd go round during testing at Monza and Modena with one front wheel probably as much as 18 inches off the ground through corners. It still had a bit of a shark-nose and was unpainted at that time.

Fantuzzi would come along, cut pieces here or bang pieces there; aerodynamic testing was largely done with

John Surtees is seen testing the first V12 250P Prototype at Modena Aeroautodromo *in late 1962. The car was based on a lengthened 246SP chassis and a new body without the 'shark nose'.*

oil that was spilled over the bodywork to see where it flowed and where it didn't flow. After I had hammered that car round and round, they went back to the factory and made the first of the 250Ps, which was a stiffened-up and generally strengthened version of what had come out of the testing. The bodywork had lost its shark-like nose and it was replaced by a straight opening early on in the testing, partly because of more effective cooling, and it was all a rush, a panic to get ready for the Sebring 12 Hours race. As happened throughout the time that I was at Maranello, I was always responsible for passing out the cars and giving them their final test – which annoyed a certain other Englishman who was there *[Mike Parkes]* – apart from the time that I was in hospital and couldn't carry out the initial testing of the 330P3.

At Sebring I was to drive with Ludovico Scarfiotti, he came to the works for a fitting and we sorted out our car, which was the third of the four built. The fourth car was so late being finished that there was no time for testing. We arrived at Sebring only to find that they had swapped the cars and given the third car to Chinetti's team and gave us the new, untried car – which wasn't really appreciated. They said I had done all the testing of the 250P and I had to sort it out. So we just got on with it in practice, I wasn't happy obviously and this was, I suppose, the first time that I crossed swords with Dragoni.

At the wheel of the Tipo 158 Formula 1 car John Surtees talks to Mauro Forghieri before the 1965 International Trophy race at Silverstone. Surtees finished second behind Jackie Stewart (BRM P261). All season Surtees complained about the engine's lack of power. (Guy Griffiths)

It was an eventful race. One of the problems that we'd encountered in testing had been fumes, which blew back in under the rear engine cover and over the cockpit, as the engine cover tended to lift. We had modified the sealing round the top of the body and the way it was held down – except for the last car. Ludovico and I were getting gassed, so we were consuming large amounts of liquid and it was very uncomfortable. We finished the race, despite some brake trouble and a couple of other niggling little problems. We'd won, only to find that our own team manager had protested us and suggested that the *NART* car had won and that the officials were a lap out on their lap-chart.

However, my then wife, Pat, was probably the best timekeeper and lap-chart keeper at the race and she had kept both an immaculate lap-chart and a record of lap times. It so happened that the official lap-chart coincided perfectly with my wife's. *NART* didn't have a proper chart; they'd been on the vino and the pasta. After this had been resolved, Ludovico and I had to go out to be presented to some American beauties, but on the way there each of us was being sick because we had been virtually gassed-out in our 250P. This was my first insight into the manoeuvres that could happen at Ferrari at that time.

One of the annoying things about the Prototype period at Ferrari was that you would go along and test and sort out the cars, only for them to be passed to Pedro Rodriguez, Graham Hill and others who drove for private teams. This, of course, was the business side of Ferrari. In addition, all the other teams, such as BRM, were concentrating on Formula 1, whereas Ferrari did almost nothing about Formula 1 and the only development that was coming along was the Michael May-designed fuel injection. It was exciting and the lads in the team were great. At this time Forghieri was not the foremost figure, he was one of the boys and he was not involved in Ferrari politics, such as massaging the American scene.

You would see people, trying to emulate Neubauer of Mercedes-Benz and being clever. This is what I think Dragoni did during his time at Ferrari. He played politics by trying to juggle the Fiat side of things, because in the background at this time was the potential Ford offer and Fiat's constant interest in the company. Dragoni had certain contacts in Turin. Old man Ferrari was doing his best to keep everything alive; I don't think I appreciated at the time how much the team was operating on a shoestring. As I see in hindsight, this excuses some of the more absurd things that happened. We were our own worst enemy, but the Prototype side was a super little team, apart from once when I lost a wheel at the Nürburgring.

In the 1963 Targa Florio my co-driver was Mike Parkes. I wasn't really on the pace; I didn't feel comfortable there and the race didn't really flow for me. I needed to spend more time on the circuit. I was a racer who adopted a slightly different attitude to my sports car driving – obviously, because of the type of racing it was. The Targa Florio was like going to the Isle of Man for the first time; the *Piccolo Madonie* circuit was all about rhythm, understanding how to approach the circuit and I don't think that I can blame anyone else because I crashed, I just made a mistake. I think that it was the only mistake I made with the Prototypes.

I would have preferred not to have co-driven with Parkes, I thought, frankly, that he was a bit of a pain; he was a good driver in saloons and Prototypes, but I would much rather have co-driven with Bandini, Scarfiotti or Willy Mairesse because they were the right sort of size. When you have two people driving a car, it does end up a compromise of how you both sit in the car. It did present a particular problem for Michael, for there was no one as tall as him.

I had Willy Mairesse as co-driver at both the Nürburgring and Le Mans. We won in the 1,000Km race. At Le Mans we were again leading and Willy was at the wheel when the fuel sloshed over and, as far as we understand it, the stop-light switch ignited the fuel as he braked to go under the Dunlop Bridge. He was badly burned; it very nearly brought his career to an end and in some ways I think, contributed to him committing suicide a few years later. He drove a few times more, but he was devastated by losing his racing career, the thing he lived for.

The Old Man agreed that I should run a Lola after I had driven a modified 250P at Mosport and Riverside at the end of 1963. We were checking out the American scene and I gave him a report as to what had happened. I told him, 'One: you haven't a big enough engine; two: the cars are too heavy. There's this new Can-Am series coming up, we need to keep development going and it helps me if I work with other people as well.' He said, 'Fine, as long as you do it privately.' That's how I came to form *Team Surtees* and went back to Eric Broadley to do development on the T70. This didn't go down particularly well with a number of people at Maranello.

We had some problems in 1964 at Sebring where my co-driver was Lorenzo Bandini and we finished third. Bandini was again my co-driver at the Nürburgring in 1964 and we were leading when the car lost a wheel. I managed to keep the car on the track, I went along it a long way and slowed down by using the hedges. It was one of only two occasions when I had a major breakage on a Ferrari; the other was at the 1964 Austrian Grand Prix when the front suspension failed while I was leading. At Le Mans in 1964 Bandini and I were leading when the fuel pipe, which ran from the top of the tank to the bottom to pick the fuel up, broke half-way up; this meant that we could only use half the tank of fuel and we dropped back to finish third. At the Reims 12 Hours race Bandini and I drove a *NART* 250LM and we finished second. I got on fine with Bandini.

It's not true that Dragoni favoured Bandini, which was just something a person who didn't know what he was talking about conjured up. Dragoni used Bandini for his own manipulations, it might have appeared that Dragoni favoured him; it was not for Bandini's sake, although at times Bandini benefited, but purely for his own juggles. I was a threat in many ways to what Dragoni was trying to establish. I was trying hard to make the team more international, as has happened in recent years. We were too isolated, we'd lost Maserati down the road, we'd lost Alfa Romeo, so we were racers isolated in the middle of Italy and falling behind. In the UK there was a hotbed of racing manufacturers all vying with each other.

At the same time I brought in Peter Jackson of Specialised Mouldings who did the Lola bodywork and we created the first glass-fibre bodies and started the first glass-fibre manufacturing at Scaglietti just down the road from Ferrari at Maranello. Peter Jackson made the first glass-fibre Prototype noses. We were going to start a joint company, but in the end Ferrari did it by itself, at first for Formula 1 and then for Prototypes. While Lola made sports cars as long as I was at Maranello, Ferrari stuck to Prototypes. They were very different animals; the sports cars were much lighter and used 5- to 6½-litre production-based engines.

Companions in anxiety – Mauro Forghieri and John Surtees in the Ferrari pit at the Le Mans Test Weekend in April 1964. (LAT)

Dragoni saw it as a bit of an intrusion that I was trying to get outside people involved in Ferrari. In a way this also started to annoy Forghieri because he thought that everything that was original was being developed at Maranello. Of course it wasn't, there was very little originality at Ferrari at that time. Ferrari did good, sound, basic engineering, but in the way of new technology, nothing much was happening.

The frustrating thing about the Prototype programme was that we so often were in a position to win Le Mans and something minor went wrong, such as in 1963 with poor Willy and in 1964 with Bandini when the petrol pipe broke off in the fuel tank. We never had any major problems, the cars were very driveable, very user-friendly, certainly we tried to develop them that way so that you could extend them and push them hard. You couldn't afford to have a Prototype that was like a Formula 1 car, getting pretty well on the knife-edge; a long-distance car has to be more forgiving.

In 1965 we came up with the twin cam per bank engines and improved aerodynamics. At Daytona that year I shared a 330P2 with Pedro Rodriguez who was a good driver. Rodriguez was a *NART* team member and this pairing was possibly a good political solution to ensure nothing like 1963 happened. We had problems with the Dunlop tyres; we tried high-lines and low-lines, but the tyres kept failing. We had the same problems in the Monza 1,000Km race and we dropped back because of tyre failure.

During my Can-Am programme, I had worked with Firestone and because of these tyre failures I went to the Old Man and told him that we needed a change of tyre supplier. I showed him what we had done testing with Firestone and he said, 'Do a test with them.' It was sad in some ways because I had known the Dunlop people for a long while, but they weren't keeping up with the opposition. I got Mr McCary of Firestone over to Italy for tests and, as a result of these, Ferrari used Firestone tyres at the 1965 Mexican Grand Prix (running the cars in the name of *NART* to avoid contractual problems), ran them in some races in 1966 and went over to Firestone completely in 1967. It was another benefit that Ferrari derived from my Can-Am programme.

By this time we were getting into such trouble with the Formula 1 cars in 1965 that I missed the Targa Florio. With Scarfiotti I won the Nürburgring 1,000Km race, and we were partners again at Le Mans. What the good thing about Ferraris was that normally they were well engineered. The various things that stopped me winning at Le Mans were silly things, the fire with Mairesse in 1963, the broken fuel pipe in 1964. The main components like engines and gearboxes were very good. At Le Mans we had a whole batch of brake discs that were cracking and all the problems stemmed from this. We even had one shatter. The result of these brake problems was that we relied on the gearbox more and more for braking and eventually this gave up.

The Ferrari 12-cylinder engine had, of course, a superb power range, it didn't rev high, and it was a fairly basic engine in 1963–64. In 1965 we had engines with twin camshafts per bank of cylinders and this, coupled with the increased capacity that was adopted for 1964, gave an increase in power and altered the characteristics of the engine. The 4-litre engine with twin camshafts per bank of cylinders had much more torque than previous Ferrari Prototype engines and you let it pull a higher gear, which would make it easier on tyres and brakes. Generally, the Ferrari Prototypes were good, steadily developed cars and very enjoyable to drive. While I was at Ferrari, we would have won every Prototype race that we entered, but for minor problems. There was never an occasion when other teams were quicker.

I stirred things up more in 1965 over the question of the Formula 1 cars, which I did not think were getting proper attention. I had won the Drivers' Championship in 1964 and it was natural to expect another good year. I said that we were playing politics with Formula 1 and it was ludicrous. We should have just concentrated on developing the flat-12 engine, but nothing in the way of development was done. We were having all sorts of problems with the flat-12s and these cars were basically the same as they were the year before. Because of a tie-up with Fiat and the fact they wanted the V8 to go in the *Dino*, Ferrari was persevering with this engine, which was no real match for the Coventry Climax V8.

Only once in 1965 did I have an engine that I believed was truly competitive and that was the flat-12 that I drove in the Italian Grand Prix just before my accident. Shortly before this race Rocchi developed a revised cylinder head with improved induction. I was in my element with this car because I was competitive. I was unhappy with what was happening inside the team and I was stressing that we should look more closely at what was happening outside Ferrari and bring other people into Ferrari. There were more pressures on me from Dragoni and others, but at the same time the Old Man was asking me to move to Italy and live there.

I did move to Italy just before my break-up with Ferrari. When I returned after my accident, I had been due to compete at Indianapolis with a Lola that I had tested before my accident. I passed the car over to Graham who won with it. The way Ferrari had treated me when I had my accident was superb. I had no personal injury accident policy and he said, 'Ferrari' and the Ferrari insurance paid all my expenses. He even offered to build me a race car with automatic transmission. I made the decision that I would stop everything else and I would concentrate on one, getting fit and two, the Ferrari cause. So the Old Man gave me a flat and I went out and bought all the furniture. I was just moving in at around the time of Monaco and Spa. This was not what some people wanted. They were concerned that I would get even closer to the Old Man.

Just after I came back from my accident, I tested the 330P3, our new Prototype for 1966. It just didn't work. We got it to work in a test just before its first race. This was where the big thing between me and Parkes happened and you've got to remember that Parkes had teamed up with Dragoni and become part of his clique. I

An Interview with John Surtees 239

asked them why it wasn't doing good lap times. You couldn't get round the *Curva Grande* at Monza and this was a really difficult fast corner then, one where you really had to get everything right. The aerodynamic balance of the P3 was just not right. I was not the engineer, I didn't pretend to be the engineer, and I was just passing information from the seat of my pants to Mauro. I was the PI system or the computer system of today. This was how Mauro and I worked together, we made changes to the P3 and it worked well.

We had atrocious weather in the P3's first race, the Monza 1,000Km and it was a race in which Dragoni's pettiness showed itself. In that race we set off as the heavens opened and during the race the windscreen wipers stopped. Dragoni suggested after the race that I had wanted to retire the car, whereas I had said that we just had to go faster, so that the rain went over the windscreen and roof in the slipstream. If we went slower in these conditions we would have actually seen less than if we went faster. We had to go faster than we wanted to, but we pulled out a big lead. Afterwards Dragoni said, 'If it wasn't for Michael, we wouldn't have won.' He completely ignored the fact that I was the one in the car at the time, worked out what we had to do and set fastest lap.

So this was the sort of thing that I had to put up with. You have to remember that Enzo Ferrari was sitting back at Maranello, waiting to hear what had happened; there wasn't full TV coverage of the races in those days. So what happened instead? He relied on Dragoni, Franco Lini and others reporting back to him and he was being fed rubbish; if only we'd had the television of today, we'd have had none of these problems. Half the problem was that the Old Man had lost touch with racing; he was too involved in politics and in keeping Ferrari afloat.

The first real problem with Dragoni was at the Monaco Grand Prix. Dragoni insisted that I drove the 3-litre V12 car. I told him, 'The 2.4-litre *Dino* was two seconds a lap faster round Modena than the current Formula 1 car. You are denying me the use of it and I'm the fastest driver. I came to Monaco to win. The V12 will break its gearbox, you have to row it along because it doesn't have enough power and it's too heavy. I know it doesn't have the power you say it has, I've been to the test shop and seen the papers. It doesn't have the 320bhp that you're talking about, it doesn't even have 300bhp.' I led the race, but predictably retired because of gearbox failure. Bandini finished second and if I had been driving the V6, we would have won.

Three weeks after Monaco I won the Belgian Grand Prix with the V12 to which a modified cylinder head had been fitted and then I went to Le Mans where I was to drive with Scarfiotti. When I arrived, Dragoni told me, 'Mr Agnelli *[President of Fiat]* is coming and so we are going to put Ludovico in for the start.' I reminded Dragoni what had happened at Monaco and then said, 'Now we come here. You said to me, "We've got to beat Ford, go out and do it." I did what you wanted, I set fastest time. There is only one way you are going to beat Ford. The Ford team is filled with racers, Gurney, Foyt and all the others. Generally, our car is pretty foolproof. You can virtually drive it like a Grand Prix car and it should last the race.

'We know very well that perhaps the Fords can be quicker, but only if they can pace themselves. None of the Ford drivers will let someone get away from them. Your only hope is for me to go "bang" right from the start as though it were a Grand Prix; that is the only way we will win this race. We have another two or three cars running at a steady pace; we go for security and if they last – and they should last, they've covered 12 hours, – we'll win. You know that at a minimum I'm a second a lap faster than Ludovico, he's just not that sort of racer. What are we trying to do? I've just came back from winning at Spa and you didn't even congratulate me.'

So I just left and drove back to the factory. I saw Enzo, and went into the problems. We'd all agreed that we would never actually spell out the final reason why the break had to be. It was not necessarily better for me, but a lot of my heart was at Ferrari. As things were there was no other decision for me to make. Dragoni did not have the power originally to do what he did, but he went back a long time in Ferrari's life and he had his contacts in Turin. It was vital for Ferrari, if he was to survive, to have the Turin involvement. It was a natural thing that should have happened in any case. I think that it was wonderful that Agnelli did his deal with Ferrari and in the end it has allowed Ferrari to have its finest hour, which we are seeing today. I said at the time of Enzo Ferrari's death, 'Ferrari's finest hour is still to come and the Old Man will be looking down and chuckling.'

It all went back to the general situation where the mechanics, the engineers, Rocchi, Salvarani and all the rest of them were on my side, but not the senior management. Just a few years ago I drove into Modena in a 300SLR Mercedes-Benz during the Mille Miglia and parked in Scaglietti's yard; all the mechanics, who were still alive from my Ferrari race team, had come out to meet me. That meant so much to me; that was the sort of relationship I had with them. Because of what had happened I – and Ferrari – lost two or three World Championships – together we could have made it. I was part of a family at Maranello. The Prototype period was one of which Ferrari could justifiably be proud and I am proud to have been part of it. My years with Ferrari, despite the problems and the ups and downs, were probably the happiest of my motor racing career.

Gozzi was involved in the decision and he came to a little celebration in my honour about three years ago and

John Surtees seen in 1964, his second year with Ferrari when he won the Drivers' World Championship. (LAT)

he said, 'It should never have happened. If Mauro Forghieri had stood up and told the truth at that time, it wouldn't have happened.' The Old Man shared responsibility for what happened to me at Maranello. His words to me not long before he died were, 'John, we must remember the good times and not the mistakes.' I think that summed it all up.

In 1970 Ferrari asked me to drive the 512S at Spa and the Nürburgring. I didn't like it at all. I gave him a long report. I said, 'The 512 is a prime example of a car that someone drives with their heart rather than their head.' Perhaps Mauro didn't like the fact my report was critical of a car that I didn't think would work. Ickx and I thought that it was in some ways like Mike Hailwood and the Honda motorcycle. Mike rode it with his heart, largely round the problems, rather than sort out the problems. Ickx would throw up his hands about the Porsche 917s being faster, but Maranello did nothing to make the 512S better. It was so aerodynamically unbalanced that all sorts of things were tagged on to it, but made no difference. It reminded me of the 330P3 when I came back after my accident.

After he left Ferrari, Surtees joined Cooper and won the 1966 Mexican Grand Prix. He continued to race Lola sports cars until the end of 1967 and also raced the Lola T70 Mark III Prototype with Aston Martin engine in 1967. He drove for Honda in 1967–68 Formula 1 racing, worked with Eric Broadley on development of the V12 Honda, won the 1967 Italian Grand Prix and finished second in the 1968 French race. During 1969 he drove for BRM in Formula 1, but the cars were uncompetitive, and he also raced a Chaparral in Can-Am. He had started his own racing car company based at Edenbridge in Kent in 1969, at first building cars for Formula 5000 and then operating a Formula 1 team for which he drove himself until the end of 1971. Thereafter he ran a very successful Formula 2 team sponsored by the Lesney 'Matchbox' toy concern. He is still based in Edenbridge and remains active in business.

An interview with Brian Redman

Works Ferrari sports car driver, 1972–73

Brian Redman and Jody Scheckter at the 1973 Watkins Glen Six Hours race. In this race Scheckter co-drove a Ford Capri RS2600 with Jackie Stewart. (LAT)

Brian Hermon Thomas Redman was born in Burnley in Lancashire on 9 March 1937. In his words, 'my education is best described as minimal.' He left school at 16 with three passes at GCE 'O' level. Then he went to a catering college in Blackpool for three years. He was not interested in catering, but the family had a chain of grocery shops and two cafés in Burnley. He then went into the Army to do his National Service. He bought a Morris Minor 1000 Traveller, driving all over the country in connection with the family business. He modified the Minor and his modifications included fitting a Shorrocks supercharger. He decided that he would better off on a track rather than driving too fast on public roads. Brian first raced the Minor at Rufforth airfield circuit on Easter Monday, 1959, was thoroughly trounced, but it whetted his appetite. At the end of 1959 he bought an 848cc Mini, modified it himself and raced it through 1960.

For 1961 he bought an ex-Leslie Johnson XK 120, raced it at one meeting at Catterick, at which it *consumed a set of tyres, and then moved on to a Morgan Plus 4 for 1962. He married in September 1962. (In Brian's words, 'I had run out of money, so there was no alternative but marriage'.) He took up Moto-cross with first a DOT and then a Greeves, but occasionally drove in car competitions. He had a chance to drive the ex-John Coombs 'Lightweight' Jaguar E-type for John Bridges and was taken on by the* Red Rose *team. He established an outstanding reputation in British racing with the E-type Jaguar in 1965 and for 1966 the team moved on to a Lola T70 with Traco-modified Chevrolet engine and did exceptionally well in British events. At the end of the year he gained a Grovewood award.*

In 1967 he drove a F2 Brabham for David Bridges until mid-season when Bridges obtained a Lola T100. By 1968 he was driving a Gulf-Ford GT40 with Jacky Ickx for John Wyer, winning at Brands Hatch and Spa. He raced a works Formula 2 Ferrari on the Sudschleife *circuit at the Nürburgring and was a works Cooper Formula 1 driver. In the 1968 Belgian Grand Prix he crashed his Cooper-BRM as the result of suspension failure and his injuries put him out of racing until the end of the year when he drove a Chevron in the Springbok series. In 1969 he partnered Jo Siffert in the works Porsche team; he again partnered Siffert at the wheel of Gulf-Porsche 917s in 1970, winning at Spa, in the Targa Florio (with a 908/3) and in Austria. He also won the 2-litre European Sports Car Championship for the British marque Chevron.*

Brian decided to retire from racing at the end of 1970, moved to South Africa, but came back after a few months because of the political situation. He drove an old McLaren M10B for Sid Taylor, but had a largely unsuccessful season. He returned to Gulf-Porsche for a 'one-off' drive in the 1971 Targa Florio, but it ended in a life-threatening accident when the steering failed. The Porsche caught fire and Brian suffered bad burns to the face, neck and hands. This chapter is based on telephone conversations, e-mails and a tape-recording, conducted during July 2003. The material used has been checked and approved by Mr Redman.

My first contact with Ferrari was when I received a telephone call in 1968 at my home in Colne. 'Brian, this is Forghieri at Ferrari. We want you to come to Modena to test the *Dino* Formula 2 car.' A week later I was at the Modena *Aeroautodromo*, being fitted into the lovely little V6 racer. It was a delight, with sure and precise handling, a gearbox second to none with lightning fast changes as quick as the hand could move.

During a short break for lunch Forghieri took me to one side and said, 'Brian, you see over there, in the raincoat.' Two hundred yards away, standing under the trees on the outside of the second turn stood a tall, white-haired figure. 'Brian,' Forghieri continued, '*this* is Signor Ferrari!' Naturally, it added a certain degree of impetus to my driving! At the end of testing, Forghieri told me we would look at the factory the following day – and then have lunch with Signor Ferrari.

On our arrival in the Maranello dining room, 12 Ferrari lieutenants fixed their quizzical gaze on me, no doubt noting how nervous I was. Enzo Ferrari finished his conversation with *Ing.* Caliri, turned to face me, shook hands and said, '*Va bene?*' and then raised his left hand, pinched me on the right cheek and added, '*Nize boy.*' Only later did I learn that this was a great compliment. I was asked to drive a Formula 2 car alongside Jacky Ickx on the South Circuit at the Nürburgring. I finished fourth and set fastest lap after a stone thrown up by Ahren's Brabham broke my goggles.

In the 1972 Spa 1000 Km race Brian Redman drove this 312PB with Merzario. They won after team-mate Ronnie Peterson went off in the wet. (LAT)

I was emotionally drained by the race and declined the invitation to continue driving for the team.

Late in the 1971 season Sid Taylor was offered a BRM P167 Can-Am car for two races at Imola and Hockenheim, both of which I won. The Imola race was held in heavy rain and the BRM was very good in the wet; I lapped the entire field. Mauro Forghieri came up to me and said, 'What are you doing next year?' I subsequently received a request to pay another visit to Maranello – and another invitation to lunch. As we went into the dining room, Forghieri turned to me and said, 'Brian, you are the only driver Ferrari ever asked twice!' Enzo Ferrari greeted me with a handshake, a warning weave of the finger – and no pinch on the cheek! Following this meeting I joined the Ferrari sports car team in Maranello's attack on the World Manufacturers' Championship.

For me, at least, Ferrari was the first team I drove for that paid any decent money, £20,000, a huge sum, for the 1972 season. With the John Wyer team I had received $1,000 a race for the long races, Daytona, Sebring and Le Mans and $700 for each of the other events. This had something to do with the reason that I went to Ferrari!

I didn't go back to Maranello for testing, but in November flew out to South Africa for the Kyalami Nine Hours race which, I guess was a shake-down for the 1972 season, where Ferrari entered two of the splendid 312PBs. I managed to put our car on pole position and Clay Regazzoni and I won, but that isn't why I remember it so well. Our hotel, the nearby Kyalami Ranch, was a sumptuous resort-style establishment where the rooms were in rondavels: African-style, separate buildings with straw roofs. There was a tremendous party to celebrate our victory, which included much horseplay involving the swimming pool, the drivers, crew-members – and various items of hotel furniture.

Afterwards, Clay decided that Mario Andretti needed a little further excitement in his life. He lit a newspaper, went to Mario's rondavel and tossed the blazing paper through the door. It was not an enraged Mario who came charging out, but another hotel guest, who showed not the slightest sign of amusement. That night we hid Clay from a search party of large African policemen and the following day he was smuggled out of South Africa.

Although Ferrari was largely unopposed in 1972, there was a very strong challenge between the drivers in the team, every body was trying to win, and I think Peter Schetty ran the team extremely well and his organisation compared very favourably with that of John Wyer and the *Gulf-Porsche* team. I had a very good relationship with all my co-drivers; I had made myself into the ideal second driver. Very often I didn't fit into the car, because Siffert (at Porsche) was smaller than me. I was often a bit crunched up with my knees under the wheel, but I never said anything.

I co-drove at the first couple of races with Clay Regazzoni and I would say that he was one of the world's great characters. He had an inclination for hitting things and going off the track, but he was a superb driver. I was very impressed at Spa in 1972 when I went to get him to go for dinner. I went to his room and he shouted 'Ciao', and there he was between the owner of the hotel and her daughter.

Sebring in 1972 was one of the big disappointments of my racing career. Clay and I were leading by a long, long way, about four laps, when the car caught fire and was burnt out. At Monza I spun at the *Curva Del Vialone* and put the car out of the race. The race was run in miserable, wet conditions, but I'd been through there on the same line 20 or 30 times before and, suddenly, boom, I spun for no apparent reason. I could never understand why I'd spun, but only a year or so ago I read in a magazine that the Ferrari team management were extremely mad at Ronnie Peterson at Monza because he'd hit Redman and knocked him off! I don't know whether that's true or not, but certainly something funny happened at Monza.

At Spa Merzario was hopeless, he didn't like the circuit and was lapped. I was leading at Spa and there was immense pressure because Peterson was catching me, even though I was going as hard I could. I came up to *Les Combes* and I saw an unusual movement in the crowd. Ever since my accident at that corner in 1968, I didn't take the normal line braking into the apex. I braked, the brakes locked, I came off the brakes, put them on again and I just made it round the corner. Ronnie never made it; he hit the barrier, and went round it like a slot car. It was a fine win for us. Another good win with Ickx at the lovely Österreichring rounded off the season.

In 1973 I continued to be partnered with Jacky Ickx. I had driven with him in 1968 with the John Wyer team, I knew him very well and I often stayed at his house in Brussels. We had an excellent relationship. Everyone has their own opinions and I think that he was the best long-distance driver in the world, perhaps ever. Although he was young, he was so calm and cool, never got flustered.

The first time I drove with him was at Kyalami in 1967 and I was stunned at the Le Mans start when he walked calmly across the road. By the time he had his belts fastened, the rest of the field had gone and he was nearly lapped. On the third or fourth lap he came in because there was something wrong with the oil pressure, it was the sender unit, but we went on to win with the Mirage. His speed in the rain, especially at Spa, was phenomenal. He was a fabulous driver, we were very friendly and I knew all his family.

I don't think that the Ferraris handled badly in 1973;

it was just that the Matras were technically more advanced. They had at least as much power, they had better aerodynamics and they had more supple suspension. They were better over the bumps and many of the tracks were very bumpy. One race in particular that I remember was the Targa Florio. I think that it was the fourth time that I raced there. I didn't claim to know the circuit, but Jacky Ickx had never raced there before. Before the race Jacky was in the car waiting to start and I said, 'Jacky, you only have to remember one thing – this is not a race.' Any way he crashed on the second lap. When he got back to the pits, I asked him if he was okay. 'Yes, Brion,' he replied, 'but I have a very big accident. I go a long, long way down a mountain.'

At the Nürburgring Caliri said to us, 'If a Ferrari is leading at the half-way mark, no other Ferrari is to pass it.' So what happened? Jacky and I are leading, but Merzario and Pace caught up with us. Merzario went hurtling past Ickx right in front of the pits. Caliri was jumping up and down and leaping around, everybody's shouting and yelling and, anyway, both cars stopped for a splash of fuel just before the end of the race. Merzario was staring down, gripping the wheel and he wouldn't look at anybody. The Ferrari people were screaming at him, 'Get out of the car!' Two burly Italian mechanics forced his hands off the wheel, grabbed him by his overalls and hauled him out of the cockpit. So we went on to win, it was not a very satisfactory race, but how many are?

Before Le Mans, Ferrari tested at the Paul Ricard circuit and on an *autostrada* near Modena, which the authorities closed specially for Ferrari. While we were at Paul Ricard, Forghieri asked me to raise myself up in the cockpit at full speed – nearly 200 mph – to see if my helmet was deflecting air from the engine intake. Instantly the pressure of the air-stream caught the peak of my helmet and I was looking at the sky! It was only with great effort, propelled by self-preservation, that I was able to get my head down.

Jacky took pole position in practice at Le Mans with our old friend Merzario alongside. Just before the start Jacky said to me, 'Brion, I wish you to start ze race.' 'What for?' was my response.' Jacky explained, 'I do not wish zu battle with Merzario.' We were both on the front row. I said to Jacky, 'There are nine Prototypes in the race and one of them will win. At the end of the first lap I shall be in ninth place.' He said, 'Good!' At seven in the evening I get a signal to pit out of sequence. Forghieri shouted, 'We must look at the brake pads. Merzario has just come in and his backing plates were welded to the discs.' By this time Merzario had lapped us, but they looked at our brakes and they reckoned that they would be all right until midnight.

Around midnight we took the lead, but then at around 2am an exhaust pipe broke and it couldn't be repaired, we had a spin and a new tail-section had to be fitted and after that the fuel tank developed a leak. We still kept driving as hard as possible, we regained time on the leaders and with just over an hour to the finish we were in second place and gaining on the leading Matra. I had finished driving, I was in the caravan changing, when in came Ickx. He said, 'We are finished, the piston has collapsed'. It was caused by the weak mixture on the cylinder on which the exhaust had broken. It was very sad, we got a standing ovation, the mechanics were crying.

That time with Ferrari was fantastic, it really brought me out of impending obscurity and at around the same time I was driving for Carl Haas and Jim Hall in America in Formula 5000 in a Lola T3300 and having a very good year of it. I lost the championship by just a few points because I missed two races driving for Ferrari. Ferrari, of course, withdrew from sports car racing at the end of 1973 and so I remained in America doing Formula 5000.

In 1977 the FCCA tried to revitalise Formula 5000 in the United States by reviving the name 'Can-AM' series and running the cars with full-width bodywork. At the first race at St. Jovite in Canada Brian was driving a Lola T333 in qualifying and, following an adjustment to the front wing, the car became airborne and landed upside down, dragging Brian for 100 yards along the track. He suffered neck, sternum and other serious injuries. On the way to the hospital the ambulance suffered a puncture while travelling at 100mph. He returned to racing in 1978, but his services were not in great demand, so he sold up his home at Gargrave in Yorkshire and worked for Carl Haas in Chicago, selling Lola cars.

Brian proposed a Lola for IMSA racing in 1982 and acted as driver and team manager for Cooke-Woods Racing and he won the IMSA Championship. He drove for the Group 44 Jaguar team in IMSA racing in 1984–86 and raced Aston Martin AMR1 Group C cars in 1989. He and his wife Marian live in Los Angeles where in 1991 he formed International Race Promotions, a company that organises and promotes historic racing events. Brian continues to compete at historic meetings and cars driven by him have included a Ford GT40 and Graham Hill's 1962 World Championship-winning BRM.

Colonel Ronnie Hoare
Founder of *Maranello Concessionaires*

A crowded pit as Joakim Bonnier is about to set off with the Maranello Concessionaires-entered 330P that he and Graham Hill drove to second place at Le Mans in 1964. The 'Colonel', in dark blazer, can be seen standing by the nose of the car with his back to the pit counter. (LAT)

The 'Colonel' ran the British Ferrari agent, *Maranello Concessionaires*, and was one of the leading private entrants of Ferraris in the 1960s. Born on 31 August 1913 in London, on his birth certificate he is called Ronald Jack Hoare, he always preferred to be known as Ronald John, but later, in motor racing circles, if you said 'the Colonel', everyone knew whom you meant. Hoare never knew his father, who was, it is believed, killed in action during the First World War. He was educated at Collett Court (the prep school for St Paul's public school in London) and subsequently at St Paul's. After leaving school his godfather, Lord Aberconway, arranged for Ronnie to be apprenticed at the Metropolitan Railway, of which he was Chairman. Ronnie's nanny remembered him coming back from work filthy and greasy.

Ronnie's mother gave him a new MG Midget for his 19th birthday and he competed with this regularly. For Ronnie, the Metropolitan Railway was not the future

246 Scarlet Passion

that he had in mind and he became a salesman at University Motors Ltd, the London area MG distributors, at their main London showrooms at 80, Piccadilly, W1. The Sales Director, Paddy Lynch, thought him to be difficult and arrogant. That was the opinion of an older man about a much younger, brash and ambitious man and, perhaps, should not be taken too seriously. It was while at University Motors that Ronnie married in 1936 for the first time but it was not a successful marriage, perhaps they were both too young and they divorced.

Ronnie, like many young men of the period, was deeply concerned about the intentions of Hitler and Nazi Germany, and the likelihood of war made him feel both excited and anxious. In 1939 he joined the Army Supplementary Reserve and following the outbreak of war on 3 September 1939 he was commissioned into a London regiment. He transferred to the Royal Horse Artillery, served in France in the early days of the war and was at Dunkirk. Ronnie re-married in 1942, but it proved another unsuccessful marriage and was dissolved.

Still in his twenties, he was a lieutenant-colonel on General Alexander's staff and then became a full colonel on General Montgomery's staff in North Africa, where he was slightly wounded. Ronnie played a significant role in planning the invasion of Sicily and was awarded an OBE. When he was on staff duty in Germany, he was awarded a CBE and was promoted to the rank of Acting Brigadier (probably the youngest ever in the British army to hold this rank). After the end of the war he held the substantive rank of major and he was posted to the 4th Regiment Royal Horse Artillery and was given command of the Eagle Troop.

He married Anne in 1949 and she proved a pillar of strength, support and commonsense throughout their marriage, which lasted forty years. There are three children, Louise, Christopher and Margaret. After a course at the Joint Services Staff College he served as AQ of the 6th Armoured Division, first at Bulford and then in Germany. During his Eagle Troop days and at Bulford, he and Anne owned what she called the 'fun' cars, including – in 1949 – a Riley MPH and the ex-Guy Templar 2.9-litre Alfa Romeo. Ronnie and Anne used to race each other on the open road, but this had to stop when he was posted to Germany. 'A Jaguar XK 120 was a happy replacement,' says Anne. Ronnie finally commanded a Royal Artillery Training Regiment at Oswestry.

He resigned his commission in 1955 and bought a one-third share in F. English Limited, the Ford main dealer in Poole where he and his wife settled. Later he bought out the other shareholders. He and his wife then moved to nearby Broadstone. Ronnie was elected a Conservative councillor on Dorset County Council and became Chairman of the Finance Committee. In his role as councillor he was also Chairman of the Hurn (Bournemouth) Airport Management Committee.

Ronnie went into partnership with Bob Gibson-Jarvie, the son of the Chairman of the United Dominions Trust finance company, and they set up the United Racing Stable, which entered Formula 2 Cooper-Climax cars in 1959 for Bill Moss, Ron Flockhart and Henry Taylor. The partnership did not work well, the team missed many races during the year and the best performance was a fourth and last place by Taylor in the poorly supported *Coupe du Salon* at Montlhéry. At the end of that year Hoare and Gibson-Jarvie went their separate ways.

Ronnie Hoare, in his early forties, at about the time of his election to Dorset County Council. (Courtesy of Mrs. Anne Hoare)

During his years at F. English Limited, Hoare owned a number of exotic cars, including Jaguar C-type XKC 048 and D-type XKD 515, a Ferrari *Testa Rossa*, and, in later days a de Tomaso Vallelunga, as well as racing a Ford GT40, at the same time as he was racing Ferraris. It was in 1959 that Ronnie's serious involvement with Ferrari started. Although a number of competition Ferraris had been bought directly from Maranello, there had been no serious attempt to market the touring cars in Britain. Brooklands of Bond Street were concessionaires for a short while and they sold one car to David Brown (Brooklands were also London Aston Martin and Lagonda distributors), but they soon lost interest.

Mike Hawthorn, the works Ferrari driver who won the Drivers' World Championship in 1958, acquired the British Ferrari agency and ran it from Tourist Trophy garage, the family business in Farnham, Surrey. Hawthorn exhibited two Ferrari 250GTs at the 1958 London Motor Show. Tommy Sopwith (son of Sopwith aircraft and Hawker Siddeley *supremo*, Sir Tom Sopwith) told Hawthorn that if he didn't sell one by the end of the show, he would take it off his hands.

Hawthorn failed to sell one of the cars, there was a spirited discussion between Tommy, Ronnie and Sir Gawaine Baillie, as to which of them would buy it, but Tommy clinched the deal at around £6,000. Tommy commented recently, 'I hated the car more than I could possibly describe. I couldn't keep it on twelve cylinders. It was arguably the first serious go that Ferrari had at making a road car. They made cars that were road-legal, but this one had a Farina coupé body and it was supposed to be a proper road car. They were, however, still quite a long way down the learning curve from making a sensible touring car.'

One evening, at about 11pm after a meeting with fellow-Ford dealers Sopwith and Elwes, Ronnie swapped his Mercedes-Benz 300SL for the Ferrari at Woking Motors (then owned by Sopwith) and drove it home to Bournemouth where he arrived at 2am. He was so excited with the car that he insisted on taking Anne out in it immediately. So they roared round the local area, Anne still in her nightdress and anxious about what people would think if they had an accident. Later, Ronnie managed to get the Ferrari running on 12 cylinders by completely replacing the wiring loom to aircraft standards. He stayed in contact with Tourist Trophy garage, which had lost its Ferrari agency after Mike Hawthorn was killed in an accident on the Guildford By-pass in January 1959.

Ronnie decided that he wanted to be the British concessionaire and after talking to John Adams who had bought Tourist Trophy garage and correspondence with the Ferrari factory, he met their commercial manager, Gerolamo Gardini, at the 1960 Brussels Motor Show.

Subsequently he flew to Italy to see Enzo Ferrari at Maranello. The Old Man asked him, 'How many cars do you think that you can sell a year?' Hoare, optimistically said, 'Four', expecting the Old Man to reject him out of hand. Instead, Ferrari was delighted, commenting, 'Marvellous; we've only sold four cars in Britain in the last ten years.'

So Hoare obtained the agency, set up Maranello Concessionaires Ltd in April 1960 and started trading in July. Ronnie Hoare never made major decisions without consulting Anne and she remembers that he was excited about obtaining the Ferrari agency, but he regarded it as something of a gamble. For some years the Ferrari sales operation was based in two bays of the premises of F. English Ltd., in Poole Road, Bournemouth. As Tommy Sopwith says, 'I would be doubtful if it made a profit for a long time. Ronnie was absolutely besotted by Ferraris. In the early days he collected most of the cars from the factory and drove them back himself.' At this time Mike Parkes, a development engineer at the Rootes Group working on the Imp project, was racing Jaguar saloons for Tommy Sopwith's *Équipe Endeavour*. Ronnie and Tommy decided that they would go 50/50 on the costs in racing a 250GT Ferrari during the 1961 season.

Ronnie bought the cars, Tommy arranged the entries and they split the expenses down the middle. The first car raced in 1961 was 250GT SWB, chassis number 2119, which had originally been supplied to the partnership of Rob Walker and Dick Wilkins; among other successes Stirling Moss had driven it to a win in the 1960 Tourist Trophy. The car and its successors were painted dark blue with a white noseband, the colours of Sir Tom Sopwith's America's Cup yacht *Endeavour*, primarily to make it easier to identify them. Later in 1961 the team took delivery of a new 250GT to more powerful *Competizione* specification, chassis number 2417, and Parkes drove this to a hard-fought second place in the Tourist Trophy at Goodwood.

A GTO followed, but after Sopwith's retirement from racing at the end of 1962, *Maranello Concessionaires* went its own way. The cars were now Italian racing red with a light blue nose-band. Ronnie had an obsession with the colour blue, especially Cambridge blue. While he was at Oswestry and he and Anne were first considering the possibility of buying into F. English Ltd, Anne was able to come to the rescue by selling some Shell shares that her father had given her. Her father, uncle, brothers and cousins had all been to Cambridge.

In particular Ronnie had great admiration for Anne's father who had been an excellent all-round sportsman and had boxed and played polo for Cambridge. The use of Cambridge blue on his cars was to show his gratitude to Anne and her family. He particularly liked wearing pale blue shirts. When Richard Attwood (who had a helmet painted in Harrow colours) and Piers Courage (who had a helmet painted in Eton colours) drove his 330P3/4 for him at Le Mans in 1967, it was in Richard's words, 'The Colonel's all-time Utopia.'

The promise given to the Old Man was fulfilled, for *Maranello Concessionaires* sold eight production cars in 1960, 14 in 1961, 18 in 1962, 24 in 1963 and total sales climbed to a giddy 51 in 1964. Ronnie Hoare's extensive racing programme had certainly helped boost sales. In 1964 *Maranello Concessionaires* raced both a 250GTO64 and a 330P Prototype and continued to race Ferraris through to the end of the 1967 season. The team made one further appearance, at Le Mans in 1972 with a *Competizione* Ferrari 365GTB4 *Daytona*, which retired because of piston failure. In Doug Nye's book, *The Colonel's Ferraris*, Ronnie explained the terms on which he and the other principal agents, *NART*, *Écurie Francorchamps* and *Scuderia Filipinetti* operated in 1963.

They were each loaned a Prototype similar to those used by the works, the cars were prepared in the customer *Assistenza* (literally 'assistance' or 'help') department on a fixed tariff regardless of the amount that needed to be done to the car. There was an option to buy the car at the end of the season. In 1963 Ferrari paid the retainers of Hoare's drivers, Joakim Bonnier and Graham Hill, and their agreed share of the prize money. *Maranello Conces-*

The first British Ferrari agent was Brooklands of Bond Street. The name 'Ferrari' was emblazoned across the facia of their premises, but only for a short while. Parked outside is the sole car delivered, a 212 Inter with Vignale body. David Brown was the buyer and it was not merely that he was indulging himself in a luxury toy, but it gave the opportunity for back-to-back comparisons with the Aston Martin DB2s that he built.

sionaires refunded to Ferrari all start, prize and bonus money, less the costs of entering the car. If there was a credit balance in the British team's favour at the end of the season, this could be set off against the purchase price of the 330P or one of the 250LMs that they had ordered.

The late Henry Manney III (European correspondent of *Road & Track*) once asked the following question in a quiz he set for the magazine: 'What did Messrs Hoare, Chinetti, Swaters and Filipinetti once have in common?' The answer he gave was: 'These gentlemen were in the unenviable position of running customers' works teams for Ferrari. Usually with second-hand equipment and a lot of static if they didn't do well. Still, some of them made money.' (Quoted by Graham Gauld in the spring 2003 issue of *Ferrari*.)

Many years later, Ronnie Hoare in his seventies, photographed when he lived a rather unhappy life in Monte Carlo. (Courtesy of Mrs. Anne Hoare)

Maranello Concessionaires opened a London service depot in Wellesley Road, Chiswick in 1964. Shaun Bealey joined the company on 1 January 1967 and, although he and Ronnie had originally planned that it would happen after 12 months, he acquired a 40% interest in the company and became Managing Director in mid-1967. Bealey used to pass Tower Garage on the Egham By-pass daily on his way to Chiswick. This elegant building (which became listed) was a Shell garage operated by the Lex Group and it sold cars and serviced lorries, but it was becoming increasingly run-down. Hoare agreed that the site would be an ideal base for the company, Lex, it was learned, wanted out and *Maranello Concessionaires* took a new lease and started trading from the premises on 1 January 1968. Despite financial ups and downs, the business flourished. Hoare and Bealey sold out to the TDK Group in 1988, mainly because of Hoare's health problems.

Outside motoring, Hoare's other interests were numerous. He was a very keen shot, although he was by no means a country person; he enjoyed photography and for ten years following the cease of *Maranello Concessionaires*' racing activities at the end of 1967, he became a devotee of Class A power-boat racing. But his real love was steam railways; when the family lived in Broadstone he had a miniature steam railway in the garden to the delight of his children.

Later he built what he described himself as the 'World's second-biggest model railway layout' and this was operated in a secure building at Poole. It was 0-gauge with a mile of electric track, perfectly accurate locomotives specially made for him by experts, rolling stock, buildings and scenery all set in the 1930s. He played with them every weekend when he was not racing. Model railway accessories were also made there for sale. A year before his death the railway was conservatively valued at £500,000.

But what of Ronnie Hoare the man? Ricard Attwood talks of the pleasure of driving for him on Page 83. Tommy Sopwith remembers Hoare as being extremely efficient, a superb 'staff officer' and a great enthusiast for cars in general and motor racing in particular. He was immensely smooth and charming and Tommy cannot remember a single argument while they were racing together. Anne Hoare remembers him as being incredibly charming, efficient, tough, but very kind. He did have his bad moments and Anne recounted to the author the time that he was staying in London and was dissatisfied with his breakfast:

'I can't remember whether it was the Savoy or the Ritz, but it was one of the two. He was unhappy with his scrambled eggs, so he sent for the chef. He told the chef exactly how he should scramble eggs. I was very glad that I wasn't there. Ronnie thought that he knew all about cooking, even though he hardly knew at home where the kitchen was. He was a very formal gentleman. When we were going out together before our marriage, he would never hold hands; certainly not kiss me in public.

'He was a stickler for good manners and when we were entertaining at Broadstone and, later, at Chute near Andover, he was insistent that everything should be precisely correct and as perfect as possible. I often regretted that he still didn't have the wonderful batman who'd served him at Oswestry. At this time I was very busy with the fast-growing family, a large house and garden and many outside commitments. He came to the house quite frequently, he always discussed important business matters with me and we telephoned each other regularly.

'Ronnie was a heavy smoker and eventually he suffered from emphysema. His doctor ordered him to smoke only one pipe-full a day, but of course he ignored that.' After selling *Maranello Concessionaires*, Ronnie went to live in Monte Carlo for tax and health reasons. He was never happy there, as the ex-patriots from Britain were not the kind of people he was comfortable in associating with. He wanted to return to England, but was too ill. Anne visited him three times and was with him when he died in 1989.

The writer is very appreciative of Mrs Anne Hoare's willingness to let him visit her at her beautiful Berkshire home and for a very informative and helpful discussion.

APPENDIX 1
Dramatis Personae
A guide to the more important personalities

AMON, CHRIS, 1943–
Amon was a driver of immense potential, which was largely unfulfilled because of a combination of bad judgement and bad luck. He was born in Bulls, New Zealand where his father ran a successful motor business. Amon raced a Maserati 250F, before coming to Europe when he was 19 and he drove in 1963–65 for *Reg Parnell (Racing)* in the lower echelons of Formula 1. His best performance was fifth place with a Lotus 25-BRM in the 1964 Dutch GP. He signed up for the works Cooper team during 1966 as a replacement for Ginther who left early in the year to drive for Honda, but then Surtees joined Cooper, and Amon drove only in the French GP (eighth). In sports car racing he did better, co-driving the winning Ford Mark II with Bruce McLaren and performing well with Group Seven McLarens in both Europe and North America.

He joined Ferrari for 1967 and after Bandini's fatal accident at Monaco and Parkes's bad crash at Spa, became the sole Maranello representative in Formula 1 that year. The V12 Ferrari was no match for the latest British cars, but Amon did well to finish third in the Monaco, Belgian, British and German GPs. He stayed with Ferrari in 1968, now joined by Jacky Ickx. At the beginning of the year Amon drove a 2.4-litre *Dino*-powered Ferrari in the Tasman series, won two races and finished second in two others. In F1 1969 was another largely unproductive year and his best performance was second place in the British GP. Although the team's Formula 2 cars were too heavy, he managed a third with one of these V6s at Barcelona.

He drove two Ferrari F2 cars with 2.4-litre *Dino* engines supplied by Ferrari and entered in the name of *Scuderia Veloce* in the 1969 Tasman series and won five races. By 1969 the V12 Formula 1 Ferrari was obsolescent and the team was pinning its hopes on the new flat-12 312B which it was intending to introduce during the year. Amon led the Spanish GP before retiring and finished third in the Dutch race, but withdrew from the F1 team after the British race. The 312B did not appear until 1970, the New Zealander had lost confidence in Ferrari (he was also becoming too 'political' in criticising the team) and left. Interestingly, Forghieri considers that of all the drivers he worked with, Amon was the very best at giving feedback to the engineers.

In 1970 Amon led the new and under-financed March F1 team and finished second in the Belgian and French GPs and third in the Canadian. He switched to Matra for 1971 and with the raucous V12 cars achieved a few places, the best of which was third in the French GP. Constantly driving uncompetitive cars had eroded Amon's confidence and ability. Amon drove for the Tecno team in 1973, but it proved to be a hopeless, disorganised shambles and he left the team – which immediately folded – in mid-season.

He then formed his own team in 1974 financed by one-time amateur Austin-Healey and Aston Martin driver John Dalton, and Gordon Fowell designed the Amon AF101 F1 car following Lotus design practice, with added special features. It was plagued by misfortune and after Amon had failed to qualify for the Italian GP, he drove BRMs in the last two races of the year. In 1976 he drove for another under-financed team, Ensign, and crashed badly twice because of structural failures. Amon returned to the team at the German GP, but after witnessing Niki Lauda's terrible, near-fatal accident, he retired from Grand Prix racing on the spot. Not long afterwards he retired from racing altogether and returned to New Zealand.

ATTWOOD, RICHARD, 1940–
The son of a Midlands car distributor, Richard was educated at Harrow school; he raced a Triumph TR3 in club events and in 1961 became a founder-member of the *Midland Racing Partnership* which initially raced Lola Formula Junior cars; it became the Lola works team in 1963, moved into Formula 2 in 1964 and was wound up in 1966. Attwood won the Grovewood Trophy in 1963, gained a testing contract with the BRM formula 1 team in 1964, but raced only once. In 1965 he drove an uncompetitive Lotus-BRM for the Tim Parnell team and raced a Ferrari for the first time at Kyalami where he co-drove Piper's 365P.

During 1966–67 he drove regularly for both *Maranello Concessionaires* and David Piper, sharing the class-winning *Dino* at Spa and the winning 365P2/3 with Piper at Kyalami in 1966; in 1967 he and Lucien Bianchi took third place with a 330P3/4 at Spa; in 1968 Richard rejoined the BRM team following the death of Mike Spence and finished second at Monaco. He was a member of the works Porsche team in 1969 and in 1970, entered by *Porsche Salzburg* and he was co-winner with Hans Herrmann at Le Mans. As a member of the *Gulf-Porsche* team in 1971 he finished second with Herbert Müller at Le Mans and with Pedro Rodriguez won the Austrian 1,000 Km race; he drove the camera car during the making of

Appendix 1 251

Steve McQueen's Le Mans film and then retired from racing at the end of 1971 to work in the family business.

BAGHETTI, GIANCARLO, 1934–96
The son of a wealthy industrialist, Baghetti was born on Christmas day and worked briefly in the family business. He started racing in 1956 with Alfa Romeos and Abarths before graduating in 1960 to a Formula Junior Lancia-Dagrada with which he won the Italian championship. During 1961 Eugenio Dragoni's *Scuderia Sant' Ambroeus* entered him with a fourth works Formula 1 Ferrari. Baghetti's first races with the Ferrari were phenomenal; he won the non-Championship Syracuse and Naples GPs early in the year and then won his first World Championship race, the French GP, after the retirement of the works cars – it was a feat that no other driver has matched.

In 1962 he was a member of the works Ferrari team and achieved no success; his season with Count Volpi's ATS Formula 1 cars in 1963 was a disaster and he had another unsuccessful year in 1964 with *Scuderia Centro-Sud*'s elderly BRMs. He continued to race works Ferrari Prototypes in 1965. Thereafter he drove only in the Italian Grand Prix in 1965–67 before retiring from racing. He once said, 'I should have retired at the end of 1961 and then everybody would have remembered me.' Baghetti died of cancer.

BANDINI, LORENZO, 1935–67
He was born in the Italian North African colony of Cyrenaica, but his family moved to Florence when he was four. At 15 he was apprenticed in Florence and started competing with a Fiat 1100 in local speed events in 1957. He entered Formula Junior with a Volpini in 1958 and raced a Stangullini Formula Junior car in 1959–60. 'Mimmo' Dei of *Scuderia Centro-Sud* entered him with a Cooper-Maserati in Formula 1 in 1961. He joined Ferrari in 1962, finishing third at Monaco and winning the non-Championship Mediterranean GP, and he stayed with Ferrari for Prototype racing until his death. Dei entered him with an ex-works BRM in 1963 and he rejoined the Ferrari Formula 1 team the following year, when he also married Margaretha. His sole Grand Prix win was in the 1964 Austrian event. He crashed and suffered burns that proved fatal in the 1967 Monaco GP. At the time his wife was expecting their first child.

BIANCHI, LUCIEN, 1934–59
Although he was born in Italy in 1934, Lucien Bianchi's family moved to Belgium when he was young. His father was an Alfa Romeo-trained mechanic and became racing mechanic to well-known Belgian driver 'Johnny' Claes. Lucien started to rally when he was 18 and also went to work for Claes, and accompanied his employer in the 1955 Liège-Rome-Liège Rally. They finished third overall and Bianchi undertook much of the driving after Claes became very ill. Claes was suffering from cancer, went into hospital immediately after the rally and died three days later.

Young Bianchi moved on to motor racing and in 1957 he co-drove a 2-litre Ferrari with one Harris at Le Mans. They finished seventh overall and won their class. The same year he partnered Olivier Gendebien to the first of three successive victories in the Tour de France. During 1960-62 he drove single-seaters for a number of teams, especially the reformed *Équipe Nationale Belge*, but his cars were uncompetitive and he had no success. He co-drove with Bonnier the winning Ferrari *Testa Rossa* of *Scuderia Serenissima di Repubblica Venezia* in the 1962 Sebring 12 Hours race.

Bianchi also competed in the United States and in 1968 he enjoyed his very best season. As a member of the uncompetitive Cooper F1 team he finished third at Monaco and sixth at Spa; he co-drove the winning Alfa Romeo 33/2 with Vaccarella and 'Nanni Galli' in the Circuit of Mugello; and at Le Mans he co-drove the winning *Gulf* Ford GT40 with Pedro Rodriguez.

He signed up with *Autodelta* for 1969 and he was killed at the Le Mans Test Weekend when his Alfa Romeo 33/3 3-litre car ran out of control at the end of the *Mulsanne* Straight and hit a telegraph pole. The car disintegrated in flames. Lucien Bianchi was a man who loved motor sport in all its forms. His brother, Mauro, was a works Alpine driver. Bianchi left a widow and three children.

BIZZARRINI, GIOTTO, 1926–
Born in Quercianella, near Livorno, he read engineering at Pisa University and after graduation taught for a short while before joining Alfa Romeo in August 1954. He moved to Ferrari in February 1957 and was a senior engineer/test driver. After working on the development of the V12 *Testa Rossa* engine, he became responsible for the development of the 250GT SWB and 250GTO models. Bizzarrini was one of those who left Ferrari in the management walkout at the end of 1961. After leaving Maranello, he was responsible for the concept of the so-called 'bread van' development of the 250GT, he became consultant to ASA (who had bought the rights to manufacture the 'Ferrarina' 849cc model) and he was a member of the ATS engineering team formed in 1962, but left after a short while.

Bizzarrini also worked for Lamborghini as a consultant on the design and development of the company's first V12 engine. Thereafter he joined Renzo Rivolta's Iso Rivolta project, worked on the original four-seater, developed the Iso Grifo A3L coupé (some of which were sold under the name 'Bizzarrini') and in 1964 left to run his own company at Livorno building Bizzarrini cars. The company failed and he became bankrupt. He then worked on the abortive AMC AMX/3 project in 1969–71 and thereafter became Professor of Engineering at Pisa and Florence universities. He retired in 1985.

BONNIER, JOAKIM, 1930–72
Born in Stockholm, he served for three years in the Swedish Navy. He drove a Citroën in ice-racing and rallying and became an Alfa Romeo dealer. In 1956 he raced a re-bodied 1953 Alfa Romeo 6C-34 coupé and a 1900 saloon. He entered a Maserati and other sports cars before becoming a member of the BRM

Formula 1 team in 1959. That year he scored BRM's first-ever Grand Prix win in the Dutch race. He was a member of the works Porsche Formula 1 and sports car teams in 1961–2. He shared the winning Ferrari with Bianchi at Sebring in 1962 and drove regularly for *Maranello Concessionaires*.

During 1963–5 he raced Cooper and Brabham Formula 1 cars for Rob Walker. He entered his own Cooper-Maserati in 1966–7 and drove a works Honda into fifth place in the 1968 Mexican GP. After this he raced Lola sports cars. Bonnier was President of the Grand Prix Drivers' Association and carried out considerable work in persuading organisers to make circuits safer. He had a wide range of business interests and was the first of a number of drivers to settle in Switzerland, living at Les Mudies with his wife Marianne and sons Jonas and Kim. He set up a team of Lola T280 3-litre cars and was killed at the wheel of one of these at Le Mans in 1972.

CHINETTI, LUIGI, 1901–94

He was born in Milan to middle-class parents; he left school at 14 and worked in the family workshops; he joined the Italian air force after WW1 and after his discharge went to work at Alfa Romeo; he was sent with the works team to the 1925 French Grand Prix (the race at which Antonio Ascari was killed in practice), and stayed in France to work on Alfa Romeo competition cars for the French agent. Chinetti enjoyed a splendid run of success with Alfa Romeos in the early 1930s. He co-drove the winning car at Le Mans in 1932 with Raymond Sommer, finished second with Philippe Varent in 1933 and won with Philippe Étancelin in 1934. He co-drove Talbots at Le Mans in 1937–39, but retired each year. After the death of Laurie Schell, he joined Lucy O'Reilly Schell at the *Écurie Lucy O'Reilly Schell* to work on the team's Delahayes that ran at Indianapolis in 1940.

Because Italy had entered WW2, he was unable to return to France and stayed in the United States during the war years. He married during this time, and after hostilities ceased returned to France and then travelled to Italy. He saw his old colleague Enzo Ferrari and obtained the East Coast agency for the new V12 Ferrari. He set up Chinetti International Motors Inc at Greenwich, Connecticut. Chinetti raced Ferraris in Europe in early post-war days and he won the Paris 12 Hours in 1948 (with Lord Selsdon) and in 1950 (with Jean Lucas); in 1949 he won Le Mans (with Lord Selsdon, but drove for 23 hours of the race) and the Belgian 24 Hours race (with Jean Lucas). Later he won the 1950 Paris 12 Hours race (with Jean Lucas), and co-drove the winning Ferrari in the 1951 Carerra Panamericana Mexico with Taruffi and finished third with Lucas in 1952.

Chinetti entered Ferraris from the late 1940s onwards, but did not form *North American Racing Team* until 1951. Although Chinetti was Ferrari's most successful sales outlet, he received little in the way of special favours from Maranello. From 1961 Mexican Don Pedro ('Papa') Rodriguez, who ran a major construction company, provided much of the finance for *NART* so that his sons, Pedro and Ricardo could race competitive cars. Nothing pleased Chinetti and the brothers more than to 'blow off' the works cars, but this meant that they totally overdrove their cars, resulting in mechanical failure. In later years *NART* earned a bad reputation for incompetent race preparation and management. The team continued to race Ferraris until 1982.

CHITI, CARLO, 1924–

Chiti was born in Pistoia, took a degree in aeronautical engineering and in 1952 joined Alfa Romeo as a trainee engineer. He was soon transferred to the racing department where he worked on the *Disco Volante* and its derivatives. Giotto Bizzarrini was a contemporary at Portello, but moved on to Ferrari where Chiti joined him in 1957. Chiti became technical director of production at Ferrari and increasingly involved in the racing side of the company's activities. He was largely responsible for the development of the Tipo 250 *Testa Rossa*, together with the rear-engined Tipo 156 Formula 1 car and the 246SP sports-racing car; the 246SP formed the basis of most Ferrari Prototypes in the early 1960s.

At the end of 1961 he was one of many senior staff to leave Ferrari and together with former team manager Romolo Tavoni he set up the ATS organisation financed by Count Volpi. Volpi lost interest in the project, left it underfunded and an inevitable failure. In 1964 Chiti rejoined Alfa Romeo as general manager of a new racing department called *Autodelta* and based at Settimo Milanese some miles from the centre of Milan. *Autodelta*'s successes were limited, except in touring car racing in which they were exceptionally successful, and Chiti left in 1984 to develop turbocharged F1 engines for Motori Moderni, a company which survived for only a short while.

COLOMBO, GIAOCCHINO, 1903–87

He was born in Legnano, about 20 miles north-west of Milan and at the age of 14 he was apprenticed in the drawing office of Officine Franco Tosi, a local engineering company. He worked on design drawings for both steam turbines and early diesel engines. He was a winner in an examination set by Societa Italiana Nicola Romeo and joined the team formed by Vittorio Jano to design and develop the Alfa Romeo P2. In 1928 Colombo became chief engineering draughtsman heading the drawing office. Much of Colombo's work was in interpreting Jano's ideas into practical, detailed drawings. He increasingly undertook more design work and when Alfa Romeo transferred racing operations to *Scuderia Ferrari*, Colombo acted in an engineering liaison role between Portello and Modena. At Modena he designed – with input from Ferrari – the Tipo 158 *Voiturette* and he was also responsible for the Tipo 308, 312 and 316 1938–39 Grand Prix cars.

Colombo remained with Alfa Romeo during the war years, acted as consultant to Ferrari in immediate post-war days and joined him on a full-time basis in 1948. Colombo was the 'father' of the V12 Ferrari engine that in improved form survived well into Prototype days. He was eclipsed at Ferrari by Aurelio Lampredi, left in late 1950 to work at Alfa Romeo once more on the later versions of the Alfa Romeo Tipo 159 and also the *Disco Volante* competition sports car. He was also consultant to Maserati (laying down the basic design of the 250F Grand Prix car), Bugatti (for whom he designed the unsuccessful Type 251 Grand Prix car) and MV Agusta.

DRAGONI, EUGENIO, 1909–74

He enjoyed a long-term friendship with Enzo Ferrari and had close connections with the Agnelli family. Dragoni had pursued a very successful business career and owned a company manufacturing cosmetics and perfumes. He was a director of *Scuderia Sant' Ambroeus*, which he controlled and managed. (*Sant' Ambroeus* [Saint Ambrose] was born in Trier, Germany, practised law in Rome, was appointed consular prefect of Upper Italy, the capital of which was Milan, in 369AD, and when the bishopric of Milan became vacant in 374 he was chosen as bishop by public acclaim, even though he was only a catechumen, undergoing religious instruction and not even baptised.) In 1961 this team ran a Formula 1 V6 rear-engined Ferrari with the less-powerful 65° engine. The driver was Giancarlo Baghetti who won the non-Championship Syracuse and Naples Grands Prix and then scored a remarkable victory in the French Grand Prix at Reims. After Romolo Tavoni left Maranello at the end of 1961, Dragoni took on the job of 'racing director' with great enthusiasm and he operated in total compliance with Enzo Ferrari's wishes.

Dragoni introduced some much-needed Ferrari discipline to the team, but his dictatorial and uncommunicative attitude offended drivers and press alike. Dragoni believed that Ferrari should be a truly national Italian team. This strongly conflicted with the attitude of John Surtees who believed that Ferrari should be international in attitude and look outwards, not inwards. This was the root cause of the conflicts between them, although other foreign drivers, notably Phil Hill, disliked Dragoni intensely. Although it was Enzo Ferrari who decided that Surtees should leave the team, it was a decision that he later regretted. He was an old man, not always thinking as clearly as he should have, and in his mind he came to believe that Dragoni was responsible for the loss of Surtees. This was the main reason why Dragoni left Ferrari at the end of 1966.

DROGO, PIERO, 1926–73

Born in Venezuela, he raced a 250 *Testa Rossa* in South America before emigrating to Italy, finishing fourth with Gonzalez in the 1958 Buenos Aires 1,000Km race. He continued to race in Italy and set up Carrozzeria Sports Cars in the via Emilia Ouest in Modena, a smaller and lesser-known coachbuilding concern. Drogo re-bodied Lloyd Casner's *Tipo 61* Maserati after the American crashed it badly at Pescara in 1961. Later he built the 'bread van' bodies on 250GT SWB chassis, and was responsible for the longer, more streamlined 'Drogo' noses fitted to a number of Ferrari 250LMs. Drogo carried out prototype work for Ferrari and he built the bodies on the first Ferrari 330P3 and the *Dino* 206S cars. He also built, to the design of Pete Brock, the coupé bodies of the *Shelby American* Daytona cars.

FERRARI, ENZO, 1898–1988

Enzo Ferrari was born on 18 February 1898 in a house on the outskirts of Modena. His father ran a metal-working business next to the family home. Initially he worked in his father's expanding firm but during the First World War he was conscripted into the Italian Army and served in a mountain artillery regiment. He became ill and was invalided out of the army and subsequently worked in Turin for a small company converting ex-military vehicles for passenger use. A chance meeting with racing driver Ugo Sivocci led to the opportunity to join the CMN company in Milan, a former aviation and engineering firm which had switched to car manufacturing. It was here that he had his first opportunity to drive in competition, but it must be remembered that although Enzo Ferrari's racing career stretched from 1919 to 1931 and was successful, it was not particularly distinguished and his real talents lay elsewhere.

Ferrari left CMN in late 1921 to join Alfa Romeo (the CMN company lasted only until 1923) and became increasingly involved in the competition side of the company's activities. It seems that it was because of poor health that Ferrari left Alfa Romeo, but became the make's agent in Bologna for the Emilia and Marche regions. In 1929 Enzo Ferrari discussed with Augusto and Alfredo Caniato, textile merchants in Ferrara, and Mario Tadini, the formation of a private racing team. After protracted negotiations *Scuderia Ferrari* was formed with effect from 1 December 1929 and set itself up in Modena. The team bought its cars from Alfa Romeo and although the Milan manufacturer continued to race cars, the company's policy was confused and uncertain. In early 1932 Alfredo Caniato bought out Mario Tadini's share in the team and later that year Count Felli Trossi bought the whole of Caniato's shares and replaced him as President.

In 1932 Alfa Romeo introduced their Tipo B *Monoposto* Grand Prix car, but these were retained and raced by the works team, *Alfa Corse*, while *Scuderia Ferrari* continued to race the older *Monza* cars. As a result of Portello's financial problems Alfa Romeo withdrew the Tipo Bs from racing at the beginning of 1933, but Ferrari's hopes that these cars would be handed over to him were misplaced. It was not until the beginning of August that Alfa Romeo released six Tipo Bs to Ferrari. Now *Scuderia Ferrari* took over technical staff formerly employed by Alfa Romeo and raced all entries on behalf of the works until the end of 1937, but Alfa Romeo held 80% of *Scuderia Ferrari* shares. On 1 January 1938 Ubo Gobbato, Managing Director of Alfa Romeo, announced that the works team, *Alfa Corse*, was being revived and would have sole responsibility for all racing activities.

Enzo Ferrari joined *Alfa Corse*, but his relations with Alfa Romeo's management became increasingly strained; he challenged management decisions and constantly waged war with Alfa Romeo technical staff, in particular Spanish engineer Wifredo Ricart. In November 1939 Alfa Romeo sacked Ferrari, but paid him substantial compensation. Ferrari then returned to Modena, having covenanted not to revive *Scuderia Ferrari* or engage in racing for four years. In Modena Ferrari set up a machine tool company, Auto Avio Costruzioni. For the 1940 closed circuit Mille Miglia, Ferrari, with assistance from Enrico Nardi, built the two Fiat-based Tipo 815 cars for Alberto Ascari and the Marchese Lotario Rangoni Machievelli. Italy entered the Second World War on 10 June 1940 and motor racing in Italy ceased. In 1944 Ferrari started to plan his own V12 cars and this book is about some of what happened thereafter. Enzo Ferrari died on 31 July 1988.

FORGHIERI, MAURO, 1935– (SEE PAGES 194–201)

GIUNTI, IGNAZIO 1941–71

At the time of his death Giunti was the most promising of young Italian drivers and so could be described as one of Enzo Ferrari's favourite sons. He was born in Rome on 30 August 1941 into a wealthy family. Giunti took up motor sport in 1961 and competed with Alfa Romeo production cars, receiving some sponsorship from tuning concerns. For 1965 he became a works Abarth driver. Carlo Chiti invited him to join *Autodelta* for 1966 and he raced works Alfa Romeo touring cars for two seasons. He won the Touring Car division of the European Hill Climb Championship in 1967.

In 1967 *Autodelta* introduced their first V8 2-litre Tipo 33 cars and although these proved very fast, but unreliable (some would say lethal), Giunti persevered all season and towards the end of the year took second place in the rather parochial Bettoja Trophy on the Vallelunga circuit at Rome. The 1968 Alfa Romeo 33/2 was a much-improved car and during the year, paired with 'Nanni' Galli, he was second in the Targa Florio and fourth at Le Mans.

Giunti stayed with Alfa Romeo for 1969 and the team raced the new 3-litre 33/3 cars. After complete failure at Sebring and Lucien Bianchi's fatal crash at the Le Mans Test Weekend, *Autodelta* withdrew the 33/3s for much of the year, but late in the season Giunti drove a 33/3 to second place behind Ickx (Mirage-Cosworth) at Imola. With an Alfa Romeo GTA he also won the European Saloon Car Championship rounds at Belgrade in the former Yugoslavia and Jarama in Spain.

For 1970 Giunti approached Ferrari and after a test session was signed on for both the Formula 1 and sports car teams. He finished fourth in the Belgian Grand Prix, but lost his Formula 1 drive to Clay Regazzoni, who was conspicuously quicker. He regularly drove the 512S Competition Sports Cars and although success largely eluded him, he shared the winning car at Sebring, the second-place car at Monza and the third-place car in the Targa Florio.

He was to drive for Ferrari in both Formula 1 and sports car racing in 1971. As recounted on page 172, he was killed in an horrific crash at Buenos Aires in January. He was engaged to the delightful and very attractive Mara Puppo. Ignazio Giunti was a thoughtful, sensitive man, lacking the rather undesirable flamboyance of some of his Italian motor racing contemporaries. Motor racing fatalities are tragic and inevitable, especially up to 20 years or so ago, but the stupidity that caused Giunti's death still angers many

GOZZI, FRANCO, 1932–
Born in Modena, he was trained as a lawyer, met Enzo Ferrari and joined the workforce at Maranello in 1960 as assistant to Sales Director Gerolamo Gardini. In 1961 Gozzi was appointed chief press officer and he became motor sport director of the racing department (Team Manager) in 1968 through to the end of 1970. He then became Enzo Ferrari's personal assistant and after Ferrari's death in 1988 he acted as consultant to motor sport director Piero Giorgo Capelli. He later became chief press officer and from 1993 was assistant to Ferrari president Luca di Montezemolo. After retiring in 1995 he acted in a consultancy capacity to Ferrari for a year. He is the author of *Memoirs of Enzo Ferrari's Lieutenant* (Giorgio Nada Editore, 2002).

HILL, PHIL, 1928–
Born at Santa Monica in California, Hill's father was the postmaster and his mother a musician. He read Business Studies at the University of Southern California, but was completely bored by the subject and left without graduating. After drifting from job to job, he settled down in the motor trade. He raced MG TC, Jaguar XK120, Alfa Romeo 8C 2900B and Ferrari Tipo 225 and Tipo 250MM cars. He had a bad crash in the 1953 Carrera Americana Mexico road race and withdrew from racing in 1954 because of stomach ulcers. In 1955 he and Carroll Shelby finished second with a private Ferrari *Monza* in the Sebring 12 Hours race, he drove a works Ferrari at Le Mans and signed up with Ferrari to race sports cars in 1956. Four times, in 1958, 1960, 1961 and 1962 he and Olivier Gendebien won at Le Mans. He drove Grand Prix Ferraris from 1958 onwards and in 1961 he won the Drivers' World Championship by one point from posthumous second-place von Trips who was killed in the Italian GP race.

Because the 1962 V6 Grand Prix cars were so uncompetitive, he and Baghetti blamed the young and relatively inexperienced Forghieri. Both of them were persuaded to drive the new ATS Formula 1 cars in 1963; these were hopelessly unsuccessful and in effect destroyed their Grand Prix careers. Hill was a works Cooper driver in 1964, drove Fords and Cobras in 1964–65 and then joined Chaparral for 1966-67. After his retirement this nervous restless man worked in American television and restored classic cars. He is a keen musician and appreciator of music – he once commented, 'I like all music except lousy music.' In May 2003 Hill was elected president of the *Club International des Anciens Pilotes Grand Prix et F1*.

HOARE, COLONEL RONNIE, 1913–89 (SEE PAGES 214–218)

ICKX, JACKY, 1945–

The Belgian, known by his team-mates in his younger days as the 'Brussels sprout' is the son of motoring journalist Jacques Ickx; he is one of the greatest drivers of his generation and the greatest Belgian driver ever. He competed in the International Six Days motorcycle event at the age of only 17 on a 50cc Zündapp, progressed to four wheels, competing with BMW 700, standard Ford Cortina and then two events with an Alan Mann-entered Lotus Cortina. He met Ken Tyrrell when he was competing with the Alan Mann car at Budapest in 1964 and Tyrrell offered him a drive in Formula 3; he was unable to accept because he had to serve his National Service in the Belgian army for 15 months. In late 1965 Tyrrell gave him a trial with a Cooper-BRM Formula 2 car, then he drove a Tyrrell-entered Matra-BRM throughout 1966 and won the European F2 Championship with one of these cars in 1967; the same year he drove a F1 Cooper-Maserati in two races and also drove Mirages for John Wyer, co-driving the winning car in four races; his most outstanding performance was a win in the Spa 1,000Km race where, in torrentially wet conditions, he outstripped the opposition.

Jacky joined Ferrari for Formula 1 and Formula 2 in 1968, but stayed with the Wyer team for sports car racing. With Ford GT40s and Brian Redman as co-driver, he won three races, including his home Spa 1,000Km event and in a difficult season with Ferrari he won the French Grand Prix at Rouen, but crashed in practice for the Canadian race, breaking a leg. Ickx moved to Brabham for 1969, winning the German and Canadian GPs and finishing second in the World Championship; with Wyer-entered Ford GT40s and Jackie Oliver as co-driver, he won at Sebring and Le Mans. He returned to Ferrari in 1970 and over four seasons drove swiftly and masterfully for the team. In F1 Ickx had a bad crash in the 1970 Spanish GP in April and suffered burns, which caused him pain for much of the year, but won the Austrian, Canadian and Mexican GPs to take second place behind the posthumous championship winner, Jochen Rindt.

Ickx failed to win a single Grand Prix in 1971, mainly because of the lack of speed and reliability of the flat-12 cars, he won only the German GP in 1972 and after a hopelessly unsuccessful year in 1973 he left Ferrari because he was 'too political' (in other words, he spoke his mind). He drove for Lotus in 1974 with little success, stayed with the team for 1975, but was 'rested' for the remainder of the season after he lost confidence in the obsolescent 72D following two drive-shaft failures. Some of Jacky's finest drives were yet to come, however, for he co-drove the winning Mirage at Le Mans in 1975, then joined the Porsche team and his further successes included co-driving the winning car at Le Mans in 1976–7 and 1981–2.

KLASS, GUNTHER 'BOBBY', 1936–67

Son of a wealthy industrialist, he was born in Stuttgart. He ran his own wholesaling business, a chain of launderettes and a nightclub. Klass started competition driving in 1961 and from 1962 drove works Porsche entries, initially in rallies, but later in circuit racing. He co-drove the fourth-place Porsche at Sebring in 1964, he finished fifth in the Nürburgring 1000Km race in 1965 and was leading the 1966 Targa Florio when his Porsche shed a wheel. Later in the year he drove Ferrari, Ford GT40 and Porsche entries for *Scuderia Filipinetti*. Ferrari signed Klass up in April 1967, primarily to help develop the *Dino* 206S, but he made few race appearances for the team. He had married at the age of 19, but was divorced and at the time of his death in practice for the Circuit of Mugello in July 1967, his son was 11 years old.

LINI, FRANCO, 1925–97

Highly respected Italian motor racing journalist who wrote for *L'Équipe* and *AutoItaliana*. He was Ferrari Team Manager in 1967 only and although he improved Ferrari's relations with the press immensely, he was out of his depth when it came to team management.

PARKES, MIKE, 1931–77

Born in Surrey, he was the son of John Parkes who later became Managing Director and Chairman of Alvis. He was educated at Haileybury and joined the Rootes Group in 1949. He started his racing career with an MG in 1952 and thereafter competed with different cars, including a Frazer Nash and then in 1957 a Lotus Eleven. He stayed with the Rootes Group until 1962 and his main contribution was his work on the Hillman Imp project code-named 'Ajax'. In the meanwhile Tommy Sopwith had been attracted by his driving abilities. He joined Tommy's team, which raced Jaguar saloons and they became good friends. He also drove the *Equipe Endeavour/Maranello Concessionaires* GT Ferraris with great élan and considerable success.

Both Ronnie Hoare and Tommy Sopwith promoted him to Ferrari. He drove works Ferraris in a few races in 1962 and then joined the *SEFAC* the following year as a production car development engineer and a works driver. While racing for Ferrari, Enzo Ferrari offered Parkes a very senior position within the company if he gave up racing. He was not willing to do so and after John Surtees left in 1966, he became a works F1 driver. In the 1967 Belgian GP, Parkes lost control on oil dropped by Jackie Stewart's BRM H16, went into a long slide and the car somersaulted. Mike suffered severe injuries that included three breaks in one leg and a compound fracture in the other. As a result he was in hospital for over a year.

As Tommy Sopwith commented, 'I tried on bended knee to persuade him to give up racing – he'd done it all, there was nothing more that he could do. With his engineering and racing background, he could have had a brilliant life at Ferrari.' Parkes returned to racing in 1969 to provide engineering support to the 312P Prototype programme, but he wanted to carry on driving. Enzo Ferrari refused to let him do this, because he regarded Parkes's engineering abilities highly, and so Mike left Ferrari. He drove for *Scuderia Filipinetti* before finally retiring from racing in 1971. He continued to live in an apartment in Modena and took charge of the Lancia Stratos rally development programme.

He was killed in a road accident near Turin in 1977 shortly before he was to become married. Tommy Sopwith was to have been the Best Man at his wedding.

PIPER, DAVID, 1930–

He was the greatest private Ferrari entrant of the 1960s and is still running his 250LM and P4 at historic meetings. Piper's first car was an ex-Hugh Hamilton, ex-Dennis Poore supercharged 750cc MG J4, which he ran in sprints and hill climbs in 1954. For 1955 he acquired the 'Empire Special', a Lotus Mark 6 with supercharged 750cc MG engine and among his successes that year was a win in the Leinster Trophy in Ireland. David co-drove Dan Margulies's Jaguar C-type (XKC 039) in the 1956 Targa Florio in which they finished ninth; during 1956–58 he toured Europe with an 1,100cc Lotus Eleven, racing weekend after weekend and living on the starting and prize money. During 1959–60 he drove front-engined Lotus 16s with limited success in Formula 1 and Formula 2 races, together with a Lotus 15 sports-racing car. He raced a Formula Junior Lotus 20 in 1961 and early 1962.

David's cars have for almost all his racing career been painted light green, simply because he likes bright colours and thought BRG sombre and gloomy (it has nothing to do with BP, his one-time sponsor). In 1962 he acquired his first Ferrari, 250GTO, chassis number 3767, a replacement followed in 1963 and in 1964 he bought a 250LM, chassis number 5897. David crashed his 250LM heavily at Snetterton in September and for the remainder of the year's races he drove a 250LM loaned by *Maranello Concessionaires*. He rebuilt his own 250LM and he and Tony Maggs finished third with it at Sebring in 1965. David raced 5897 through to 1966, the year in which he acquired 8165, the last 250LM to be built. By this time he was also racing a 365P, later upgraded to 365P2 specification which he crashed heavily at the Crystal Palace in 1967. From 1966 onwards he drove for *Maranello Concessionaires* and at the end of 1967 he bought the British team's P3/4.

David drove a works Porsche 917 at the Nürburgring in 1969 (at this time the handling was so bad that the works drivers refused to race it) and he raced works 312Ps at Spa and Le Mans. David bought a Porsche 917 in late 1969 and with this, co-driving with Richard Attwood, scored his fifth win in the Kyalami Nine Hours race. During the making of Steve McQueen's *Le Mans* film he crashed, perhaps because of loss of concentration, injuring his right leg. Although the injury was not severe, he caught an infection in a French hospital and the leg had to be amputated below the knee. David's love of Ferraris has persisted over the years and many of the period have passed through his hands. He still owns 250LM, 8165, which he has extensively modified and it is the fastest of its type to survive. At his Surrey workshop he has built three 330P 'replicas'.

REDMAN, BRIAN 1937– (SEE PAGES 210–213)

REGAZZONI, GIANCLAUDIO 'CLAY', 1939–

Clay Regazzoni is a charismatic, exuberant man despite his terrible accident. He was born 5 September 1939 in Lugano, Switzerland where his father was a coachbuilder who ran his own business. He came from a big family, he was one of five children, and he left school at 18 to work in the family business. He started competing with an early Austin-Healey Sprite and then with a Mini Cooper 'S'. Then he raced in Formula 3 with de Tomaso and Brabham cars, in late 1966 to early 1967 he drove works Formula 3 Tecno cars and stayed with Tecno in 1968. Franco Gozzi asked him to drive Formula 2 Ferraris in 1969, but the cars were uncompetitive and he drove in only four races.

In 1970 Regazzoni drove for both Tecno in Formula 2 and for Ferrari in Formula 1. He had an exceptionally successful year, winning the Italian GP and finishing third in the Drivers' Championship (it was the year in which Jochen Rindt was posthumous Champion) and he also won the European Formula 2 Championship. He stayed with Ferrari in 1971–72 and his sports car drives are narrated in this book; in Formula 1 in 1971 his best performances were third places in the South African and Dutch GPs, together with a win in the non-Championship Race of Champions at Brands Hatch. He had a poor year in F1 in 1972, was dropped by Ferrari for 1973 as part of an economy drive at Maranello and had a hopelessly unsuccessful season at BRM.

He returned to Ferrari for 1974–76 and apart from providing good back-up for Niki Lauda, he won the 1974 German GP and took three second places. In 1975 he won the Italian GP and he finished his career at Ferrari in 1976 with a win in the United States GP West at Long Beach and took second places at Zolder, Zandvoort and Monza. Clay was always a hot-tempered driver and he had more than his reasonable share of accidents. He drove without much success for the small Ensign team in 1977 but he returned to Ensign in 1980. At Long Beach he was holding what seemed to be an assured fourth place when he crashed heavily, possibly because of structural failure. He suffered injuries that left him paralysed from the waist down. Prior to this accident he had been a keen sportsman, who played football and tennis, rode and swam.

RODRIGUEZ, PEDRO, 1940–71

In his native Mexico both Pedro and his brother Ricardo (born two years later) were racing prodigies. Both raced motorcycles in Mexico and South America and then drove Ferraris for *NART* (their father sponsored the cost of the entries). Ricardo was killed in practice for the 1962 United States Grand Prix and Pedro retired from racing, but only briefly, for he reappeared at the 1963 Daytona race which he won with a 250GTO. He also won the sports car Canadian Grand Prix that year and won both races again in 1964 (the Daytona race co-driving with Phil Hill). In 1964 he also drove a Tipo 156 Ferrari in the Mexican Grand Prix. During the next two seasons he sank into obscurity, but he joined the Cooper F1 team for 1967 and scored an unexpected win in his first race. He achieved little else that year – apart from his presence in the team angering Jochen Rindt – for the Cooper-Maseratis were uncompetitive. Most of his sports car drives were with *NART*. He drove BRM Formula 1 cars in 1968, finishing third in both the Dutch and Canadian GPs and co-drove with Lucien Bianchi the winning Wyer-entered Ford GT40 at Le Mans.

In 1969 he became a Ferrari works driver, racing the 312Ps all year, and in Grands Prix from the British GP until the end of the season. During his early years Pedro drove with very little restraint and little consideration for the mechanics of his car, but he had matured considerably by 1970. That year he returned to BRM, winning the Belgian GP and finishing second at Watkins Glen, together with some other good places. During 1970 he enjoyed great rivalry in the *Gulf-Porsche* team with Jo Siffert and proved himself to be perhaps the greatest sports car driver ever. With Leo Kinnunen as co-driver he won at Daytona, Brands Hatch, Monza and Watkins Glen, as well as finishing second in the Targa Florio with a Porsche 908/03. The following year with Jackie Oliver as co-driver he won at Daytona, Monza, Spa and the Österreichring. Pedro Rodriguez was a man of tremendous charm and personality; most women found him exceptionally attractive. When he crashed with fatal results at the Norisring in 1971, he was greatly mourned.

SCARFIOTTI, LUDOVICO, 1933–68

The grandson of the first president of Fiat, 'Lulu' or 'Dodo', as he was known, was born in Ancona, the son of a wealthy cement manufacturer. He first raced in 1953 with a Fiat 500 'Mouse', moved on to an 1100 (with which he won his class in the 1956 Mille Miglia), then raced a Fiat 8V Zagato and drove works OSCAS in 1958–59. He drove works sports Ferraris in 1960, finishing fourth in the Targa Florio with Mairesse. In 1961 he was racing again for OSCA. With a works-supported *Scuderia Sant' Ambroeus* Ferrari *Dino* he won the European Hill Climb Championship in 1962. He became a regular member of the Ferrari sports car team in 1963 and won the Sebring 12 Hours race (with Surtees), finished second in the Targa Florio (sharing the driving with Bandini and Mairesse) and won at Le Mans (with Bandini). A week later he finished sixth with a V6 Ferrari in the Belgian GP but crashed heavily in practice for the French Grand Prix and temporarily retired from racing.

He returned in 1964 and with Ferrari sports cars he was second at Sebring and won the Nürburgring 1,000Km race (co-driving with Vaccarella in both). In 1965 he again won the European Hill Climb Championship for Ferrari and finished second at Monza and won the Nürburgring 1,000Km event (co-driving in both with Surtees). He was involved in a bad crash at Le Mans in 1966, but won that year's Italian Grand Prix with a V12 Ferrari. In 1967 he finished second in the Daytona 24 Hours, Monza and Le Mans races (all co-driving with Parkes). For 1968 'Lulu' joined Porsche and also drove works Cooper-BRMs in Formula 1. He crashed with his Porsche in practice for the 1968 Rossfeld hill climb and was killed instantly. Outside motor racing he was an enthusiastic skier and very fond of music. He left a widow and two children.

SURTEES, JOHN, 1934– (SEE PAGES 202–207)

SWATERS, JACQUES, 1926–

He studied law and while a student bought a pre-war MG, which with Paul Frère as co-driver he ran in the 1949 24 Hours' race at Spa. He owned *Garage Francorchamps* in Belgium and in 1952 he and Charles de Tornaco raced Tipo 500 Formula 2 Ferraris under the name *Écurie Francorchamps*. He became Ferrari agent for Belgium and Luxembourg in 1954. *Écurie Francorchamps* moved on to sports Ferraris and entered both Tipo 750 *Monza* and Tipo 250 *Testa Rossa* cars. During the years of Prototype racing Swaters ran his team on much the same lines as *Maranello Concessionaires*, but he persisted longer and entered a 512S/512M in 1970–71. He has a vast collection of Ferrari memorabilia. In May 1998 Ferrari UK Ltd (*Maranello Concessionaires*) bought *Garage Francorchamps* and Swaters opened a *Galleria Ferrari Francorchamps* dedicated to Ferrari, Ferrari cars and memorabilia. There is frequent confusion between *Écurie Francorchamps* and *Équipe Nationale Belge*. The latter was the racing name of Joska Bourgeois of the Belgian Motor Company, who was the Belgian Jaguar agent and entered Jaguars at Le Mans and elsewhere.

APPENDIX 2
Specifications of Ferrari Prototypes, Competition sports cars and GT cars, 1962–73

GRAND TOURING CARS

250GT SWB, 1960–63
Engine: Front-mounted 60° V12 of 2,953cc (73 x 58.8mm), with single overhead camshaft per bank of cylinders chain-driven from the nose of the crankshaft, two valves per cylinder, single plug per cylinder, 9.2:1 compression ratio, three Weber 38DC twin-choke carburettors and a power output of 280bhp at 7,000rpm.
Transmission: 4-speed in unit with the engine.
Chassis: Twin-tubular with front suspension by double wishbones and coil springs and rear suspension by rigid axle and semi-elliptic leaf springs.
Body: Coupé, steel with aluminium-alloy doors, bonnet and boot panels (road cars); aluminium-alloy (competition cars).
Dimensions: Wheelbase: 7ft 10.5in (2,400mm). Front track: 4ft 5.2in (1,350mm). Rear track: 4ft 5in (1,350mm). Dry weight (steel/alloy body): 2,240lb (1,016kg), (aluminium-alloy body): 2,130lb (965kg).

250GTO, 1962–64
Engine: Front-mounted 60° V12 of 2,953cc (73 x 58.8mm), with single overhead camshaft per bank of cylinders chain-driven from the nose of the crankshaft, two valves per cylinder, single plug per cylinder, 9.8:1 compression ratio, six Weber 38DCN twin-choke carburettors and a power output of 300bhp at 7,500rpm.
Transmission: 5-speed in unit with the engine.
Chassis: Twin-tubular with front suspension by double wishbones and coil springs and rear suspension by rigid axle and semi-elliptic leaf springs.
Body: Coupé, aluminium-alloy
Dimensions: Wheelbase: 7ft 10.5in (2,400mm). Front track: 4ft 5.2in (1,350mm). Rear track: 4ft 5in (1,350mm). Dry weight: 2,000lb (910kg).

COMPETITION SPORTS CARS

246SP, 1961–62
Engine: Rear-mounted 65° V6 of 2,417cc (85 x 71mm), with twin overhead camshafts per bank of cylinders chain-driven from the nose of the crankshaft, two valves per cylinder, twin plugs per cylinder, 9.8:1 compression ratio, three twin-choke Weber 42DCN carburettors and a power output of 270bhp at 8,000rpm.
Transmission: 5-speed in unit with the final drive.
Chassis: Multi-tubular space-frame with independent front and rear suspension by double wishbones and coil springs.
Body: Open two-seater, aluminium-alloy.
Dimensions: Wheelbase: 7ft 7.5in (2,325mm). Front track: 4ft 1.5in (1,260mm). Rear track: 3ft 11.25in (1,200mm). Overall length: 13ft 4in (4,065mm). Height: 3ft 5.5in (1,055mm).

248SP and 268SP, 1962
Engine: Rear-mounted 90° V8 of 2,458cc (77 x 66mm), with a single overhead camshaft per bank of cylinders chain-driven from the nose of the crankshaft, two valves per cylinder, single plug per cylinder, 9.8:1 compression ratio, four twin-choke Weber 40DC carburettors and a power output of 250bhp at 7,400rpm. (NOTE: The 268SP had a capacity of 2,644cc (77 x 71mm) and a power output of 265bhp at 7,000rpm).
Transmission: 5-speed in unit with the final drive.
Chassis: Multi-tubular space-frame, independent front and rear suspension by double wishbones and coil springs.
Body: Open two-seater, aluminium-alloy.
Dimensions: Wheelbase: 7ft 7.75in (2,330mm). Front track: 4ft 0.5in (1,230mm). Rear track: 3ft 11.25in (1,200mm). Overall length: 13ft 3.8in (4,060mm). Width: 4ft 10.2in (1,480mm).

Dino 196SP, 1962
Engine: Rear-mounted 60° V6 of 1,983cc (77 x 71mm), with a single overhead camshaft per bank of cylinders chain-driven from the nose of the crankshaft, two valves per cylinder, single plug per cylinder, 9.8:1 compression ratio, three twin-choke Weber 40DC carburettors and a power output of 210bhp at 7,500rpm.
Transmission: 5-speed in unit with the final drive.
Chassis: Multi-tubular space-frame, independent front and rear suspension by double wishbones and coil springs.
Body: Open two-seater, aluminium-alloy.
Dimensions: Wheelbase: 7ft 7.3in (2,320mm). Front track: 4ft 0.5in (1,230mm). Rear track: 3ft 11.25in (1,200mm).

PROTOTYPES (V12)

330TRI, 1962
Engine: Front-mounted 60° V12 of 3,967cc (77 x 71mm), with single overhead camshaft per bank of cylinders chain-driven from the nose of the crankshaft with two valves per cylinder, single plug per cylinder, 9.3:1 compression ratio, six twin-choke Weber 42DCN carburettors and a power output of 390bhp at 7,500rpm.
Transmission: 5-speed in unit with the engine
Chassis: Multi-tubular space-frame, independent front and rear suspension by double wishbones and coil springs.
Body: Open two-seater, aluminium-alloy.
Dimensions: Wheelbase: 7ft 9in (2,100mm). Front track: 4ft 4.5in (1,330mm). Rear track: 4ft 4in (1,320mm).

250P, 1963
Engine: Rear-mounted 60° V12 of 2,953cc (73 x 58.8mm), with single overhead camshaft per bank of cylinders chain-driven from the nose of the crankshaft with two valves per cylinder,

single plug per cylinder, 9.5:1 compression ratio, six twin-choke Weber 38DCN carburettors and a power output of 310bhp at 7,500rpm.
Transmission: 5-speed in unit with the final drive.
Chassis: Multi-tubular space-frame, independent front and rear suspension by double wishbones and coil springs.
Body: Open two-seater, aluminium-alloy.
Dimensions: Wheelbase: 7ft 10.5in (2,400mm). Front track: 4ft 5.25in (1,350mm). Rear track: 4ft 4.75in (1,330mm). Dry weight: 1,520lb (690kg).

250LM, 1963–68
Engine: Rear-mounted 60° V12 of 3,285cc (77x 58.8 mm), prototype had engine of 2,953cc (73 x 58.8mm), with single overhead camshaft per bank of cylinders chain-driven from the nose of the crankshaft with two valves per cylinder, single plug per cylinder, 9.7:1 compression ratio, six twin-choke Weber 38DCN carburettors and a power output of 320bhp at 7,500rpm (prototype had power output of 300bhp at 7,500rpm).
Transmission: 5-speed in unit with the final drive.
Chassis: Multi-tubular space-frame, independent front and rear suspension by double wishbones and coil springs.
Body: Coupé, aluminium-alloy (note two cars had glass-fibre bodies).
Dimensions: Wheelbase: 7ft 10.5in (2,400mm). Front track: 4ft 5.25in (1,350mm). Rear track: 4ft 4.75in (1,340mm). Length: 13ft 11in (4,270mm). Width: 5ft 6.9in (1,700mm). Height: 3ft 8in (1,115mm). Weight: 1,874lb (850kg).

275P and 330P, 1964
Engine: Rear-mounted 60° V12, 275P: 3,285cc (77 x 58.8mm). 330P: 3,967cc (77 x 71mm) with single overhead camshaft per bank of cylinders chain-driven from the nose of the crankshaft with two valves per cylinder, 9.8:1 compression ratio (275P), 9:1 compression ratio (330P), six twin-choke Weber carburettors, 38DCN (275P), 42DCN (330P), power output of 320bhp at 7,700rpm (275P), 390bhp at 7,500rpm (330P).
Transmission: 5-speed in unit with the final drive.
Chassis: Multi-tubular space-frame, independent front and rear suspension by double wishbones and coil springs.
Body: Open two-seater, aluminium-alloy.
Dimensions: Wheelbase: 7ft 10.5in (2,400mm). Front track: 4ft 5.25in (1,350mm). Rear track: 4ft 4.75in (1,340mm).

275P2 and 330P2, 1965
In most respects, other than engines with twin overhead camshafts per bank of cylinders and revised open bodywork, these cars were similar to the 275P and the 330P. Both models had six twin-choke Weber 40DCN/2 carburettors. The 3.3-litre 275P2 had a power output of 350bhp at 8,500rpm and the 330P2 had a power output of 370bhp at 8,200rpm.

365P and 365P2, 1965
In most respects these cars were similar to the 330P, except an engine of 4,390cc (77 x 81mm) and a power output of 380 bhp at 7,200rpm. The 365P retained bodywork of the 330P-style, while the 365P2 had the latest style of body fitted to the 330P2.

330P3, 1966
Engine: Rear-mounted 60° V12 of 3,967cc (77x 71mm), with twin overhead camshafts per bank of cylinders chain-driven from the nose of the crankshaft, two valves per cylinder, twin plugs per cylinder, 11.4:1 compression ratio, Lucas indirect fuel injection and a power output of 420bhp at 8,000rpm.
Transmission: 5-speed in unit with the final drive.
Chassis: Multi-tubular space-frame with stressed aluminium-alloy panelling and with bonded glass-fibre floor structure, independent front and rear suspension by double wishbones, coil springs anti-roll bar.
Body: Open two-seater or coupé, aluminium-alloy.
Dimensions: Wheelbase: 7ft 10.5in (2,400mm). Front track: 4ft 5.25in (1,350mm). Rear track: 4ft 4.75in (1,340mm). Length: 13ft 8in (4,165mm). Width: 5ft 10in (1,780mm). Height: 3ft 2.8in (985mm). Weight: 1,588lb (720kg).

365P2/3
In most respects these cars were similar to the 365P and 365P2, except for bodywork of the latest style as fitted to the 330P3.

330P4, 1967
Engine: Rear-mounted 60° V12 of 3,967cc (77 x 71mm), with twin overhead camshafts per bank of cylinders chain-driven from the nose of the crankshaft with three valves per cylinder, two plugs per cylinder, 10.5:1 compression ratio, Lucas indirect fuel injection and a power output of 450bhp at 8,200rpm.
Transmission: 5-speed in unit with the final drive.
Chassis: Multi-tubular space-frame with stressed aluminium-alloy panelling and with bonded glass-fibre floor structure, independent front and rear suspension by double wishbones, coil springs and anti-roll bar.
Body: Open two-seater or coupé, aluminium-alloy.
Dimensions: Wheelbase: 7ft 10.5in (2,400mm). Front track: 4ft 10.75in (1,490mm). Rear track: 4ft 9.25in (1,455mm). Length: 13ft 11.5in (4,255mm). Width: 6ft 4in (1,930mm). Height: 3ft 4in (1,015mm). Weight: 1,762lb (799kg).

330P3/4, 1967
These cars were 330Ps brought up to P4 specification, except that they used six twin-choke Weber 42DCN carburettors and were fitted with ZF five-speed gearbox (in place of the Ferrari-built gearbox of the 330P3 and 330P4).

312P, 1969
Engine: Rear-mounted 60° V12 of 2,989cc (77 x 53.5mm), with twin overhead camshafts per bank of cylinders chain-driven from the nose of the crankshaft, four valves per cylinder, single plug per cylinder, 11:1 compression ratio, Lucas indirect fuel injection and a power output of 420bhp at 9,800rpm.
Transmission: 5-speed in unit with the final drive.
Chassis: Multi-tubular space-frame with stressed aluminium-alloy panelling, independent front suspension by double wishbones and coil spring/damper units, independent rear suspension by single upper links, reversed lower wishbones, radius rods and coil spring/damper units.
Body: Open two-seater or coupé, glass-fibre with detachable nose and tail sections.
Note: first car originally fitted with aluminium-alloy body. Coupé bodies used only at Le Mans.
Dimensions (open cars): Wheelbase: 7ft 8.5in (2,370mm). Front track: 4ft 10.5in (1,485mm). Rear track: 4ft 11in (1,500mm). Overall length: 13ft 10.5in (4,230mm). Width: 6ft 6in (1,980mm). Height: 2ft 11in (890mm). Dry weight: 1,497lb (679kg).

PROTOTYPES (V6)

166P, 1965
Engine: 65° V6 of 1,593cc (77 x 57mm), with twin overhead camshafts per bank of cylinders chain-driven from the nose of the crankshaft, two valves per cylinder, two plugs per cylinder, 9.8:1 compression ratio, three twin-choke Weber 38DCN carburettors and a power output of 190bhp at 9,000rpm.
Transmission: 5-speed in unit with the rear axle.
Chassis: Multi-tubular space-frame, independent front and rear suspension by double wishbones and coil springs.
Body: Coupé and open two-seater, aluminium-alloy.
Dimensions: Wheelbase: 7ft 4in (2,235mm). Front track: 4ft 5.2in (1,350mm). Rear track: 4ft 5.2in (1,350mm). Length: 12ft 2in (3,810mm). Width: 5ft 2in (1,575mm). Height: 3ft 1.8in (960mm). Weight: 1,290lb (585kg).

206S, 1966–68
Engine: 65° V6 of 1,987cc (86 x 57mm), with twin overhead camshafts per bank of cylinders chain-driven from the nose of the crankshaft, two valves per cylinder, two plugs per cylinder, 10.8:1 compression ratio, three twin-choke Weber 42DCN carburettors and a power output of 218bhp at 9,000rpm.
Transmission: 5-speed gearbox in unit with the final drive.
Chassis: Multi-tubular space-frame with stressed aluminium-alloy panelling, bonded glass-fibre floor structure, independent front and rear suspension by double wishbones, coil springs and anti-roll bar.
Body: Coupé, aluminium-alloy.
Dimensions: Wheelbase: 7ft 5.8in (2,280mm). Front track: 4ft 5.5in (1,360mm). Rear track: 4ft 5.3in (1,350mm).

CAN-AM

612P, 1968–72
Engine: 60° V12 of 6,222cc (92 x 78mm), with twin overhead camshafts per bank of cylinders chain-driven from the nose of the crankshaft, four valves per cylinder, single plug per cylinder, 10.5:1 compression ratio, Lucas fuel injection and a power output of 620bhp at 7,000rpm. From the last Can-Am race in 1969 onwards the works cars had 6,780cc (92 x 85mm engine).
Transmission: 4-speed in unit with the final drive.
Chassis: Multi-tubular space-frame with stressed aluminium-alloy panelling, front suspension by double wishbones and coil spring/damper units, rear suspension by single upper links, reversed lower wishbones, radius rods and coil spring/damper units.
Body: Glass-fibre with detachable nose and tail sections.
Dimensions: Wheelbase: 8ft 0.4in (2,500mm). Front track: 1968: 4ft 11.8 in (1,510mm). 1969: 5ft 3in (1,600mm). Rear track: 1968: 5ft 1.1in (1,550mm). 1969: 5ft 3in (1,600mm). Overall length: 1968: 13ft 4.5in (4,080mm). 1969: 13ft 9.4in (4,200mm). Width: 1968: 6ft 10.6in (2,100mm). 1969: 7ft 4.2in (2,240mm). Height: 2ft 11in (890mm). Dry weight: 1968: 1,750lb (794kg). 1969: 1,543lb (700kg).

GROUP FIVE SPORTS CARS

512S and 512M, 1970–71
Engine: 60° V12 of 4,994cc (87 x 70mm), with twin overhead camshafts chain-driven from the nose of the crankshaft, four valves per cylinder, single plug per cylinder, compression ratio of 11.5:1, Lucas indirect fuel injection and a power output of 550bhp at 8,500rpm (later increased to 575bhp, 512M, 600bhp).
Transmission: 5-speed in unit with the final drive.
Chassis: Multi-tubular space-frame with stressed aluminium-alloy panelling; independent front suspension by double wishbones, coil springs and anti-roll bar; independent rear suspension by single upper links, reversed lower wishbones, coil springs and anti-roll bar.
Body: Coupé and open two-seater, stressed aluminium-alloy centre-section, glass-fibre nose and tail sections.
Dimensions: Wheelbase: 7ft 10.5in (2,390mm). Front track: 4ft 11.7in (1,520mm). Rear track: 4ft 11.5in (1,510mm). Length: 13ft 3.8in (4,060mm). Width: 6ft 6.7in (2,000mm). Weight: 1,850lb (838kg).

PROTOTYPES/SPORTS CARS (Flat-12)

212E, 1969
Engine: Horizontally opposed 12-cylinder of 1,991cc (65 x 50mm), twin overhead camshafts per bank of cylinders gear-driven from the rear of the crankshaft, with two valves per cylinder, two plugs per cylinder, 11:1 compression ratio, Lucas indirect fuel injection and a power output of 300bhp at 11,800rpm.
Transmission: 5-speed in unit with the final drive.
Chassis: Multi-tubular space-frame with stressed aluminium-alloy panelling, bonded glass-fibre floor section, independent suspension front and rear by double wishbones, coil springs and anti-roll bar.
Body: Two-seater, aluminium-alloy.
Dimensions: Wheelbase: 7ft 10.5in (2,400mm). Front track: 4ft 6.2in (1,377mm). Rear track: 4ft 8in (1,412mm). Weight: 500kg (1,002lb)

312PB, 1971–73
Engine: Horizontally opposed 12-cylinder of 2,991cc (78.5 x 51.5mm), twin overhead camshafts per bank of cylinders gear-driven from the rear of the crankshaft, with two valves per cylinder, two plugs per cylinder, 11.5:1 compression ratio, Lucas indirect fuel injection and a power output of 450bhp at 10,800 rpm.
Transmission: 5-speed in unit with the final drive.
Chassis: Multi-tubular space-frame with stressed aluminium-alloy panelling, independent front suspension by double wishbones, coil springs and anti-roll bar, independent rear suspension by single upper links, reversed lower wishbones, twin radius rods and anti-roll bar.
Body: Open two-seater, stressed aluminium-alloy centre-section, glass-fibre nose and tail sections.
Dimensions: Wheelbase: 7ft 3.4in (2,220mm). Front track: 4ft 8.1in (1,425mm). Rear track: 4ft 7.1in (1,400mm).

APPENDIX 3
Championship Results 1962–73

PROTOTYPE CHAMPIONSHIPS, 1962–64

Challenge Mondiale de Vitesse, 1962–66

1962
1st Ferrari, 40 points; 2nd Porsche, 23 points; 3rd Alfa Romeo, 7 points

1963
1st Ferrari, 36 points; 2nd Porsche, 17 points; 3rd Jaguar, 5 points

1964
1st Ferrari, 34 points; 2nd Porsche, 18 points; 3rd Shelby American Cobra, 11 points

Prototypes Trophy, 1963–66

1963
1st Ferrari, 72 points; 2nd Porsche, 30 points; 3rd René Bonnet, 19 points

1964
1st Porsche, 34.8 points; 2nd Alpine, 9.6 points; 3rd Austin-Healey, 1.6 points (Note: Ferrari was not eligible as no Ferrari Prototypes ran in the Targa Florio)

1965
1st Ferrari, 58.5 points; 2nd Porsche, 30.4 points; 3rd Ford, 19.6 points

1966
1st Ford, 38 points; 2nd Ferrari, 36 points; 3rd Chaparral, 10 points

Speed and World Challenge Cup, 1967

In 1967 the Group Six Championship was extended to cover the Daytona, Sebring, Monza, Spa, Targa Florio, Nürburgring, Le Mans and BOAC '500' races. Only the best five results counted and the points system had been revised as follows: First: 9 points; Second: 6 points; Third: 4 points; Fourth: 3 points; Fifth: 2 points; Sixth: 1 point.

1967
1st Ferrari, 34 points; 2nd Porsche, 32 points; 3rd Ford, 22 points

GRAND TOURING CAR CHAMPIONSHIP 1962–65

Division III, Over 2,000cc

1962
1st Ferrari, 45 points; 2nd Jaguar, 16 points; 3rd Chevrolet, 9 points

1963
1st Ferrari, 126 points; 2nd Jaguar, 28 points; 3rd Shelby American Cobra, 24 points

1964
1st Ferrari, 84.6 points; 2nd Shelby American Cobra, 78.3 points; 3rd Jaguar, 6.6 points

1965
1st Shelby American Cobra, 90 points; 2nd Ferrari, 71.3 points; 3rd Jaguar, 7.2 points

SPORTS CAR MANUFACTURERS' CHAMPIONSHIP, 1968–71

The cars admitted to Championship events were Group Three Grand Touring cars of unlimited cylinder capacity, Group Four Competition Sports Cars up to 5,000cc and Group Six Prototypes up to 3,000cc. The minimum production for Competition Sports Cars was 50 in 1968 and thereafter 25. Points were awarded on the basis of First: 9 points; Second: 6 points; Third: 4 points; Fourth: 3 points; fifth: 2 points; Sixth: 1 point.

1968 (Based on the best five performances)
1st Ford, 45 points; 2nd Porsche, 42 points; 3rd Alfa Romeo, 15½ points

1969 (Based on the best five performances)
1st Porsche, 45 points; 2nd Ford, 25 points; 3rd Lola-Chevrolet, 20 points

1970 (Based on best seven performances)
1st Porsche, 63 points; 2nd Ferrari, 39 points; 3rd Alfa Romeo, 10 points

1971 (Based on best eight performances)
1st Porsche, 72 points; 2nd Alfa Romeo, 51 points; 3rd Ferrari, 26 points

THE WORLD CHAMPIONSHIP FOR MAKES, 1972–73

The cars admitted to Championship events were Group Five Sports cars up to 3,000cc, Group Four Special Grand Touring Cars of unlimited cylinder capacity and the organisers could also admit Group Two Special Touring Cars, but cars in the last category were not eligible for Championship points. Events in the series had a minimum length of 1,000km or a minimum duration of six hours. Points were awarded on the basis of First: 20 points; Second: 15 points; Third: 10 points; Fourth: 8 points; Fifth: 6 points; Sixth: 6 points; Seventh: 4 points; Eighth: 3 points; Ninth: 2 points; and Tenth: 1 point.

1972 (Based on eight best performances)
1st Ferrari, 160 points; 2nd Alfa Romeo, 85 points; 3rd Porsche, 66 points

1973 (Based on best seven performances)
1st Matra, 124 points; 2nd Ferrari, 115 points; 3rd Porsche, 82 points

APPENDIX 4
Ferrari Chassis Information

250GTO AND 330SA

Apart from the four prototype cars, total Ferrari production of GTOs and derivatives amounted to 40 cars: of these 33 were of the original type first seen at the Ferrari Press Conference in February 1962; three cars of the original type were built with 4-litre engines; three 250GTO64s were also built (and others rebuilt in this form); and there was one 3-litre car built with LMB body.

1737GT: Based on the 400 *Superamerica*, this prototype had a short-wheelbase chassis, 3-litre engine with triple carburettors and roadster body.

2429GT: Similar to 1737GT above, but fitted with coupé body.

2643GT: Experimental *berlinetta* with Pininfarina body and raced at Le Mans in 1961.

2649GT: This prototype was built in early 1961, driven by Tavano/Baghetti at Le Mans and sold to Luigi Chinetti in January 1962. Stirling Moss drove it to fourth place overall and a win in the GT class at Daytona.

3175GT: Pre-production prototype distinguished by unusual nose design. Willy Mairesse tested it extensively and Stirling Moss tested it in September 1961.

3223GT: This car was displayed at the Ferrari Press Conference in February 1962 and retained by the works until June. Thereafter it was sold to Chinetti's *NART* team and extensively raced in the United States.

3387GT: Sold to *NART* in March 1962, made its race debut at Sebring where Phil Hill/Olivier Gendebien drove it into second place overall; it was raced extensively by *NART*.

3413GT: Sold in Italy to Edoardo Lualdi and raced extensively by him. It passed through the ownership of Gianni Bulgari and Corrado Ferlaino; Ferlaino sent the car to Scaglietti in late 1963 and it was re-bodied as a 250GTO 64.

3445GT: Originally ordered by Luciano Conti, on behalf of *Scuderia Serenissima Repubblica di Venezia*. In late 1964 Ulf Norinder bought 3445 and had a very stylish body for road use built by Drogo. The body was extensively damaged in a road accident in 1976 and some years later this car was rebuilt in what was substantially original GTO style.

3451GT: Sold to Pietro Ferraro in April 1962 and bought back by the factory in September 1962. Sold on by Ferrari, it subsequently had several different owners and was extensively raced.

3505GT: Sold in Britain to the *UDT-Laystall* team. Apple green with green cloth upholstery (according to the records). Raced extensively and its successes included a win by Innes Ireland in the 1962 Tourist Trophy. Sold by Stirling Moss and *UDT-Laystall* in 1963.

3527GT: Sold to Gottfried Kochert in Vienna in May 1962, bought back by the factory in October 1962 and immediately sold on to Jacques Swaters. *Écurie Francorchamps* raced it extensively. In 1965 Swiss coachbuilder Hermann Graber carried out internal and external modifications to make the car more suitable for road use. It was restored to original exterior form in 1984, although the Graber interior was retained.

3589GT: RHD. Delivered to Ronnie Hoare of *Maranello Concessionaires* and owned jointly with Tommy Sopwith's *Équipe Endeavour*. Mike Parkes raced it extensively in British events. In November 1962 Tom O'Connor (*Team Rosebud*) bought it and entered it for Innes Ireland at the Nassau Speed Week.

3607GT: It was originally delivered to Ferdinando Pagliari, but he sold it to *Scuderia Repubblica di Venezia* in 1963. Subsequent owners included Jacques Swaters, Jess Pourret and Pierre Bardinon.

3647GT: RHD. Delivered to *Bowmaker Racing* in 1962 (but, it was owned by *Maranello Concessionaires*). John Surtees crashed it in the 1962 Tourist Trophy. After repairs it was sold to Prince Zourab Tchokotoua and driven for him by Tommy Hitchcock, but loaned back to *Maranello Concessionaires* in the early part of the 1963 season. Hitchcock crashed it at both the Nürburgring and in the Tourist Trophy in 1963.

3673LM: Works car with 4-litre engine and Mairesse/Parkes drove it into second place in the 1962 Nürburgring 1,000Km race. It retired because of overheating at that year's Le Mans race where Bandini/Parkes drove it. It was sold subsequently to Pietro Ferraro. In 1964 it was fitted with a 3-litre engine and gearbox and it was raced in 1965 in Italian events by Ferdinando Latteri.

3705GT: Delivered to Jean Guichet in June 1962 and retained by him into 1973. With this car Guichet/Noblet finished second overall at Le Mans in 1962.

3729GT: Delivered to John Coombs via Roy Salvadori and raced in British events with very limited success. Sold to Robert Perry and then John Pearce, who installed the engine in a Cooper chassis for Formula 1. Pearce reunited engine and car and it was then sold to Neil Corner. Jack Sears bought it and retained it for many years.

3757GT: Delivered to *Écurie Francorchamps* in June 1962, extensively and successfully raced. Owned by Nick Mason of *Pink Floyd* from 1978. (See article in *Car*, January 1979.)

3767GT: *Maranello Concessionaires* ordered this car for David Piper. Piper drove it back from Maranello and he raced it extensively in 1962 and early 1963.

3769GT: Originally delivered to Fernand Tavano in June 1962. Sylvain Garant bought it and competed with it until it was badly damaged in a competition accident. Engine removed and installed in 3451GT. It was later restored using the engine, gearbox and final drive from 3451.

3809GT: Originally delivered to Kalman von Csazy (Switzerland) and raced on a fairly regular basis.

3851GT: Delivered to Jo Schlesser/Henri Oreiller, France. Oreiller crashed with fatal results at Montlhéry in October 1962. The car was rebuilt at the factory, sold to Paolo Colombo who competed with it extensively in Italy.

Appendix 4   263

3869GT: RHD. Exhibited at Earls Court 1962 by *Maranello Concessionaires* and sold in 1963 to Ron Fry who competed with it in many minor events until the end of 1964.

3909GT: Delivered to Edgar Berney in Switzerland in September 1963. Its best performance was a win at Spa in 1963 (Siffert). In 1989 it was sold in England to a Japanese buyer for £10 million.

3943GT: Delivered in France to Pierre Noblet and extensively raced by him until 1965.

3987GT: Delivered to Chinetti in October 1962 and sold immediately to John Mecom Jnr. Ricardo and Pedro Rodriguez drove it to win the 1962 Paris 1,000Km race at Montlhéry before it was shipped to the United States. Roger Penske drove it to a win in the 1962 Nassau Tourist Trophy. Subsequently Penske and Augie Pabst raced it for Mecom in the United States.

4091GT: It was originally delivered in November 1962 to Sergio Bettoja of *Compagnia Romagna Alberghi Roma* and retained by it until February 1964. It was then sold to *Scuderia Sant' Ambroeus*, rebuilt as a 250GTO64 and thereafter extensively raced.

4115GT: It was originally delivered in December 1962 to Hermann Cordes in Germany and had a very limited racing history.

4153GT: Originally delivered to Pierre Dumay in Belgium in June 1963 and then sold on to Jacques Swaters later that year. Its successes in 1963 included fourth overall at Le Mans (Dernier/Dumay) and Bianchi/Berger drove it to an outright win in the 1964 Tour de France.

4219GT: Delivered to Chinetti and registered in the name of Mamie Reynolds; it was driven to a win in the 1963 Daytona race by Pedro Rodriguez; sold by Reynolds in 1963.

4293GT: Originally ordered (it is believed) by *Scuderia Sant' Ambroeus*, but delivered instead to Jacques Swaters in April 1963. Successes included first in the 1963 Spa GT race (Mairesse) and second overall by 'Beurlys'/Langlois van Ophem in the 1963 Le Mans race. Sold in the United States in late 1963.

4399GT: RHD. It was delivered to *Maranello Concessionaires* for the 1963 season and extensively raced by Graham Hill and Mike Parkes. It was retained by the team for 1964 and rebuilt in 250GTO64 form.

4453SA: It was delivered to Mamie Reynolds early in 1963 and driven at Sebring by Bandini/Parkes (retired) at Le Mans by Guichet/Noblet (retired).

4491GT: RHD. This car was delivered to David Piper in June 1963 and extensively and successfully raced by him through to the end of 1964. It was sold to Peter Sutcliffe for 1965 and he continued its successful racing career.

4561SA: Car with 4-litre engine specially built in 1963 for then Ferrari director Paul Cavalier. Colonel Ronnie Hoare bought it in 1964 and retained it until 1965.

4619SA: Parkes drove this car at the Le Mans Test Weekend in 1963. It was never raced and the factory sold it in November 1963 to Cantiere del Timavo SpA at Trieste and it was resold in France the following month.

4675GT: Delivered in May 1963 to Annunziata and sold in September 1963 to Guido Fossati and Ariberto Francolini. It was rebuilt in 250GTO64 form and it continued a long and successful racing career until 1966.

4713GT: This was the 3-litre car built in 250LMB form with *Lusso*-style body. It was delivered to *NART* just before the 1963 Le Mans race and driven by Gregory/Piper to sixth place. Roger Penske drove it to eighth place in the Tourist Trophy. It enjoyed a very considerable racing history in the United States.

4725SA: RHD. This was the fully trimmed 4-litre car with glass windows and screen and some steel panelling delivered to *Maranello Concessionaires* in 1963. Sears/Salmon drove it to fifth place at Le Mans and Bandini finished eighth with it in the Guards Trophy at Brands Hatch. *Maranello Concessionaires* detuned it, including fitting three carburettors and sold it to Pierre Bardinon.

4757GT: This car was delivered in 1963 to the *Scuderia Serenissima Repubblica di Venezia* and Carlo Abate enjoyed many successes in minor events. Bandini/Tavano drove it in the 1963 Tour de France, but Bandini crashed heavily during the night and Tavano suffered a broken arm. After repairs Jacques Swaters bought it in May 1964 and sold it on to fellow-Belgian, Marquet.

5095GT: This car was delivered to *Scuderia Serenissima Repubblica di Venezia* in September 1963 and Lucien Bianchi/Carlo Abate drove it into second place in the 1963 Tour de France. Volpi sold it to the *Automobile Club de l'Ouest* in March 1964 and they later used it as a training car at their racing drivers' school on the Bugatti circuit at Le Mans.

5111GT: Delivered new to Jean Guichet and driven by him and José Behra to win the 1963 Tour de France. Guichet/de Bourbon-Parme finished second with it in the 1964 Tour de France.

5571GT: This was the first of the 250GTO64 cars; Chinetti took delivery in February 1964 and *NART* raced it until February 1965. Phil Hill/Pedro Rodriguez drove it to a win in the 1964 Daytona Continental 2,000Km event.

5573GT: This 250GTO64 was registered to *SEFAC Ferrari* in June 1964 and delivered to *NART* the same month. It was frequently raced – and frequently crashed. Surtees drove it in the 1964 Tourist Trophy.

5575GT: This was the last 250GTO64 and delivered to Jacques Swaters. It passed, nominally at least through the ownership of two Belgians, then back to Swaters. It achieved a number of good class performances and Lucien Bianchi/'Vic' drove it to second place overall and a class win in the 1964 1,120-mile (1,800km) Tour of Belgium.

246SP, 196SP, 248SP, 268SP and 286SP

0790: This was originally a 246SP. During 1961 it won the Targa Florio (von Trips/Gendebien/Ginther) and finished third in the Nürburgring 1,000Km race (Ginther/Gendebien/von Trips). Hill/Gendebien drove it to a win in the 1962 Nürburgring 1,000Km race and Parkes won the 1962 Guards Trophy at Brands Hatch with it. For 1963 it was fitted with a 2-litre engine, became a 196SP, and driven by Lualdi to eighth place for *Scuderia Sant' Ambroeus* in the European Hill Climb Championship.

0796: This was originally a 246SP. It ran in the Targa Florio and Nürburgring 1,000Km races in 1961, but retired in both events. P. Hill/R. Rodriguez drove it into second place in the 1962 Daytona Three Hours race, it won the Targa Florio driven by Mairesse/R. Rodriguez/Gendebien and it retired in the hands of the Rodriguez brothers at Le Mans. It formed the basis of the first 250P tested by Surtees in late 1962.

0798: It first appeared at the Le Mans Test Weekend in 1962 in 248SP form. It was fitted with a 268SP engine for Le Mans, driven by Baghetti/Scarfiotti, but retired. Driven by Bandini for *NART* at the 1962 Bahamas Speed Week. Thereafter sold to 'Buck' Fulp.

0802: It was on display at Ferrari's Press Conference in February 1962 with a 268SP engine. It appeared at the 1962 Targa Florio, but Phil Hill crashed heavily in practice because the throttle stuck open and he non-started. It was rebuilt for 1963 with 196SP engine and driven by Bandini, Scarfiotti and Mairesse into second place in the Targa Florio. It was sold to Chinetti minus engine in August 1963 and rebuilt with a coupé body.

0804: This car was a 196SP displayed at the Ferrari Press Conference in February 1962. Driven to second place by Bandini/Baghetti in the 1962 Targa Florio. Driven by Baghetti/Bandini in the 1962 Nürburgring 1000Km race, but retired. Scarfiotti then drove the car in the 1962 European Hill Climb Championship entered by *Scuderia Sant' Ambroeus*. It was then exported to the United States (*NART*) and 'Buck' Fulp drove it into fourth place in the Governor's Trophy, Nassau in December. John Godfrey (author of *Ferrari Dino* SPs) bought it in 1969.

0806: This car was built in 248SP form and was air-freighted to the United States in March 1962; 'Buck' Fulp/Bob Ryan drove it into 13th place in the Sebring 12 Hours race. It was returned to the factory and fitted with a 196SP engine and sold to Darold (Doug) Thiem in Milwaukee.

250P

0796: As stated above, this car started life as a 246SP and formed the basis of the first 250P. Works car.

0810: Works car. Parkes/Maglioli drove it to third place at Le Mans in 1963.

0812: Works car. Surtees/Mairesse drove it at Le Mans in 1963, but it caught fire and was substantially destroyed.

0814: Works car. Scarfiotti/Bandini drove it to a win at Le Mans in 1963.

250LM

5149: Red. The chassis was slightly different from production models. It was originally fitted with a 3-litre engine, Pininfarina body with spoiler in rear of roof, all instruments in front of driver. Exhibited at Paris Salon in October 1963 and then at Turin, London and Brussels. Bought by *NART*. Damaged in fire at Sebring, 1964 and later rebuilt.

5841: Red. Delivered to *Scuderia Filipinetti* and sold by it in 1966 to French collector Pierre Bardinon.

5843: Red. Loaned to *Écurie Francorchamps* in May 1964, later repainted yellow, raced regularly, bought from Ferrari in November 1964 and sold in the United States in 1966.

5845: Early history is not known, but it was sold to American Arthur Swanson, raced briefly in Europe and then taken to the United States.

5891: Red. Left-hand drive. Date of manufacture: 6 April 1965. Delivered to *Scuderia Filipinetti* and raced extensively. Sold in 1969 to Pierre Bardinon who resold it in 1970.

5893: Red. Delivered to *NART*. Drogo nose fitted shortly after delivery. It was the winning car at Le Mans in 1965 and it was raced by *NART* until 1970. It is believed that this car was sold to Greg Young in 1970, sold back to *NART* and then sold via Kirk White to the Indianapolis Motor Museum.

5895: China red. Date of manufacture: 30 April 1964. Delivered to *Maranello Concessionaires* and raced by them until June 1965. In September 1965 it was sold to Peter Clarke and raced by him until it was badly damaged in a South African race in 1968.

5897: Green. Ordered through *Maranello Concessionaires* by David Piper and delivered to him in July 1964. Piper crashed it heavily at Snetterton in September 1964. It was rebuilt for 1965 with an unnumbered chassis supplied by the works and raced extensively in 1965–66. In 1966 Piper sold the car to Jeff Edmonds and it was destroyed in a transporter fire at Silverstone in 1967. This car was later rebuilt.

5899: Red. Date of manufacture: 16 May 1964. It was delivered to *Scuderia Filipinetti* and raced by them in 1964. Werner Biedermann bought it early in 1965. He competed in Swiss hill climbs with the car until he crashed it badly in a road accident. Fellow-Swiss Hans Illert, bought it, shortened the chassis and fitted a Porsche *Carrera* 6 body. Herbert Müller and others drove it in Swiss hill climbs. After a chequered life it was restored in the late 1970s.

5901: China red. Fitted with centre-lock alloy wheels. Date of manufacture: 24 September 1964. It was delivered to *NART* and raced by them until after the 1966 Daytona 24 Hours race. Thereafter it passed through the hands of many owners.

5903: Red. Left-hand drive. Date of manufacture: 30 January 1965. It was fitted with a Drogo nose. Sold to Irene Gaessly in Rome and thereafter it passed through the hands of many owners.

5905: Red. Delivered to *Scuderia Filipinetti* on 24 March 1965, but sold almost immediately to Swiss hill climb specialist Heinrich Walter who competed with it extensively. It was badly damaged in an accident, ran at a couple of meetings in open form, repaired and then badly damaged in a fire following another accident. Thereafter it also passed through the hands of many owners.

5907: China Red. It was delivered to *Maranello Concessionaires* on 1 July 1964. They raced it a couple of times and it won the 1964 Reims 12 Hours race. It was loaned to David Piper for a couple of races and then sold in late 1965 to Bernard White (*Team Chamaco Collect*). It was bought by Richard Attwood in November 1967 and he sold it to Sir Anthony Bamford in September 1969.

5909: Red. Date of manufacture: 27 May 1964. Delivered to *NART* who ran it at Le Mans and Reims in 1964. It was sold to Bob Grossman in late 1964 and he raced it during late 1964 and sold it in 1965 as he had ordered a Ford GT40. Thereafter it had many owners.

5975: Red. Sold to Helge Pehrsson, Sweden in early 1965 and raced by him in a few club events. He sold the car in late 1967 to the Schlumpf brothers and it is now in the French National Motor Museum/Collection Schlumpf at Mulhouse.

5995: LHD. Metallic silver-grey. Sold in 1965 by the factory to Count Volpi. Loaned by him to Roberto Benelli, who drove it in minor races. Volpi had the car modified for road use and changes included large Plexiglas rear window, air conditioning, electric windows and cast magnesium-alloy wheels. It subsequently passed through the hands of many owners.

6023: Yellow. Date of manufacture: 30 August 1964. It was sold to *Écurie Francorchamps* in September 1964 and the Belgian team raced it through to 1966. It was exhibited on the Ferrari stand at the 1966 Brussels Motor Show. It passed through the hands of several owners, including David Piper.

6025: White with blue stripe. Special Pininfarina-bodied car built in road trim and exhibited at the 1965 Geneva Salon and the New York Auto Show. Luigi Chinetti bought and kept it until 1971. Various subsequent owners.

6045: Colour and date of manufacture not known. It was delivered in 1965 to Bill Harrah of Reno, Nevada, Ferrari dealer and owner of the Harrah Car Collection. It was retained by Harrah for road use until 1966 and then sold to Dr. Hart Isaacs. Car badly damaged in a road accident and burnt out. This car was broken up for spares.

6047: Red. The first known owner was John Mecom Jnr in late 1964 and his *Mecom Racing Team* entered the car in races from the autumn of 1964 through to early 1965. It was sold to Bill Harrah, Reno, Nevada for use as a road car and then had various owners.

6051: China red. Delivered to *Maranello Concessionaires* on 8 September 1964 against an order placed by Viscount Portman. He sold it in May 1965 to Roy Salvadori who sold it on to Jackie Epstein (son of sculptor Jacob Epstein) who raced it through to 1966. It was then bought by David Prophet who raced it at events in 1967. Prophet fitted a Drogo nose, but with larger than usual air intake and minor body modifications. Prophet then sold the car on and it had a number of different owners.

6053: China red. Date of manufacture: 30 June 1964. Ordered by George Drummond through *Maranello Concessionaires*. Extensively raced by Drummond and others 1965–67. Fitted long nose. Thereafter various owners.

6105: China red. Ordered by *Maranello Concessionaires* for Ron Fry and delivered in September 1964. Loaned back for display at the 1964 London Motor Show. Fry had it registered RON 54. He competed with the car in numerous minor events between September 1964 and September 1966. *Maranello Concessionaires* exhibited it again at the 1966 London Motor Show and eventually sold it early in 1968 to David Skailes who fitted a Drogo nose and Campagnolo magnesium-alloy wheels. Skailes sold the car in October 1968 to Jack Maurice, who called it *The Duchess* and competed with it extensively and successfully in hill climbs until 1975. Thereafter various owners.

6107: Red. Date of manufacture: 23 July 1965. Delivered new to Ferrari dealer Charles Rezzaghi, San Francisco and sold new to Steve Earle, Los Angeles who had it repainted metallic dark blue and used it only on the road. Earle wanted to sell the car from late 1966 and in March 1967 he sold it to Ecuadorians Guillermo Ortega and Fausto Merello who raced it with John Gunn under the name *Raceco Racing Team*. They entered it at Daytona and Sebring 1968, Daytona 1969. Sold on to the UK and then Japan.

6119: Red. Glass-fibre body. Sold in 1964 to Georges Filipinetti for use by *Scuderia Filipinetti*. Raced in Paris 1,000Km race in October 1964 and throughout 1965. Sold for 1966 to Swiss Pierre de Siebenthal who entered it at Monza and Nürburgring 1966 and thereafter driven in Portuguese events by Antonio Peixinho. Ran at Monza 1000Km 1967 and fitted that year with long nose by Sbarro. It was badly damaged in an accident, stored in dismantled form and later sold. Various owners.

6167: Light metallic green. Delivered to William H. Lowe, Australian Ferrari importer, Melbourne for sale to David McKay. McKay cancelled order when the 250LM could not be homologated and after Lowe had the car in his showroom for many months it was returned to the factory and fitted with a Drogo nose. This 250LM was repainted china red and delivered to *Maranello Concessionaires* for the 1967 season. Mike Parkes fitted it with a re-profiled more aerodynamic nose-section. It was extensively raced, including a win by Attwood in the Group Four sports car race at the British Grand Prix meeting, and then sold in September 1967 to Paul Vestey. Vestey raced the car until co-driver David Piper crashed it heavily in the 1968 Targa Florio. The car was rebuilt with a replacement chassis (said to be from 6053) and a glass-fibre body built by Piper and installed by Scaglietti and Drogo. Vestey/Pike drove it painted mauve at Le Mans in 1968 and thereafter it was sold in the United States.

6173: Red. Date of manufacture: 1 April 1965. Delivered to *Scuderia Sant' Ambroeus*. Eduardo Lualdi-Gabardi drove it in minor Italian races and hill climbs with great success and Taramazzo/Sigala also raced it in the 1965 Monza 1,000Km and Targa Florio races. At a time not known a Drogo nose was fitted. It was sold to Swiss Ferrari dealer Peter Monteverdi, Basle who modified it for road use by a Dr. Hopf. Sold in the United States, badly damaged in an accident, restored and various owners thereafter.

6217: Colour not known. Date of manufacture: 1 April 1965. It was fitted with a Drogo nose at the factory. Sold to Canadian Michael McDonald. Modified for road use by fitting different exhaust and 275GTB4 clutch. Sold in 1970 and thereafter various owners.

6233: Red. Glass-fibre body. Date of manufacture: June 1965. Delivered to Chris Cord, United States, sold in October 1965 and thereafter various owners.

6???: Delivered to *Écurie Francorchamps* on 22 April 1965. Raced in a few events 1965–66. It was sold to Tony Dean and, apparently, engine from 6023 installed at the time of sale. Subsequent owners included Neil Corner, Richard Crosthwaite and David Piper. Thereafter sold to Australia.

6321: Red. Date of manufacture: October 1964. Delivered to Ferrari dealer William Lowe, Melbourne to the order of David McKay. Spencer Martin raced it for McKay very extensively and very successfully in Australia in 1965–66. Jackie Stewart/Andy Buchanan drove it to a win in the 1966 Surfers Paradise 12 Hours race. Andy Buchanan leased the car from McKay and he (and other drivers on his behalf) raced it in 1967. It won the Surfers Paradise 12 Hours race again that year. After the 1967 season the car was sold to Ashley Bence, Sydney and L. Geoghegan and I. Geoghegan drove it to a win for him in the 1968 Surfers Paradise Six Hours race. McKay bought the car back and retained it for many years.

8165: Red. The last 250LM to be built and it was loaned to *Scuderia Filipinetti* in 1966. Factory modifications included lower front, larger air intakes, fog lights under Perspex covers, modified suspension and, according to one source, fuel injection. Mairesse/Müller drove it in the 1966 Nürburgring 1,000Km race and thereafter it was sold to David Piper who repainted it in his usual light green. When Piper bought the car, it was on carburettors and with no sign of fuel injection ever being fitted. Piper raced the car until his accident in 1970, extensively modifying it to improve roadholding and to reduce weight. He returned to historic racing with the car in 1980 and still owns it.

275P and 330P

0812: Works 275P car. Baghetti/Maglioli drove it at Le Mans, but it was eliminated by an accident.

0814: 330P supplied to *NART* in 1964, initially on loan; Rodriguez/Hudson drove it at Le Mans; Rodriguez and Fulp drove it in North America.

0816: Works car. First raced by Mike Parkes as a 250P with 4-litre engine at Reims and

Silverstone in July 1963. It was rebuilt as a 275P and re-bodied by Fantuzzi for 1964. Scarfiotti/Vaccarella drove it to second place at Sebring and Guichet/Vaccarella drove it to a win at Le Mans.

0818: 330P initially supplied to *Maranello Concessionaires* on loan and delivered direct to the 1964 Sebring 12 Hours race. It was retained and raced by the British team through 1965 and then sold to Dick Protheroe who rebuilt it and incorporated aerodynamic modifications proposed by Mike Parkes. Protheroe crashed it with fatal results while practising for the Tourist Trophy in April 1966.

0820: Works 275P. Parkes/Scarfiotti drove it at Le Mans in 1964. It retired because of oil pump failure.

0822: Works 330P. Surtees/Bandini drove it to third place at Le Mans in 1964.

0824: Works 330P. Rebuilt as a 365P with 4.4-litre engine for 1965; loaned to *Scuderia Filipinetti*, but burnt out following Tommy Spychiger's fatal crash in the 1965 Monza 1,000Km race.

275P2/330P2

0820: Works 275P2 converted from 275P. Parkes/Scarfiotti drove it at Le Mans in 1965. It retired because of oil pump failure.

0828: Works car first raced in 275P2 form in the Targa Florio by Bandini/Vaccarella who won; fitted with 4-litre engine for the Nürburgring 1,000Km race and it won again driven by Surtees/Scarfiotti. Surtees/Scarfiotti drove it at Le Mans, but eventually retired because of gearbox trouble. For subsequent history, see below.

0832: Works car raced in 275P2 form by Bandini/Biscaldi at Le Mans in 1965, but retired because of valve trouble.

0836: Works 330P2 driven by Guichet/Parkes at Le Mans in 1965 and retired because of cylinder head gasket failure. It was subsequently rebuilt in 365P2 form (see below).

365P2

0828. Supplied in 1966 to *Écurie Francorchamps*; this car was updated to 365P2/3 specification for Le Mans in 1966 with 330P3-style body and some P3 chassis modifications.

0832: Rebuilt from 275P2 (see above) and supplied to *Scuderia Filipinetti*.

0836: Supplied in 1965 to *Maranello Concessionaires*; it retired at Le Mans driven by Bonnier/Piper, but Surtees/Parkes drove it to second place in the Reims 12 Hours race. David Piper bought this car in July 1965 and his successes included a win in the Kyalami Nine Hours race. The car was updated to 365P2/3 specification for Le Mans in 1966 with 330P-style body and some P3 chassis modifications. Piper crashed it in 1967 at the Crystal Palace; it was rebuilt and bought by Dan Margulies for 1968. After three-four months Margulies sold it to Neil Corner.

0838: Supplied in 1965 to *NART*; Rodriguez/Vaccarella drove it to seventh place at Le Mans and Rodriguez/Guichet won the Reims 12 Hours' race with it. Rodriguez drove it to third place in the Canadian GP. This car was updated to 365P2/3 chassis specification for Le Mans in 1966 and was fitted with a long-tail body by Piero Drogo.

330P3 and 330P3/4 (412P)

0844: Works P3 in 1966. Bandini/Guichet drove it at Le Mans, but retired because of transmission trouble. It was a *NART* entry for Rodriguez/Ginther at Le Mans in 1966. It was rebuilt as a P3/4 (412P) for *NART* for 1967.

0848: Works P3 in 1966. Scarfiotti/Parkes drove it at Le Mans, but were eliminated by an accident. It was rebuilt as P3/4 for *Scuderia Filipinetti* for 1967.

0850: Works P3 in 1966, rebuilt as P3/4 for *Écurie Francorchamps* for 1967.

0854: Works P3 in 1966, rebuilt as P3/4 for *Maranello Concessionaires* for 1967. Attwood/Bianchi drove it to third place in the Spa 1,000Km race and sixth place in the BOAC 500 race. *Maranello Concessionaires* sold it to David Piper who raced it for several years.

330P4

0846: Works car. Driven at Le Mans in 1967 by Amon/Vaccarella, but retired because of overheating.

0856: Works car. Entered at Le Mans in 1967 by *Écurie Francorchamps* and driven into third place by Mairesse/'Beurlys'.

0858: Works car. Driven into second place at Le Mans in 1967 by Scarfiotti/Parkes.

0860: Works car. Driven at Le Mans by Klass/Sutcliffe, retired because of fuel-feed problems.

0900: David Piper built this car up, basing it on the suspension and original body of a P4 rebuilt for Can-Am racing. Enzo Ferrari agreed to build a new chassis, which was given this number. Still owned by Piper.

312P

0868: Original works prototype that first appeared at Sebring. It crashed heavily at Monza with Pedro Rodriguez at the wheel. It is believed that a new car with coupé body was built with the same chassis number and incorporating parts from the original 0868. After the Le Mans race it was sold to *NART*.

0870: First appeared at Brands Hatch and raced regularly thereafter. It was fitted with a coupé body for the Le Mans race and afterwards it was sold to *NART*.

512S

1002: *Spyder*. Originally red, later yellow with central green stripe. Works car raced at Sebring 1970. Sold to Spanish *Escuderia Montjuich*. Raced at Le Mans and afterwards in 1970 by Juncadella. Rebuilt in Feb–March 1971 as 512M *berlinetta* and raced by Juncadella.

1004: *Berlinetta*. Originally works car. Ickx/Schetty drove it at Daytona and Surtees/Schetty at Monza. Ferrari then sold it as a chassis with mechanical components and body panels to Jacques Swaters. It passed in 1971 to *Herbert Müller Racing* who built it up with components from other cars to produce a car with the chassis number 1016, but it was not raced.

1006: *Spyder*. Supplied to *NART* and raced extensively throughout 1970–71. Then various owners including Harley Cluxton (1971) and Steve Earle (1972).

1008: *Berlinetta*. Red with white nose, lower side panels and central stripe and narrow turquoise blue line at the centre of the stripe. *Scuderia Filipinetti*. Raced at the Nürburgring 1970 by Müller/Parkes and Le Mans 1970 with long tail by Bonnier/Wisell. Sold to *Herbert Müller Racing*, converted to 512M, driven by Moretti/Zeccoli at Monza and destroyed in Rodriguez's fatal crash at the Norisring.

1010: *Spyder*. Works car raced in 1970 at Sebring (Andretti/Merzario), Brands Hatch (Ickx/Oliver), Nürburgring (Giunti/Merzario), Watkins Glen (Ickx/Schetty), Watkins Glen

Can-Am (Ickx). Rebuilt as 512M and driven by Ickx/Giunti (Austria and Kyalami 1970), Merzario (Imola Interserie, 1971). Rebuilt as Can-Am car (712P) driven by Andretti, 1971 and thereafter sold to *NART*.

1012: *Spyder*. Works car raced in 1970 by Amon/Merzario (Brands Hatch), Vaccarella/Giunti (Targa Florio) and Giunti/Merzario (Nürburgring).

1014: *Berlinetta*. Red with central dark blue stripe edged with white stripes. Delivered to *NART* who raced at Daytona (Gurney/Parsons) and after rebuild at works with long tail it was driven at Le Mans by Sam Posey/Ronnie Bucknum. At Daytona this car had a bulge on the driver's side of the roof to clear Gurney's head. Rebuilt as 512M and sold to Greg Young who raced it with various co-drivers in 1971.

1016: *Berlinetta*. Red with white nose, lower side panels and central stripe, with narrow turquoise blue line at the centre of the stripe. Delivered to *Scuderia Filipinetti* and raced regularly by the Swiss team. It was fitted at the works with a long tail for Le Mans 1970 and raced there by Mike Parkes/Herbert Müller. For 1971 it was sold to *Herbert Müller Racing* and driven in a number of events by Wiesendanger/Kocher (co-driver Gregory in Austria).

1018: *Spyder*. Red with yellow nose-band, fins and central stripe. Delivered to George Loos's *Gelo Racing*. Raced regularly, but with little success in 1970, including Le Mans where *Scuderia Filipinetti* entered it. Rebuilt as 512M for 1971 and continued to be raced without success.

1020: *Berlinetta*. Not raced in 1970 but rebuilt as 512M for *NART* for 1971 and driven by Posey/Revson (Daytona), Revson/Savage (Sebring), Posey/Adamowicz at Le Mans and Posey/Bucknum (Watkins Glen). In 1974 driven by Chinetti Jnr/Paul Newman/Phil Hill it set International Class records at Bonneville Salt Flats.

1022: (See 1032)

1024: 512S *Berlinetta*, but never raced in that form, rebuilt for 1971 as a 512M and sold to *Scuderia Brescia Corse*. Mainly driven by 'Pam', but Facetti co-drove with him at Monza and Casoni in Austria.

1026: *Berlinetta*. The works entered this car in 1970 at Daytona (Andretti/Merzario/Ickx), Sebring (Vaccarella/Giunti/Andretti), Monza (Amon/Merzario), Spa (Giunti/Vaccarella) and Le Mans (Derek Bell/Ronnie Peterson). Sold to Jacques Swaters for use in the making of the *Le Mans* film and destroyed. Subsequently resurrected.

1028: *Spyder*. The works entered this car in 1970 at (Vaccarella/Giunti) and then sold it to *NART*. Used in the making of *Le Mans*. Rebuilt after filming as a *spyder*, crashed at Sebring 1971, rebuilt as 512M and driven at Le Mans by Craft/Weir.

1030: *Berlinetta*. Yellow, delivered to *Écurie Francorchamps*. Driven at Spa by Bell/Fierlandt. Fitted at works with long tail for Le Mans 1970 and driven there by Hughes de Fierlandt/Alistair Walker. Subsequently ran at Kyalami 1970 (Bell/Fierlandt), Buenos Aires and Daytona 1971 (Gosselin/Fierlandt). Thereafter rebuilt as 512M and sold to Alain de Cadenet. Raced at Le Mans, Watkins Glen Six Hours and Can-Am 1971 and sold to Neil Corner.

1032: Red. Corrado Manfredini bought three 512S 'packages'. 1032 was delivered first, monocoque wrecked at Daytona and rebuilt with the monocoque from 1022. Both cars were *berlinettas*. When the car was rebuilt to 512M specification for 1971, the monocoque from 1050 was used. The car was raced in 512S form as both 1032 and 1050. Its history was dismal apart from a win at Mount Fuji in Japan.

1034: *Berlinetta*. Red. Works long-tail car driven by Merzario/Regazzoni at Le Mans in 1970 and crashed. The car was destroyed and dismantled.

1036: *Berlinetta*. Red. Used by the works for testing and as a team spare. Sold to Solar Productions for the making of the *Le Mans* film. Sold for 1971 to *Herbert Müller Racing*. Raced in Can-Am in 1974 with 512M specification, *spyder* body, cut-down windscreen and various sizes of engine.

1038: *Berlinetta*. Red. Driven at Spa by Ickx/Surtees and at Le Mans 1970 by Jacky Ickx/Peter Schetty. After Ickx's bad crash it was written off.

1040: *Spyder*. Red. Sold in 512S form to Earle Cord Racing and driven in Can-Am events by Adams. Rebuilt in the United States by Roger Penske to 512M specification using drawings supplied by Forghieri. It became the Sunoco-Ferrari.

1042: *Spyder*. Red. The works entered this car in 1970 at Sebring Ickx/Schetty, Monza (Giunti/Vaccarella/Amon), Nürburgring (Schetty/Ickx) – [crashed in practice by Schetty], Watkins Glen (Andretti/Giunti), Watkins Glen Can-Am (Andretti) and Imola (Merzario/Giunti).

1044: *Berlinetta*. Red. The works entered this car in 1970 at Spa (Merzario/Schetty) and Le Mans (Vaccarella/Giunti). It was converted to 512M specification and sold to *Herbert Müller Racing*; extensively raced 1971–72 and crashed heavily by Müller in the 1972 Nürburgring Interserie race. Badly damaged and burnt out, but restored by Müller.

1046: According to factory records, this car was dismantled once the 512S had been homologated. It may have formed the basis of the 512S *Modulo* show car exhibited by Pinin Farina at the 1970 Geneva Salon.

1048: Red. Works *berlinetta* used as a test and spare car. During 1970 Ferrari sold it to *Scuderia Filipinetti*. The team ran it in 1971 at Buenos Aires and Monza for Bonnier/Parkes on both occasions. It then was modified by Parkes for Le Mans and is sometimes known as the 512F.

1050: (See 1032)

Bibliography

Bluemel, Keith and Pourret, Jess G. *Ferrari 250GTO* (Bay View Books, 1998)
de Hartog, Jack Hoobs, de Biolley, Rodolphe and Olczyk, Philippe *Bizzarrini: The Genius Behind Ferrari's Success* (There is no publisher's acknowledgement other than a web-site address, 2001 – copyright date only)
Ferrari, Enzo, (English translation) *My Terrible Joys* (Hamish Hamilton, 1963)
Fitzgerald, Warren W. and Merritt, Richard F. *Ferrari: The Sports and Gran Turismo Cars* (Bond Publishing Company, 1968/Patrick Stephens, 1979)
Godfrey, John *Ferrari Dino SPs* (Patrick Stephens, 1990)
Gozzi, Franco *Memoirs of Enzo Ferrari's Lieutenant* (Giorgio Nada Editore, 2002)
Henry, Alan *Flat-12 – The Racing Career of Ferrari's 3-Litre Grand Prix and Sports Cars* (Motor Racing Publications, 1981)
Henry, Alan, *Ferrari, The Grand Prix Cars* (Second Edition, Hazleton Publishing, 1989)
Massini, Marcel with Box, Rob de la Rive *Ferrari 250LM* (Osprey Publishing, 1983)
Moity, Christian *The Le Mans 24-Hour Race, 1949–73* (Edita SA/Patrick Stephens, 1974)
Moss, Stirling with Nye, Doug *My Cars, My Career* (Patrick Stephens, 1987)
Nye, Doug *The Colonel's Ferraris* (Ampersand Press, 1980)
Orsini, Luigi and Zagari, Franco (English text edited by Doug Nye) *The Scuderia Ferrari* (Osprey Publishing, 1981)
Pourret, Jess G. *Ferrari 250GT Competition Cars* (Foulis/Haynes Publishing, 1987)
Pritchard, Anthony *Ford Versus Ferrari: The Battle for Le Mans* (Pelham Books, 1968)
Pritchard, Anthony *Sports Car Championship* (Robert Hale, 1972)
Tanner, Hans, with Nye, Doug *Ferrari* (Fifth Edition, Foulis/Haynes Publishing, 1979)
Venables, David *First Among Champions: The Alfa Romeo Grand Prix Cars* (Haynes Publishing, 2000)
Wimpflen, Janos L. *Time and Two Seats* (Motorsport Research Group, 1999)
Wyer, John *The Certain Sound* (Edita SA/Automobile Year, 1981)
Magazines include *Autosport, Cavallino, Ferrari* (the magazine of the Ferrari Owners' Club of Great Britain), *Ferrarissima, Motor Racing, Motor Sport, Prancing Horse* (the magazine of The Ferrari Club of America), *Road & Track, The Autocar, The Motor.*

Index

Abarth cars: 84, 95, 163
Abate, Carlo: 26, 27, 28, 29, 31, 33, 35, 56, 58, 61
AC Cobra cars: 60, 84
Ahrens, Kurt: 158, 168, 170, 175, 176, 179
Alan Mann Racing: 97, 98, 101, 106, 156
Alfa Romeo cars:
 Giulia TI: 137
 33: 117, 118, 121–2, 127–8
 33/2: 166
 33/3: 168, 170, 178, 180, 185, 188, 190, 191, 209, 210
 33TT3: 209, 210, 216, 217, 224
 33TT3: 209, 210, 216, 217, 224
 33TT12: 221, 222, 223
Adamowicz, Tony: 164, 165, 180, 183, 188, 192
Amon, Chris: 89, 90, 92, 97, 105, 108, 115, 116, 118, 119, 124, 125, 126, 128, 129, 147, 149, 150, 157, 158, 160, 161, 162, 168, 173, 176, 251
Andretti, Mario: 97, 98, 106, 117, 118, 125, 126, 140, 152, 157, 158, 162, 168, 169, 170, 177, 186–7, 188, 191, 192, 209, 210, 211, 222, 231
Angolan Grand Prix: *1964*, 135; *1965*, 140
Aston Martin cars:
 DBR1: 26
 DB4GT: 27, 49, 133, 134
 DB4GT Project 214: 31, 34, 35, 38
 Project 215: 60–61
ATS cars: 17, 31
Attwood, Richard: 38, 61, 82, 90, 98, 100, 103, 107, 108, 109, 111, 116, 117, 120, 122, 124, 125, 126, 128, 129, 131, 137, 139, 140, 142, 143, 144, 145, 168, 170, 175, 176, 190, 191, 251–2
Austrian Sports Car Grand Prix, *1965*: 92, 139
Austrian 1,000Km race: *1970*, 178; *1971*, 185, 185; *1972*, 217; *1973*, 224

Baghetti, Giancarlo: 41, 46, 47, 49, 56, 82, 84, 88, 89, 90, 92, 100, 101, 124, 228, 252
Bandini, Lorenzo: 38, 46, 47, 49, 50, 53, 56, 57, 60, 61, 63, 82, 84, 88, 89, 90, 92, 97, 98, 100, 101, 104, 107, 116, 118, 119, 120, 125, 137, 140, 237–8, 252

Barcelona 1,000Km race: *1971*, 185
Bell, Derek: 165, 173, 175, 176, 179, 188, 190, 210, 216, 217
Beltoise, Jean-Pierre: 140, 168, 188, 220, 221, 222, 223, 224
'Beurlys' (Jean Blaton): 24–5, 26, 29, 31, 38, 41, 60, 92, 98, 109, 116, 120, 124, 126, 130, 134, 137
Bianchi, Lucien: 23, 25, 26, 27, 29, 32, 33, 35, 38, 39, 45, 92, 98, 101, 106, 117, 120, 122, 125, 130, 134, 137, 252
Biscaldi, Giampero: 41, 88, 92, 98, 98, 100, 101
Bizzarrini, Giotto: 17, 26, 31, 252
BOAC 500 race: *1967*, 128–30; *1969*,157; 1,000Km race: *1970*, 170; *1971*, 188; *1972*, 212
Bondurant, Bob: 38, 39, 87, 89, 90, 92, 98, 140
Bonnier, Joakim: 38, 39, 45, 46, 50, 56, 57, 63, 89, 90, 91, 97, 100, 103, 107, 134, 176, 180, 181, 190, 214, 216, 217, 252–3
Bridgehampton 'Double' 500Km race: *1963*, 61; *1964*, 39, 85, 134; *1965*, 94; Can-Am race, *1968*, 149
Broadley, Eric: 7, 64, 105, 230, 237
Bucknum, Ronnie: 90, 106, 108, 125, 126, 169, 176, 177, 188
Buenos Aires 1,000Km race: *1970*, 168; *1971*, 180, 188; *1972*, 209

Caliri, *Ing.* Gaicomo: 155, 218, 241, 243
Casoni, Mario: 92, 98, 100, 101, 117, 118, 121, 127, 128, 131, 137, 139, 185, 192, 217
Casner, Lloyd: 60, 88
Cesana-Sestriere hill climb: 1965, 95; 1966, 113; 1967, 131; 1969, 163
Cevert, François: 178, 217, 220, 221, 222, 223, 224
Chaparral cars: 7, 53, 88, 94, 95, 97, 98, 103, 107, 111, 116, 117, 118, 120, 121, 122, 125, 126, 128, 129, 136, 146
Chinetti, Luigi: 133, 146, 147, 149, 231, 232, 253
Chiti, Carlo: 7, 14, 43, 117, 216, 227, 228, 235

Clermont-Ferrand races: *1956*, 25; *1961*, 29; *1966*, 140–1
Colombo, Giaocchino: 9, 253–4
Coppa Inter-Europa race: *1957*, 23; *1959*, 26; *1960*, 27; *1963*, 34–5; *1964*, 134
Courage, Piers: 108, 124, 168

Dallara, *Ing.* Gianpaolo: 227
Da Silva Ramos, Hermanos: 24, 25
Davis, Colin: 26, 28, 31, 33, 90, 100
Daytona Continental Three Hours race: *1962*, 29, 44–5; Challenge Cup: *1964*, 133; 2,000Km race: *1964*, 36; *1965*, 87; 24 Hours race: *1966*, 97, 140; *1967*, 116–7; *1969*, 156–7; *1970*, 164, 168–9; *1971*, 165; Six Hours race, *1972*, 188, 209
De Adamich, Andrea: 122, 168, 178, 180, 185, 188, 190, 191, 209, 216, 217, 222, 223
De Fierlandt, Hughes: 173, 176, 177, 179, 180, 183, 214
Della Casa, Ermanno: 17, 90
Deserti, Bruno: 90
Dijon 1,000Km race: 1973, 220
Donohue, Mark: 97, 98, 106, 125, 126, 136–7, 156, 180, 182, 183, 185, 191, 232
Dragoni, Eugenio: 46, 81, 90, 95, 104–5, 115, 229, 230, 236, 238, 239–40, 254
Drogo, Piero: 31, 96, 116, 254
Ducarouge, Gérard: 218
Dumay, Pierre: 60, 134, 137, 140
Dulon cars: 188, 189

Earl, Steve: 152
Eaton, George: 165, 183
Écurie Francorchamps: 31, 38, 41, 91, 92, 98, 103, 107, 109, 111, 116, 120, 124, 131, 134, 135, 136, 140,143, 173, 175, 176, 180, 185, 258
Edmonton Can-Am race: *1971*, 152
Elford, Vic: 128, 158, 160, 168, 170, 171, 175, 176, 177, 180, 188, 191, 216
English Limited, F.: 98, 101
Epstein, Jack: 121, 130, 140, 145
Équipe Endeavour: 27, 29, 31, 35, 36

Escuderia Montjuich: 176, 177, 180, 181, 183
Essex Wire Corporation: 98, 101, 106
Enna Cup, City of: *1965*, 137, 139
Elkhart Lake Can-Am race: *1969*, 149; *1971*, 185

Facetti, Carlo: 38, 209, 223
Fantuzzi, Medardo: 235–6
Ferrari, Enzo: 8, 9, 12, 13, 15, 17, 19, 39–40, 43, 49–50, 81, 104–5, 109, 114, 115, 148, 149, 168, 175, 220, 227, 230, 231, 232, 233, 235, 237, 239–41, 243–4, 254–5
Ferrari, Laura: 17
Ferrari, Piero Lardi: 19
Ferrari single-seater racing cars:
 340 Formula 1: 11
 375 Formula 1: 11
 500 Formula 2: 12
 625 Formula 1: 12, 13
 553 Formula 1: 13
 312B Formula 1; 163–4, 168, 186–7, 232
 312B3 Formula 1: 232
 312T Formula 1: 232–3
Ferrari V12 sports cars:
 125: 9–10
 159: 10
 166 *Inter*: 10
 166 *Mille Miglia*: 10
 195 *Sport*: 10
 195 *Inter*: 10
 212 *Inter*: 10–11
 212 *Export*: 11
 250 *Sport*: 11
 342 *America*: 11
 375 *Le Mans*: 11
 375 Plus: 12
 410 *Sport*: 12
 250 *Mille Miglia*: 11, 21
 290 *Mille Miglia*: 14, 86
 315 *Sport*: 14
 335 *Sport*: 14
 250 *Testa Rossa*: 7, 14, 16, 23, 26, 29, 33, 44, 45, 46, 49, 52, 58, 61
Ferrari four-cylinder sports cars:
 625 *Sport*: 14
 735 *Sport*: 12
 750 *Monza*: 12
 860 *Monza*: 12
 500 *Mondial*: 12–13
 500 *Testa Rossa TRC*: 13
Ferrari six-cylinder sports cars:
 118 *Le Mans*: 13
 121 *Le Mans*: 13
Ferrari V6 sports cars:
 Dino 296S: 15
 Dino 196S: 15–16

Dino 246S: 16
Dino 246SP: 16–17, 43, 44, 46, 47, 49, 52–3
Dino 196SP and S: 43, 46, 50, 56
Dino 248SP: 43, 46, 61
Dino 268SP: 43, 46, 47, 49
Dino 286SP: 43
Ferrari V12 *Gran Turismo* cars
 250 *Europa*: 21, 23
 250GT: 14, 21–6
 250GT SWB: 17, 26–9, 35, 36
 250GT 'Breadvan': 31, 33
 250GT *Spyder California*: 25–6
 250GTO: 17, 29–36, 43, 45, 49, 54, 58, 61, 82, 84, 133, 135
 250GTO64: 36, 39–40, 82
 275GTB: 40, 91, 108, 126, 137
 250GTO 4-litre: 46, 47
 330TR1-62: 46, 49, 53, 54, 58, 228
 330LM/SA: 53, 54, 58, 59, 61
 250LMB/SA: 60
 365GTB/4 *Daytona*: 152
Ferrari Prototypes:
 250P: 33, 36, 52–7, 60–1. 62, 230, 235–6, 237
 250LM: 36, 84, 88, 91, 92, 101, 111, 132–45, 166
 275P: 38, 62, 63, 81, 82, 84, 87, 230
 330P: 62, 63, 82, 84, 87, 88, 89, 92, 94, 99, 134, 136, 137, 230
 275P2: 88, 89, 90, 92
 330P2: 86–7, 88, 89, 90, 91, 92, 137, 139, 230, 239
 Dino 166: 86, 88, 90
 Dino 206S: 95, 97, 98, 99–101, 103, 104, 105, 113, 117, 118, 121–2, 127–8, 130, 131
 365P: 88, 89, 91, 137, 139
 365P2: 88, 91, 92, 94–5, 97, 99, 101, 144
 365P2/3: 97, 98, 101, 103, 104, 107–9, 111, 116, 117
 330P3: 96, 98–9, 100, 101, 103, 104, 105, 107, 230, 239–40
 330P4: 114–29, 147, 231
 330P3/4 (412P): 116–31, 147
 P5: 152
 312P, 154–165, 231
 312PB, 186–92, 209–225, 244–5
Ferrari Flat-12 sports car:
 212E *Montagna*: 158, 231
Ferrari Can-Am cars:
 350 Can-Am: 147, 148

612P/Can-Am: 148, 152, 155
712P: 150, 152
512P: 152
Ferrari Competition Sports Cars:
  512S: 166–183, 231-2
  512M: 178–185, 188, 231
Ford Advanced Vehicles Ltd: 64, 90, 92, 100, 106, 118
Ford France: 90, 92, 106, 125, 127, 131
Ford Motor Company: 17, 19
Ford cars:
  GT40: 7, 36, 61, 64, 81, 82, 84, 87, 88, 89, 90, 92, 95, 99, 100. 101, 103, 105, 106, 118, 126, 136, 140, 143, 156, 157, 166
  Mk II: 91, 92, 96, 97, 98, 101, 105, 106, 108, 116, 140, 144
  Mk IIB: 125–6, 127, 128, 131
  J-car: 98
  Mark IV: 117, 118, 125–6
Forghieri, Mauro: 43, 49, 52, 101, 104, 114, 116–7, 147, 148, 149, 150, 158, 162, 163, 168, 169, 174, 175, 176, 181, 226–233, 235, 236, 238, 241, 244, 245
Foyt, A.J.: 116, 117, 118, 125, 126
Fraschetti, Andrea: 13, 14
Freiburg Hill Climb: *1962*, 50; *1965*, 95; *1966*, 113; *1969*, 113
Frère, Paul: 23, 25
Fry, Ron: 140
Fulp, Bob: 45, 63, 84, 134

Gaisberg Hill Climb: *1965*, 95; *1966*, 113
Galli, Nani: 188, 191, 216
Ganley, Howden: 192, 217, 222
Gardner, Frank: 92, 101, 106, 125, 131, 139
Garnier, Peter: 23
Gavin, Bill: 55, 149
Gelo Racing: 170, 176, 177, 178, 181, 183, 185
Gendebien, Olivier: 14, 17, 22–3, 24, 25, 26, 27, 29, 31, 45, 46, 47, 49, 228
Gilberti, Frederico: 17, 90
Ginther, Richie: 17, 26, 33, 82, 87, 88, 103, 104
Giunti, Ignazio: 168, 169, 170, 171, 172, 173, 175, 176, 177, 178, 189, 188, 232, 255
Gobbato, *Dottore* Piero: 90
Gobbato, Ubo: 90,105
Gonzalez, Froilan: 12, 13
Goodwood races: *Easter 1962*, 51; *Easter 1963*, 33; *Easter 1964*, 38
Gosselin, Gérald: 137, 140, 180
Governor's Cup, Nassau: *1963*, 61; *1964*, 84
Gozzi, Franco: 17, 104–5, 149, 157, 158, 230, 240–1, 255
Grant, Jerry: 38, 97, 98, 106, 135
Gregory, Masten: 14, 31, 60,
82, 99, 116, 137, 189, 182, 183
Grossman, Bob: 38, 87, 94, 106, 135
Guard's Trophy, Brands Hatch: *1962*, 49; *1963*, 61; *1964*, 84; *1965*, 92, 139
Gulf Racing Team/Gulf Research Racing: 155, 157, 161, 168, 169, 170, 171, 173, 174, 175, 176, 177, 178, 180, 183, 185, 188, 189, 190, 191, 209, 217
Guichet, Jean: 27, 29, 31, 33, 35, 38, 39, 49, 58, 82, 84, 89, 90, 92, 100, 101, 116, 118, 121, 122, 124, 137
Gurney, Dan: 38, 44, 46, 59, 61, 87, 88, 98, 106, 116, 117, 125, 126, 168

Hailwood, Mike: 192, 220, 222
Hall, Jim: 7, 53, 59, 88, 95, 97, 116, 117, 118, 136
Hansgen, Walter: 61, 84, 87, 97, 98, 134, 135, 136–7
Harrah, Bill: 147, 148, 149
Hawkins, Paul: 105, 120, 121, 125, 126, 131, 139, 140, 143, 145
Hawthorn, J.M.: 12, 13, 15
Herbert Müller Racing: 180, 181, 185
Herrmann, Hans: 46, 95, 100, 101, 120, 131, 158, 161, 170, 175, 176
Herzog, René, 180, 181, 185
Hezemans, Toive: 170, 188, 190, 191
Hill, Graham: 32, 34, 38, 39, 45, 46, 53, 54, 61, 62, 63, 81, 82, 84, 88, 90, 106, 134, 136, 217, 222
Hill, Phil: 16, 17, 23, 26, 31, 36, 38, 44, 46, 47, 49, 57, 58, 63, 82, 84, 90, 92, 97, 103, 107, 116, 117, 118, 120, 121, 122, 125, 128, 134, 228, 255
Hoare, Colonel 'Ronnie': 31, 32, 33, 35, 59, 61, 62, 98, 99, 231, 246–50
Hobbs, David: 61, 104, 125, 137, 180, 181, 185, 191
Holman & Moody: 97, 98, 195, 118, 120, 125
Hugus, Ed: 27, 31, 87
Hulme, Denis: 105, 120, 125, 137, 143, 149, 176, 177
Hutcherson, Dick: 105, 108

Ickx, Jacky: 106, 118, 120, 128, 130, 131, 143, 157, 161, 168, 169, 170, 173, 174, 175, 176, 178, 180, 188, 189, 191, 192, 209, 210, 212, 213, 214, 215, 216, 218, 220, 221, 222, 223, 224, 225, 233, 244–5, 256
Imola 500Km race: *1970*, 177–8; *1972*, 218; Shell Cup: *1971*, 181; Interserie race: *1971*, 185, 191
International Martini Racing Team: 177, 179, 180, 183, 188, 191, 223
Ireland, Innes: 25, 27, 31, 32, 33, 34, 38, 45, 49, 84, 92, 95, 106, 137, 228

Jacaponi, *Ing.* Stefano: 163, 231
Jano, *Cavaliere Ing.* Vittorio: 9,13
Jarier, Jean-Pierre: 152
Jennings, Bruce: 116, 117, 125, 126
Jaguar E-type cars: 27, 33, 35, 36, 57, 84, 87, 133, 134
Jenkinson, Denis: 13
Johnson, Bob: 38, 87, 116, 117, 125, 126
Juncadella, José: 176, 177, 178, 180, 181, 183, 185

Kauhsen, 'Willi': 177
Kamm, Wunibald: 31
Kelleners, Helmut: 176
Klass, Günther: 100, 116, 117, 118, 121, 124, 127, 128, 131, 256
Kolb, Charles: 41, 104, 117, 134
Klondike Can-Am race, Edmonton: *1969*, 149
Kyalami Nine Hours race: *1964*, 134–5; *1965*, 95; *1966*, 109–11, 143; *1967*, 131; *1969*, 168; *1970*, 179; *1971*, 191, 244; *1972*, 218

Laguna Seca Can-Am race: *1970*, 152; *1971*, 152
Lampredi, Aurelio: 9, 11, 13
Larrousse, Gérard: 161, 177, 180, 188, 191, 214, 217, 220, 221, 222, 223, 224, 225
Le Mans 24 Hours race: *1949*, 10; *1953*, 11; *1954*, 12; *1955*, 13; *1956*, 14; *1960*, 26–7; *1961*, 28–9; *1962*, 31; *1963*, 33, 236; *1964*, 38; *1965*, 41, 90–2, 137; *1966*, 103–8, 140; *1967*, 123–6; *1968*, 145; *1969*, 145, 161; *1970*, 165, 176–7; *1971*, 181; *1972*, 216–7; *1973*, 223–4, 245
Le Mans Practice Weekend: *1961*, 28; *1962*, 45; *1964*, 64, 134; *1965*, 88; *1966*, 98; *1967*, 118; *1970*, 170; *1971*, 181
Le Mans Three Hours race, *1971*, 181
Ligier, Guy: 90, 92, 100, 106, 125, 127, 128, 134, 144
Lindner, Peter: 57, 84
Lini, Franco: 115, 230, 256
Linge, Herbert: 161
Lola cars:
  Generally: 17, 95, 146, 147, 148, 235
  GT: 7, 35, 58, 60, 61, 64, 105, 230
  T70: 94, 111, 137
  T70 Mark III GT: 105, 118, 120, 121, 122, 125, 126, 127, 128, 131, 145
  T70 Mark IIIB GT: 156, 166
  T280 and T282: 209, 210, 214, 217, 224
Loos, George: 170, 176, 177, 178, 181, 183
Los Angeles Times Grand Prix, Riverside Raceway: *1967*, 147; *1969*, 150; *1970*, 152; *1971*, 152; *1972*, 185
Lottery Grand Prix, Monza: *1958*, 26
Lotus cars:
  Eleven: 25
  19: 31, 49, 87
  19B: 44, 88
  23: 46, 61
  30: 84, 92 139
Lyons, Pete: 148, 152, 180

Madrid Six Hours race: *1970*, 178
Maggs, Tony: 33, 58, 134, 136, 137
Maglioli, Umberto: 13, 31, 56, 58, 60, 63, 82, 88, 89, 92, 134
Mairesse, 'Willy': 25, 26, 27, 29, 33, 41, 46, 53, 54, 56, 57, 60, 92, 99, 100–1, 104, 109, 116, 120, 124, 126, 137, 140, 228, 236–7
Manfredini, Gianpiero: 168, 170, 176, 178, 181, 182, 183, 188
Maranello Concessionaires: 27, 29, 31, 32, 33, 35, 36, 38, 39, 49, 59, 61, 63, 82, 84, 90, 91, 92, 94, 98, 99, 101, 103, 104, 107, 108, 120, 124, 128, 129, 134, 135, 137, 139, 140, 231, 248–50
Marko, Helmut: 177, 191, 216, 217
Maserati cars
  250F: 13
  300S: 22, 23
  350S V12: 14
  Tipo 61 'Bird-cage': 14
  Tipo 151: 49, 53, 61, 82, 84, 88
Maserati-France: 49, 82
Matra cars
  MS620: 107, 140
  MS630/650: 168
  MS660: 178, 188
  MS670: 209, 217, 220, 221, 222, 223, 224, 225, 244
McLaren, Bruce: 34, 82, 84, 88, 89, 90, 92, 94, 97, 105, 108, 117
McLaren cars: 94, 146, 147, 149, 150, 152, 177
McClusky, Roger: 125, 126
McKay, David: 140, 142, 145
McQueen, Steve: 170
Mecom, John Jr: 33, 84, 88, 136
Mercedes-Benz cars:
  300SL: 22, 23
  W196: 13
  300SLR: 13
Merzario, Arturo: 163, 168, 169, 170, 173, 175, 176, 178, 181, 188, 189, 213, 216, 218, 220, 222, 223, 224, 225, 245
Mexican Grand Prix: *1962*, 33; *1964*, 84
Michigan Can-Am race: *1969*, 150

Mid-Ohio Can-Am race: *1971*, 185
Miles, Ken: 39, 87, 88, 97, 105, 108, 136
Mille Miglia race: *1948*, 10; *1949*, 10; *1950*, 11; *1951*, 11; *1952*, 11; *1953*, 11; *1954*, 13; *1955*, 13; *1957*, 14; *1956*, 22–23; *1957*, 14, 23; *1958* (rally): 25
Minneapolis Tribune Can-Am, Donneybrooke: *1970*, 152
Mirage cars: 118, 120, 122, 125, 130, 131, 209, 210, 216, 217, 218, 220, 222, 224, 225
Mitter, Gerhardt: 90, 95, 100, 113, 118, 119, 121, 122, 131, 160, 163
Monaco Grand Prix: *1955*, 13; *1966*, 240; *1967*, 120
Monterey Grand Prix, Laguna Seca: *1967*, 147; *1969*, 150
Montseny Hill Climb: *1969*, 163
Mont Tremblant races: *1964*, 84, 134; Player's 200: *1965*, 94
Mont Ventoux Hill Climb: *1962*, 50; *1965*, 95; *1966*, 113; *1969*, 113
Monza 1,000Km race: *1965*, 88, 137; *1966*, 98, 140, 240; *1967*, 118–9; *1969*, 157–8; *1970*, 170; *1971*, 188–9; *1972*, 213, 220–2, 244; *1973*, 220–2
Moretti, Gianpiero: 168, 170, 176, 178, 181
Mosport Park Can-Am race, *1967*, 147; *1971*, 152
Moss, Stirling: 13, 23, 26, 27, 28–9, 31, 45, 60, 228
Motschenbacher, Lothar: 152, 185
Mugello, Circuit of: *1965*, 137; *1967*, 127
Muir, Brian: 106–7, 125
Müller, Herbert: 88, 89, 99, 101, 104, 117, 118, 121, 122, 124, 127, 128, 140, 170, 172, 173, 175, 176, 189, 181, 185
Munari, Sandro: 216, 217

Nassau Trophy: *1963*, 61; *1964*, 84, 135; *1967*, 111; Tourist Trophy: *1961*, 29
Neerpasch, Jochen: 106
Nicodemi, Tonino: 137
Noblet, Pierre: 24, 26, 29, 31, 33, 49, 58
Nocker, Peter: 31
Norisring Interserie race: *1971*, 185
North American Racing Team: 28, 31, 33, 38, 39, 45, 49, 53, 58, 59, 61, 82, 84, 88, 91, 94, 97, 103, 104, 107, 116, 117, 118, 121, 124, 134, 137, 140, 145, 147, 148, 152, 164, 165 168, 169, 176, 180, 182, 183, 188
Nürburgring 1,000Km race: *1953*, 11; *1958*, 24; *1959*, 26; *1960*, 26; *1961*, 17, 28; *1962*, 31, 46; *1963*,

Index 271

33, 57–8; *1964*, 38, 81, 134; *1965*, 41, 90, 137; *1966*, 103, 140; *1967*, 122; *1969*, 160–1; *1970*, 175; *1971*, 190–1; *1972*, 216; *1973*, 223, 245

Oliver, Jack: 157, 170, 180, 185, 190
Olthoff, Bob: 58
Ollon-Villars Hill Climb: *1962*, 50; *1965*, 95; *1966*, 113; *1969*, 163
Oreiller, Henri: 33
Oulton Park GT race: *April 1961*, 36

Pabst, Augie: 27, 33, 35, 54
Pace, Carlos: 217, 218, 220, 222, 224, 225
'Pam' (Marsilio Pasotti): 181, 185
Paris 12 Hours race: *1949*, 10
Paris 1,000Km race: *1960*, 27; *1961*, 29; *1962*, 33; *1963*, 33; *1964*, 39, 84, 134; *1967*, 130–1; *1970*, 178; *1971*, 185
Parkes, Mike: 28, 31, 32, 33, 34–5, 38, 46, 49, 53, 54, 55, 57, 60, 61, 62, 63, 82, 89, 90, 97, 98, 99, 100, 101, 103, 104, 105, 107, 116, 118, 119, 120, 124, 125, 128, 133, 137, 139, 158, 164, 170, 172, 173, 175, 176, 180, 181, 183, 185, 188, 231, 236, 240, 257–8
Parma-Poggia di Berceto Hill Climb: 1962, 50
Parsons, Chuck: 124, 156, 164, 165, 168
Patria, Franco: 84
Pau Grand Prix: *1958*, 24
Penske, Roger: 33, 54, 58, 185, 232
Pescara 12 Hours race: 1953, 11
Pescara Sports Car Grand Prix: *1961*, 29
Pescarolo, Henri: 168, 178, 180, 182, 183, 190, 217, 220, 221, 222, 223, 224, 225
Peterson, Ronnie: 168, 176, 185, 191, 192, 209, 210, 212, 213, 214, 216, 217, 218
Pierpoint, Roy: 109–110
Pinin Farina (from *1961* Pininfarina): 11, 12, 21, 22, 23, 26, 29, 40, 53, 130, 133, 135, 154–5
Piper, David: 32, 33, 34, 38, 60, 87, 91, 94, 95, 98, 99, 101, 103, 108, 109, 110, 116, 117, 118, 119, 120, 122, 125, 128, 129, 131, 134, 135, 136, 137, 139, 140, 142, 143, 144, 145, 158, 161, 164, 168, 183, 192, 258
Porsche cars:
 Generally: 38, 45, 46, 50, 56, 57, 81, 90, 95, 98, 100–1, 108, 113, 118, 119, 120, 121, 122, 126, 127, 128, 129, 131, 137, 152

907: 156
910: 189
908: 156, 157, 158, 160, 162, 181, 217
908/03: 172–3, 175, 190, 191, 209, 213
917: 140, 158, 166–7, 168, 169, 170, 171, 172, 173, 175, 176, 177, 178, 180, 183, 185, 188, 189, 190, 191, 192
911 *Carrera*: 220, 223
Porsche Konstruktionen (Porsche Salzburg): 168, 176
Protheroe, Richard: 33, 99
Posey, Sam: 145, 148, 152, 164, 169, 176, 177, 180, 183, 185

Redman, Brian: 101, 131, 157, 158, 160, 168, 170, 173, 175, 176, 177, 178, 191, 192, 209, 210, 212–3, 214, 215, 216, 217, 218, 220, 221, 222, 223, 225, 242–5
Rees, Alan: 118, 120
Regazzoni, Clay: 176, 181, 188, 189, 191, 192, 209, 210, 212, 213, 214, 215, 216, 217, 218 223, 224, 244, 258
Reims 12 Hours race: *1957*, 23; *1958 (GT cars)*, 25; *1964*, 38, 84, 134; *1965*, 92, 137; *1967*, 127, 144
Reims Prototype and GT race: *1963*, 34–5, 61
Revson, Peter: 98, 101, 106, 170, 180, 209
Renolds, Mamie Spears: 33
Reutemann, Carlos: 220, 221, 224, 225
Ricart, Wifredo: 9
Rindt, Jochen: 90, 92, 97, 106, 118, 119, 134, 137
Road America 500 Race, Elkhart Lake: *1964*, 134; *1968*, 148; Can-Am race: *1972*, 152
Road Atlanta Can-Am race, Georgia: *1971*, 152
Rocchi, *Ing.* Franco: 227, 232, 235. 239, 240
Rodriguez, Pedro: 29, 33, 36, 38, 39, 44, 45, 46, 47, 49, 53, 54, 58, 61, 63, 82, 84, 87, 88, 91, 92, 94, 95, 97, 98, 104, 107, 116, 117, 118, 124, 125, 128, 133, 134, 135, 136, 137, 139, 140, 148, 157, 158, 160, 161, 162, 168, 169, 170, 171, 173, 174, 175, 177, 180, 185, 188, 190, 191, 238, 258–9
Rodriguez, Ricardo: 29, 33, 45, 47, 49
Roger Penske Racing Team: 152, 156, 180
Rossfeld Hill Climb: *1965*, 95; *1966*, 113; *1969*, 163
Rouen Grand Prix: *1959*, 26
Roy Hesketh Race, Pietermaritzburg: *1965*, 140
Ruby, Lloyd: 87, 97, 117, 118, 125, 126

Salmon, Mike: 38, 59, 101, 104, 134, 137, 143
Salvadori, Roy: 27, 31, 34, 35, 81, 134
Salvarini, *Ing.* Walter: 227, 232, 235, 240
Sanderson, Ninian: 69
Savage, 'Swede', 180
Scaglietti: 14, 22, 23, 26, 29, 41, 133
Scarab-Chevrolet-Zerex car: 84, 134
Scarfiotti, Ludovico: 33, 38, 39, 47, 49, 50, 53, 54, 56, 57, 60, 63, 81, 82, 84, 88, 90, 95, 97, 98, 99, 100, 101, 103, 104, 107, 113, 116, 118, 120, 124, 125, 126, 127, 128, 129, 134, 147, 236, 258
Scarlatti, Giorgio: 26, 31
Schenken, Tim: 210, 216, 218, 220, 221, 222, 224, 225
Schetty, Peter: 158, 161, 163, 168, 169, 170, 171, 173, 175, 176, 177, 192, 209, 210, 213, 217, 218, 220, 244
Schuppan, Vern: 220, 222
Scott-Brown Memorial Trophy, Snetterton: *1964*, 134
Scott, Skip: 98,101, 106
Scuderia Brescia Corse: 131, 185
Scuderia Filipinetti: 88, 99, 101, 104, 117, 118, 121, 122, 124, 127, 128, 134, 137, 140, 170, 172, 175, 176, 180, 181, 182, 183, 185, 188
Scuderia Piccho Rosso: 168, 170, 176, 177
Scuderia Sant' Ambroeus: 50, 95, 98, 100, 107, 137, 140, 254
Scuderia Serenissima Repubblica di Venezia: 31, 33, 45
Scuderia Veloce: 142
Sebring 12 Hours race: *1957*, 14; *1958*, 24; *1959*, 26; *1960*, 26; *1961*, 17, 27–8; *1962*, 31; *1963*, 33, 45, 53, 236; *1964*, 38, 63, 134; *1965*, 88, 136; *1966*, 97, 140; *1967*, 117; *1969*, 157; *1970*, 164–5, 169–70; *1971*, 165, 180, 188; *1972*, 210, 212, 244
Seidel, Wolfgang: 23, 24, 31
Sestrieres Rally : *1957*, 23
Sharp, Hap: 53, 88, 94, 97, 121, 136
Shelby American Cobra cars: 7, 36, 38, 39, 40, 41, 63, 88, 139
Shelby American Racing Team: 87,88, 90, 92, 97, 105, 106, 125
Shelby, Carroll: 36, 87, 88, 133
Schlesser, Jo: 27, 28, 33, 38, 39, 81, 82, 84, 87, 107, 116, 125, 126, 127, 128, 144
Sears, Jack: 34, 36, 38, 41, 59, 61

Sicily, Tour of: *1955*, 13; *1956*, 22; *1957*, 23
Sierre-Montana-Crass Hill Climb: *1964*, 39, 134
Siffert, Jo: 120, 121, 127, 131, 157, 160, 168, 169, 170, 173, 175, 176, 177, 178, 179, 181, 188, 189, 190, 191
Sighala, Oddone: 137, 140
Silverstone: GT race, *May, 1962*, 31; Sports car and GT race: *July, 1963*; Group Four race: *April, 1967*, 143
Simon André: 27, 32, 60
Soisbault, Annie: 134
Sopwith, Tommy: 31, 33, 35, 248, 256, 257
Spence, Mike: 116, 117, 118, 120, 121, 122, 125, 128, 139
Spa 500Km race: *1964*, 38; *1965*, 137
Spa 1,000Km race: *1966*, 101, 140; *1967*, 119; *1969*, 158, 160; *1970*, 173–5; *1971*, 181, 189–90; *1972*, 213, 244; *1973*, 222–3
Spoerry, Dieter: 106, 126, 137
Spychiger, Tommy: 88, 89
Stabilimenti Farina (coachbuilder): 10
Stewart, Jackie: 82, 90, 128, 129, 134, 142, 213
Stardust Grand Prix, Las Vegas: *1967*, 147; *1968*, 148
Steinemann, Rico: 126
Stommelen, Rolf: 121, 188, 191, 209, 221, 222, 223, 224
STP Challenge Trophy, Bermuda: *1971*, 152
Sunoco-Ferrari: 180, 181, 185–8, 191, 232
Surfer's Paradise 12 Hours race: *1966*, 142–3; *1967*, 145
Surtees, John: 7, 33, 38, 53, 54, 56, 57, 60, 61, 62, 63, 81, 82, 84, 87, 88, 89, 90, 91, 92, 94, 95, 98, 99, 101, 103, 104, 109, 115, 118, 119, 122, 125, 128, 168, 173, 175, 176, 228, 229, 230, 234–41
Sutcliffe, Peter: 95, 101, 106, 113, 124, 126, 128, 129, 130, 134, 137, 140, 143
Swaters, Jacques: 231, 258

Taramazza, Luigi: 25, 38, 137, 140
Targa Florio: *1955*, 13; *1959*, 26; *1960*, 16, 26; *1961*, 28; *1962*, 31; *1963*, 55–6; *1965*, 89, 137; *1966*, 140; *1967*, 121–2; *1969*, 158; *1970*, 190; *1972*, 214, 216; *1973*, 223, 245
Taruffi, Piero: 13, 14, 22, 23
Tavoni, Romolo: 17
Tavano, Fernand: 33, 38
Tchokotoua, Prince Zourab: 33, 38
Team Chamaco Collect: 140
Thompson, Dick: 41, 106,

118, 119, 120, 122, 125, 128
Tour de France: *1956*, 23; *1957*, 23; *1958*, 25; *1959*, 26; *1960*, 27; *1961*, 29; *1962*, 33, 46; *1963*, 35; *1964*, 39, 81; *1966*, 100–1; *1967*, 121–2
Tourist Trophy: *1954*, 12; *1955*, 13; *1960*, 27; *1961*, 29, 31; *1962*, 31–2; *1963*, 34; *1964*, 84, 134; *1965*, 137; *1966*, 99–100
Trento-Bondone Hill Climb: *1962*, 50; *1965*, 95; *1966*, 113; *1969*, 163
Trintignant, Maurice: 12, 13, 13, 23, 25, 29, 90, 92

UDT-Laystall Racing Team: 31, 228

Vaccarella, Nino: 38, 46, 53, 54, 56, 57, 63, 81, 82, 84, 88, 89, 90, 91, 98, 101, 104, 118, 121, 124, 134, 137, 168, 170, 172, 173, 174, 175, 183, 185, 188, 190, 191, 216, 217, 223
Vallelunga Six Hours race: *1973*, 220
Van Lennep, Gijs: 128, 190, 191, 210, 216, 217
Van Ophem, Gérald Langlois: 31, 60, 134, 137
Veiga, Garcia: 165
Vignale (coachbuilder): 11
Vila Real Grand Prix: *1971*, 185
Villoresi, Luigi: 12, 22
Volpi, Count Giovanni Volpi di Misurata: 17, 31
Von Trips, Wolfgang: 14, 16, 17

Watkins Glen Six Hours race: *1970*, 177; *1971*, 185, 191; *1972*, 217–8; *1973*, 225
Watkins Glen Can-Am race: *1968*, 149; *1970*, 177; *1971*, 152, 185; *1972*, 152
Walker, Alistair: 176
Walker, Rob: 27, 28, 92
Wascher, Jacques: 22, 23
Weir, David: 183, 185
Whitmore, Sir John: 89, 90, 92, 101, 106
Wilkins, Dick: 27, 28
Williams, Jonathan: 117, 121, 128, 129, 147, 148, 170
Wisell, Reine: 176, 209
Woolfe, John: 161
Wyer, John: 64, 82, 84, 88, 118, 120, 125, 129–30, 136, 168, 170, 209, 216

Yorke, David: 168
Young American Racing Team: 180
Young, Greg: 180
Yeoman Credit Racing Team: 235

Zagato (coachbuilder): 22
Zeccoli, Teodoro: 145, 181
Zolder Grand Prix: *1964*, 134
Zolder Interserie race: *1971*, 181